Sunset

Western Garden Annual

1998 EDITION

By the Editors of *Sunset Magazine* and Sunset Books

Gazing globe reflects golden daylilies (page 203).

Sunset Publishing Corporation ■ **Menlo Park, California**

LEIGH BEISCH

Flower pot filled with handy garden trowels (page 234).

SUNSET BOOKS

Director, Sales & Marketing
Richard A. Smeby
Editorial Director
Bob Doyle
Production Director
Lory Day
Art Director
Vasken Guiragossian

STAFF FOR THIS BOOK

Managing Editor
Suzanne Normand Eyre
Contributing Editors
Philip Edinger
Helen Sweetland
Cornelia Fogle
Indexer
Pamela Evans
Production Coordinator
Patricia S. Williams

SUNSET PUBLISHING CORPORATION

President/Chief Executive Officer
Stephen J. Seabolt
VP, Chief Financial Officer
James E. Mitchell
VP, Consumer Marketing Director
Robert I. Gursha
VP, Manufacturing Director
Lorinda Reichert
VP, Editor-in-Chief, Sunset Magazine
Rosalie Muller Wright
Managing Editor
Carol Hoffman
Senior Editor, Gardening
Kathleen Norris Brenzel

Another Year of Good Gardening

This *Western Garden Annual,* like its four predecessors, enfolds between two covers the entire body of gardening and outdoor living material from the prior year's issues of *Sunset Magazine.* In 12 chapters, one for each month of 1997, you will find combined all of the garden-related material presented in the various regional editions of the magazine.

Each month begins with the Garden Guide mini-articles, which comprise a potpourri of "you-should-be-aware-of" points of interest specific to the month or to the gardening period just ahead. The Garden Notebooks section offers personal tips, anecdotes, and question-and-answer features from the *Sunset* garden editors who cover the West. Separate garden Checklists for each region capsulize garden activities appropriate to each month. Lavishly illustrated full-length articles conclude each chapter's offerings.

Throughout these chapters, plant performance and gardening activities are keyed to numbered climate zones. Those 24 zones, covering the entire West, are described and mapped in the sixth edition (1995) of the *Sunset Western Garden Book.*

Front cover: Bouquet of roses, alstroemeria, New Zealand tea tree, red anemone, and red-flowering currant. Cover design: Vasken Guiragossian. Photographer: John Humble.

Back cover: Wheelbarrow bouquet (see page 212), Rob Proctor.

Endpapers: (hardcover edition): *Galium odoratum,* David McDonald.

All material in this book originally appeared in the 1997 issues of *Sunset Magazine.*

Sunset Western Garden Annual was produced by Sunset Books. If you have comments or suggestions, please let us hear from you. Write us at:

Sunset Books
Garden Book Editorial
80 Willow Road
Menlo Park, CA 94025

First printing March 1998
Copyright © 1998 Sunset Publshing Corporation, Menlo Park, CA 94025. First edition. All rights reserved, including the right of reproduction in whole or in part in any form.

ISSN 1073-5089
Hardcover edition: ISBN 0-376-06108-1
Softcover edition: ISBN 0-376-06109-2

Printed in the United States.

Contents

A Special Year in the Garden

From January's ebullient cyclamen to December's illuminated saguaro, this has been another distinctly diverse Western gardening year. And as usual, the array of opportunities from mountains to seashore, desert to redwood forest have been reported by the voice of Western gardening, *Sunset Magazine.* What to grow and how to grow it, new tools, new books, creative garden design—for decades, novice and experienced gardeners alike have turned to *Sunset* for reliable information about these topics.

The 12 months of 1997 delivered a mixed salad of feature material for readers to savor. For the first time, garden design and designers were accorded Western Garden Awards, showcasing stellar examples of style and innovation as a stimulus to any gardener's imagination. Among plants that reach perfection in parts of the West, we call attention to primroses and dahlias. And easterners transplanted to warm-winter West Coast communities discovered some low-chill lilacs that could remind them of home. Natural air-conditioning was high-

A formal arbor surrounded by lush roses brightens this English-style garden in Napa, California. For more information, see page 192.

lighted in a major article on planting the West's best shade trees; addressing gardeners with established trees was "How to Prune a Tree—Properly."

For culinary gardeners, the year offered a bumper crop of information—on tomatoes, corn, melons, offbeat potatoes, herbs, antique apples, and growing vegetables in hanging containers. Also featured were contemporary organic gardening successes and how to plant a garden that would not become a banquet for deer. Garden technicians were treated to evaluations of rotary tillers and cordless mowers, a presentation of the latest in sprinklers—even advice on constructing a temporary "blow-up" greenhouse from plastic sheeting.

And as always, each month gardeners throughout the West could turn to the Garden Guide for enticing tidbits ranging from labor-saving tips and tools to shows, tours, and events of special interest. Garden Checklists for each of the West's gardening regions address planting and maintenance activities best done during that month.

Think of this compilation of the 1997 garden year as a 352-page epicurean feast. Discover, or rediscover, the unique gardening opportunities of the West—and the pivotal role that *Sunset Magazine* plays in their development.

NORMAN A. PLATE (2)

For colorful winter bloom indoors, try cyclamen (see page 11).

January

gardenguide

NORMAN A. PLATE

Trouble-free indoor trees

Ficus benjamina is a temperamental leaf-dropper. But six new varieties, just as handsome, are tougher

Weeping fig (*Ficus benjamina*) is a popular house plant, but growing it can be frustrating. This glossy-leafed tree drops leaves—sometimes defoliating almost completely—with the slightest change in temperature, light, or soil moisture.

Now, much tougher ficus trees are available. As green and attractive as the old favorite, the new varieties stand up to moderately low light and humidity, and even fluctuations in soil moisture.

This group of patented trees, called Ficus of the Future, includes six new varieties. The three pictured are, from left, *F. maclellandii* 'Amstel King' with 5-inch-long droopy, leathery green leaves; *F. benjamina* 'Monique', a bushy plant with ruffled, glossy green leaves; and *F. b.* 'Rianne', whose branches zig and zag, making it look like old bonsai. The three others are *F. b.* 'Indigo', whose leaves emerge a deep green, darkening to a glossy variegated blue-black; 'Midnight', whose leaves begin green, then turn a solid blue-black; and 'Wiandi', which is similar to 'Rianne'.

Overwatering poses the only threat to these trees, which like to go almost dry between waterings.

If your nursery doesn't have Ficus of the Future, it can order them wholesale from Hesketh Growers (800/342-8775).

by **LAUREN BONAR SWEZEY**

tools

Japanese pruning saws can make your pruning jobs much easier. The one shown at right, a Shark Saw Series CleanCut Pruning and Multipurpose Saw by Takagi Tools, cuts through branches as easily as a knife cuts through butter. When not in use, the blade folds into the handle.

What makes this tool so different from other pruning saws is its blade, which is made of chromium-impregnated high-carbon steel. Because of the steel's strength, the blade can be made thinner than other kinds of saw blades, which means it causes less friction during cutting. Also, the teeth are straight, not "set" (bent out to the left and right), so cuts can be thin and precise without tearing the branch.

Every tooth on the blade is diamond-wheel ground, which makes the blade very sharp. And each tooth has three cutting edges instead of the typical two. Because the blade is so sharp, it has a safety lock to fasten it open or closed.

The chromium finish inhibits rusting. To maintain the blade, just clean off any debris and wipe the blade with vegetable oil after each use. With minimal care, a heavily used blade will last at least five years. After that, the blade can be popped out and replaced—it can't be sharpened.

The saw is available for $27 to $30 (additional blades cost about $16) at garden centers and some home centers. If you can't find one, call Takagi Tools (800/777-5538) to locate a supplier near you. — *L. B. S.*

CATALOG *news*

Arena roses

If you love David Austin English roses, you'll love Arena Rose Co.'s catalog. Arena propagates 60 different Austin varieties and has one of the broadest selections of field-grown English roses produced in the United States. Virtually all of Arena's Austins originated from cuttings taken from the Huntington Botanical Gardens' rose collection. In the catalog, luscious color portraits show each variety. Be prepared to drool. You'll want all of the plants. Fortunately, the honest text accompanying the photos cools the blood a bit. Comments like "stretches out in temperate climates" and "requires watchful protection from mildew" help sort out the must-haves from the merely gorgeous. Arena also propagates antique roses and some modern roses that display old-fashioned charms. For a catalog, send $5 to 536 W. Cambridge Ave., Phoenix, AZ 85003, or call (602) 266-2223. — *Sharon Cohoon*

new **CARNATION**

'Velvet 'N Lace'

This pretty flower has the rich coloring of a gorgeous ball gown with a ruffled petticoat showing.

Double, 1½-inch-diameter flowers grow on 12-inch-tall stems and appear throughout the summer in mild climates; they have a wonderful sweet-and-spicy fragrance.

Sow the seed indoors in small pots. Grow seedlings in bright light, such as a west-facing window, until the plants are strong enough to transplant outdoors (plants should be bushy and at least several inches tall). Gradually acclimate them to full sun. Plant them in well-drained soil rich in organic matter. As the plants start blooming, pick off old flowers to encourage repeat blooming.

Seed is available from *Park Seed Co.,* Cokesbury Rd., Greenwood, SC 29647; (800) 845-3369. A packet of seed costs $1.80 plus shipping. — *L. B. S.*

NORMAN A. PLATE

DEIDRA WALPOLE

designing with **CACTUS**

Down at the Rancho

"We're going for Ansel Adams rather than the Kodachrome moment," says John Schoustra, chief horticulturist at Rancho Los Alamitos, a historic estate in Long Beach. "Many cactus gardens are based on the annual bedding plant approach," he explains. "They rely on strong color contrasts." But the cactus garden at the Rancho uses subtler strategies to command visitors' attention. Plant colors harmonize, flowing from silver through blue-gray, gray-green, and blue-green like the half-tone shifts in an Adams print. And, as with Adams's photographs, textures are emphasized. Steel-smooth leaves of agave play against the fleshy rosettes of aeonium and the warty surfaces of *Cereus peruvianus* 'Monstrosus'. Shapes tend toward the boldly sculptural: artichoke globes, fat cylinders, slender columns, and bayonet-like blades.

The important thing about the Rancho Los Alamitos cactus garden is that, first and foremost, it's a garden, not just a collection of interesting plants. The number of species in it isn't the point, Schoustra says. What matters is that cactus are used the same way any other landscaping material would be. They serve as companion plants, ground covers, accent pieces, and backbones for borders.

Rancho Los Alamitos is open 1 to 5 Wednesdays through Sundays. Guided tours of the adobe ranch house (circa 1800), early-20th-century barns, and blacksmith shop leave every 30 minutes; the last tour begins at 4. Garden tours are self-guided. (The Rancho also has a rose garden, a geranium walk, and a cutting garden.) The Rancho is at 6400 Bixby Hill Road in Long Beach. (Enter through the residential security gate at the intersection of Anaheim Rd. and Palo Verde Ave.) Admission is free.

—*Jim McCausland*

Easy and colorful winter bloom indoors

Few indoor plants produce flowers without extra light, and fewer still bloom through winter. Cyclamen is a beautiful exception (see photo on page 6).

The most common cyclamen for indoor use (*C. persicum* and its hybrids) is usually sold by size rather than by name, but sometimes you'll find plants sold as florists' cyclamen or tagged with the name of a particular series.

All the plants in a series grow to roughly the same size, but flower in different colors. In the Sierra series, for example, you can choose among 14 colors, including 'Sierra Lilac', 'Sierra Scarlet', and 'Sierra White'.

At the tall (9-inch) end are Gradation (intensely colored with frosty white edges) and Sierra (clear colors) hybrids. In the medium range (7 inches), try Laser (clear colors, subtle scent). And at the short end (5 inches), look for Dressy and Miracle (clear colors).

All have heart-shaped green leaves with beautiful white variegation. Plants are sold in 4- and 6-inch containers.

Cyclamens grow well on a windowsill and can flower continuously for several months. For longest possible bloom period, let cyclamen plants dry out between waterings and apply half-strength fertilizer twice a month. In summer, tops may die back. At that time, put the plants in a shady spot outdoors and water occasionally. Leaves should reemerge in fall, and flowers will follow in winter. — *J.M.*

A bumper crop of All-America winners

The number of new All-America Selections has been increased to six for 1997—twice as many as last year—with judges picking three flowers and three vegetables based on their performances in trial gardens.

'Cajun Delight' okra. Most varieties need lots of summer heat. 'Cajun Delight' comes to harvest less than two months after being planted in warm soil.

'Crystal White' zinnia (*Z. angustifolia*). Tougher and smaller than common garden zinnias (*Z. elegans*), 'Crystal White' stands up better in heat, is much less susceptible to powdery mildew, and grows 10 inches tall. It has daisylike white flowers and a trailing habit.

NORMAN A. PLATE

'Dynamo' cabbage. As big as softballs and 2 to 2½ pounds each, these compact heads are ready to harvest about 70 days after transplanting. The blue-green leaves are crunchy and sweet.

'Gypsy' baby's breath (*Gypsophila muralis*). This perennial baby's breath, about a foot tall, is a good choice for containers. It bears ¼-inch pink flowers.

'Prestige Scarlet' cockscomb (*Celosia cristata*). This new cristata, called multiflora, bears a heavy crop of small, cock's comb–like flowers. 'Prestige Scarlet', the first multiflora, can set a border ablaze with its 3-inch deep-red blooms.

'Siam Queen' basil. This Thai basil has darker leaves, flowers, and stems than sweet basil, and very full flavor with anise overtones. It can reach 3 feet tall and 2 feet wide. — *J. M.* ◆

Lilies that won't stain noses

You can spot avid lily gardeners by the saffron-colored pollen staining their noses and hands, and often their clothes. To get lilies without the pollen, try a double-flowered variety. 'Double Latté' (creamy orange with rose overlay), 'Strawberry Vanilla Latté', and 'Typhoon'(peachy pink) are good ones. Double-flowered lilies have no pollen because their anthers and stamens have been converted to petals (that's why the flowers are doubles). Or try a sterile, single-flowered variety such as 'Hodge Podge' (creamy yellow centers with deep pink edges), 'Red Ticklers' (bright red), or 'Snowbrook' (white).

If you can't find these varieties in local nurseries, you can order the bulbs from B & D Lilies, Box 2007, Port Townsend, WA 98368; (360) 385-1738. —*J.M.*

A witch hazel as bright as sunshine

Chinese witch hazel (*Hamamelis mollis*) will burst into bloom this month with yellow flowers that look like small tassels and carry a strong, spicy fragrance. For the most intense yellow blooms, look for *H. m.* 'Sunburst'.

The plant will grow into a 10- to 15-foot multistemmed tree (a few plants reach 30 feet). The roundish leaves are about 4 to 6 inches long and have a slightly rough texture. In mild-winter areas of the Northwest and Northern California, you can plant witch hazels in bloom now (they are not hardy in coldest-winter climates, *Sunset* zones 1–3).

Expect to pay $12 to $40 for a 1-gallon plant. You can mail-order witch hazel from Gossler Farms Nursery, 1200 Weaver Rd., Springfield, OR 97478; (541) 746-3922. Catalog costs $2.

— *Steven R. Lorton*

Pacific Northwest Garden Notebook

by **STEVEN R. LORTON**

Ialways urge gardeners to learn the botanical names of the plants they grow or want to grow. There are lots of good reasons. The most important is getting the plant you want. When you ask for mondo grass, for example, you might be given any number of species. But go to a nursery and ask for *Ophiopogon planiscapus* 'Nigrescens' and you'll be sure you're getting the plant that forms 8-inch-tall, foot-wide tufts of glistening black grassy leaves.

Once you know the botanical name, you can look the plant up quickly in any reference to find out exactly how to grow it. And no matter where you travel in the world, botanical names are the same, so you'll be able to "talk plants" even if you can't speak a particular foreign language.

I know it sounds hard to do, but it isn't. Start with a single genus name: a good one is *Acer*—maple. Then you add species names (just like you're learning the first names of each member of the Jones family). The bigleaf maple is *Acer macrophyllum*. The skinny little vine maple in the entry is *Acer circinatum*. And the beautiful maple with the flaky cinnamon-colored bark that you're longing to grow is *Acer griseum*. There, you've already nailed three maples. When you use botanical names around other gardeners, they'll assume that you're a horticultural genius.

When my son, John, was little, I'd show him a tree and say the botanical name several times. He'd repeat it and practice it. When, at random, I pointed to a given plant and he came up with the correct botanical name 10 times in a row (during a period of two weeks or so), I gave him a dollar. It worked like a charm. Now when he walks through a garden, he can tick off the plants' names as if he'd grown up in a nursery.

•

MARINA THOMPSON

If you're looking for terra-cotta pots, head over to Herban Pottery, a new store in Seattle's Wallingford District with a great selection. Owner Alison Rae Ogden shops for imports in more than 20 countries, including England, Italy, Mexico, Portugal, Spain, and Sri Lanka. Herban's high-quality containers come in all sizes and styles—from baroque to contemporary. Most are fired at high temperatures so they'll stand up to the Northwest's cold, wet winters. Masonry sealer for frost-proofing pots is also available. The shop is at 250 N.E. 45th Street, and it's open 10 to 6 Tuesdays through Saturdays, noon to 5 Sundays.

THAT'S A GOOD QUESTION

Q: No matter what I do, my bamboo palm drops its lower leaves. I use a little more water, I use a little less, I fertilize a bit more, I hold off … what's wrong?
— *Sam Kwong, Walla Walla, Washington*

A: Nothing is wrong. Your bamboo palm (*Chamaedorea erumpens*) is just doing what comes naturally. This plant grows 4 to 5 feet tall (occasionally taller) and forms clumps of stems. As the plant grows, the lower leaves drop off, making the clusters of stems look like clumps of bamboo. This palm can take low light, though it does best with some direct sunlight. An east- or southeast-facing window is perfect. In direct south or west light, it will probably get scorched. Grow it in a generous container filled with a rich, loose commercial potting mix. Feed the plant from April through October. Keep the soil moist, but make sure that drainage is good.

Northern California Garden Notebook

by **LAUREN BONAR SWEZEY**

Some gardeners find January a rather dull time of year in the garden because few plants are blooming and many are devoid of leaves. Not me. January is pruning time, and pruning's my thing. Give me a small tree, shrub, or rose—I'll chop into anything. Don't get me wrong, I'm not a hacker. There's a definite art and science to pruning. I find the challenge of molding and forming plants into beautiful shapes as exciting as a sculptor might.

But pruning shears are powerful weapons. Make the wrong cut and you can wreck a plant's shape for years. Before you make your first cut, you need to learn how to prune properly. One place to get hands-on pruning instruction is at a pruning workshop; community colleges, community garden centers, and some nurseries offer them at this time of year. Pruning manuals are also helpful.

One new book to consider is *Johnson's Guide to Gardening: Pruning, Planting, and Care,* by Eric A. Johnson (Ironwood Press, 2968 W. Ina Rd., #285, Tucson, AZ 85741, 1997; $16.95). The 160-page softcover book is filled with the latest information about where to make pruning cuts and how to shape plants. It also provides plenty of tips on proper planting methods and plant care for dry-climate landscape plants.

TIME TO ADJUST YOUR AUTOMATIC WATERING SYSTEM?

Automatic watering systems can be both a help and a hindrance. They help by keeping the garden watered when you're on vacation or don't have time to water the garden yourself. They hinder when you forget to adjust the automatic controller as the weather cools, or to turn it off during

MARINA THOMPSON

rains. Time and time again, I've seen sprinklers spewing out water while it's pouring rain in midwinter. We Northern Californians may be well past our drought emergency of previous years, but we should still conserve whenever possible (in some communities, water can be pretty expensive too!). If you haven't checked your automatic controller lately, take a look. Is it on? Should it be? If the soil remains moist between storms, turn off the system. If it's not raining and plants need water, you may need to readjust the controller's schedule. Try to determine how long the soil stays moist, then schedule the timer to go on at the appropriate frequency.

THAT'S A GOOD QUESTION

Q: We just planted a new ginkgo and wonder about care its first winter. When should we fertilize it, and what about watering if the rains don't come? Should we mulch the base? — *Paul Simon, Los Altos Hills*

A: All plants, regardless of their adaptability to drought, need water at least through the first season after planting. New plants have restricted root systems and don't have access to water in the surrounding soil until the roots penetrate the area. So if rain is lacking, you definitely need to water. Test soil moisture in the rootball by sticking your finger into it. When it feels barely moist, it's time to water (make sure the irrigation water soaks into the rootball and doesn't just roll off the top). Mulch the soil to conserve moisture between rains. If you didn't apply fertilizer at planting time, apply it in late winter just before growth begins (mix it into the top few inches of soil around the rootball).

Southern California Garden Notebook

by **SHARON COHOON**

Many books about rose care read like war manuals. Stockpile weapons, they exhort. And don't wait for an invasion to use those fungicides and insecticides. Conduct monthly preemptive strikes. Mix solutions, don protective gear, and attack with spray guns. March forth and exterminate. It sounds exhausting. If all this were truly necessary, I'd just wave the white flag, surrender my roses, and be done with it.

Fortunately the rose garden doesn't have to be a battlefield. Not, that is, if you select disease-resistant roses and are willing to live with a little imperfection. I'm reminded of this every time I walk out my back door and admire my never-been-sprayed 'Iceberg' and 'Bonica' roses. They bloom their hearts out and get better all the time despite being treated almost as casually as salvias.

Another reminder is Jan Weverka's monthly newsletter, *The Rose Garden*. Weverka grows roses beautifully. I know. I've visited her garden. And she uses the roses in her floral-design business. Yet her method is purely organic. She relies on birds, toads, lizards, and beneficial insects to keep bad bugs in check, and water washes on winter mornings and summer evenings to subdue mildew. She spends her energy amending the soil rather than spraying chemicals. Her newsletter extols the virtues and pleasures of composting, mulching with alfalfa hay, and starting a wormery. I read her monthly missives with pleasure, never fail to learn something new, and always set them down wanting more, not fewer, roses.

The Rose Garden costs $15 a year. To subscribe, write to Jan Weverka, 783 Oakglade Dr., Monrovia, CA 91016.

MARINA THOMPSON

YELLOW POPPIES, ANYONE?

Last year I grew the annual California poppy *Eschscholzia caespitosa* and was thoroughly smitten with it. I found something very endearing about these pale yellow flowers with their fernlike gray-green foliage. I started with nursery plants, but I want more this year, so I'm going the seed route. I picture these dainty poppies billowing out around my multicolored freesias like a tutu of yellow tulle. But they would look equally gorgeous skirting blue babiana. It's not too late to sow seeds. Wildflowers germinate quickly this wet month. Order *E. caespitosa* from Larner Seeds (Box 407, Bolinas, CA 94924; 415/868-9407).

THAT'S A GOOD QUESTION

Q: My blue hydrangeas turned pink last year and wiped out the great apricot-blue color scheme I'd worked out. How can I turn them blue again?

— *Carla Robertson, Los Angeles*

A: A little jolt of acid applied now ought to do the trick. Flower color in garden hydrangeas is determined by soil pH. Shrubs grown in neutral or alkaline soils produce pink or red blossoms; those grown in acidic soils produce blue or purple. Our soil is alkaline. So blue hydrangeas planted in it eventually revert to pink if the soil isn't regularly acidified. To turn your hydrangeas blue again, supplement regular fertilizer with one tablespoon of aluminum sulfate per gallon of water. Treatment needs to occur well ahead of bloom time to affect color. Feed when you prune. Prune the same time as you do roses.

Planting

☐ **DECORATE WITH ORCHIDS.** Nurseries and florists stock a number of blooming orchids this month. Liven up your living room with a corsage orchid (*Cattleya*), miniature cymbidium, moth orchid (*Phalaenopsis*), *Oncidium*, or pansy orchid (*Miltonia*). All of these orchids need bright light indoors. Cool temperatures prolong bloom. Move cymbidium plants outdoors when bloom is over (protect them from frost).

☐ **PLANT ANNUALS.** Zones 7–9, 14–17: For midwinter bloom, buy 4-inch instant color (smaller plants will just sit until spring). Stuff plants into containers or set them out in flower beds. Try calendula, candytuft, cineraria, dianthus, English daisy, English and fairy primroses, Iceland poppy, pansy, snapdragon, stock, and viola.

☐ **PLANT BARE-ROOT.** Zones 7–9, 14–17: This is the prime month to buy and plant dormant fruit and shade trees, roses, shrubs, and vines. Bareroot plants cost less and adapt more quickly than container plants. It's best to plant immediately upon arriving home from the nursery, but if you can't plant for a few days, temporarily lay plants on their sides in a shallow trench (in a pinch, a bucket will do) and cover them with moist sawdust or soil—a process called heeling in.

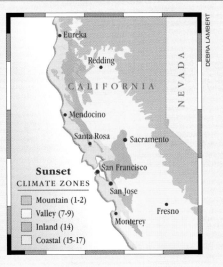

Sunset
CLIMATE ZONES

☐ Mountain (1-2)
☐ Valley (7-9)
☐ Inland (14)
☐ Coastal (15-17)

☐ **PLANT BERRIES AND VEGETABLES.** Zones 7–9, 14–17: Artichokes, asparagus, blackberries, grapes, raspberries, and strawberries are all available bareroot this month. For a treat, try 'Olallie' blackberry. The huge, 1½-inch-long berries are sweet and succulent, and the plant is well adapted to Northern California.

Maintenance

☐ **CARE FOR LIVING CHRISTMAS TREES.** If you haven't done so already, move your living Christmas tree outdoors. If the tree is rootbound, transplant it into a larger container or trim off some of the rootball and replant with fresh potting mix. Water thoroughly. Give the tree partial sun to begin with, then move into full sun after a week or two. Rinse off the foliage and thoroughly soak the soil.

☐ **CUT BACK HYDRANGEAS.** Zones 7–9, 14–17: Cut back to 12 inches stems that have bloomed. For the largest flowers next spring, reduce the number of stems; for more numerous medium-size blooms, keep more stems.

☐ **PRUNE.** Zones 7–9, 14–17: This is prime time for pruning dormant deciduous plants such as flowering vines, fruit and shade trees, grapes, and roses. Use pruning shears for small cuts, up to about ⅜ inch in diameter (good-quality shears can prune branches up to ¾ inch in diameter). Use loppers for cuts ⅜ inch to 1 inch in diameter. Use a pruning saw for branches more than 1 inch in diameter. Wait to prune spring-flowering plants such as lilac and Japanese snowball until after they bloom.

Pest control

☐ **SPRAY FOR PEACH LEAF CURL.** Zones 7–9, 14–17: If you haven't applied your first spray for peach leaf curl (a fungus that causes distorted leaves), do so now. Spray with lime sulfur now, and then again in early spring when buds begin to swell but before they open. Use a spreader-sticker to improve coverage, and spray when rain isn't predicted for at least 36 hours.

☐ **SPRAY ROSES.** Zones 7–9, 14–17: To control overwintering insects such as aphids, mites, and scale, spray rose plants with a dormant oil, thoroughly covering the trunk, branches, and twigs.

Planting

☐ **ORDER SEEDS.** Place orders for warm-season flowers and vegetables. (Mail-order catalogs offer a much wider choice than seed displays in grocery stores and most nurseries.) Start seeds indoors as soon as they arrive and you'll have seedlings ready to transplant to the garden in early spring.

☐ **PLANT WINTER ANNUALS.** It's not too late to plant colorful annuals and perennials to bloom now and into early spring—especially in mild coastal areas. Nurseries offer calendulas, cinerarias (frost-tender), dianthus, English daisies, Iceland poppies, larkspur, lobelia, nemesia, pansies, primroses, snapdragons, stock, sweet alyssum, sweet peas, and violas. In the low desert (Palm Springs), also plant petunias.

☐ **PLANT WINTER VEGETABLES.** Final crops of seedlings—broccoli, brussels sprouts, cabbage, and cauliflower—can go in now. Start beets, carrots, leaf lettuces and other greens, radishes, and turnips from seeds. Plant seed potatoes and leek and onion sets.

☐ **SHOP FOR BARE-ROOT PLANTS.** Most nurseries have great supplies of healthy rose plants. You'll also find perennial vegetables such as artichokes, asparagus, and rhubarb; fruits such as cane berries, grapes, and strawberries; and ornamentals such as wisteria vines and deciduous shade trees. In the hottest inland areas, such as Palm Springs, look for stone fruit, apple, and fig trees along with roses.

Sunset
CLIMATE ZONES

1-3   7-9   11   13   14-24

☐ **SHOP FOR SUCCULENTS.** Winter-blooming succulents are another option for brightening the winter garden. They look particularly at home in drought-tolerant Mediterranean-style settings. Look for flowering aloes, echeveria, and kalanchoe, among others, at your nursery.

☐ **SHOP FOR SUMMER BULBS.** Nurseries have good supplies of summer-blooming bulbs in stock now. Choices include acidanthera, amaryllis, tuberous begonias, caladium, calla, canna, crinum, crocosmia, dahlia, gladiolus, lilies, nerine, and tigridia.

Maintenance

☐ **BEGIN DORMANT-SEASON PRUNING.** Prune deciduous trees, fruit trees, grapes, roses, shrubs, and vines this month before new growth begins. Make sure saws, loppers, and shears are sharp before starting. Wait until late spring after flowers fade to prune trees and shrubs grown primarily for their spring flowers.

☐ **GROOM CAMELLIAS.** If camellia blight is a problem (petals turn brown and rot in the center), keep ground beneath plants clean by removing fallen flowers and leaves promptly. Pick infected flowers from plants.

☐ **WATER NATIVE PLANTS.** In winter, native plants can best absorb and store water for summer. If rains have been light or nonexistent, give plants slow, deep soakings now through early spring as needed.

Pest control

☐ **APPLY DORMANT SPRAY.** Spray deciduous flowering and fruit trees with dormant oil to smother overwintering insect pests such as scale, mites, and aphids. For fungal diseases such as peach leaf curl, mix lime sulfur or fixed copper into the oil. Spray the branches, crotches, trunk, and ground beneath the tree's drip line. If rain occurs within 48 hours of spraying, repeat treatment. Near the coast, if plants aren't leafless (especially 'Anna' apple), withhold water to force dormancy before spraying.

Planting

□ **ORDER SEEDS, SPRING PLANTS.** Place catalog orders for seeds and plants early for best selection; that's especially true if you want specialty varieties (like Chinese vegetables, old roses, or rare plants). For seedlings, figure out when you can plant outdoors, then count backward about five weeks. That's when to sow seed indoors.

□ **SOW PERENNIALS.** In milder parts of the intermountain West, start perennials such as delphinium, hellebore, veronica, and viola in a coldframe or greenhouse for planting when at least two sets of true leaves appear (and, in coldest areas, when ground can be worked).

Maintenance

□ **CARE FOR HOLIDAY PLANTS.** Some tabletop Christmas plants (like poinsettias) aren't worth trying to save for another year. But others, like cyclamen, Christmas cactus, and kalanchoe, go on and on. Wash them off under a barely warm shower, feed kinds that carry fruit or flowers, and put in a bright place out of drafts and away from heating and air-conditioning sources. After danger of frost is past in spring, you can move these outside for the summer.

□ **CARE FOR LIVING CHRISTMAS TREES.** They need light, so you should move them outside as soon after Christmas as possible. Start them off in a place that's shaded from midday and afternoon sun (under a tree is nice), moving them into full sun after a couple of weeks. You can also plant your tree outside after the ground thaws if it's among the varieties that thrive where you live; otherwise, keep the tree in the container and protect it from prolonged hard frost. Some out-of-range trees can live on for years as potted plants.

MONTANA
Helena •
• Boise
IDAHO
WYOMING
Cheyenne •
NEVADA
Salt Lake City
Denver •
• Reno
UTAH
COLORADO
Las Vegas

Sunset
CLIMATE ZONES
☐ 1-3   ▨ 10-11

DEBRA LAMBERT

□ **CHECK STORED BULBS, PRODUCE.** Look over any tender corms, tubers, and produce that you have stored, checking for shriveling and rot. You can usually reverse shriveling by sprinkling on a little water. Discard anything that shows signs of decay except dahlia tubers: you can cut the bad spots out of those, dust with sulfur, and store apart from the rest.

□ **FERTILIZE ASPARAGUS.** After the ground thaws, top-dress with rotted manure or organic mulch mixed with a complete fertilizer.

□ **PRUNE TREES, SHRUBS.** Start pruning in the high desert and the mildest parts of the intermountain West when daytime temperatures are well above freezing. Cut out dead, diseased, crossing, and closely parallel branches, then prune for shape.

□ **TUNE UP TOOLS.** Spring will be here before you know it. Sharpen shovels and hoes, rub down wooden handles with linseed oil, and replace or hone blades on dull pruning shears.

□ **WATER HOUSE PLANTS.** When it's not raining, low humidity is usually the rule in much of the West. That, combined with house heat, means that plants will dry out more quickly than usual unless you have a humidifier. Check soil often, and water when the top of the soil has dried out. Water less and plants will die from thirst. Water more and waterlogged roots will rot and, ironically, the plant will also die, from thirst.

Pest control

□ **INDOOR PLANTS.** Examine house plants regularly for aphids, scale insects, spider mites, and mealy bugs. Rinse infested plants with lukewarm water, then spray them with insecticidal soap.

Planting

☐ **BARE-ROOT STOCK.** Berries, cane fruits, fruit trees, roses, and shade trees are all in nurseries now. Bare-root plants are relatively inexpensive and can be planted in unamended native soil. Decide what you want, dig a hole, then buy your tree. Have the nursery pack the roots in damp peat moss or sawdust for the trip home: if unprotected roots dry out between the nursery and your garden, the plant will likely die.

☐ **CHILLED BULBS.** If you refrigerated bulbs of tulips or other spring-flowering plants to provide pre-planting chill, take them out after six weeks, plant them in well-amended soil, and water well; shoots should emerge from the bulbs in a month or two.

☐ **VEGETABLES.** In the low desert, sow seeds of eggplant, melons, peppers, and tomatoes in flats now for transplanting outside when the weather warms up. In intermediate and low deserts (zones 12 and 13), set out short-day onions such as Texas Grano types, which form bulbs when daylight lasts only 10 to 12 hours.

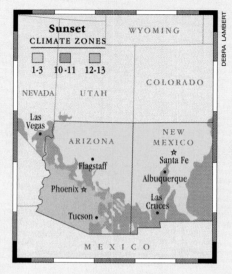

☐ **WINTER COLOR.** Nurseries offer plenty of choices for winter color, including bachelor's button, calendula, cineraria, cyclamen, English daisy, pansy, primrose, snapdragon, sweet alyssum, and wallflower.

Maintenance

☐ **FEED CITRUS TREES.** Applied now, fertilizer will be effective when citrus starts to bloom. Water trees first, then a day later apply ammonium sulfate at the following rates: 2½ pounds for grapefruit trees; 4 pounds for oranges and tangerines; and 5 pounds for lemons. Water again after feeding.

☐ **PROTECT CITRUS FRUIT.** When temperatures drop below 25° for more than two hours, most citrus fruits are damaged. When temperatures below 28° are predicted, cover trees at night with cloth (old sheets are fine) and uncover them in the morning. If fruit is damaged, pick and juice it within 24 hours.

☐ **MULCH.** To keep weeds down and the ground moist, spread a thick layer of mulch around shrubs and trees, and in vegetable and flower beds.

☐ **PRUNE ROSES.** If you're pruning hybrid tea roses, cut plants back to the three to five strongest canes. Cut top growth back by about a third.

Planting

☐ FRUITS AND BERRIES. Plant apples, berries, figs, grapes, jujubes, peaches, pears (both Asian and European), pecans, persimmons, plums, and sour cherries this month. Most are available as bare-root stock, but some are sold in containers.

☐ ONIONS. In both central and South Texas, plant short-day onions such as Texas SuperSweet, which forms bulbs even when daylight lasts only about 10 to 12 hours.

☐ ORNAMENTALS. Plant ornamental trees, shrubs, and vines now from bare-root stock.

☐ ROSES. They're available bare-root and in containers this month. Plant right away.

☐ ORDER SEEDS, SPRING PLANTS. Place catalog orders for seeds and plants early for best selection; that's especially true if you want specialty varieties (like Chinese vegetables, old roses, or rare plants). For seedlings, figure out when you can plant outdoors, then count back about five weeks. That's when to sow seed indoors.

Maintenance

☐ CARE FOR CHRISTMAS PLANTS. Some tabletop Christmas plants (like poinsettias) aren't worth trying to save, but ones like cyclamen, Christmas cactus, and kalanchoe go on and on. Wash them off under a lukewarm shower, feed kinds that carry fruit or flowers, and put in a bright place out of drafts and away from heating and air-conditioning sources. After danger of frost is past in spring, move them outside for the summer.

☐ PRUNE TREES, SHRUBS. On a day when temperatures are above freezing, cut out dead, diseased, crossing, and closely parallel branches, then prune for shape.

Pest control

☐ INDOOR PLANTS. Examine house plants regularly for aphids, scale insects, spider mites, and mealy bugs. Sometimes the first sign is sticky honeydew on pot rims and leaves; it's exuded by feeding insects. Rinse infested plants with lukewarm water from the shower, then spray with insecticidal soap.

☐ TREES AND SHRUBS. Apply dormant oil to deciduous trees and shrubs to kill overwintering insects, eggs, and larvae, reducing your insect problems next season. ◆

Crown jewels of the cool season

Primroses shine in the garden or in containers,
from winter into spring

ike bright jewels spilled over the dark earth, primroses add sparkle to the winter garden. The flowers come in shades of amethyst, citrine, garnet, sapphire, and pink tourmaline; some are even edged with gold or silver. Yet for all their delicate beauty, not even frost and rain can take the luster off these garden gems.

Most gardeners grow primroses from plants, not seeds. In mild-winter areas of California and the Southwest, the plants are on the market from October through early spring. Early in the season, you can buy them in flats, six-packs, or 4-inch pots.

In mild parts of the Pacific Northwest, primroses show up mostly in 4-inch pots from New Year's through early spring. In snowy-winter areas, plants appear in late February or March.

As bedding plants or in containers, primroses look great. Regular feeding promotes bloom. Bedding plants do best with an application of complete, controlled-release fertilizer every three months or so. For container plants, apply a complete, half-strength liquid fertilizer twice a month.

THE STARS OF PRIMROSE LANE
Plants are often sold simply as English primroses, fairy primroses, or obconi-

For a royal border along a path, plant acaulis primroses (one flower per stem) and polyanthus types (multiple blooms).

cas. English types take more sun (in warmer climates, give them filtered sun in the hottest part of the day); fairy primroses and obconicas do best in light shade. The chart on page 22 shows you which kinds grow best in your *Sunset* climate zone.

English types have outsold other primroses for decades, and their flowers come in a wide range of brighter colors than you'll find in fairy primroses or obconicas. English primroses come in two types: acaulis and polyanthus.

Acaulis primroses usually have just one flower per stem, and the stems are only about 3 inches long. Breeders are concentrating on acaulis types, and their work shows: the flowers are very large, and the colors are exquisite. There are many hues of burgundy, red, pink, bronze, brown, yellow, apricot, white, and blue.

In the landscape, acaulis primroses tend to make a big splash of bloom early, then follow with more sporadic flowers throughout the season. They'd bloom more heavily and longer if it weren't for a rain-induced mold called botrytis. You can limit it by faithfully deadheading faded blooms.

Because of the botrytis problem and because acaulis blooms aren't tall enough to be seen easily from a distance, we recommend them for container plantings. Given protection from rain, they're perfect in wide bulb pots and front porch flower boxes. They

by **JIM McCAUSLAND**

NORMAN A. PLATE

NORMAN A. PLATE

also make good indoor plants if you can give them plenty of light.

Polyanthus hybrids flower on 8-inch stems and thrive just about anywhere. Look for Concorde, Pacific Giant, or Santa Barbara hybrids. The color range is almost unlimited.

Because polyanthus bloom stalks stand tall in the landscape, they show up well in flower beds.

Fairy primrose (Primula malacoides), a frost-tender species, likes mild-winter climates. It bears delicate whorls of bloom on 15-inch stems. The widely available Prima series has especially clear colors.

Because of fairy primrose's susceptibility to snails, slugs, and frost (28° is its lower limit), the popularity of this plant is declining in parts of the West.

P. obconica, sometimes called German primrose, is a rising star among the primroses sold in mild-winter parts of Arizona, California, and Texas. *Sunset's* head gardener, Rick LaFrentz, raves about this plant. "Of all the primulas we've grown, the obconicas are the most resistant to snails and slugs, and flower the longest. They start in October and bloom until we dig them up in May."

The obconicas come mostly in white and pastel shades of pink, salmon, magenta, orange, and blue.

Until recently, growers didn't like obconicas because their leaves give some people an itchy rash. But Goldsmith Seeds, a wholesale grower in Gilroy, California, came up with Libre, a nonallergenic obconica series that's free of primin (an alkaloid); these plants are easier to handle. ◆

Brimful with blooms, this pot combines tall strains, including Prominent (top left) and Pacific Giant (top center), with shorter Danova and Pageant primroses.

4 PRIMROSES at a GLANCE

	SPECIES	ZONES	PLUSES AND MINUSES
ENGLISH TYPES	Primula polyantha	1-10, 12-24	Polyanthus types are more widely adaptable than any other primrose, and they stand up best in the landscape. Moderate susceptibility to snails and slugs.
	P. vulgaris (P. acaulis)	1-6, 14-17, 21-24	Acaulis types are widely used indoors and out, but subject to botrytis, which damages or destroys crowns. Moderate susceptibility to snails and slugs.
FAIRY PRIMROSE	P. malacoides	8-9, 12-24	Most successful as an outdoor annual. Blooms December through April in California. Very susceptible to snails and slugs.
GERMAN PRIMROSE	P. obconica	4-9, 15-24	Good outdoors and in; can bloom almost year-round in either place. Leaves of most kinds cause an itchy skin rash for some people. Lower susceptibility to snails and slugs.

NORMAN A. PLATE

How to prune a tree...properly

Three steps to a better-looking (and healthier) tree: make big cuts, make small cuts, then thin

A healthy, well-shaped tree is a valuable asset to your landscape. Besides adding beauty to your garden and neighborhood and providing shade on hot summer days, it can also add thousands of dollars of equity to your property.

To maintain a tree's health, you need to prune its canopy periodically. Routine pruning will keep the tree shapely and free of dead and dying branches, which can invite disease; it will also prevent wind damage.

Pruning isn't complicated, but it may

take a little practice to develop an eye for good tree shape and form. It's best to tackle only small to medium-size trees yourself and leave the large trees for arborists. If you're wary of making any cuts at all and prefer to deal with an arborist, it's still useful to learn

by LAUREN BONAR SWEZEY

1

2

3

PETER CHRISTIANSEN (5)

something about the pruning process. A little knowledge will help you ask the right questions and determine whether your arborist is qualified to do the job.

The best time to prune trees is winter (early spring in cold climates), when they're dormant.

TOOLS OF THE TRADE

Start with the proper ladder, suggests arborist Kevin Raftery of Palo Alto, who helped us prune the hawthorn tree shown on these pages. "The closer you can get to what you're cutting, the less strain on your body. Orchard ladders, which have three legs, are best (you can rent one); stepladders, which have four legs, can tip over. Make sure the ladder is planted firmly on solid ground." You may need to actually climb into the tree to make some out-of-reach pruning cuts.

To make cuts efficiently, Raftery uses a variety of tools: Japanese handsaw, pole pruner, loppers, and pruning shears. Pole pruners are especially useful when

you're working among thorny branches. Loppers work well on thornless trees.

To save energy on a big job, Raftery sometimes uses a chain saw. "But you have to be very careful not to injure nearby branches and yourself," he says.

Gardeners working at home may not have many tools on hand, but you can get by with just a handsaw and pruning shears. You may want to rent or borrow a pole pruner to reach high branches.

One last critical piece of equipment, says Raftery, is a pair of sunglasses: "They help keep the dust out of your eyes and protect them from glare."

1. MAKE THE BIG CUTS

Before you cut anything, stand back and look at the tree. Identify the principal framework (main branches) that you'll probably want to keep. Raftery advises caution when deciding what and how much to prune: "You may want to leave questionable branches and then come back and assess them later after you've cleaned up some of the tree. It's better

to underprune than overprune."

Then make your big cuts using a pruning saw. On the overgrown hawthorn shown here, Raftery had to cut out a few large branches. But small cuts heal more quickly, so it's best to prune frequently enough (once a year) that large cuts aren't necessary. (Sealants, which can seal in moisture and diseases, are no longer recommended for cuts of any size.)

To remove a large branch (more than 2 inches in diameter), make a cut on the underside of the branch about 12 inches from the crotch; cut a quarter of the way through. Then start on the top side of the branch and make a second cut an inch (toward the branch end) from the undercut; cut all the way through. Finally, remove the branch at the crotch by cutting just beyond the branch's bark ridges.

2. REMOVE WATERSPROUTS

After making the major cuts, remove most of the watersprouts (stems that

Before it was pruned, this hawthorn (left) was overgrown, full of watersprouts. After pruning (right), its scraggly growth is gone. The tree is well balanced, with space between branches for air circulation. Five months later (page 25), it's gorgeous.

rise vertically from branches) in the center of the tree. Watersprouts are weakly attached and can cause massive tangles and poor air circulation.

"In a tree as overgrown as this hawthorn, it helps to first clear out the center of the tree so you can see what you're doing," says Raftery. You may have to cut the watersprouts in two or three places just to get them out of the tangled interior and to avoid breaking branches you want to keep. "It's a little like alligator wrestling," he says.

Remove almost all of the vertical sprouts, except ones that would leave gaping holes in the tree's canopy. Step back often to reassess what you're doing.

3. THIN BRANCHES AND BRANCH TIPS
Use pruning shears (or a pole pruner) to thin growth on branch ends to reduce their weight. Also remove crossing and broken branches. Make your cuts just above a side branch or a bud that grows in the direction you want the branch to grow. Pruning to a bud

that faces down will encourage horizontal growth, and a bud facing up will encourage upright growth.

Never lop off the tops of branches to reduce a tree's height. You'll only encourage weakly attached, vertical growth the following season. To reduce a tree's height, always cut back to a lateral (horizontal) branch ⅓ to ½ the diameter of the one you're cutting.

Heavy pruning promotes much new growth. The following summer, you'll need to remove new vertical sprouts. ◆

Forced hydrangeas can make the transition from indoors to the garden. For details, see page 32.

PAUL HAMMOND

February

gardenguide

CHAD SLATTERY

Stars of the scrub

Leucospermum and other unthirsty plants burst into bloom
at Buena Creek Gardens this month

by **SHARON COHOON**

Showy isn't the first adjective that comes to mind when you describe scrub plant communities such as Southern California's chaparral. *Subtle* is more like it. But the drought-tolerant garden at Buena Creek Gardens in San Marcos is living proof that showy and scrub are not mutually exclusive terms. This month grevilleas, shrubs from the Australian scrub community, bear large clusters of red, coral, and magenta flowers. South African proteas and leucospermum sport exotic thistlelike blooms in shocking shades of orange, yellow, and hot pink. And the blue of California ceanothus, the star of our own chaparral, provides a cool counterbalance.

Steve Brigham, the nursery's owner, amassed this collection of knock-your-socks-off flowering plants from Mediterranean climates around the world and planted them out in the most inhospitable section of the nursery—a granite shelf nearly devoid of nutrients. Then, to further test their mettle, he experimented to see just how much neglect the plants would survive (near total, it turns out).

Brigham never feeds or deadheads these plants. For the first five years, he didn't prune them. And he rarely waters them. "Twice last year," he says. (Yes, you read that right.)

Many of these plants could take richer soil and more water than he gives them. They just wouldn't last as long. Under those conditions, Brigham says, "they live fast, die young, and look glorious until the end."

To find out more about the glamorous side of these drought-tolerant plants, contact Brigham for information about tours of his garden; telephone (619) 744-2810. The nursery is located at 418 Buena Creek Road, San Marcos.

tools

TRANSPLANT SPADE

CURTIS ANDERSON

Every now and then a really smart gardening tool comes along that makes you wonder how you ever got along without it. This new transplant spade, from Lee Valley Tools, is one of them.

Its blade is 3 inches narrower than the standard 8-inch blade, 11½ inches long, and curved rather than flat. Shaped for precise work, this tool is perfect for digging planting holes in tight places and for transplanting perennials in a flower border without fear of damaging surrounding plants. The tubular, steel-reinforced handle is strong but light. In fact, the entire tool weighs just 4 pounds.

The transplant spade is available in rust-free, easy-to-clean stainless steel ($25, plus shipping) or stronger high-carbon steel ($15, plus shipping) from Lee Valley Tools (800/871-8158). — *Lauren Bonar Swezey*

Perfect penstemons

NORMAN A. PLATE

Last winter, *Sunset* test garden coordinator Bud Stuckey sowed seeds of 'Early Bird Mixed' penstemon, hoping that by fall he might have some healthy, good-size plants and a few blooms. Much to his surprise, the penstemons were blooming profusely by early summer. And the gorgeous flowers—in red, pink, cerise, light purple, and white—were huge (2 inches wide).

'Early Bird Mixed', a hybrid penstemon, has been bred for an early show of large flowers on smaller plants (ours grew to 2 feet tall).

Now's the time to start your own penstemons from seed. Sow the seeds in containers indoors or in a greenhouse. After they germinate, move the seedlings to an area that gets bright light. Keep the soil moist, but not wet. Fertilize with a dilute solution of fertilizer.

When the seedlings are well developed and the weather is mild, set them outdoors in a protected area and slowly introduce them into full sun during a period of a week or so. Then plant them in well-amended soil.

Penstemon seeds are available from Thompson & Morgan, Box 1308, Jackson, NJ 08527; (800) 274-7333. A packet costs $2.65, plus shipping. — *L. B. S.*

TIPS, TRICKS & SECRETS

Forcing buds into bloom

Nothing can make you feel more like spring is on its way than a big vase filled with leafless branches covered with swelling buds that burst into bloom inside the house. The process of forcing deciduous flowering shrubs to bloom in late winter has delighted gardeners for centuries.

Among the plants that respond well to forcing are forsythia and flowering varieties of crabapple, cherry, plum, and quince. Simply cut some branches and put them in a vase of warm water indoors. If the buds are exceptionally tight and dry (usually when the weather is very cold), they may be slow to open, or worse yet, dry up and drop from the branch. To prevent this, give branches with tight buds a moisturizing bath. Fill a bathtub or large pan with lukewarm water, submerge the branches, and let them soak for several hours or overnight. Remove them from the water, let them drip dry, then put them on display. Don't crowd stems into vases; leave room for buds to open. Often, forced branches will put on a show for a couple of weeks. — *Steven R. Lorton*

'Bolivian Rainbow' ornamental pepper

One of the most eye-catching plants in *Sunset's* test garden last summer was a chili pepper. 'Bolivian Rainbow' bears 1-inch-long pods that start out metallic purple, then gradually turn yellow and finally red at maturity. The effect of the chili's purple-yellow-red rainbow is set off by the purple-tinged foliage of the plant, which grows 2 to 3 feet tall.

The fruits appear prolifically all summer. They can be eaten fresh at any color stage, but they have the hottest flavor—and that is *very hot*—when they reach the ripe, red stage. The pods can also be dried or pickled.

Because of its ornamental qualities, 'Bolivian Rainbow' can easily move out of the vegetable patch into flower beds.

If you want to grow 'Bolivian Rainbow', you'll have to start from seed. Sow the seeds in flats indoors about six weeks before the last spring frost. When the seedlings reach about 2 inches tall, transplant them into small pots. Harden off the plants by gradually exposing them to ever-brighter light outdoors, then set them in a spot that gets full sun. Fertilize the plants regularly, especially when young, and don't let them dry out.

'Bolivian Rainbow' is available from Seeds of Change, Box 15700, Santa Fe, NM 87506; call (800) 957-3337 for a free catalog. — *Lance Walheim*

Change of scene for potted hydrangeas

Floral shops and nurseries are full of foil-wrapped pots of hydrangeas this time of year. You'll find two types in bloom: those with standard flowers, and lace cap hydrangeas with clusters of small fertile flowers surrounded by a ring of big sterile blossoms.

Both types come in whites, blues, pinks, and bicolors. The lace cap hydrangeas in 6-inch pots featured on page 26 are about a year old. Greenhouse growers force them to flower young, but the plants won't stay small very long; most eventually grow into 4- or 5-foot shrubs.

In most parts of the West, except the desert and the coldest-winter areas, forced hydrangeas can easily make the transition from indoors to the garden. While the plants are still indoors in pots, water them when the top ½ inch of soil dries out; be sure to snip off flower clusters when they're past their prime.

Then in May, after all danger of frost is past, allow hydrangeas to harden off, or gradually acclimatize, to outdoor conditions on a patio or deck that gets filtered sun. You can plant hydrangeas in the ground right after they've hardened off, or keep them in pots all summer and plant them after the weather starts to cool off in the fall. They take full sun in mild climates along the coast and partial shade where summers are hot.

In snowy-winter areas, mound leaves over the plants in fall to protect them over winter against damage from hard freezes.

Hydrangea flower color is, to a degree, dependent on soil pH (acidity or alkalinity). Acid soil makes flowers blue; alkaline soil makes them pink. If you have acid soil and blue flowers, you can get pink blossoms by amending the soil with lime before you plant. If you have alkaline soil and pink flowers, you can get blue ones by feeding with an acid fertilizer such as aluminum sulfate.

— *Jim McCausland*

plant **PROFILE**

'Summer Icicle', a chilly euphorbia

A fiery Indian curry tastes twice as good with a soothing dish of cucumber-and-yogurt raita alongside to balance the curry's heat. The warm scarlets, oranges, and sulfur yellows of summer flowers benefit from a cool counterbalance, too. *Euphorbia marginata* 'Summer Icicle' performs this task beautifully.

The top leaves of this tall summer annual (18 to 24 inches) are icy white with a mint-green center stripe. It's a look cool enough to chill out the hottest marigolds, zinnias, and celosias.

'Summer Icicle' keeps its cool in flower arrangements, too. Sear the stems with a hot flame or dip them in boiling water immediately after cutting, and they'll last a week if not longer.

Seedlings in 4-inch pots, occasionally available at nurseries, are worth a try. But 'Summer Icicle' is best started from seed. Be patient, though. Compared with many annuals that shoot up seedlings quickly, *E. marginata* is poky (seeds take as long as 28 days to germinate). Sow seeds outdoors when soil temperatures begin to warm up (60° to 75°). Or start indoors and transplant outdoors after danger of frost is past. Plant euphorbia where its bare legs will be masked by other foliage.

If you can't find seed at your usual sources, order 'Summer Icicle' from Thompson & Morgan, Box 1308, Jackson, NJ 08527; (800) 274-7333.
— *S.C.*

Pacific Northwest Garden Notebook

by S T E V E N R. L O R T O N

Twenty-five years ago this month—on Valentine's Day, to be exact—I walked into the Northwest Bureau of *Sunset Magazine* to start my life as a garden writer. Through the years, so much has changed in the horticultural world that when I look back, I'm amazed.

Gardening is now the number one leisure activity in the United States. We've gone from liberally spraying hazardous pesticides like DDT to using organic, environmentally safe controls. Waves of new plants have been introduced—annuals, perennials, grasses, roses, conifers, and many great vegetables. And native plants have taken their rightful place in our gardens. We've shown a much deeper regard for our water supply—and the lack of it—by cutting back on lawns and instead developing gardens that are water-wise.

But for me, the most exciting change of all has been the growth of the youth gardening movement. So here's my silver anniversary wish: that everyone reading this column make an effort to get one child started in gardening. If we want the next generation to be committed to the health of our planet, a good place to start is with one easy-to-grow plant and a tiny plot or pot of soil. It could be as simple as planting sunflower seeds in a 1-gallon can. You might contact a nearby elementary school to see if the teachers would be interested in having someone help students with a hands-on project such as making saucer gardens with sempervivums and succulents (ask a parent group, nursery, or garden club to donate the materials).

IF YOU LOVE TREE PEONIES, MEET MR. ROGERS

My friend Rick Rogers, a great plantsman, has just opened a new nursery in Sherwood, Oregon, called Brothers Herbs & Peonies. Rick will be selling both, but what he's best known for is his excellent selection, propagation, and cultivation of tree peonies. Rick loves these plants not only for their huge and handsome blooms but also for their three-season foliage show (which often culminates in vivid autumn color) and

their winter form. Rick's catalog will be out this month. You can read about the plants and place an order for fall delivery of rootstock. For a catalog, send $2 to Brothers Herbs & Peonies, 27015 S.W. Ladd Hill Rd., Sherwood, OR 97140; (503) 625-7548.

HELLO, ALASKA GARDENERS

This issue marks the return of Alaska to Sunset's Pacific Northwest Garden Guide. In addition to covering British Columbia, Washington, and Oregon, the checklist on this page now includes Alaska (see map on page 37). Naturally, Alaska claims some of the Northwest's most intrepid and resourceful gardeners—and with such a short growing season, they have to be. Yet some of the biggest vegetables and most beautiful flowers we've ever seen were in Alaska gardens.

We're eager to hear from Alaska gardeners: What are your tricks and secrets for growing great crops? What are your favorite short-season vegetable varieties? If you have a particularly prolific garden, we'd like to see it. Send your tips and color snapshots to Alaska Gardens, *Sunset Magazine*, Suite 600, 500 Union St., Seattle, WA 98101. Please include a daytime telephone number.

THAT'S A GOOD QUESTION

Q: When I buy pots of blooming daffodils and tulips this month, can I plant them outdoors while they're in bloom? — *Marie Nelson, Eugene, Oregon*

A: You can plant them outdoors in the Pacific Northwest's milder climates (*Sunset* zones 4 through 7). In the coldest climates (zones 1 through 3), the plants will freeze and turn to mush if they're set out now, so enjoy them indoors. In my gardens in Seattle and the Skagit Valley, I often knock the bulbs out of their pots and plant them in the ground—and they don't miss a beat.

Northern California Garden Notebook

by LAUREN BONAR SWEZEY

The other day, I was explaining to a nongardening friend why gardening is so satisfying. It's good for the body, I told her. After shoveling, bending, and planting all day, my muscles know they've been exercised! Gardening can be good for the environment (I don't keep an arsenal of pesticides in my cupboard). And the gardeners I meet in my wanderings are about the nicest people around—always willing to share treasured plants.

But, I explained, what really excites me about gardening is the occasional happy accident—a favorite plant popping up in a place where I hadn't planted it. Last summer, I discovered catmint blooming in a pot with an apricot-colored miniature rose and another poking up through an ornamental oregano. The color combinations were stunning. Then my *Geranium endressii* 'Wargrave Pink' seeded itself next to a boulder on the edge of a gravel path. I couldn't have chosen a better location if I had planted it myself. I even found a coral *Salvia coccinea* 'Brenthurst' popping up in a pot of blue pansies. I was thrilled.

Then there are those lovely wanderers, like gaura and *Verbena bonariensis,* that border on invasive. They reseed themselves so readily that my relationship with them isn't always easy. On the other hand, they're so gorgeous in bloom, I can excuse their forwardness. I just make sure to rout out excess seedlings.

I don't think I persuaded my friend to plant an acre of vegetables, but I could tell she was intrigued by the notion of growing plants. So I promised to give her some gaura seedlings. I just hope that she still thinks of me as a friend when she finds dozens of little happy accidents all over her yard next spring.

MARINA THOMPSON

A NEW BOOK FOR HERB LOVERS

Herb gardening has become a popular pastime in recent years, and publishers have taken advantage of this trend. Now you can find dozens of herb books to choose from. One new book I find particularly informative for the beginning herb gardener is *The Herb Gardener: A Guide for All Seasons,* by Susan McClure (Storey Communications, Pownal, VT, 1996; $29.95; 800/441-5700). The 236-page book is divided into five helpful sections—from herb-gardening basics to a guide to individual herbs. The only oversight—the author left out of the appendix my favorite mail-order nursery: Mountain Valley Growers, 38325 Pepperweed Rd., Squaw Valley, CA 93675; (209) 338-2775.

THAT'S A GOOD QUESTION

Q: My front lawn has been ruined by red-earthworm mounds. I tried Diazinon granules, but they didn't work. Should I use the stronger liquid Diazinon I can get from the farm supply store? — *Gerry Hermsmeyer, Napa*

A: I'm sure it's frustrating to have mounds in your lawn, but earthworms are very beneficial to the soil and important for the long-term health of your lawn. They aerate the soil, improve soil drainage, and encourage microbial activity. Worm activity near the surface is only temporary. When soil is waterlogged from excess rain, worms tunnel up and spend more time near the soil surface. When rains subside, the worms tunnel deeper. Don't use Diazinon. Not only is it not registered for use on earthworms, it will kill all of them and your lawn will suffer. A better solution is to just rake the mounds down.

Southern California Garden Notebook

by **SHARON COHOON**

Cymbidium stems in a bud vase on your bathroom counter are a glorious way to start a cold, gray, wet winter day. They can turn your whole mood around. I owe the pleasure of this experience entirely to one man—the orchid hobbyist who persuaded me not to give up on them.

My first experience with cymbidiums, you see, wasn't exactly positive. They refused to rebloom. I fussed and fiddled. I mixed red potions and blue. And the orchids just sat there, boringly green. Disgusted, I prepared to chuck the lot. Fortunately, though, I complained to this man first.

"Stop hovering!" he ordered. "Just toss a little Osmocote in the pots every spring and be done with it. That's what I do." It sounded too easy. But it worked. And without my shadow looming over them, my cymbidiums have bloomed every year since.

Incidentally, if you haven't tried it, you might be surprised to know that cut cymbidium stems last six weeks or longer in a vase. Makes them a bargain, not a luxury, wouldn't you say? So why weather another winter without them?

MARINA THOMPSON

SPEAKING OF SHOWS . . .

Wet winters aren't all bad. They produce gorgeous camellias, for instance. See the best blossoms of the year at shows at the Huntington Botanical Gardens or Descanso Gardens this month. Call (818) 405-2141 for details on the Huntington camellia show. For information on the Descanso Gardens show, call (818) 952-4401.

ALOHA, HAWAII GARDENERS

Welcome to the Southern California/Hawaii edition of *Sunset.* You enjoy the kinds of gardens the rest of us would love to have. So go ahead. Make our day. If you garden in the Hawaiian Islands, tell us about your garden triumphs, your great plant collections, how well you're succeeding with native plants or with exotics such as orchids or mangoes, or how you've made your garden a special place—on a tight lot or in difficult terrain. If you have good garden ideas to share with other *Sunset* readers, send letters and photographs, if you have them, to the address listed below. *Mahalo.*

THAT'S A GOOD QUESTION

Q: My purple fountain grass looks bedraggled and unkempt. What should I do?

A: Trim the whole plant back and let it make a fresh start. Purple fountain grass and other warm-season grasses like miscanthus need serious shearing once a year to remain graceful and healthy, according to ornamental-grass specialist John Greenlee of Greenlee Nursery in Pomona. The shearing is a substitute for the grazing and periodic burning that would occur in a natural grassland, he says. Using sharp pruning shears, cut the grass back to a few inches above the ground now, before new growth emerges. New foliage will cover up those pruning scars quickly.

Westerner's Garden Notebook

by **JIM McCAUSLAND**

Perhaps nothing is as closely linked to a garden's success as the weather. For that reason I keep a homemade weather station in my back garden. By checking the station every evening and keeping weather records, I've learned that I average 25 percent more rain, have cooler temperatures, and get more snow than the nearest big airport (just 20 miles away). It's the kind of vital information I could get no other way.

The weather station was easy to make. I just sunk a pressure-treated, 8-foot 4-by-4 about 18 inches into open ground about 20 feet from the nearest building. I hung a minimum-maximum thermometer on its north side, a jumbo rain gauge on its south side, and a windsock from a cross member. I also tacked a yardstick against its east side to measure snow. You can find minimum-maximum thermometers at hardware stores and garden centers. The best rain gauge I've ever seen is from Productive Alternatives ($29.95, no credit cards), Box 329A, Fergus Falls, MN 56537; (218) 736-5668.

THE WELL-FEATHERED GARDEN

Nothing adds more life to a garden than the birds that inhabit it. With that in mind, Jan Mahnken wrote *The Backyard Bird-Lover's Guide* (Storey Publishing, Pownal, VT, 1996; $24.95). This book can help you get more birds to call your garden home.

Different sections of the book explain how to provide food, water, and nest boxes for birds. And when they come,

MARINA THOMPSON

scan the book's field-guide chapter (which fills more than half of this 310-page book) to identify them. The watercolors and descriptions of 135 common garden birds are perfect for beginning bird-watchers.

But the most valuable part of the book may be its appendix, which lists common types of bird feed—from seeds to fruits and nuts—and what birds they attract. The guide also includes habitat requirements for each of the birds listed, so you can tailor your garden to the creatures you want to have living there. To order the book directly from the publisher, call (800) 441-5700.

THAT'S A GOOD QUESTION

Q: I refer to my *Sunset Western Garden Book* regularly. I have a couple of questions about terminologies that are used. What is meant by "tender perennial" (petunias)? What is meant by "perennial grown as summer annual" (pansies, Mexican sunflowers)? — *Susan Alls, Colorado Springs, Colorado*

A: A tender perennial is one that freezes out easily, so most people use it as an annual (they grow it during the warm season, then let it die when frost comes) or expect it to be a perennial only in frost-free gardens. A perennial grown as a summer annual is exactly the same thing. In areas that never get frost, some tender perennials (like Madagascar periwinkle, also known as *Vinca rosea*) can go on for years.

Planting

☐ **BARE-ROOT.** In zones 4–7, plant bare-root cane berries, trees, shrubs, and vines. Buy early. It's best to plant them as soon as you get them, but if you can't, pack their roots in damp compost, sawdust, wood shavings, or soil and keep them moist in a place out of direct sun. In the coldest climates (zones 1–3), bare-root planting comes later in the spring.

☐ **PEAS.** You can plant peas outside this month in zones 4–7. Give them a head start by soaking them in water overnight, then placing them between layers of damp paper towel on a cookie sheet. Set them in a warm place. Once they have sprouted, plant them in the ground.

☐ **PRIMROSES.** You'll find blooming plants in 4-inch pots all over this month. Slipped into baskets or repotted in decorative containers, they make great Valentine's Day gifts. Keep them well watered. One way is to fill a sink or dishpan with water and set the primroses in it, with the water covering the top of the soil. Let them soak for several hours or even overnight. Groom the plants: pick off blooms and foliage as they fade. Give the plants a complete liquid plant food (12-12-12 is a good choice) diluted to half-strength to encourage a second and third crop of blossoms. In zones 4–7, you can plant primroses outdoors in a shady spot after the indoor show is over.

Maintenance

☐ **EXAMINE STORED BULBS.** Take a look at bulbs you've been storing through the winter. If any are shriveled, sprinkle a bit of water on them to plump them up. If any show signs of rot, toss them out. However, if dahlia tubers show signs of rot, cut out all the bad spots, dust tubers with sulfur, and store them apart from other bulbs.

☐ **FEED HOUSE PLANTS.** With short days and low winter light, most plants don't need to be fed, but do fertilize any that are blooming, fruiting, or showing signs of growth (the standard feeding schedule for indoor plants is April through October).

☐ **PRUNE ROSES.** Washington's Birthday is the traditional day to prune roses in the milder climates of the Northwest (zones 4–7). Remove injured or dead canes, then cut the remaining canes back to a length of 6 to 8 inches. Finally, shape plants so that canes face up and out in a vase shape. In zones 1–3, wait until April to prune roses.

Pest and weed control

☐ **BATTLE SLUGS.** You may think you got all the slimy demons last fall, but plant a blooming primrose out in the garden and the next morning you'll probably grieve over the chewed-up skeleton of a plant. Whatever your weapon (bait, traps, or beer), use it liberally now. As the days warm, little slugs crawl out ready to eat. Take care to keep poison bait well away from pets and children.

☐ **WEED.** Any weeds you pull now will not be around to mature and scatter seeds later, and they won't gobble up soil nutrients to compete with desirable plants.

Planting

☐ **PLANT FOR SPRING BLOOM.** Zones 7–9, 14–17: Some choices include calendula, candytuft, cineraria, dianthus, English daisy, English and fairy primroses, forget-me-not, Iceland poppy, pansy, *Primula obconica,* snapdragon, stock, and viola.

☐ **PLANT FLOWERING CHERRIES.** Zones 7–9, 14–17: Plant several kinds for staggered bloom. Early blooming: single, pink *Prunus yedoensis* 'Akebono'; double, dark pink *P. serrulata* 'Royal Burgundy'. Midseason: bright pink 'Beni Hoshi'; double, rose pink 'Kwanzan'. Late: semidouble, light pink 'Shogetsu'.

☐ **PLANT PERENNIALS.** Zones 7–9, 14–17: For spring-blooming perennials try alstroemeria, bergenia, bleeding heart, brunnera, campanula, candytuft, catmint, columbine, coral bells, delphinium, dianthus, diascia, foxglove, poppy, and violet.

☐ **PLANT VEGETABLES.** Zones 7–9, 14–17: Set out roots of artichokes and asparagus, and seedlings of broccoli, cabbage, cauliflower, celery (only in zones 15–17), green onions, and lettuce. From seed, try beets, carrots, chard, lettuce, peas, and spinach. Sow seeds of eggplant, pepper, and tomato indoors with bottom heat (use a heating coil or set containers on a water heater until the seeds germinate, then move them into bright light); allow six to eight weeks to reach transplant size.

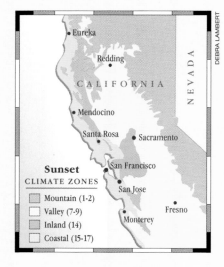

Sunset
CLIMATE ZONES
☐ Mountain (1-2)
☐ Valley (7-9)
☐ Inland (14)
☐ Coastal (15-17)

☐ **SET OUT EVERGREEN VINES.** Zones 7–9, 14–17: Good choices are fragrant, yellow-flowered Carolina jessamine (*Gelsemium sempervirens*); white-flowered evergreen clematis (*C. armandii*); pinkish purple–flowered *Hardenbergia violacea* 'Happy Wanderer'; pink-flowered *H. v.* 'Rosea'; fragrant, pinkish white–flowered *Jasminum polyanthum;* violet trumpet vine (*Clytostoma callistegioides*). All are very vigorous, growing at least 15 to 20 feet.

☐ **START SUMMER-BLOOMING BULBS.** Zones 7–9, 14–17: Plant tuberous begonias, callas, cannas, dahlias, gladiolus, tigridias, and tuberoses.

Maintenance

☐ **CUT BACK FUCHSIAS.** Zones 7–9, 14–17: To stimulate new growth, cut back woody stems to the main branches, then remove interior twiggy and dead growth. Cut back container fuchsias to the pot rims.

☐ **REPOT CYMBIDIUMS.** If your cymbidiums are bulging out of their containers, it's time to repot them. It's best to do this between mid-February and early July. Repotting too late in the season will prevent next season's bloom. It may also make cymbidiums that live outdoors more susceptible to cold. Use a medium bark or cymbidium mix. Cut off dead roots; discard soft or rotted bulbs.

Pest control

☐ **CONTROL SLUGS AND SNAILS.** Zones 7–9, 14–17: As nighttime temperatures rise, snails and slugs become more active and can quickly consume favorite plants, especially tender young seedlings. To apply bait without it contacting the soil, use a liquid type and place it on a shingle on top of the soil; cover it with another shingle.

☐ **SPRAY FOR PEACH LEAF CURL.** Zones 7–9, 14–17: Around mid- to late February, when buds are beginning to swell, apply a dormant spray to prevent peach leaf curl—a fungus that distorts peach leaves and destroys the fruit. Use lime sulfur with a spreader-sticker to improve coverage; do not spray when rain is predicted within 36 hours.

Planting

☐ **PLANT ANNUALS.** Coastal and inland gardeners can fill in bare spots in the garden with calendula, cineraria, Iceland poppy, nemesia, pansy, primrose, snapdragon, stock, sweet pea, and viola.

☐ **PLANT PERENNIAL WILDFLOWERS.** In the low desert (zone 13), plant coreopsis, desert marigold, evening primrose, penstemon, and salvia.

☐ **PLANT SUMMER BULBS.** Continue to set out caladium, calla, canna, crocosmia, dahlia, eucomis (pineapple flower), gladiolus, tigridia, tuberose, and tuberous begonia. Glads planted now will bloom before thrips strip and distort foliage in summer.

☐ **PLANT WINTER VEGETABLES.** Gardeners in coastal, inland, or high desert areas (zones 22–24, 18–21, and 11, respectively) can continue to sow seeds of cool-season plants, including beets, carrots, celery, chard, endive, kale, head and leaf lettuces, mustard, onions, peas, potatoes, radishes, spinach, and turnips. Annual herbs like chervil, chives, dill, and cilantro can also be sown. Broccoli, cauliflower, and other cabbage-family vegetables are best planted from seedlings this late in the season. In the low desert (zone 13), many warm-season vegetables, including tomatoes and peppers, can go into the ground after midmonth.

Sunset CLIMATE ZONES

1-3 7-9 11 13 14-24

☐ **PLANT WINTER-FLOWERING VINES.** Add some eye-level color to the winter garden with flowering vines. Good choices are yellow Carolina jessamine (*Gelsemium sempervirens*), purple-flowered *Hardenbergia violacea,* pink jasmine (*Jasminum polyanthum*), and orange flame vine (*Pyrostegia venusta*).

Maintenance

☐ **FEED PERMANENT PLANTS.** Feed ground covers, perennials, roses, shrubs, and trees. One quick way to fertilize is to scatter all-purpose granular fertilizer on the ground just before a storm is expected and let the rain water it in. For more gradual and consistent feeding, apply a slow-release fertilizer such as cottonseed meal, well-rotted manure, bone meal, or compost.

☐ **GROOM WINTER ANNUALS.** To keep your fall-planted annuals, like pansies, going strong, remove the spent flowers, pinch off weak growth, and feed them with a liquid fertilizer.

☐ **PRUNE DORMANT PLANTS.** If you didn't get to it last month, prune deciduous trees, fruit trees, grapes, roses, shrubs, and vines before the weather warms and growth begins.

☐ **TEND LAWNS.** Fertilize cool-season lawns every six weeks, and water if rains are inadequate; mow with blades set at 1½ to 2 inches. Warm-season lawns will begin to grow midmonth along the coast and early next month inland; dethatch, fertilize, and water them. If desired, apply a preemergence herbicide by midmonth to control crabgrass.

Pest and weed control

☐ **APPLY FINAL DORMANT SPRAY TO FRUIT TREES.** This is your last chance to smother overwintering insect pests such as scale, mites, and aphids with horticultural oil while trees are still leafless. Spray when the growth buds begin to swell but before they color and open. For fungal diseases such as peach leaf curl, add lime sulfur or fixed copper to the oil, following package directions. Spray the branches, crotches, trunk, and ground beneath the tree out to the drip line. If rain occurs within 48 hours of spraying, repeat the treatment.

Planting

☐ **BARE-ROOT PLANTS.** If the soil can be worked where you live, now is the time to plant bare-root stock. Nurseries carry small fruits like grapes and strawberries; cane fruits like blackberries and raspberries; all kinds of ornamental, fruit, and shade trees; and even vegetables like asparagus and horseradish.

☐ **ORDER SEED.** Place your seed orders for spring planting this month, before suppliers run out of popular and unusual varieties.

☐ **VEGETABLES.** Indoors or in a greenhouse, start cool-season vegetable seeds like broccoli, cabbage, cauliflower, Chinese vegetables, kale, and lettuce about six weeks before planting time in your area.

☐ **WILDFLOWERS.** Sow seeds of hardy wildflowers in prepared, weeded soil. If you sow at three-week intervals, you'll get a succession of bloom from most wildflowers this spring and summer, but some of the perennials and biennials common to most wildflower mixes won't bloom until their second growing season.

Maintenance

☐ **CLEAN HOUSE PLANTS.** Sponge off big leaves to remove dust. For small plants in pots, cover the soil with plastic wrap, then spray them with lukewarm water under the shower. Prune out yellowing and dead leaves. If plants are losing too many leaves, short days are likely the problem: consider installing artificial light.

Sunset
CLIMATE ZONES
☐ 1-3   ▨ 10-11

☐ **FEED BEARDED IRISES.** Late in the month, sprinkle a complete fertilizer on top of the soil over the rhizomes and water it in well.

☐ **FEED ROSES.** Pick a day late in February when nighttime temperatures are forecast to remain above freezing. Water established plants, let the soil drain, apply a complete fertilizer, and water again.

☐ **PREPARE BEDS.** As soon as the ground can be worked, dig or till compost or other organic matter into the soil to prepare flower and vegetable beds for spring planting. If you live where spring comes late, you can even dig in manure that's not fully rotted yet; by planting time, it will have mellowed out enough to nourish plants without burning them.

☐ **PROTECT SEEDLINGS.** In the coldest parts of the West, late frost can come any time and nip tender seedlings. Order cloches or floating row covers now so you'll have them when you need them. Windbreaks are also essential to keep tender seedlings from drying out: you can protect your garden plot by planting a double row of Siberian peashrubs (*Caragana arborescens*) and pines on the windward side of the area you plan to protect.

☐ **TIDY UP GREENHOUSES.** Before you start annuals and vegetables, wash pots and flats with a mild mixture of household bleach and water. Replace potting soil and check heating cables, heaters, vents, weather-stripping, and glazing. There's still time to make repairs before sowing.

Pest control

☐ **MONITOR HOUSE PLANTS.** Inspect leaves for aphids, telltale webs of spider mites, and the sticky honeydew that signals scale insects. Spray pests off leaves with lukewarm water; scrape off scale insects if necessary. If you choose to spray with an insecticide, first cover the plant with a plastic garment cover (the kind you get from dry cleaners) to confine the spray.

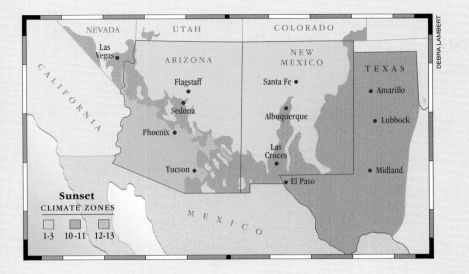

DEBRA LAMBERT

Planting

☐ **BARE-ROOT PLANTS.** Plant bare-root grapes, strawberries, blackberries, and raspberries; all kinds of ornamental, fruit, and shade trees; and even asparagus and horseradish.

☐ **GROUND COVERS, VINES.** In zone 11 (Las Vegas), set out Hall's honeysuckle, *Vinca major,* or *V. minor.* In zones 12 and 13, plant these plus perennial verbena, star jasmine, and trailing indigo bush (*Dalea greggii*). In colder zones, plant after danger of hard frost is past.

☐ **PERENNIAL WILDFLOWERS.** In zones 12 and 13 (Phoenix, Tucson), set out evening primrose, desert marigold, paperflower (*Psilostrophe cooperi*), penstemon, and salvia for spring bloom.

☐ **VEGETABLES.** In zones 11–13, sow cucumber, eggplant, melons, pepper, squash, and tomato indoors for transplanting after danger of hard frost is past. Sow root crops (beets, carrots, radishes), spinach, and peas in prepared garden soil. In zone 10 (Sedona, Albuquerque, Las Cruces, El Paso), start seeds of cool-season crops (broccoli, cabbage, cauliflower, Chinese vegetables, and lettuce) indoors late in the month.

Maintenance

☐ **CHECK DRIP SYSTEMS.** Clean or replace drip system filters, then turn on the system and check each emitter. If you find one that can't be unclogged, install a new emitter next to it.

☐ **FEED BEARDED IRISES.** Late in the month, sprinkle a complete fertilizer over iris rhizomes and water it in thoroughly.

☐ **FEED ROSES.** On a day late in February when nighttime temperatures are forecast to remain above freezing, water established plants, let the soil drain, apply complete fertilizer, and water again.

☐ **FEED WINTER RYE LAWNS.** In zones 12 and 13, apply 2½ pounds of ammonium sulfate per 1,000 square feet of lawn, and water it in well.

☐ **PREPARE BEDS.** Get flower and vegetable beds ready for spring planting by digging compost or other organic matter into the soil. If the soil is very alkaline in your garden, adjust the pH and increase fertility by adding 2 pounds of ammonium phosphate and 3 pounds of soil sulfur per 100 square feet. In Las Vegas, the native soil is so poor that the county extension office recommends planting in raised beds of imported soil only.

Pest control

☐ **CHECK HOUSE PLANTS.** Inspect leaves for aphids, telltale webs of spider mites, and the sticky honeydew that can signal scale insects. Spray pests off leaves with lukewarm water. Scrape off any scale insects.

☐ **CONTROL APHIDS.** In zones 12 and 13, check new growth for aphids. Blast them off with a jet of water and follow up with insecticidal soap.

THE *new* Western

Around the West, regional styles are redefining the garden—its design, its purpose, its plantings

Forward-thinking landscape professionals around the West have taken inspiration for years from the West's natural beauty and from the plants that grow here naturally—rather than from moister climates to the east, where endless green lawns and picture-perfect delphiniums grow effortlessly.

Now this quiet revolution is quickening. We've entered the age of the Northwest garden, the Southwest garden, the California garden, the mountain garden—embracing the land, the climate, and the cultural heritage. Our landscaping styles are as different from each other as they are from those in England and in the rest of America.

Gardeners have come to terms with the futility of growing tropicals where conifers reign supreme, or of carpeting the desert with lawn. We're using native plants or plants that are well adapted to conditions where we live. Many of our gardens are lawnless. Even outdoor art— whether a rustic wood carving of a Spanish padre or an aged copper temple bell from Asia—often hints at the heritage of a region.

Our gardens are still extensions of our houses—to be furnished and accessorized as much as indoor rooms. But now our gardens touch the land lightly.

MICHAEL THOMPSON

Garden

"Nature doesn't serve us, we serve nature," says Seattle landscape architect Robert Chittock.

Bright deciduous azaleas flame like fire against the serene backdrop of a mirror-smooth pond and a Japanese-style pavilion.

Year-round splendor

by **STEVEN R. LORTON**

Landscape designer Terry Welch's garden in Woodinville, Washington (also shown on pages 42 and 43), combines the rugged lushness of a Northwest rain forest with the tailored serenity of a Japanese garden. And by choosing just the right plants, Welch created a retreat that looks as pleasing in winter as it does in summer. Bark, foliage, conifers, the sculptural forms of leafless trees, and frost-browned grasses all spice the garden in winter as much as dazzling flowers do in spring and summer.

Handsome plantings stand out against rich backgrounds: swaths of lawn and water, stands of dark green Western hemlock, and a screen of alders that's rich green in summer, tawny and bare in winter. Broad-leafed evergreens are everywhere.

Upon this canvas, Welch put bold strokes of color, grouping several plants of the same species for visual impact. For its brilliant white bark, he planted *Betula jacquemontii* in groves. Along the pond in winter, waves of gold and crimson are produced by yellowtwig and redtwig dogwoods. Near the pond in spring, rhododendrons and deciduous azaleas erupt in brilliant yellows and reds.

MICHAEL THOMPSON

A sheltered bell and weathered fences (above) give this section of the garden a Japanese look.

Weeping copper beeches (Fagus sylvatica 'Purpurea Pendula') and Japanese maples are living sculptures in a wide bed before tall Douglas firs (above right). Blue-flowered Lithodora diffusa grows in front.

Mossy vine maple branches (right) arch dramatically over longleaf mahonia (M. nervosa) and three kinds of ferns (deer, sword, and lady) in a garden corner that mimics a Northwest rain forest.

Low-growing rhododendrons (left), crowned with spring blooms, edge a small pond and smooth, bluish boulders.

Rhododendrons abound

by PAMELA CORNELISON

The *grandes dames* of the Northwest landscape take center stage in this enchanting garden near Bellevue on the east shore of Lake Washington—the perfect setting for rhododendrons of all kinds. In spring, lightly ruffled blossoms in colors ranging from creamy white to pink, red, and yellow bring alive the softly textured background of green foliage. Owners Ned and Jean Brockenbrough created the garden to show their rhododendrons and azaleas to best advantage.

The lake-facing front of the house is the showplace; here the Brockenbroughs blend the rhododendrons with dogwoods, ferns, and deciduous azaleas whose bare-in-winter branches

add seasonal interest between ever-green plants. To give the garden a lush, woodland look, Ned trims the bottom branches from some of the rhododen-drons so he can grow anemones, dwarf kinnikinnicks, and maidenhair ferns beneath them.

The Brockenbroughs consider their garden a work in progress, and for good reason. In a test garden behind the house, Ned hybridizes and pro-duces many varieties of rhododen-drons each year, and he's always eager to try out his ready supply of seedlings. If a plant doesn't perform well in a new setting, there's always an understudy waiting in the wings in this back garden to replace it. ◆

Rhododendron 'Pink Pearl' and 'Beauty of Littleworth', along with pink dogwood, brighten the garden in spring behind low-growing azaleas (left). Sword ferns and lily-of-the-valley grow between boulders.

Blooming mounds of white rhododendrons (including R. yakushimanum, R. mucronulatum 'Sekidera', and R. pseudochrysanthum) flank the steps and terrace (right).

MICHAEL THOMPSON

The test garden blooms in a carnival of color (above) against a backdrop of Western red cedar and native hemlock.

CALIFORNIA LANDSCAPES

"I like gardens that connect their owners with the real world of earth, weather, seasons, and change," says San Francisco landscape designer Chris Jacobson.

Spa-turned-pond nestles in a private pocket of the garden. Small rocks, flagstone, and boulders add textural interest and blend with the muted tones of the lavender and grasses.

Water soothes the soul

by **PETER O. WHITELEY**

California's early mission courtyards inspired the design of this multilevel garden in Saratoga, California (also shown on pages 48 and 49). Like those at the missions, this peaceful retreat adapts well to the dry but ocean-tempered climate. Native and Mediterranean plants mingle in rock-edged raised beds. There is no lawn. Water is used judiciously—just enough to calm the soul. It animates the garden with trickling sounds as it spills from a fountain into a shallow, rock-lined "rill" (a sunken irrigation ditch). From there it rushes into a pond that was formerly an inground spa.

Broad paths of permeable paving—flagstone and decomposed granite—replaced an old concrete patio. The concrete was recycled to form walls for the raised beds. A cap of flagstone and a veneer of dry-stacked rocks mask the stacked concrete to give the raised beds a finished look.

To blend new flora with established plantings—hollyleaf cherries, maytens, and oleanders—landscape designer Chris Jacobson chose a palette of drought-tolerant plants: daylilies, fortnight lilies, lavenders, ornamental grasses, rosemary, succulents, and verbena. Lush ferns thrive in shady pockets. Angel's trumpets bloom in summer. Rill, walls, and gate were built by Dave Romeri. To save water, all plants are irrigated with a drip system.

SAXON HOLT

Garden paths (above) flow around a center raised bed planted with feathery mayten trees, squat mugho pines, silvery lamb's ears, and spiky fortnight lilies.

Fragrant angel's trumpet adds a touch of color to a raised bed (above right). The flagstone cap on the wall serves as a garden bench.

Sturdy but delicate-looking native giant chain ferns (right) highlight border plantings that include Japanese maple, mondo grass, and fountain grass (Pennisetum setaceum 'Rubrum').

Bog in a pot (left): tall, sculptural horsetails thrust from an antique pot.

Mediterranean living in an urban Eden

by **SHARON COHOON**

editerranean gardens often have two personalities. The side presented to the public is reserved and restrained. But the private side—hidden behind walls and seen only by family and friends—is rich, sensual, and luxurious. The garden designed for this Spanish mission–style house in North Hollywood by landscape architect Jerry Williams exhibits this attractive double nature.

The front garden, seen by motorists and pedestrians, is pleasant but deliberately low-key. Plants are soft and

subtle in tone, durable in disposition, and Mediterranean in origin—lavender, olive, rosemary, sea lavender, and society garlic. Blue-greens and silver-grays predominate. Flowers are few—mostly in soft purple shades. Watering and maintenance are minimal.

But when you step inside the garden at the rear of the property, you enter into another world where plants are boldly textured, brightly colored, and tropical in effect. There, foliage tones shift toward emeralds and apple greens. Rich fragrances perfume the air,

and the burble of running water soothes the spirit.

Such dual-personality gardening makes perfect sense in an urban environment, says Williams. Save the splash—and save on maintenance—for the private areas you really use. ◆

High walls protect this backyard oasis (left) from public view. King and queen palms add texture; flowers such as angel's trumpets add fragrance and color. Concrete triangles lead to a pond (below), where a small stone cherub sits in the shade of Australian tree ferns (Cyathea cooperi).

What the world sees is a low-maintenance Mediterranean garden (above). A soothing palette of silvers, blues, and grays complements this Spanish-style house on a small city lot.

ROB PROCTOR

MOUNTAIN STATES

"A garden is the foreground for the natural landscape," says landscape architect Chris Moritz of Bigfork, Montana. "Plants needn't be native to the region, but they need to blend with the background."

An arbor of gathered branches bridges a tiny stream where geese forage among ox-eye daisies.

Ranch dressing

by **ROB PROCTOR**

When Laurie and John McBride bought a ranch near Snowmass, Colorado, their friends and family wondered if this city couple had lost their marbles. But Lost Marbles Ranch (also shown on pages 54 and 55) is flourishing. A backdrop of deep-blue mountains, green pastures, and ever-changing sky sets the stage for a garden of drama and whimsy.

To frame vistas and mark entrances, Laurie's father, John Mack, built the charming arbors from branches he gathered. A stone wall that encircles the vegetable and cutting garden retains heat, an important consideration for a high-altitude garden with a short growing season. "I trick my lavender to bloom by planting it near rocks," explains Laurie. A scarecrow called Camilla presides over the produce, aided by family dogs and ducks in the war against visiting deer and elk. Groves of quaking aspen highlight the garden but are carefully placed not to screen the view from favorite seating areas.

Laurie enjoys creating visual puns, such as fencing one of her flower borders with iron headboards salvaged from the barn. "A proper bed deserves a proper headboard," she explains. Her love of watercolor painting drove her to begin gardening. "I needed subject material," she laughs. Soon she began to express her artistry in the garden, favoring easy-care perennials like ox-eye daisies, poppies, bellflowers, shrub roses, pansies, and columbines that thrive in the cool temperatures under sunny skies.

Brick and stone patio (left) for dining and entertaining extends from the house. Rustic accessories—twiggy chair and country birdhouse—add to the patio's casual ambience.

Daisies and columbines self-sow beneath quaking aspens (above right).

Pinks, lavender, and herbs thrive with young fruit trees against a wall that offers an enticing view through antique glass (right). Family pets have the run of the place.

ROB PROCTOR

A Rocky Mountain border

by **ROB PROCTOR**

Just as forests flow into meadows in parts of the Rocky Mountains, so conifers give way to curving perennial borders in Bea Taplin's garden on a gentle slope in Cherry Hills Village, Colorado. "Taking advantage of the vistas has been my priority," says Taplin.

Terraces of native stone provide structure and an easy transition between the classic clapboard house and a flax-filled field below. Pines and blue spruces stamp the garden as a Colorado original and enhance the vibrant colonies of stalwart perennials. A limited color palette and contrasting plant shapes and textures create an air of casual elegance.

Pink, yellow, and blue flowers show Taplin's preference for pastels, but dashes of scarlet and orange enliven the mix. The white blossoms of Asiatic lilies, baby's breath, and daisies sparkle among pale yellow yarrows, royal blue delphiniums, and brassy daylilies and ligularias. The emerald lawn—a playground for children and pets—further sets off the colorful,

gently curving borders.

Shrub roses and lilacs screen a vegetable garden from the main garden. Taplin's granddaughter tends her own small plot there, alongside rows of vegetables and flowers for cutting. "I love bouquets in the house," says Taplin, "but the real pleasure is in growing flowers for them." ◆

Spikes of golden ligularias and mulleins, blue delphiniums, and pink checkerblooms (left) line the walk to the pool and stand out handsomely against the backdrop of conifers.

A selected palette of gold, white, and pink benefits from a splash of red-orange Asiatic lilies (above top).

An inspired combination of Asiatic lilies, baby's breath, and yarrows (above) sparkles in the sylvan setting.

ROB PROCTOR

CHARLES MANN

THE SOUTHWEST

"What's unique about the Sonoran Desert is its abundance of plants, including large cactus and other succulents," says landscape architect Carol Shuler of Scottsdale, Arizona. "For desert gardens, plants should complement such natives in color, texture, and scale."

Young saguaros poke through boulders beside a desert wash. The tallest saguaro was already growing on-site when the garden was installed.

Taming nature

by **PAMELA CORNELISON**

Sculptural lines and subdued colors give the Scottsdale, Arizona, garden (pictured below and on pages 60 and 61) the look of untamed desert. But in fact, designer John Suarez carefully planned it to blend harmoniously with the surrounding Sonoran Desert.

The garden visually flows from inside the house to the desert. Chocolate flagstone paves interior and exterior floors and paths. Adobe walls snake along the patio, their gentle curves embracing clusters of prickly pear, saguaro, and barrel cactus, or pots of red geraniums. Pyracantha, the only ex-otic landscape plant here, billows over the wall, bright with cloud-white flowers in spring. A small ramada with an "old pueblo" look shelters a patio dining area and fireplace.

Beyond the wall, native plantings meander along a wash of river rock placed at the garden's lowest point for surface drainage. Small outcroppings of desert plants and well-worn boulders complement the textures and gentle contours of house and patio walls. Delicate-looking sweet acacia trees and sturdy saguaros add vertical accents to the rolling landscape.

Desert sun sparks a ghostly glow over spines of teddybear cactus (Opuntia bigelovii), a sculptural, treelike Arizona native.

Easy enchantment

When Santa Fe residents were called upon to cut their water use by 25 percent, Ann Mehaffy redesigned her garden to suit the region's persistent drought while maintaining a sense of place. She created meandering pathways of crushed Santa Fe brown gravel, planted unthirsty perennials and trees, and reduced her full-size vegetable garden to a small corner of the yard. Planting areas were mulched with straw, and new soaker hoses replaced the old drip system.

The new design has been so successful that Mehaffy has cut her residential

water use by 50 percent. And except for occasionally deadheading spent blooms or moving an errant volunteer or two, she finds her garden maintenance-free. She also had some fun with the design by incorporating whimsical touches, such as a brilliant red gate in a wall of terra-cotta, an umbrella that appears to float above the ground, and a metal handprint that waves through the windowed door to the vegetable garden.

Pink saponaria, ribbon grass, red spikes of knotweed, and lemon yellow toadflax add rich textures (above).
A tranquil "streambed" of gravel (right) meanders past Russian sage, Jupiter's beard, and Shasta daisies.

CHARLES MANN

Living alfresco on the Sonoran Desert

The desert flows seamlessly into this garden in Tucson—through walls designed to pass each other without touching. The token fencing between them is just enough to satisfy pool code requirements.

That's the way the owners—transplanted Californians—wanted it. When they first moved to the Southwest, they were mesmerized by the stark, dramatic beauty of the Sonoran Desert and wanted their garden to preserve the character of the site.

Landscape designer Paul Serra designed the garden to take advantage of the sloping site. He separated areas of activity into three different levels. On the top level, closest to the house, an outdoor kitchen has everything the owners need for complete meal preparation: wet bar, ice maker, sink, refrigerator, barbecue grill, and storage cabinets. Flagstone steps lead down to the midlevel pool, which is edged with boulders to give it the look of a natural pond. A waterfall cascades from the spa over native stone to the pool. On the lower level, the desert takes over. A "desert walk" wanders among palo verde trees and other native plants that are regularly visited by hummingbirds.

Throughout the garden, *bancos* (low seat-walls) provide extensive seating. In one area, they're grouped around a firepit that provides warmth on chilly evenings. ◆

Boulders and plants—cycads, euphorbias, justicias, lantanas, verbenas, and blue Salvia clevelandii—give the pool the look of a wild desert oasis.

NEW SUNSET BOOK *for* **WESTERN GARDEN MAKERS**
The gardens pictured on these pages are among more than 40 Western gardens featured in the new *Sunset Western Landscaping Book.* A companion to the *Sunset Western Garden Book,* this 416-page book focuses not just on plants but on landscape design. Glossy color photographs show great gardens from each region. Plans for parts of gardens, such as beds and borders, and for whole gardens—designed for us by Western landscape professionals—are included. Other chapters provide planning help, show finishing touches that make a garden special, and offer landscaping solutions to problems that affect garden design in the West, such as drought, erosion, floods, pollen, lack of privacy, smog, wildfires, and winds. The book ($29.95) is now available in bookstores and nurseries.

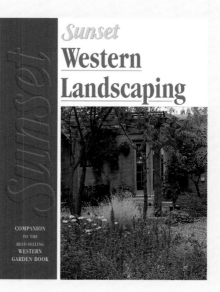

CHARLES MANN

Yes, we have blue potatoes

The freshest, most colorful crops are easier than ever to grow.
Here's a spud-lover's guide to the perfect potato patch

One spring, when I was 7, my grandfather gave me a potato and told me to put it in the ground. I did. Three months later, I happened upon the biggest, most verdant weed I'd ever encountered. What could it be—I wondered—and would it harm my potato? Well, Grandpa set me straight: that "weed" *was* my potato! And on that day, a gardener was born.

I think I must have planted a 'Russet Burbank' (I still remember the fluffy white flesh of the baked spuds), and for years it never occurred to me that there were any other kinds—not red, yellow, or blue potatoes. Yet all those colors and many new and antique varieties are on the market today. Order them now and plant in March (or as soon as the soil can be worked).

Many gardeners grow several varieties simply because different colors are fun to serve together. We know of one patriotic chef who celebrates every Fourth of July with a potato salad made of red, white, and blue spuds.

But there's more to potatoes than color, of course. Just taste for yourself. It's hard to beat the delicate flavor of new potatoes or a big, fluffy baker.

Last year, we grew a slew of potatoes in *Sunset's* trial garden in Menlo Park, California, and in a home garden on Puget Sound in Washington, then invited a panel of potato lovers to taste them in our test kitchen (for the results, see page 68). In addition to differences in color, flavor, and texture, we found great variability in the sizes of potatoes at harvest. Some varieties produced lots of marble-size tubers along with the full-size spuds we expected; others tended to bear more evenly.

GROWING TIPS

Each potato tuber is a complete package, containing enough water and nutrients to get the plant off to a good start. It just needs well-drained soil and full sun. In temperate climates, irrigation isn't an issue; for many farmers and gardeners, potatoes are dryland crops. One to 2 inches of water per month between planting and harvest is enough to produce a crop.

How to start: You can plant any untreated potato to start, or "seed," a new potato plant. My strategy is to plant these potatoes, known as seed potatoes, whole if they're small, or cut into egg-size chunks if they're larger. Before you plant chunks, place the fresh-cut tubers in a dry, shady spot for a few days to allow them to form calluses over the cuts. All else being equal, uncut seed potatoes will give slightly greater yields than chunks.

Some people presprout their potatoes (a process called "chitting") by putting them out in a cool, dry, frost-free place for a few days before planting. If you want fewer, bigger potatoes at harvest, break off all but one or two of these sprouts. For more, smaller potatoes, don't break off any sprouts.

Yields: As a rule of thumb, a pound of seed potatoes will produce 15 to 25 pounds of potatoes at harvest. If you plant chunks, figure that each start will produce 3 pounds of potatoes.

Rows or hills: There are several basic planting techniques, each with an infinite number of permutations. In row gardens, plant tubers or chunks 4 inches deep and 18 inches apart in rows 2 feet apart. If you'd prefer to plant in hills, mound soil as you would for squash and plant three or four seed

by **JIM McCAUSLAND**

NORMAN A. PLATE

hot POTATOES

'ALL BLUE'

'FRENCH FINGERLING'

'ALL RED'

'RUSSET NORKOTAH'

'ANOKA'

'YELLOW FINN'

The harvest of spuds comes in a spectrum of colors, from deep blue to buttery yellow. For culinary notes on these varieties, see the chart on page 68.

CURTIS ANDERSON (6)

potatoes in each hill. You can also plant potatoes in compost piles or in soil-filled tires. Generally, the more space you give the plants to develop (up to 3 square feet per plant), the higher the yields will be at harvest.

The soil should be well drained and reasonably fertile. I always till well-rotted manure or compost into the ground before I plant.

When potato plants reach 4 to 6 inches tall, mound soil up around each plant, leaving about half the top unburied. Do this in the morning, when plants are standing up straight (they sometimes sprawl during the day). Keep hilling plants up until about 8 to 12 inches of soil covers the seeds. Then let the plants mature.

Pests: Gophers can be a problem in some areas (they took a big bite out of the crop in our Menlo Park test garden). In the worst circumstances, you may have to line the bottom and sides of your planting bed with hardware cloth, or even plant in barrels. You can avoid most disease problems by plant-

Cut big seed potatoes into chunks (top) for planting. When plants reach 4 to 6 inches tall, mound soil up around them.

ing only certified seed potatoes.

Harvesting: When plants flower, you can harvest a few new potatoes from around the edge of each plant. New potatoes aren't just small potatoes—they're immature spuds whose sugar

hasn't yet converted to starch, as it has in fully developed tubers. That's why new potatoes are deliciously sweet and why they're best when used immediately after harvest.

After the tops of the plants die down, push a potato fork (a spading fork or pitchfork will do) into the soil around the perimeter of each plant. Rock it back and forth to break small roots connecting the potatoes, then leave the potato patch alone for a week to give the skins a chance to harden up—this way the spuds won't bruise when you dig them up and they'll keep longer.

SOURCES

Nurseries and garden centers offer the most popular kinds of seed potatoes. To get more exotic varieties, order by mail. These two suppliers offer the best selection in the West (catalogs are free): Garden City Seeds, 778 Highway 93 N., Hamilton, MT 59840, (406) 961-4837; and Ronniger's Seed Potatoes, Star Route 40, Moyie Springs, ID 83845. ◆

19 CHOICE POTATOES *and* HOW THEY PERFORM

	VARIETY	CULINARY NOTES	GARDEN NOTES
Blues	'All Blue'	Good mashed, fried, and in potato salad.	Blue inside and out. Midseason.
	'Caribe'	Scored well when boiled; good for mashing.	Blue skin, white flesh. High yields. Early.
Fingerlings	'Anna Cheeka's Ozette'	Firm and meaty; buttery flavor. Warty-looking skin is very tender.	Brought to the Northwest from Peru by 18th-century Spanish explorers; still grown by Native American gardeners. Late.
	'Butterfinger'	Second-best boiled potato.	Late.
	'French Fingerling'	Scored well when boiled.	Finger-shaped tubers. Midseason to late.
	'German Yellow'	Great color and flavor. Second-best baker.	Crescent-shaped tubers. Late.
	'Red Thumb'	Great flavor.	Red inside and out. Late.
Reds	'All Red'	Best boiled potato.	Red inside and out. Midseason.
	'Buffalo'	Creamy and moist; tasty skin.	Midseason.
	'Reddale'	Good boiled or baked.	Early.
	'Red LaSoda'	A little dry; good, firm, thin skin.	Midseason.
Russets	'Nooksack'	Good baked or mashed; creamy texture, thick skin.	Does well in wet areas. Late.
	'Russet Burbank'	Classic baker. Good-flavored skin and flesh.	Midseason.
	'Russet Norkotah'	Fine baker. Mealy texture and thin skin.	Early.
White	'Anoka'	Highly rated baker. Creamy texture, very soft skin.	Consistent producer of medium to large tubers. Early.
Yellows	'German Butterball'	Best baker. Good skin flavor.	Late.
	'Island Sunshine'	Good baked or mashed.	From maritime Canada, it grows well everywhere and resists late blight. Midseason.
	'Yellow Finn'	Good baked or mashed.	Midseason.
	'Yukon Gold'	Good all-purpose potato; high-scoring baker. Great color, creamy texture, and soft skin.	Bred in Canada for short growing seasons. Early.

DEIDRA WALPOLE

'Lavender Lady' bears 6-inch-long clusters of blooms starting in early spring.

Lilacs for mild climates

Flowers as pretty as party dresses, with a gently sweet fragrance reminiscent of Grandma's dressing table, make lilacs sentimental favorites. In a world that swirls around us too fast, lilacs spark nostalgia—possibly for a place where they once flourished, or perhaps for another era.

But this nostalgia isn't easy to create everywhere. In mild-winter climates, you can't pop just any lilac (*Syringa vulgaris*) into the ground and expect an exuberant show of blooms come midspring. You'll need to buy low-chill varieties.

Why? Because most lilacs prefer the kind of winter chill that sends us scrambling for heavy wool coats. Not so the low-chill varieties.

The first low-chill lilac, called 'Lavender Lady', was developed in Southern California 30 years ago by Walter Lammerts, a researcher and hybridizer with Rancho del Descanso—a former wholesale nursery that's now the site of Descanso Gardens, a botanical garden open to the public. "Walter was an excellent hybridizer," says Bob Boddy, son of the nursery's owner. "He came up with a progeny of 350 potentially outstanding low-chill lilacs." Although many varieties of lilacs are sometimes

attributed to Lammerts, 'Lavender Lady' and 'Angel White' were his only direct creations.

But other descendants from the original plantings have been introduced through the years by Descanso's staff. The lilacs—often referred to as Descanso Hybrids—now number a dozen or so, and many of them can still be seen growing at the gardens (1418 Descanso Dr., La Cañada Flintridge; 818/952-4400).

HOW TO GROW THE BEST FLOWERS

Like roses, lilacs are a bit greedy. To produce an abundant crop of flowers, they need plenty of sun. They also need space; crowding reduces air circulation and makes them more prone to powdery mildew. In mild Southern California, avoid planting them near lawns; year-round watering can prohibit dormancy and flowering.

Unlike many plants that thrive in rainy Eastern climates, lilacs prefer the arid West's alkaline soil. It's generally not necessary to add soil amendments at planting time unless the soil is very sandy or heavy clay.

After planting and until plants are established, water regularly to keep the soil moist but not soggy. In Southern California, after the third season of growth, hold off watering starting in late September to induce winter dormancy (colder winter temperatures throughout most of Northern California induce dormancy naturally, so it's not necessary to cut off water). If winter rains are sporadic, begin watering again when the buds start to swell (around late February).

Fertilize lilacs in late winter with an organic fertilizer such as blood and bone meal, or with a commercial product.

After lilacs bloom, remove the spent flowers where the leaves join the stems just above the points where next year's flowers are forming; leaving spent flowers on the plants can inhibit next year's bloom. Don't prune lilacs heavily (or later than June) or you'll cut off developing flower buds. To control growth and shape the plants, pinch back new shoots. ◆

Low-chill lilacs

Many nurseries offer these plants. If you can't find the variety you want, ask your nursery to order it from L. E. Cooke Co. in Visalia, California (wholesale only).

DESCANSO HYBRIDS
'Angel White': Mildly fragrant white flowers develop on the upper branches of a thick, bushy shrub that grows 8 to 10 feet tall. Selected and introduced from Lammerts' original plants by Monrovia Nursery. "The idea was to name it after the baseball team and call it 'Los Angeles Angels'," says Boddy. But it didn't get registered that way.

'California Rose': Mildly fragrant medium pink flowers appear in profusion on a vigorous shrub that grows 8 to 10 feet tall.

'Lavender Lady': Lavender flowers with good fragrance develop on a shrub about 8 to 10 feet tall. **'F. K. Smith'** and **'Sylvan Beauty'** are similar, but the flowers on 'F. K. Smith' are a bit lighter on an 8- to 10-foot-tall plant, and 'Sylvan Beauty' has pinker, more open blooms on a 10- to 12-foot-tall plant.

OTHER LOW-CHILL LILACS
'Blue Skies': Very fragrant lavender flowers appear on an 8-foot-tall plant. Heavy bloomer. No need to adjust water to induce dormancy. Developed by rose hybridizer Ralph Moore in Visalia, California.

'Esther Staley' (*Syringa hyacinthiflora*): Very showy, pure pink flowers with good fragrance develop on rounded shrubs that grow to about 8 feet tall.

'Excel' (*S. hyacinthiflora*): Light lavender flowers with good fragrance appear on rounded shrubs 8 feet or taller. Massive bloomer. Blooms earlier than the others listed (late February or early March).

by **LAUREN BONAR SWEZEY**

NORMAN A. PLATE

Mini-tillers are made for light cultivation and turning amendments into loose soil.

The power to turn the earth

Mechanical tillers can break up soil without breaking your back—or your budget

Turning soil ranks as horticulture's dirtiest but most essential task. The act itself—the clod-breaking, soil-loosening clash of earth and steel—can be satisfying, but it doesn't need to be backbreaking. It all depends on the tool.

For gardeners with more than a small area of earth to work, a mechanical tiller can make the job almost worth looking forward to: in two to three hours, you and a machine can transform a lawn or fallow ground into a garden bed. Then, after plants are growing, bring back the tiller every couple of weeks to eliminate weeds and make the earth more receptive to rainfall and irrigation.

Most of these machines fall into one of three classes: mini-tillers, front- or mid-tined tillers, and rear-tined tillers. Use the right tiller for the right purpose

by **JIM McCAUSLAND**

and you'll be a happy gardener. But if you get it wrong, you'll rue the day you bought before you thought. You can rent most kinds of tillers, although minis are scarce.

THE MIGHTY MINIS

Mini-tillers are the newest and fastest-growing class of tillers/cultivators. Though the minis seem impossibly small, their engines pack a lot of power. Think of them primarily as cultivators that can also handle light tilling. You can use one to blend manure into a vegetable plot, for example, but if you plan to break up lawn or virgin ground, a bigger unit is a better choice.

Most minis till about 8 inches deep and have a tilling width of 6 to 12 inches—about half that of full-size tillers. Because they're small and have front tines, these machines are easy to control: you can get in close to fences, walls, and plants, and simply pick the tiller up and move it when you come to the end of a dead-end row (none has reverse gears). However, since minis are lightweight—most weigh in at 19 to 25 pounds—they tend to bounce when they hit hard soil.

Some models, such as the Mantis, rest on their rotating tines, which propel the tiller forward as it digs. Other minis, like those made by Homelite and Troy-Bilt, have wheels that support part of the tiller's weight as the tines dig (the Mantis also has optional wheels).

Minis cost $170 to $350; they are seldom available as rentals. The two-cycle engines run on a mix of gasoline and oil. They have enough horsepower to allow them to convert into other garden machines; with attachments, minis can become edgers, hedge trimmers, lawn dethatchers, and more.

FRONT- OR MID-TINED TILLERS

Far heavier and more powerful than minis are the front- or mid-tined tillers. They offer a tilling path at least 8 to 12 inches deep and 10 to 36 inches wide, and they can work right up to obstacles. On the downside, they take more muscle to operate than other kinds of tillers. If you use one to break fallow ground, you'll be very sore by the time

Mini-tiller: Mantis (below left) sells for $299 plus shipping from manufacturer, $319 from retailers. Front tines: Ariens model FT516 (right) sells for $590. Rear tines: Troy-Bilt Pony (below right), with electric starter, sells for $1,450.

you're done. Experience and good soil, however, make them easier to operate.

These tillers sell for about $250 to $1,050, with rentals running about $40 to $60 a day. Some models have a reverse gear, which is useful for backing out of tight spots; most have only one forward gear, with speed controlled by the throttle. Some front-tined units have attachments: aerators, finger tines for seed-bed cultivation, and even furrowers.

THE SODBUSTERS:
REAR-TINED TILLERS

When it's time to call in the heavy artillery, use rear-tined tillers, which propel themselves through the garden with the aplomb of small tractors. The biggest and best of these practically drive themselves, requiring little extra muscle from the user. If you have sod to break, rent one of these and the job will fly by. Most have a maximum tilling depth of about 8 inches and a width of 14 to 34 inches. Because rear-tined tillers have wheels and motor in front of the tines, they can't till right up to obstacles.

Rear-tined tillers are priced from $650 to $2,000 (you can expect to pay at least $1,000 for a good one); rentals cost $50 to $90 per day. Be sure to get one with multiple forward gears and a reverse gear, since these large units are not easy to push under your own power.

Oddly, smaller rear-tined tillers take

more strength to keep on track, perhaps because their lighter weight causes them to jump over stones and hard earth instead of settling into it. (One tiller company executive told us flatly that "the ability to till is a function of weight.") Yet smaller rear-tined tillers make up one of the fastest-growing segments of the market, probably because their price range is comparable to that of good front-tined tillers.

Several optional attachments are available, ranging from plows to dozer blades; some Troy-Bilt models can even be converted to chippers/shredders.

SOURCES

Various brands of tillers are sold at home and garden supply centers, hardware and department stores, and nurseries. A few brands are sold by mail.

Ariens offers front- and rear-tined tillers; call (800) 678-5443.

BCS America makes large rear-tined tillers; (800) 543-1040.

Echo makes one mini-tiller; (800) 432-3246.

Garden Way sells rear-tined and mini-tillers under the Troy-Bilt label; (800) 828-5500.

Hoffco sells the Li'l Hoe, a mini-tiller; (800) 999-8161.

Homelite, a subsidiary of John Deere, sells one mini-tiller; (800) 242-4672.

Honda Power Equipment sells front- and rear-tined tillers; (800) 426-7701.

Husqvarna makes all classes of tillers; (800) 438-7297.

John Deere offers one front-tined and two rear-tined models; (800) 537-8233.

MacKissic sells front-tined Merry Tillers; (610) 495-7181.

Mantis sells mini-tillers and attachments; (800) 366-6268.

MTD Products offers front- and rear-tined tillers under Yard-Man and Cub Cadet labels; (800) 800-7310.

Sears sells all classes of tillers under the Craftsman label. Contact your local Sears or order from the catalog; (800) 948-8800.

Snapper sells front- and rear-tined tillers; (770) 957-9141. ◆

CURTIS ANDERSON

DALE LAFOLLETTE

Inside the dome, a tentlike coldframe provides extra warmth for heat-loving seedlings.

A blow-up greenhouse for around $200

Summer crops get off to a fast start inside a plastic dome

With the steady patience of the plant scientist he is, Robert Buker of Vancouver, Washington, has spent more than 30 years perfecting a pet project—an inflatable greenhouse. The one shown here covers more than 1,400 square feet and costs about $200. Frameless, strong, and reusable, it takes only six hours to set up and 20 minutes to take down.

It also gives Buker's summer garden a big head start. In February, he erects the greenhouse over the site of the garden and starts summer flowers and crops from seed. When the weather warms in May, he takes it down. Vegetables grown in the earth beneath the dome don't need transplanting, and he harvests ripe tomatoes and melons by midsummer.

The 33- by 43-foot dome is formed from a 40- by 50-foot sheet of 6-mil ultraviolet-resistant plastic, which is guaranteed to last for three years. Nursery supply firms sell 40- by 100-foot sheets for about $120; Buker cuts them in half

by **JIM McCAUSLAND**

(he bunches up the excess at the corners). The edge of the plastic sheeting is stapled or taped to a ¾-inch strip of wood that fits snugly into a 1- by 1-inch channel running around the outside of the greenhouse's curblike concrete foundation. Just 6 inches deep and 4 inches wide, the foundation took Buker about two days to build and cost $20. (He says the structure could be scaled down to 8 by 16 feet and still function well.)

When the plastic dome is fully inflated, the greenhouse has 10 feet of headroom at its center. The dome is kept inflated by a ¼-hp electric fan (less than $50), which runs 24 hours a day, blowing outside air into the dome to maintain static pressure (see drawing at top). Although the fan never stops, Buker says, it costs less than $3 a month to operate.

At one corner of the greenhouse, a door (shown above) opens inward, so the air pressure inside the dome will keep it closed. A lath strip seals the plastic sheeting around the outside of the door frame.

To minimize heat fluctuations, Buker dug an 11- by 22- by 2-foot pond at one end of the greenhouse and lined it with plastic. The water in the pond absorbs heat during the day and releases it at night. There is no other heat source.

The air pressure inside the greenhouse must be regulated: too much pressure would put too much strain on the fan's motor or burst the plastic canopy. To check the pressure, Buker puts a straw into a glass of water inside the greenhouse and pokes the top of it through a pea-size hole in the plastic. If the water in the straw rises more than ¾ inch, the air pressure is too high, so Buker slides the fan away from the air-inlet tunnel to lower the water level in the straw to between ½ and ¾ inch.

The greenhouse has two notable weaknesses: it is difficult to cool on warm days, and the fan must stay on. But even if a power failure shuts off the fan and causes the dome to deflate, plants aren't damaged by the lightweight plastic sheet.

Buker has produced a video and booklet on building the greenhouse, which he sells for $29.95. To order, call toll-free (888) 246-1999. ◆

Inflated by air pressure, the dome covers the garden plot in early spring.

Parabola-shaped door is mounted in a plywood frame (about $20).

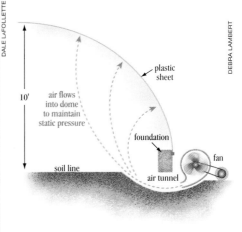

DALE LaFOLLETTE

DEBRA LAMBERT

10'

air flows into dome to maintain static pressure

plastic sheet

foundation

soil line

air tunnel

fan

Beautiful Swiss chard is delicious, nutritious, and easy to grow. Learn more about this prolific producer on page 80.

BEN WOOLSEY

March

gardenguide

CHAD SLATTERY

"Bali" in a pot

This bougainvillea blooms prolifically

by **SHARON COHOON**

Bougainvillea isn't exactly litter-free. It blooms vigorously and sheds just as copiously. So it wouldn't seem a good choice for a poolside pot. Unless—like the Rancho Santa Fe, California, homeowner this pool belongs to—you happen to see that litter as an asset rather than a nuisance.

"My client likes the way the red flowers look floating on top of the black-bottomed pool," says landscape architect Stephen Adams of Adams Design Associates. "She thinks it looks like Bali. So do I."

Adams bought a 15-gallon plant already trained in a bonsai shape, but you can create your own "tree." Start with a young plant and regularly prune off all the stems but the central leader until the plant reaches about 3 feet tall. Then prune the top to encourage side branching and a woody, supportive trunk.

The contrasting white apron skirting the pot is sweet alyssum. "Most people cut it back," says Adams, "but if you leave alyssum alone, it builds up on itself and spills out like a fountain. When it gets too shaggy, just pull it out and start over."

Growing a bougainvillea in a pot is easier if you choose the right varieties. The following shrubby types adapt best to life in containers.

'Crimson Jewel'. Blooms heavily over a long season.

'Hawaii' (also known as 'Raspberry Ice'). Red bracts and leaves with golden yellow margins; new leaves are tinged red. Regardless of its tropical name, it's one of the hardiest.

'La Jolla'. Bright red bracts.

'Rosenka'. Golden flowers age to bright pink.

'San Diego Red'. Deep red bracts over a long season. Leaves hold well during cold winters.

tool

The Soil Scoop, new from Garden Works, makes you nearly as efficient at digging as a gopher or a terrier. The general-purpose digging tool has a deep bowl-shaped head with a sharply pointed tip and serrated edges. You clasp it bowl side down for digging—just the opposite of the way you'd hold a trowel. It feels awkward for all of 10 seconds, then it begins to feel like a natural extension of your hand. It's versatile and handy—use it to dig holes, create seed furrows, weed in tight spaces, and saw through rootbound soil, or for jobs you could do if you'd been born with claws.

The Soil Scoop is made of stainless steel with a solid birch handle. If it's not available at your local garden center, call Garden Works at (206) 455-0568 to order. The scoop costs $15, plus $3 shipping.

— *S. C.*

CURTIS ANDERSON

'Lovely Fairy' and 'Royal Bonica'

When it comes to low-maintenance but still ravishingly beautiful roses, 'The Fairy' has few rivals. This pale pink polyantha, hybridized in 1932, is every bit as tough, disease-resistant, and floriferous as the new generation of landscape roses. 'Bonica', the first shrub rose to win an All-America Rose Selection award (1987), may be its only competitor.

If you're a fan of these roses, you'll be pleased to know that both are now available in new colors. 'Lovely Fairy' (shown immediately below), from Young's American Rose Nursery, is a compact grower and heavy bloomer like its parent, 'The Fairy', but it has dark pink rather than pale pink blossoms. 'Royal Bonica' (bottom), from Conard-Pyle Co., also has dark pink rather than pastel flowers. But it's a slightly larger plant, with larger blooms, than its parent, 'Bonica'. — *S. C.*

NORMAN A. PLATE (2)

COOK'S *choice*

It's a banner year for veggies

As you're buying seeds for this year's vegetable garden, keep your eyes open for some of the ground-breaking new varieties that are available.

'Ambercup', an orange buttercup squash, yields heavily. With fine-textured flesh and high sugar content, it's good both baked and mashed. Fruits average about 3 pounds each. This is a fairly long-season variety, so start it early, allowing at least four months between planting and harvest. (In short-summer climates, start seeds indoors early to get a crop.) Seed of 'Ambercup' is sold by W. Atlee Burpee & Co. (800/888-1447) and Harris Seeds (800/514-4441).

'Big Chile', an early and large Anaheim-type chili, can grow 10 inches long and 2 inches wide, and weigh 4 ounces. It's a heavy bearer. Mature fruits ripen red, but most gardeners pick and eat them green. They have fairly mild heat and are good roasted and peeled. Allow about 10 weeks from transplanting to harvest. Seed of 'Big Chile' is sold by Tomato Growers Supply Co. (941/768-1119); garden centers may sell plants in containers.

'Monet', an all-green leaf lettuce, looks as if it belongs in the ornamental garden. But the story is really in its texture, which is unusually crisp for a leaf lettuce. To enjoy the beauty of its textured globes, plant 'Monet' seeds a little farther apart than you would standard leaf lettuces (8-inch intervals should be about right). Sow successive crops for a long harvest season, but remember that later plantings need more shade to keep plants from bolting (going to seed) and turning bitter. Seed of 'Monet' is sold by Shumway Co. (800/322-7288); look for seedlings at garden centers. — *Jim McCausland*

A colorful garden tapestry

"Give me lots of orange," Caroline West instructed landscape designer Susanne Jett when West decided to get rid of her lawn and put in more sustainable landscaping. "And no pastel pinks," she added. This was just the opposite of what Jett was used to hearing from clients. But, having seen the inside of West's home in Santa Monica, Jett wasn't surprised. West's walls are covered with North African and Central and South American textiles suffused with flame reds, glowing golds, hot oranges, and strong violets.

Jett created a complementary "garden tapestry" of drought-tolerant plants with strong personalities and vivid blooms, like the fluorescent-blue spikes of pride of Madeira and the bright orange

WILLIAM B. DEWEY

whorls of lion's tail. She contrasted them with foliage plants that have sculptural qualities, like New Zealand flax. Then she wrapped them around a horseshoe-shaped space surfaced with decomposed granite and encircled by a recycled broken-concrete, dry-stack wall. The enclosure shields the space from a busy street. And the new landscaping saves water. By Jett's estimation, water usage has dropped from 13,200 gallons per month to 2,500, and even less in the winter. — *S. C.*

If your trees suffered winter storm damage

This winter in the Pacific Northwest was a whopper: cold, snowy, wet, and windy. If your trees lost big limbs, you probably removed the windfall already. But if you didn't cut the trees' broken ends smooth, you need to do that now. If you wait until trees leaf out, you'll face additional problems. It's better to prune a tree before new foliage starts to emerge, so you won't be knocking off buds and damaging good foliage.

After you prune, the trees will start sending up new shoots around the wounds. You'll want to let some of these new shoots grow, and you'll want to prune others out. If the wounds are splintery, it will be harder to prune, and a ragged wound is more vulnerable to the entry of diseases and pests.

When new shoots emerge, you may want to let them develop for a growing season or two, then look at their form and remove them when you've got a better idea of their eventual impact on the tree's shape.

If you lost the top, or crown, of a tree (conifers with their single leaders are the biggest problem), cut the leader at an angle just below the break. An angled cut keeps water from standing on the wood and creating pockets of rot. In a year or two, the tree should send out several new leaders. Unless you want what is called a wolf tree (a multi-stemmed conifer), select the strongest, most vertical leader and then prune

off the others. This single leader will grow straight and strong, and eventually you'll have a plant with a slight crook in its trunk but an otherwise normal form.

For more help, see "How to Prune a Tree … Properly" in the January chapter, page 25. — *S. R. L.*

Old-fashioned seeds

"Ten ought to do it," said Charles B. Ledgerwood, measuring out individual 'Bingo' tomato seeds. "That will be 30 cents, please." Never seen 'Bingo' in nursery racks or catalog pages? Neither had I. Even Tomato Growers Supply Company, whose catalog lists 26 pages of tomatoes, doesn't carry it. But Ledgerwood does. And 'Bingo', he told me, is the crème de la crème of tomatoes among truck farmers. My inquiries at the local farmers' market the following week bore this out. Then Ledgerwood gave me another great tip: growing cantaloupe is possible in my coastal-zone garden as long as I plant the 'Hayogen' variety. 'Hayogen' is another seed you aren't likely to find anyplace else.

If you haven't visited Ledgerwood's seed store in Carlsbad, California, remedy the situation at once. He's got a lot more tips—he's been selling seeds at this location for 64 years—and the general-store atmosphere is just too much fun to miss. Walk in, look through three-ring binders, ask questions and confer, decide what you want and how much, and watch your choices being scooped out of bins, weighed and measured, and packaged and labeled.

I don't know of another place where you can still buy seeds this way—or for these prices. (A quarter ounce of wildflower seeds cost me 75 cents.) Charles B. Ledgerwood Seeds is at 3862 Carlsbad Boulevard (between Redwood and Tamarack avenues). Drive slowly; it's easy to miss. Store hours are 8:30 to 5:30 Mondays through Saturdays; (619) 729-3282. While you're there, pick up Ledgerwood's useful Southern California vegetable-planting and flower-planting calendars. — *S. C.*

An amaryllis superstar

Fifteen years ago, *Sunset* garden writer and editor Dick Dunmire received a bulb of a large red amaryllis from a friend. He planted the bulb in an 8-inch terra-cotta pot, and just weeks later, it developed a couple of flower stalks. When the blooms faded, he cut off the stalks to see whether the bulb would rebloom the following year.

Not only did the plant bloom again—regularly, year after year—but the bulb formed offsets and produced many more flower stalks. Last season, Dunmire's amaryllis put on quite a show—seven blooming flower stalks (five stalks and two buds are showing in the photograph at right), each with three or four flowers.

What's Dunmire's secret for getting so much production from a single bulb? "I don't do much to it," says Dunmire (now retired) of his incredible bulb. "I keep the pot on my front porch, which gets full sun in the morning and full shade in the afternoon, except in December and January, when I move it into a cold greenhouse for protection." (Since many people don't have a greenhouse, Dunmire suggests bringing the pot indoors during the coldest months to protect it from frost.) He rotates the pot regularly so all sides get sun, and waters when the top of the soil feels dry.

He fertilizes the plant twice a year, first in February when new growth begins and again about two months later—with "whatever I happen to have around." (A complete, high-nitrogen fertilizer in powder form, which dilutes in water, is his current plant food.)

The bulbs never go completely dormant. As leaves turn yellow, he snips them off.

Even though the bulbs are increasing in number, Dunmire hasn't yet divided them because they still make such a good display in the single pot. Eventually, after they've filled the pot completely, he'll transplant them into a larger container.

— *Lauren Bonar Swezey*

A single mature amaryllis bulb can produce multiple flower stalks up to 3 feet tall.

Lavenders galore

Lavender is undoubtedly at the top of most gardeners' list of favorite perennials. Hundreds of kinds are grown throughout the world.

Dutchmill Herbfarm, a nursery in Forest Grove, Oregon, grows 152, "give or take five or six," says owner Barbara Remington. Her collection includes lavenders from Africa, Australia, England, France, Germany, India, and Spain, including the Canary Islands.

Remington's grandmother began the collection in about 1929. Since 1973, Remington has added to it and sold lavenders by mail and at the nursery.

What's her favorite? "The one that's in bloom," she jokes, adding that among her favorites are *Lavandula intermedia* 'Grosso' (very fragrant) and red-and-violet butterfly lavender (*L. stoechas* 'Papillon'), which attracts butterflies like a magnet.

Remington sells 20 to 30 less-common lavenders a year by mail, shipping them in spring and fall. One-gallon plants cost $9 each (minimum order is six plants), plus 20 percent for shipping. For a plant list, send a self-addressed, stamped envelope with two 32-cent stamps to the nursery at 6640 N.W. Marsh Rd., Forest Grove, OR 97116; (503) 357-0924. — *L. B. S.*

NORMAN A. PLATE

TEST GARDEN *picks*

'Dolly' dwarf phlox

Last spring, *Sunset* test garden co-ordinator Bud Stuckey picked up jumbo packs of a new *Phlox drummondii* called 'Dolly' (pictured above) at the flower trials at Sakata Seed in Morgan Hill, California. They looked promising, so he planted them. "Gorgeous," he pronounced a few weeks later. These phlox were so completely covered with flowers you couldn't see the foliage.

'Dolly' is a dwarf phlox, growing only 6 to 8 inches tall. The seeds germinate easily, and the plants are extra-early flowering (from sowing to flowering takes about 90 days). They also come in a handsome range of single colors—burgundy, deep rose, purple, red, sky blue, and white—and as a mix. 'Dolly' flowers don't need deadheading to continue blooming until the end of summer (in hot summer climates, they may fade a bit earlier).

Sixpacks of 'Dolly' should be available this year at many nurseries. If you can't find plants, grow 'Dolly' from seed (order as soon as possible from Stokes Seeds, Box 548, Buffalo, NY 14240; 716/695-6980). — *L. B. S.*

COOK'S *choice*

The beauty of chard

Not only is Swiss chard a delicious and nutritious crop, but it is easy to grow, produces prolifically, and is beautiful. You can even grow red, white, and yellow chards in the same row and harvest their leaves to mix into colorful dishes. The stems and leaves of red chard are so attractive that plants can be used as color accents in ornamental beds.

You can plant chard from this month all the way into mid-July. Give it full sun and rich, loose, quick-draining garden soil. Sow the seeds ½ inch apart in a ½-inch-deep furrow and cover them with soil. The seedlings will be up in about a month. Thin the plants so that they are about 1 foot apart—and protect them from slugs.

About 2½ months after planting, you can begin harvesting the outside leaves for eating, leaving the center leaves to mature. The plants will produce their fleshy stalks and foliage until the first hard frost. In mild-winter climates, these plants will live over winter.

Chard seed is easy to find. Nursery racks and seed catalogs are filled with choices. Many varieties have been bred to be heat resistant. 'Fordhook Giant' and 'White King' both have broad, meaty white stalks with crinkly, dark green leaves on 2-foot-tall plants. 'Rhubarb' and 'Ruby' chard, as well as a variety named 'Vulcan', have glowing ruby-red stalks and either dark green or burgundy-red leaves.

Territorial Seed Company (Box 157, Cottage Grove, OR 97424; 541/ 942-9547, free catalog) sells a variety of chard called 'Dorat' with pale, yellow-green leaves and very wide, snow-white stalks. Park Seed Company (1 Parkton Ave., Greenwood, SC 29647; 800/845-3369, free catalog) sells a plant called 'Swiss Chard of Geneva', which is exceptionally hardy. — *S. R. L.*

English delphiniums: more flower power

British gardeners are rightly proud of their delphiniums, and English breeders are constantly hybridizing new plants. Breeders have already succeeded in developing the large-flowered English delphinium strain of *D. elatum*. Bred for beauty as well as vigor, plants of this strain are starting to appear in the American market, and they may give our Pacific strain delphiniums a run for their money.

Planted this spring, these English delphiniums can grow to 5 feet by midsummer and 6 feet by next year. The 3-inch-wide flowers come in blue, cream, lavender, pink, purple, and white, including some bicolors. The blooms are so large and profuse, they completely hide the stem.

These plants need full sun and rich, well-drained soil. You must remove all but three shoots from the first year's new growth, and all but five of the strongest stems in subsequent years.

Plants of the English strain will be sold by some nurseries. Or order by mail from Jackson & Perkins (800/292-4769). — *J. M.* ◆

MICHAEL THOMPSON

Pacific Northwest Garden Notebook

by **STEVEN R. LORTON**

One day this month, I'll look out the window of our house in Washington's Skagit Valley to see my neighbors Dan and Evelo Adkinson coming up the lane with armloads of switches. I'll holler, "Yahoo!" loud enough to make the dog start barking and dash out of the house to meet them.

The Adkinsons have a number of apple trees. At the first of the month, they'll give them an annual pruning, removing all the suckers that shoot up from the major limbs. They'll set the long, straight, and sturdy sticks aside for me. Some are as wide as a broomstick at the base end. Within two days I'll have them cut into garden stakes that are 18, 24, or 36 inches long. I'll use these to protect newly planted annuals and perennials, mark vegetable rows, support top-heavy lilies, and make little fences to divert our dog, Rio. There are a million uses for these natural stakes, which weather and visually disappear in the garden. If you want to turn a gardener into a devoted friend, take a tip from the Adkinsons. Prune your apple trees and give him or her a bundle of switches.

LEOPARD'S BANE IS A PERENNIAL CLASSIC

Early last spring, I rediscovered a great old perennial—*Doronicum,* commonly called leopard's bane. It blooms early in the spring, sending up bright, glossy yellow, daisylike flowers on 8- to 10-inch stems. The blooms rise above clumps of rich green heart-shaped leaves. The plants like to be out of direct sun. I set out three plants from 4-inch pots in a north-fac-

ing bed planted to fill in around the base of a piece of sculpture. By the time the *Doronicum* is finished, hosta leaves and new fern fronds are opening. Leopard's bane grows in all Northwest climate zones.

THAT'S A GOOD QUESTION

Q: Every spring in flower shops and grocery stores, I see beautiful heathers with upright plumes of flowers. They look great, then I plant them out and they never come back. What's wrong?
— *Byron Elmendorf, Bellingham, Washington*

A: What you are undoubtedly getting is a plant called *Erica persoluta.* This South African heather with stiff, upright branches filled with feathery foliage and masses of rose—and occasionally white—flowers is not hardy anywhere in the Northwest. It is sold as a seasonal pot plant like poinsettia or the big lacy mums that unsuspecting gardeners set out each year but never see again. Treat this heather as an annual unless you have a greenhouse or a very bright sunroom, in which case you could give it a try indoors. Repot the plant (usually grown in mix with a very high peat content that dries out quickly) in a generous pot with good drainage and a good indoor plant mix. Give it plenty of sun and water, as it is intolerant of drought. Fertilize it on the same schedule you do other house plants. If you transplant the heather successfully and it responds well to its location, it will form a clump of 2-foot-tall plumes and may bloom annually.

Northern California Garden Notebook

by **LAUREN BONAR SWEZEY**

Through the years, I've seen landscapes in all shapes, sizes, and styles—large, traditional gardens worthy of the Windsors; daring, eclectic landscapes where even Andy Warhol might have felt at home; and fascinating native gardens suitable for the Euell Gibbonses of the world. But I've never been as bowled over by a group of landscape designs as I was when I reviewed the entrants in the Western Garden Design Awards contest (see the winners starting on page 90).

They're anything but run-of-the-mill. The 16 award winners break molds. Each design is innovative—sometimes even revolutionary. Take the seemingly simple water feature on page 105 by San Francisco designers Delaney, Cochran, & Castillo. Water flowing from the black bowl is in continuous movement but seems to disappear into the gravel. The oversize chessboard (pages 90 and 91) designed by Yountville, California, landscape architect Jack Chandler is both whimsical and entertaining.

Other projects are beautiful, functional, and environmentally sensitive. San Francisco landscape architect and juror Cheryl Barton praised the designers of all three problem-solving gardens (pages 106–108) for reclaiming space normally dedicated to the automobile. Landscape architect Ronnie Siegel used buffalo grass—which takes much less water than a traditional lawn—in her garden (page 106).

MARINA THOMPSON

PUTTING THE RAIN TO WORK

Here's a great tip my father shared with me years ago. An easy way to fertilize a lawn or planting bed is to scatter the fertilizer between two closely spaced rainstorms. This way you know you're applying fertilizer to a well-watered plant (fertilizer applied to a thirsty plant can burn it), and the rain does the work for you by watering it in well.

THAT'S A GOOD QUESTION

Q: I was surprised at the answer to the question about sources for old-fashioned roses by mail in your December 1996 Garden Notebook column. The most famous and complete mail-order source for antique roses is Roses of Yesterday and Today in Watsonville [which wasn't listed]. They have an amazing collection of old-fashioned roses, from Portlands and bourbons to albas and noisettes. They have many unusual modern roses as well.
— *Carroll Woods, Menlo Park*
A: Unfortunately, Roses of Yesterday and Today has announced that it will not be shipping roses by mail this season and did not want to be listed as a mail-order source. However, you can still buy roses at its nursery in Watsonville (802 Brown's Valley Rd.; 408/724-3537).

Southern California Garden Notebook

by **SHARON COHOON**

Remember the line "When E. F. Hutton talks, people listen" from the old television commercial? Well, that's how I reacted when Steve Brigham and Dave Fross both mentioned the same perennial as their favorite plant of the year. You don't get tips like that every day. So I dropped everything and ran out and bought "stock."

Brigham owns Buena Creek Gardens, a retail nursery in San Marcos. Fross owns Native Sons, a wholesale nursery in Arroyo Grande. Both men have long histories as plant scouts of the first order. And—I won't keep you in suspense any longer—the plant they've both been smitten with is (drum roll, please) *Thalictrum delavayi* 'Hewitt's Double'.

The tall, dainty flower spikes that billow above the maidenhair-fern-like foliage of this 5-foot-tall perennial "look like steel blue BB pellets in bud, then open to a stunning lavender-blue," says Brigham. "More mauve-pink, I'd say," says Fross, though he's equally unstinting in his praise. "When it's in bloom, 'Hewitt's Double' stops you in your tracks. Everyone wants it," he says. An easy, undemanding plant, too, I've found.

Still-cool soil and increasing hours of daylight make March a great month for planting perennials. One to consider: white heliotrope. It's even more fragrant than the dark purple varieties, says Joe Brosius of Magic Growers, a wholesale nursery in Pasadena. Plant it under a deciduous tree and let the low-growing perennial develop its full spread, he suggests. Or

plant a row at the front of a border, where it will look like a frilly lace cuff. That's the way I saw it used in a display at the Western Nursery and Garden Expo in Las Vegas. Very pretty.

Or try the perennial that Judy Wigand (of Judy's Perennials nursery in San Marcos) says she can't propagate fast enough: *Pelargonium sidoides*. It grows to about 1½ feet tall and has neat little leaves like nutmeg geranium, though a shade bluer, with small burgundy flowers floating a foot above. Rarely out of bloom and very tough, it's even said to withstand frost.

THAT'S A GOOD QUESTION

Q: The cymbidium I received as a present several years ago is busting out of its pot. When is the best time to repot, and what kind of potting mixture should I use for it?

A: The best time to repot cymbidiums is as soon as the flower stems are spent, says grower Pat Rowland (of the Rowland Collection). No need to wait for the flower stalk to deteriorate—it doesn't provide nourishment to the plant the way bulb foliage does. So snip off the stalk and get busy. If you repot by April 1, there's an 85 percent chance you won't miss a year's bloom, says Rowland. If you want to divide the plant, keep a minimum of three bulbs bearing foliage in each division. Use a commercial orchid potting mix or try Rowland's formula: ¼-inch fir bark (60 percent), #3 perlite (30 percent), and horticultural charcoal (10 percent).

Westerner's Garden Notebook

by **JIM McCAUSLAND**

In March, everything changes. The ground goes from frozen or sodden to crumbly and soft, and deciduous tree canopies suddenly become scaffolding for hazy green clouds of swelling leaf buds. Best of all, by month's end the days are once again longer than the nights, and we're back into the season of light, warmth, and growth.

Always one to get at least part of the garden off to a fast start, I usually buy a couple of flats of cool-season annuals (pansies, primroses, calendulas, English daisies, or whatever else looks good) to put by my front door. The sight of blooming flowers on frosty mornings usually stimulates me to get into the garden to prepare the soil, slip some bare-root plants into the earth before the winter planting season ends, and do some general cleanup. In the low desert, it's already time to plant warm-season crops.

COLDFRAMES KEEP YOUNG CROPS WARM

If frost is still a regular visitor in your garden, I recommend a coldframe for starting crops. You can make one from used brick or concrete block with an old window on top. The masonry absorbs heat all day and radiates it back to the plants inside all night. You just have to keep the top propped open when the weather heats up to keep the plants inside from cooking. If you live in the low or intermediate desert zones, it makes more sense to use one of the new double-walled plastic coldframes, which you can simply break down and put in the garage when hot weather arrives.

GOOD PLANS FOR VEGETABLES

Vegetable-garden preparation is next on my list. This year there's a great new booklet to help beginning gardeners. *Planning an Idaho Vegetable Garden,* by Susan Bell, Michael Colt, Dale Wilson, and Hugh Homan (University of Idaho Col-

lege of Agriculture, Moscow, 1996; $4) covers everything from bed preparation to fertilizing. To get a copy, send $5 (Idaho residents, add 25 cents tax) to Agricultural Publications, Moscow, ID 83844.

PAPER "HATS" FOR TRANSPLANTS

Last spring I watched a gardener friend fold sheets of newspaper into the cone-shaped hats that kids make on rainy days. (He told me he'd learned how to make them in 4-H.) Then he set them over his transplants on cold nights, holding down the edges with a little earth. They were perfect, cheap hot caps—ones kids love to make for the asking.

VIOLAS WITH NEW FACES

To my delight, violas have been making a comeback, with some very interesting new varieties showing up. There's a new hybrid line from Goldsmith Seeds (wholesale only) called the Penny series, which includes 'Penny Azure Wing', 'Penny Primrose', 'Penny Violet Beacon', 'Penny Violet Flare', 'Penny Yellow', and a mixture of the five colors, with flowers up to 1½ inches across. Penny will be sold as bedding plants for areas in the garden that get filtered sunlight or bright shade.

THAT'S A GOOD QUESTION

Q: More grocery stores are selling "cluster tomatoes" for as much as $3 a pound. Is this a "hothouse" variety, or could I get seed and grow it?

A: These are currant tomatoes (*Lycopersicon pimpinellifolium*), tiny Andean cousins of standard tomatoes (*L. lycopersicum*). Two mail-order sources are Nichols Garden Nursery (1190 N. Pacific Highway, Albany, OR 97321; 541/928-9280) and Johnny's Selected Seeds (Fosshill Rd., Albion, ME 04910; 207/437-4301). Their catalogs are free.

Planting

☐ **SUMMER BULBS, CORMS, TUBERS.** Zones 4–7: After midmonth you can plant summer-blooming bulbs of acidanthera, callas, crocosmia, gladiolus, ranunculus, and tigridia. If, after planting, an unusually hard frost is predicted, cover beds with an inch of organic mulch.

☐ **NEW LAWNS.** All Northwest zones: You can start a new lawn now. Spade and rake the top 6 to 12 inches of soil to a fine consistency and amend it with organic matter. Next, lay sod or rake in a seed mix of bent, blue, fescue, and rye grasses. In zones 4–7, blue grass should be the predominant seed. Water the newly planted lawn regularly.

☐ **SOW COOL-SEASON CROPS.** Zones 4–7: Sow beets, carrots, chard, lettuce, peas, radishes, spinach, and most members of the cabbage family.

☐ **START WARM-SEASON CROPS.** All zones: Start seeds of tomatoes, peppers, and other warm-season crops indoors—on windowsills, in sunrooms, or in greenhouses. When the weather warms, you can plant seedlings out.

Maintenance

☐ **CLEAN UP ROCK GARDENS.** Spring bloom will start soon. Take time this month to examine plants for loose or exposed roots (winter freezing and thawing often heaves out the shallow-rooted plants). Push soil down around

them. Replace soil washed away by winter rains. Snip off winter-battered foliage. Weed.

☐ **DIVIDE PERENNIALS.** Zones 4–7: Dig, divide, and replant summer- and fall-blooming perennials early this month

and you'll still enjoy bloom this year. Zones 1–3: Wait until April to divide plants. In all Northwest zones, wait until fall to divide spring-flowering perennials so you won't lose a year's worth of bloom.

☐ **FERTILIZE LAWNS.** All zones: Start feeding lawns this month. Use a fertilizer with a 3-1-2 ratio of nitrogen, phosphorus, and potassium. Apply ½ pound of actual nitrogen per 1,000 square feet of turf.

☐ **PRUNE CLEMATIS.** Zones 4–7: Cut back summer-flowering plants now. After pruning, scatter a handful of fertilizer at the base of plants (10-10-10 is a good choice). Zones 1–3: Do this job after danger of a hard freeze has passed. All zones: Prune back spring-flowering varieties as soon as they finish blooming.

Pest and weed control

☐ **CONTROL SLUGS.** Zones 3–7: Moist March weather brings out hungry slugs in all sizes; whatever your method (bait, beer, or handpicking), control them before they reproduce.

☐ **PULL WEEDS.** To eliminate a weed with a long taproot (like a dandelion), use an old butcher knife. Stick the blade straight down in the ground along the root and wiggle it back and forth a few times. Then pull firmly and steadily on the plant. It should lift right out, root intact.

Planting

☐ **PLANT TUBEROUS BEGONIAS.** Zones 7–9, 14–17: When pink buds appear in the concave part of a tuber, plant the tuber in a container filled with potting soil. Barely cover it with soil mix, then soak with water. Set the pot in filtered shade. Don't water it again until the top of the soil feels dry. Zones 1 and 2: Start tubers in a greenhouse or indoors in a cool, dry place. When leaves appear, place in bright but indirect light and keep at 65° to 70°. Move outdoors when danger of frost has passed.

☐ **SET OUT POTATO TUBERS.** Zones 7–9, 14–17: Try potatoes in different colors, such as yellow 'Bintje' or 'Yukon Gold'; 'All Red' or 'Reddale'; 'All Blue' or 'Caribe'; or pinkish red, yellow-fleshed 'Desiree'. Ronniger's Seed Potatoes (Star Route 40, Moyie Springs, ID 83845; free catalog) sells 75 varieties by mail.

☐ **SET OUT SCENTED GERANIUMS.** Zones 7–9, 14–17: Shop for these fragrant-leafed plants at nurseries now. Dozens of scented geraniums (which are pelargoniums, not true geraniums) are available. Scents include apple, apricot, peppermint, nutmeg, and rose.

☐ **SHOP FOR NURSERY PLANTS.** Zones 7–9, 14–17: Look for plants with healthy foliage. If plants have green leaves, they should be a deep color, not pale or chlorotic. Avoid plants with brown leaf edges and dead or damaged branches. To avoid purchasing root-bound plants, choose plants that are in scale with the size of the pot and make sure no roots are growing out the bottom. The biggest plant is not always the healthiest one.

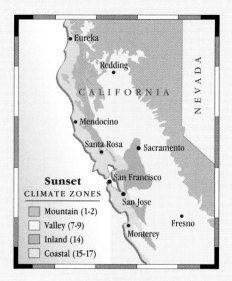

Sunset CLIMATE ZONES
- Mountain (1-2)
- Valley (7-9)
- Inland (14)
- Coastal (15-17)

Maintenance

☐ **AMEND SOIL.** Zones 7–9, 14–17: Before planting, amend fast-draining or heavy clay soils with compost, ground bark, or other organic material to improve soil texture and water retention. If you use ground bark or another wood product, make sure it has been nitrogen-stabilized (read the label or ask the supplier). Otherwise, the mulch will retard plant growth. If it hasn't, add a high-nitrogen fertilizer, such as 20-10-10 (use 2½ to 5 pounds per 500 square feet).

☐ **AVOID VITAMIN B-1.** Contrary to popular belief, vitamin B-1 does not prevent transplant shock in plants. According to university research, only those vitamin B-1 products that contain low amounts of fertilizers benefit young plants. To help transplants get off to a good start, water them with a low-nitrogen fertilizer, such as fish emulsion.

☐ **FERTILIZE.** Zones 7–9, 14–17: Feed roses when spring growth starts. Give lawns, annual flowers, vegetables, berries, citrus, and fuchsias high-nitrogen fertilizer. Apply acid fertilizer to azaleas, camellias, and rhododendrons when bloom finishes. Use liquid or controlled-release fertilizer on plants in containers. Give citrus an extra boost with a foliar feeding of a liquid fertilizer containing iron and other micronutrients.

☐ **HANG CODLING MOTH TRAPS.** To help monitor codling moth activity in apple trees and reduce the population of moths, hang two codling moth pheromone traps per tree before flowers appear. Traps can be purchased at garden centers and through many garden tool catalogs.

☐ **MONITOR SPRING RAINS.** Zones 7–9, 14–17: Weather can be variable this month, and rains may not supply enough moisture to plants. Check moisture in the root zones by digging into the soil with a trowel.

Planting

☐ **PLANT PERENNIALS.** Nurseries are fully stocked with blooming perennials, making this an excellent time to plant. Good choices include asters, *Brachycome multifida,* columbine, coral bells, diascia, dianthus, geraniums, penstemon, salvia, scabiosa, and thalictrum.

☐ **PLANT AZALEAS AND CAMELLIAS.** Select plants while they're still in flower, and plant them as soon as possible. Plants are dormant during bloom, but they begin growing again soon after flowering. Amend the soil well with organic material and a soil acidifier such as oak leaf mold or peat moss. Plant both azaleas and camellias a bit high so that the tops of the rootballs are an inch or so above ground after the soil settles.

☐ **PLANT HERBS.** Plant young chives, parsley, rosemary, sage, sorrel, tarragon, and thyme. Sow seeds of chervil, cilantro, and dill.

☐ **PLANT WARM-SEASON ANNUALS.** As weather warms, replace fading winter-spring annuals with summer bedding plants. Choices include ageratum, amaranth, coleus, lobelia, marigolds, nasturtium, nicotiana, petunias, phlox, and verbena. In the high desert (zone 11), set out marigolds, petunias, and zinnias late this month.

☐ **SOW FLOWER SEEDS.** Coastal gardeners (zones 22–24) can sow seeds of

aster, cleome, cosmos, lobelia, lunaria, marigold, nicotiana, sunflower, and zinnia in flats or directly in the garden spots where you want them to grow. Inland gardeners (zones 18–21) should wait until at least midmonth. In cold areas, sow seeds of alyssum, calendula, candytuft, clarkia, and larkspur.

Maintenance

☐ **FERTILIZE PLANTS.** Ground covers, shrubs, perennials, and ornamental and fruit trees are all putting out new growth and will benefit from feeding. The exceptions are California natives and drought-tolerant Mediterranean plants. Wait until flowering ends to feed azaleas and camellias. A quick way to fertilize is to scatter all-purpose granular fertilizer on the ground before

a storm is expected and let the rain water it in. Or water it in with the sprinkler.

☐ **PRUNE EVERGREENS AND ORNAMENTALS.** Before spring growth surges, prune evergreen shrubs such as boxwood. After flowers fade, prune to shape ornamental flowering fruit trees such as cherry, crabapple, peach, and plum. On frost-tender plants such as bougainvillea, calliandra, citrus, and natal plum, remove damaged wood and shape plants as new growth appears.

☐ **FEED LAWNS.** Both warm and cool-season turf grasses will benefit from an application of high-nitrogen fertilizer now.

Pest Control

☐ **MANAGE SNAILS.** Control them now to reduce their numbers for the rest of the year. If you find small holes in foliage and slime trails in flower beds and vegetable gardens or on young plants, hunt for snails at night. Handpick, trap by allowing them to collect on the underside of a slightly elevated board, or use commercial snail bait.

☐ **CONTROL APHIDS.** These sucking pests are attracted to tender new growth; dislodge with a strong blast of water from a hose. On delicate blossoms, mist with insecticidal soap; or wear thin disposable plastic gloves and remove aphids with your fingers.

Planting

☐ **BARE-ROOT PLANTS.** Set out bare-root stock of plants from strawberries and horseradish to fruit and shade trees early this month. Bare-root plants cost less than those sold in containers, and they adapt more quickly to native garden soil. It's essential to bring home nursery plants with their bare roots wrapped in damp cloth or sawdust: if they dry out before planting, they'll die.

☐ **COOL-SEASON ANNUALS.** In many areas, nurseries sell flats of cool-season annuals this month. Plant annuals in a warm or protected part of the garden and water them in well, and you'll have color until warm-season annuals take over after all danger of frost is past.

☐ **LAWNS.** When you overseed, be sure to sow the same kind of grass that is already growing there. Otherwise the texture and color of the new grass will contrast with the old, like mismatched paint. Keep all newly sown areas well watered until the grass is tall enough to mow.

Maintenance

☐ **DIVIDE PERENNIALS.** In zone 10 (around St. George, Utah), dig and divide clumping perennials like bearded iris, chrysanthemum, and daylily. Use a spade to cut them apart.

☐ **FEED EVERGREENS.** Sprinkle high-nitrogen fertilizer over the root zones and water it in well.

Sunset
CLIMATE ZONES

☐ 1-3 ☐ 10-11

☐ **FEED SHRUBS.** Do this on a mild day when temperatures are well above freezing. Apply high-nitrogen fertilizer to early-flowering shrubs as soon as they've finished blooming. Feed roses right away.

☐ **FERTILIZE BERRIES.** Blackberries, blueberries, and raspberries can all use a feeding this month with either high-nitrogen fertilizer or well-aged manure.

☐ **MAKE COMPOST.** As you get the garden in shape for spring and summer planting, use the weeds to start a compost heap. Layer green weeds with dry leaves, straw, or sawdust, then turn the pile weekly with a pitchfork and keep it damp; compost should be ready in a few weeks.

☐ **PREPARE BEDS.** Dig composted manure (or garden compost) into planting beds to get them ready for spring planting. For bad soil, till 4 to 6 inches of organic matter into the top foot of soil. Rake amended beds, water them, and let them settle for a week before planting.

☐ **PRUNE FROST-DAMAGED PLANTS.** Once buds start to swell, you'll clearly see which twigs and branches didn't survive winter frosts. Then you can cut them away.

☐ **TRIM ORNAMENTAL GRASSES.** When new growth appears at the base of the plant, cut back the old grass so the plant won't look ratty.

Weed control

☐ **HOE WEEDS.** Hoe weeds now while they're young and shallow-rooted. If you wait until they form deep taproots, they'll rise—and you'll weed—again. If weeds germinate between the time you prepare a flower bed and plant, hoe them off lightly without disturbing more than the top ½ inch of soil. If you weed more deeply or till, you'll just bring up a fresh batch of weed seeds.

☐ **START A BRUSH PILE.** Use woody and thorny prunings that would decompose too slowly in a compost pile. The brush provides cover for birds and wildlife.

Planting

☐ **ANNUALS.** Zones 10–11: Plant cool-season annuals now. Zones 12–13: Set out warm-season flowers, such as blackfoot daisy (*Melampodium leucanthum*), celosia, gomphrena, lisianthus, Madagascar periwinkle, marigold, portulaca, and salvia. When you take a plant out of its container for planting, butterfly the rootball and rough up its edges.

☐ **CITRUS TREES.** Zones 12–13: This is a good month to plant Algerian tangerine, Arizona Sweets oranges, 'Kinnow' mandarins, and 'Marsh' grapefruit.

☐ **GROUND COVERS.** Zones 12–13: Among ground covers to set out this month are aptenia, calylophus, dwarf rosemary, lantana, Mexican evening primrose, verbena, and vinca.

☐ **HERBS.** Plant all kinds of perennial culinary herbs now. Grow them in containers if you don't have room in the garden.

☐ **PERENNIALS.** Aster, autumn sage (*Salvia greggii*), chrysanthemum, coreopsis, feverfew, gerbera, helianthus, hollyhock, penstemon, Shasta daisy, and statice can all go in now, as can ornamental grasses.

☐ **SUMMER BULBS.** You can shop for caladium, canna, and crinum this month, but wait until soil warms to 65° before planting. Set out bearded iris, dahlia, and gladiolus now, staking tall varieties as you plant.

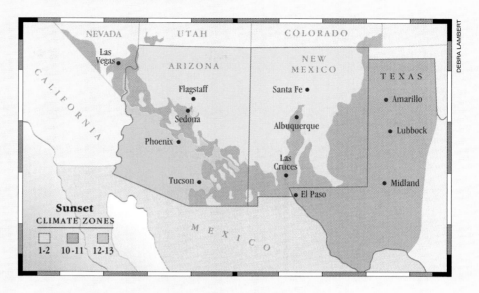

NEVADA · UTAH · COLORADO

CALIFORNIA

Las Vegas •

ARIZONA

NEW MEXICO

Flagstaff •

Santa Fe •

TEXAS

Sedona •

Albuquerque •

• Amarillo

Phoenix •

• Lubbock

Las Cruces •

Tucson •

• Midland

El Paso •

MEXICO

Sunset
CLIMATE ZONES

☐ 1-2   ■ 10-11   ☐ 12-13

DEBRA LAMBERT

☐ **VEGETABLES.** Zones 10–11: Sow cool-season vegetables in the garden now, and sow warm-season vegetables indoors for transplanting after danger of frost is past. Zones 12–13: Sow seeds of black-eyed peas, bush varieties of string beans and limas, cucumbers, melons, soybeans, summer squash, and sweet corn. Set out plants of peppers and tomatoes now, but be ready to cover young plants with cloth or plastic if frost threatens.

☐ **VINES.** Good choices include Boston ivy, Carolina jessamine, Japanese honeysuckle, Lady Banks' rose, silver lace vine, trumpet creeper (*Campsis radicans*), Virginia creeper, and wisteria. In zones 12 and 13, wait another month to plant tender vines like bougainvillea, *Mandevilla* 'Alice du Pont', and queen's wreath.

Maintenance

☐ **CARE FOR HERBS.** Cut back perennial herbs like mint and sage—the ones that die back or look ratty in winter—then fertilize and water. Mint often dies back from the center. Reinvigorate it by stabbing a sharp shovel straight down through the roots several times in a crosshatch pattern.

☐ **DIVIDE PERENNIALS.** Zones 10–11: Dig and divide clumping perennials like bearded iris, chrysanthemum, and daylily. Use a spade to cut them apart.

☐ **TRIM ORNAMENTAL GRASSES.** When new growth appears at the base of the plant, cut back the old grass so the plant won't look ratty.

Sunset

1997 Western Garden Design Awards

W G D

16 winning gardens reveal bold new directions in landscape design

Welcome to *Sunset's* first-ever Western Garden Design Awards. On the following pages, you'll discover a spectacular array of gardens from around the West—from the high desert of Santa Fe to the mild Southern California coast to the verdant Pacific Northwest—that are bold, distinctive, and well suited to their sites and regions. • These gardens represent the best of several hundred entries submitted by landscape architects in six categories—Outdoor Living, Regional Gardens, Water Conserving, Decoration, Small Space, and Problem Solving. Five jurors (listed on page 98), all landscape professionals, chose these gardens during a two-day judging last April at *Sunset's* headquarters in Menlo Park, California. These jurors were impressed by the quality and inventiveness of the designs and by the exceptional use of regional plant material. • Each garden tells its own tantalizing story. And each contains great ideas you can use in your own garden. *by* L A U R E N   B O N A R   S W E Z E Y

▌Outdoor Living: St. Helena

Out of Tuscany

Excellent craftsmanship made this Mediterranean-inspired garden in St. Helena, California, a unanimous choice of the jury. The 1920s home had spectacular views but little usable outdoor space. At the request of the owners, Yountville landscape architect Jack Chandler updated the front entry and created space for entertaining and games. Family and visitors can now relax around an expanded terrace, enjoy an outdoor dining room with kitchen, and indulge in chess, table tennis, tennis, swimming, and horseshoes.

"The Tuscany-inspired hillside pergola with its accompanying sculptured chess terrace invokes images of grand afternoons spent amongst the oaks," exclaimed one juror. Another juror thought the "scale and proportion of the steps, walls, and pergola are particularly elegant, but the grand chess game keeps the garden from taking itself so seriously!"

NORMAN A. PLATE

Whimsical metal chess set, designed and fabricated by Jack Chandler, not only is functional but also provides a focal point in the garden. Fountain grass and viburnum border the steps.

Poolside plantings recall history

"Charming and functional," the jurors said of this backyard in one of Sacramento's oldest neighborhoods. Owners Robin and Tom Guistina wanted the garden to reflect a sense of history. So landscape

A low stucco wall defines one edge of a small dipping pool and forms the front side of a raised planter. An arbor and shrubs help screen the garage from view.

architect Gary Orr chose design styles and plants that might have been used in the 1920s, when the house was built. Boxwood hedges establish "a historical planting framework," and the pool appears to have been an old reflecting pond. The curved concrete patio is chemically stained to look aged. Square columns support passion vine.

"This designer really responds to the clients' needs," one juror said of this garden and the one at right, also designed by Orr.

"Ruined walls" define the garden

"Playful and provocative" is how one juror described this landscape in Carmichael, California, created by Sacramento landscape architect Gary Orr. The owners of the garden wanted an untraditional landscape with traditional amenities: a patio for entertaining, an arbor with a removable fabric shade cover, a lawn, and a pond. The "ruined walls" are designed to represent the remnants of a building or another structure whose lower level was flooded to become the decorative pond. Great attention to detail keeps the deep-blue plastered walls from looking too artificial: they are streaked with a variety of concrete stains to make them appear old, and the "broken" tops were hand-tooled from mortar.

A sculptured wall with window (top) bridges a decorative pond and offers glimpses into the garden beyond. When the fountain is on, water flows from the window. A colored-concrete patio (bottom) provides seating in sun and shade.

JAY GRAHAM (3)

TERRENCE MOORE

■ Regional Gardens: Santa Fe

Stonehenge hillside, Southwest-style

"Really, really daring," an amazed juror said of what he called the "exploded Stonehenge hillside" designed both for erosion prevention and for effect. At its pinnacle is a hot tub with fabulous views. This Santa Fe hilltop garden, designed by landscape architect Faith Okuma of Design Workshop, reflects the native New Mexico terrain. Surrounding the house is a wild, colorful, natural-looking planting of native and drought-tolerant shrubs, perennials, and grasses. Off the back patio, the landscape is punctuated by a small green oasis of lawn and lush plants—an allusion, says the designer, to New Mexico's heritage of enclosed courtyard gardens.

Local moss rock (above) forms steps to the hot tub at the top of the hill and helps retain soil. California poppies, pineleaf penstemon, and Verbena bipinnatifida grow below the spa. 'Stella de Oro' daylilies and red valerian bloom along the left side of the steps. Mock strawberry and woolly thyme fill in the nooks and crannies of the lower stone wall below the buffalo grass lawn.

Blue oat grass, catmint, and Mexican evening primrose soften the hard lines of large boulders (left). Behind, dwarf blue rabbit brush and Caryopteris clandonensis provide yellow and blue fall color. A native blue gramma grass lawn edges the colorful plantings.

Inspired by a cool desert canyon

A wonderfully inviting desert space created on a small, barren Tucson lot was a natural winner from landscape designer Jeffrey Trent and Oasis Gardens Landscaping. "Soft textures of bamboo muhly (*Muhlenbergia dumosa*) and horsetail harmonize with the bold forms of cactus and granite boulders," said a juror. This garden demonstrates that even a very small space can be appealing, and can contain regionally appropriate materials. The lot was transformed by Trent and Oasis into a landscape reminiscent of a desert canyon with steep slopes, granite boulders, and a small pool with trickling water.

Granite boulders edge a small pool (left), which is flanked by a lush-looking planting of bamboo muhly, desert spoon, horsetail, Justicia spicigera, ocotillo, and primrose jasmine. Large barrel cactus grow in pots.

Arizona mesquite trees form a canopy over a border of foliage and flowering plants (below), including yellow brittlebush, purple Dalea frutescens, bamboo muhly, and red Salvia greggii.

TERRENCE MOORE (2)

Celebrating the Northwest's wild landscape

"Precise and well tailored," a garden that "blends perfectly with the Northwest environment," jurors said of this Seattle garden. Landscape architects Randall Allworth and Tom Berger integrated Northwest and Asian plant materials to create a sequence of seasonal color and fragrance. Fullmoon maple, Japanese snowdrop tree, and mountain hemlock form the understory for two huge

existing bigleaf maples. Basalt columns are a sculptural counterpoint to the massive maple tree trunks. Although the garden is well tailored, it's not intended to be formal. Deer fern, hellebores, and trillium soften the ground plane; blue star creeper, woolly thyme, and Corsican mint fill gaps between the pavers.

Large basalt columns are softened by grassy-looking Kaffir lily leaves. Blue star creeper, Corsican mint, and woolly thyme grow between acid-etched concrete pavers.

ALLAN MANDELL (2)

The sight and spirit of water

Clarity, simplicity, and serenity of design and materials give this garden designed by Faith Okuma a surreal quality. It "evokes the vastness of the surrounding desert without losing the human scale," remarked a juror. "Extremely brilliant in spite of its austerity," noted another. The residence is composed of a main house and garage complex along with a separate guest house. Each area features water prominently—a fountain (designed by DeWindt & Associates) or pool—to contrast with the arid site and to celebrate the spirit and presence of water. In summer, the entrance courtyard is shaded by the lush foliage of cottonwoods and locust trees. In winter, the trunks of the deciduous trees exhibit a strong architectural framework. The vote was unanimous for this garden's "gutsy moves" (a black water trough in the desert?), its restrained yet innovative design, and its Zen quality.

Lush cottonwood trees preside over a large entry courtyard, whose dominant feature is a massive, long black fountain. Water flows over its spillwaylike edges.

The Jury

Cheryl Barton, FASLA
Landscape Architect
San Francisco, CA

Ned Gulbran, ASLA
Landscape Architect
Seattle, WA

Bob Perry, ASLA
Landscape Architect
Claremont, CA

Lauren Bonar Swezey
Sunset Senior Writer
Menlo Park, CA

Greg Trutza, ASLA
Landscape Architect
Phoenix, AZ

TERRENCE MOORE

Garden rooms with a Mediterranean sensibility

A vision of abundance and voluptuous growth despite minimal water requirements for the ornamental grasses and perennial flowers made jurors unanimously sing this Seattle garden's praises. "Transplanted gardeners who have watched their Northwest plants wither begin to understand that little rain falls here between May and September," explains one juror. "So, despite its soggy reputation, Seattle is a good place to practice water conservation." Landscape designer Nancy Hammer took cues from the site's hot southern exposure and Mary and Jim Scurlock's love of Italian gardens to create a soft-hued, Mediterranean-inspired series of garden spaces. Profuse foliage and flowers encircle visitors on the crushed-stone terrace designed for entertaining and dining. Pots informally scattered throughout the beds and terraces enhance the garden's casual atmosphere.

ALLAN MANDELL

A sunken shade garden (above) planted with camellias, lamiums, maples, and nandinas sits between the house and the garage studio. Pink ivy geranium tumbles from a pot at rear.

A sun terrace (left) is bordered by green and purple fountain grass and giant feather grass. Variegated wallflower (Erysimum linifolium) blooms in a container at left.

The Mediterranean-style entry garden (right) contains voluptuous flowering perennials, including (from bottom right) yellow gloriosa daisy, purple Russian sage, purple aster, and coral-flowered Sedum spectabile.

Sculpted wall recalls an ancient bath

"A bold design statement!" a juror said of the wall relief that edges this pool in Laguna Hills, California. The design of the plant-shaped bas-relief tiles recalls ancient grottoes and public baths. Laguna Beach landscape architect Jana Ruzicka designed the pool for the Miller-Leverette garden, working with artists Leah Vasquez and Julia Klemek to create the wall. Most impressive is how "the sculpted forms capture changing light conditions and continually transform the space," said another juror. All were impressed by the arduous task of incorporating tiles in a curved pool wall.

A bold, sculptural water trough

A 60-foot-long water trough designed to catch the eye of visitors also caught the eye of all of the jurors. One juror saw the extremely bold water feature at the Kitchell residence in Paradise Valley, Arizona, as a modern adaptation of linear water channels that have historically served as water-delivery systems. Scottsdale landscape architect John Douglas designed the powerful sculptural piece to provide a focus for the long, narrow backyard, to visually connect separate patio areas, and to complement the mountain view. He purposefully selected subtle, long-lived, no-maintenance materials to create the water feature—brown-dyed concrete with a lining of natural black slate.

Water cascades out of a wall into a narrow water trough that starts at the east side of the garden and runs west to end in a small pond 60 feet away. Desert spoon, red fairy duster, and prickly pear cactus soften the trough's hard lines.

Glowing late-afternoon sun lights up the curved pool walls decorated with plant-shaped bas-relief tiles. On a calm day, the pool is like a reflecting pond, mirroring the intricate tile design. Lavender spills over the wall's top.

NORMAN A. PLATE

TERRENCE MOORE

Long wood walkway leads visitors from the house to a flagstone patio in the center of the 20- by 30-foot garden. Birches underplanted with perennials surround the patio.

NORMAN A. PLATE

▌Small Space: San Francisco

Visual trickery enhances the space

"Strong diagonals set in motion by the design made this garden intriguing," a juror said of Scott Murray and Peter Corippo's San Francisco garden, designed by landscape architect Randy Thueme. Thueme's intention was to de-emphasize the awkward offset property lines by shifting the garden's orientation away from the fence. In the process, said one juror, "he also made the space seem larger than it is because all parts of the garden cannot be seen simultaneously." A circle of birch trees adds a sense of enclosure and privacy from neighboring buildings.

Sunken patio creates the room

Clean, classic, and quietly elegant is how jurors described Judy and Richard Keene's Berkeley garden. In particular, they were impressed with the curved steps and sunken bluestone patio that give the space a "sense of room." San Francisco landscape architect Ron Lutsko Jr. created a feeling of intimacy and privacy from tall neighboring houses by enclosing the perimeter of the garden with a wisteria-covered trellis. Stunning white flowers drape from the trellis in spring.

This sunken bluestone patio edged with tufted hair grass (Deschampsia caespitosa) and other lush greenery provides a serene spot for outdoor dining. A wisteria-covered trellis wraps around three sides of the garden and continues across the house.

Artistry in neon light

The artistic effect of this small San Francisco garden captured the imagination of the jurors. "The black, green, and white garden is a real art statement," said one juror. "There is real mystery in the fountain," said another. "A sense of yin and yang emerges." Designers Delaney, Cochran, & Castillo created a Buddhist's garden—a place for meditation and reflection—for Cangioli and Raphael Che. Water from the 7-foot-diameter black concrete bowl seems to disappear into the surface of the gravel. A pink halo of neon light emanates from its edges.

Stone stairs lead down to a Buddhist's garden surrounded by giant timber bamboo and accented with a mysterious-looking 7-foot-diameter tsukubai. Black concrete benches provide seating for quiet contemplation.

NORMAN A. PLATE (2)

Reclaiming the driveway

"A wonderful example of re- claimed landscape space on a tight site," one impressed juror said of this garden. Owner and land- scape architect Ronnie Siegel's chal- lenge was to make the greatest use of an odd-shaped flag lot. One way she ac- complished this was to reposition the driveway and turn part of it into a stone garden with pea gravel paving. She also earned kudos from the jury for the re- designed front entry and the environ- mentally appropriate, water-conserving lawn of buffalo grass.

RONNIE SIEGEL

▲ Before   ▼After

NORMAN A. PLATE

A new arbor, a pared-down brick patio, and lush plantings of water-conserving native and Mediterranean plants bring new life to a formerly drab entry.

Outdoor living on a tight slope

STEPHEN SUZMAN

▲ Before   After ▶

The elegant and well-proportioned transition from top to bottom of a very difficult slope made jurors take notice of the Colton garden in San Francisco. The challenge for landscape architect Mimi Lyons and landscape designer Stephen Suzman was to create a social space for outdoor entertaining and children's play on a site that, besides being steep, is long, shady, and windy. They accomplished it by carving out a brick terrace off the kitchen, building low retaining walls for seating, and developing a lawn terrace for play. Sunny space on the roof of a new garage at the bottom of the slope wasn't wasted—raised beds and pots make it a rooftop garden for herbs, vegetables, and flowers.

New French doors lead from the kitchen to a brick terrace surrounded by rhododendrons, Japanese maples, and other lush shade plants. At the end of the long walkway is a garden on the roof of the garage.

NORMAN A. PLATE

LIESEL EISELE

Toning down the driveway

"Everything but the driveway is noticed," a juror said of this St. Helena, California, garden that used to be mostly a driveway that extended to the barn as well as the garage. "Now the experience of this space is of plants, paths, and seating." And that's exactly what landscape architect Liesel Eisele intended. The garage, behind the house, cuts the garden into two segments, so the only way to create a garden that was not all concrete without moving the garage was to make the driveway subtler. Eisele used decomposed granite, a curving colored-concrete path that directs the eye to the back of the garden, and borders filled with greenery. ◆

▲ Before ▼ After

NORMAN A. PLATE

A path of colored concrete winds through a decomposed-granite driveway. The driveway, the lawn, and an abundance of water-conserving plants replace a scruffy driveway that once led to both the barn and the garage.

Fantasy in grass

A love affair with ornamental grasses transforms a Southern California garden

RANDY LEFFINGWELL

Walking into the wildly romantic garden that surrounds—some might say engulfs—John Greenlee's house is like stepping into Henri Rousseau's painting *The Dream*. Isn't that one of Rousseau's startled lions poking its head out from behind Greenlee's stand of golden bamboo? No. Moving closer, we find it's only a rusty metal sculpture. The sculpture is the first of many pieces that lie half-hidden in Greenlee's verdant jungle, like clues to a mystery. One of the clues is a portable sculpture—an abandoned vintage lawn mower with an attached stylized head that wears a devilish grin. It's easy to imagine that the head is mocking the machine. And if it is, it's an apt metaphor for Greenlee's horticultural mission. But more about that later.

First we venture deeper into the tangle of green. What's that ahead, dangling from the trees? Aren't those cannonball-size fruit the same out-of-scale oranges Rousseau painted? No, if anything, they're stranger. They're golden Victorian gazing globes, objects we're accustomed to seeing mounted firmly to pedestals rather than suspended from tree limbs. And look, there in that open-sided utility shed. Could that be a mermaid on the grass-skirted bed? Of course not. Just because Greenlee calls this structure the "Mermaid House" doesn't mean she's real. She's just a figment of our imagination stimulated by the fantasy around us. Isn't she?

by **SHARON COHOON**

This grass-skirted bed—despite the "Sleep, sleep, per chance" placard above it—wasn't made for anything as functional as sleeping. It's purely for fun. 'Mermaid' rose vines form the "walls" in this little grass shack.

Fanciful "Mermaid House" (above) was once an ordinary utility shed. The siding was replaced with a wire grid and climbing roses.

Greenlee is the founder of Greenlee Nursery in Pomona, California, and author of *The Encyclopedia of Ornamental Grasses* (Rodale Press, Emmaus, PA, 1992; $29.95). The first nurseryman on the West Coast to laud the virtues of ornamental grasses in the landscape, Greenlee has more recently been in the vanguard of the movement to replace water- and chemical-dependent turf grasses with more self-sustaining native grasses and sedges. It's time to knock the habit of evergreen turf, he maintains. It's an unnatural act, and exacts too steep a price, he says. We pump tons of fertilizer into the earth to make the grass grow, and drench the soil with herbicides and pesticides so nothing else will. Then we mow it all down and start over. The "jack it, gack it, and whack it" syndrome, he calls it.

Greenlee urges people to liberate themselves from the perpetual care of a traditional lawn, and spend the time unleashing their garden fantasies. Abandon the mower, and make room for mermaids.

RANDY LEFFINGWELL

In John Greenlee's garden, an allée of golden bamboo (left) ends at a mirror, which visually extends it. A mysterious face (center) peeps out from the grasses at the bottom of a miniamphitheater. Greenlee (right) takes a rare break in the miniamphitheater, which was designed in part to collect that rare Southern California commodity—rainwater.

GREENLEE'S GRASS PICKS

To most of us, a meadow is at least an acre large. But to John Greenlee, alias "The Grassman," a meadow is in the mind. Even a narrow parkway strip or tiny island surrounded by flower beds can evoke the feeling of a meadow if it's planted with the right grasses, says Greenlee. Following are his recommendations for a meadow look in a variety of spaces. All of the accent grasses listed provide showy material for bouquets.

EVERGREEN GRASSES TO SIMULATE A NATURAL MEADOW
All grow 1 to 2 feet tall and should not be mowed.

- European meadow sedge (*Carex remota*): sun or shade.
- Berkeley sedge (*Carex tumulicola*): sun or shade.
- Maires fescue (*Festuca mairei*): good choice for desert.
- Autumn moor grass (*Sesleria autumnalis*): sun.
- Meadow moor grass (*Sesleria heuffleriana*): sun.

MEADOW GRASSES TO WALK ON
All grow 4 to 8 inches tall and can be left alone or mowed occasionally.

- Mosquito grass (*Bouteloua gracilis*): dormant in winter, good in the desert; sun.
- Buffalo grass (*Buchloe dactyloides*): dormant in winter, good in the desert; sun.
- California meadow sedge (*Carex pansa*): creeping evergreen grass; sun or shade.
- Valley meadow sedge (*Carex praegracilis*): creeping evergreen grass; sun or shade.
- Catlin sedge (*Carex texensis*): clumping evergreen grass; sun or shade.

ACCENT GRASSES FOR SUNNY MEADOWS OR BORDERS
- Eulalia or Japanese silver grass (*Miscanthus sinensis*): 5 to 6 feet tall.
- Evergreen miscanthus (*Miscanthus transmorrisonensis*): 3 feet tall; one of the best maiden grasses for small gardens.
- Deer grass (*Muhlenbergia rigens*): 3 to 4 feet tall.
- Fountain grass (*Pennisetum*): many varieties; 1 to 4 feet tall, depending on variety.
- Giant feather grass (*Stipa gigantea*): 2 to 3 feet tall (6 feet when in bloom).
- Mexican feather grass (*Stipa tenuissima*): 1 to 2 feet tall.

ACCENT GRASSES FOR SHADY MEADOWS OR BORDERS
All grow 2 to 3 feet tall.

- Fall-blooming reed grass (*Calamagrostis arundinacea brachytricha*): an asset in woodland plantings.
- Drooping sedge (*Carex pendula*): likes moisture; good along paths or walks.
- Northern sea oats (*Chasmanthium latifolium*): good in damp locations or by pond edges.

WHERE TO BUY GRASSES
Good retail nurseries will special-order ornamental grasses from wholesale suppliers if they don't have any in stock. Or contact one of the following mail-order nurseries:

Digging Dog Nursery, Box 471, Albion, CA 95410; (707) 937-1130.

Greenlee Nursery, 257 E. Franklin Ave., Pomona, CA 91766; (909) 629-9045.

Heronswood Nursery Ltd., 7530 288th St. N.E., Kingston, WA 98346; (360) 297-4172. ◆

Pots of colorful gerberas (also called South African daisies) appear in nurseries around the West this month (see page 116).

NORMAN A. PLATE

April

gardenguide

NORMAN A. PLATE

Floral fireworks

The secret to this Laguna Beach garden's bold color palette? In a word, annuals

by **SHARON COHOON**

Neutral colors are not San Dee Frei's style. She's a trade show booth designer, so it's her job to make sure people notice her customers' booths before anybody else's. To do that she makes them bold and bright. She works with intense color all day long. So you might think she'd want a break from all that intensity in her off-hours. But her garden in Laguna Beach explodes with color.

"Give me color—and lots of it—and year-round," Frei told garden designer Carol Muñoz of Carol's Pots & Stems in Irvine when she asked for her help in creating a picture-perfect front-yard garden. Muñoz warned Frei that the level of

gear

CURTIS ANDERSON

Wonder Gloves are not cute. They look like heavy-duty dishwashing gloves. But use them awhile and you stop noticing, because they work so beautifully. The slim cut of their fingers doesn't hamper manual dexterity. So jobs like weeding and transplanting—even seed sowing—are a snap. The snug wrists and tall cuffs are also nice features. They keep out dirt and keep hands clean. Hands stay warm and dry, too, thanks to Wonder Gloves' vinyl coating and cloth lining. That's a comfort when tackling cold, wet jobs like dividing water lilies or planting a bog garden. If you can bear to part with them long enough, you can even launder Wonder Gloves in the washing machine.

The gloves come in one color (terra-cotta orange) and four sizes: small (great for petite hands), medium, large, and extra-large. If they're not available at your local garden center, order directly from Garden Works; (206) 455-0568. A pair costs $9, plus $1.50 shipping. — *S. C.*

---

color she was demanding meant using lots of annuals. And that annual-based gardens were high-maintenance propositions. And that Frei was committing herself to a regime of deadheading and fertilizing to ensure long bloom periods—and that she would need to replace her color crops frequently nonetheless. But Frei didn't flinch. "Just give me color, lots of color," she insisted despite these measures.

Muñoz put in daffodils, ranunculus, freesias, and tulips by the bushelful. And lots of sweet peas and delphiniums. And many flats of snapdragons, pansies, lobelia, and sweet alyssum. And only perennials that bloomed their hearts out, like alstroemeria, feverfew, and Santa Barbara daisies. And just a touch of soothing gray 'Powis Castle' artemisia to keep all that color from going over the top. When she was finished, the small garden was as packed with flowers as a French nosegay.

And Frei tends it contentedly. She relies on Muñoz to replace the color when necessary and help with maintenance, but she spends up to three hours a day deadheading and fertilizing to keep her garden in perfect flower. "I know most people hate these routine chores," says Frei. "But I love neating up the garden. I find it very relaxing. Plus it gives me a great excuse to be out here."

Wisteria in pots

Chinese wisteria (*W. sinensis*) is dramatic enough when it's trained as a tree, but a pair of 50-year-old plants blooming in containers (shown below) doubles the spectacle. Seattle landscape architect R. David Adams found the two plants growing in a garden about a decade ago. He dug them up, pruned their roots, and transplanted them into big Italian terra-cotta pots.

You could adapt Adams's idea to start a similar project on a smaller scale. Begin with a plant in a 5-gallon (or larger) container. Put a wood stake in the middle of the pot and train the vine to twine up around the stake to a height of about 3 feet. Pinch off side shoots as they emerge. Allow the top to branch out, but keep pinching it back. The idea is to develop a sturdy, self-supporting trunk as fast as possible, and to do this you'll have to sacrifice blossoms for a few years. Once the trunk reaches the desired thickness (this may take five years), you can allow the plant to bloom.

W. sinensis is hardy enough to grow in all Western climate zones, but in cold-winter areas, move plants in pots to a frost-free place to keep roots from freezing.

To keep a potted wisteria going strong, make sure that it is watered regularly and fed with a balanced fertilizer immediately after blooming, and again in late July or early August. — *Steven R. Lorton*

BEN WOOLSEY

BOOKS

On salvias

Have you resisted planting salvias in your garden because (a) the number of choices was simply too overwhelming, (b) information about plant care was entirely too slim, or (c) companion planting ideas were even harder to come by? Well, stop. With the release of *A Book of Salvias: Sages for Every Garden,* by Betsy Clebsch (Timber Press, Portland, 1997; $29.95), you're running out of excuses. Clebsch, who grows salvias by the hundreds on her sunny hilltop in Northern California, has been passionately studying salvias since the late 1960s, and she has distilled her knowledge into this long-awaited book (the first devoted to the species).

Clebsch narrows the huge field of 900 species to 100 or so of the best choices for home gardens, describing each plant in detail. Color photos show most of them. She provides care instructions and inspiring planting ideas. One dynamite color combination (blue–chamois yellow): plant *Salvia azurea grandiflora* on either side of a 'Buff Beauty' rose and weave its long, willowy stems through the rose canes. There are charts indicating the best salvias for shade, for containers, and for cold areas.

Clebsch has thought of everything. Check out her book, available in bookstores later this spring. You can order it by calling (800) 327-5680. — *S. C.*

Hail to gerbera, queen of the daisies

Among the native plants of South Africa that have won a place in Western gardens, the Transvaal daisy, or gerbera, is perhaps the most irresistible. This month, as pots of gerberas appear in nurseries around the West, you'll probably be tempted to take home a few of these most regal of daisies. Their big, vibrant blooms are standouts in containers or beds, and their lasting quality in a vase makes them favorite cut flowers.

Thanks to breeders, gerberas are bearing more and consistently larger flowers than ever before, and in a wider range of colors. Pictured on page 116 (clockwise from left) are 'Festival Yellow', 'Mardi Gras Salmon Shades', 'Festival Golden Yellow', 'Masquerade Red', 'Masquerade White', and 'Festival Rose'. Most have 3- to 4-inch blooms, and some, like the Festival series, come in more than a dozen colors. The flowers have either light or dark centers (called "eyes" by breeders), regardless of flower color. Dark eyes, like the ones in the Masquerade series, are currently rising in popularity.

Mardi Gras, a new semidouble strain, comes in golden yellow, rose shades, salmon shades, and orange (more colors are scheduled for future release). The yellow, salmon, and orange flowers have light eyes, while the eye of the rose type is dark.

Gerberas bloom in six-week cycles from late April until the weather cools down in fall. To keep flowers coming, feed twice a month during the bloom period with half-strength liquid fertilizer, and water only after the top half-inch of soil has dried out.

Most gardeners grow gerberas as annuals in containers, but they are actually tender perennials that grow well in the ground in mild-winter parts of the West (*Sunset* climate zones 8, 9, and 12 through 24). Plant gerberas in loose, rich, fast-draining soil in full sun (filtered sun in hot-summer places), but to avoid rot be sure that soil never covers the crown of the plant.

— *Jim McCausland*

The Northwest's hardy palm

Once, the windmill palm (*Trachycarpus fortunei*) was merely a curiosity in Pacific Northwest gardens. You'd see a single specimen of this fan-leafed palm, with its dark, hairy trunk, standing alone in a garden or by a house, looking exotically out of place. Now gardeners are mixing them with conifers and using them as backbone plants in "tropical" borders—the latest landscaping craze.

Windmill palm is hardy in *Sunset* climate zones 4 through 7. Though established trees can survive temperatures well below freezing, younger plants may suffer from a severe cold spell. To help winterize a young palm, plant it in March after the danger of a hard freeze is past, so it will have three full seasons to establish roots and adjust to its new environment before the mercury drops.

Nurseries sell *T. fortunei* in 1- and 5-gallon (and larger) cans. It needs full sun and rich, loose soil that drains quickly. Fertilize plants the same way you do other broad-leafed evergreens. Where winters are warm, the windmill palm can reach 30 feet tall. — *S. R. L.* ◆

Pacific Northwest Garden Notebook

by **STEVEN R. LORTON**

In 1970, while I was serving in the United States Army in South Korea, I ran an education center for soldiers. That experience permanently altered the way I look at life and the way I garden. I was constantly amazed at how the Koreans managed to adapt their gardening to the demands of their harsh cold-winter, hot-summer climate, which is not unlike that of eastern Washington and Oregon. At that time, the scars of the Korean War were still visible everywhere on the land, but the resilient Koreans had made great progress in greening up their country. They planted the quick-rooting, fast-growing Lombardy poplar (*Populus nigra* 'Italica'), often from 18-inchswitches that they jabbed deep into the ground in early April. Many of those cuttings took hold and grew. Slower-growing trees like Japanese red pine (*Pinus densiflora*) were also planted, but while they were inching along, plumes of the poplars lined the roads and provided windbreaks. I've started many Lombardy poplars since then, planting cuttings as I saw the Koreans do.

To conserve space, the Koreans planted rambling vines of pumpkin, squash, and gourd in spring, training them on strings up the sides and along the eaves of their one-story houses so that, as the vines crept, their big leaves covered the roof and cooled the house during the summer. The fruits grew plump, fully supported by the roofs. When frost killed the vines, the growers climbed to the rooftop, harvested the fruits, and cleaned off the vines just as they would clear a bed on the ground. I have a shed whose roof has a gentle pitch, and this summer I'm going to grow a roofful of pumpkins and squash.

MARINA THOMPSON

And this month, around my garden pond in Washington's Skagit Valley, I'll sow some cosmos, and as I do, I'll be thinking about Korea yet again. Pinwheel blooms of bright cosmos (*C. bipinnatus*) popped up everywhere in Korea—from school yards to the fringes of rice paddies. Occasionally, I'd see a person with one cut blossom, seldom more. Flowers were religiously left on the plants to form seed and self-sow.

THAT'S A GOOD QUESTION

Q: I keep hearing about a new perennial, 'Husker Red' or something. What is it?

— *Pamela Carter, Whidbey Island*

A: The Perennial Plant Association (PPA) proclaimed *Penstemon digitalis* 'Husker Red' its plant of the year for 1996. I bought several plants in 4-inch pots to give them a try. Following the instructions of the PPA, I gave them full sun and rich, quick-draining soil. Mine grew 2 feet tall their first year (established clumps are said to reach 4 feet tall). The stalks were straight and sturdy, the leaves were dark bronzy red, and the blossoms, which lasted several weeks, resembled tiny pinkish cream snapdragons. With a name like 'Husker Red', you might guess that this plant was developed at the University of Nebraska. If you can't find plants in local nurseries, one good mail-order source is Joy Creek Nursery, 20300 N.W. Watson Rd., Scappoose, OR 97056; (503) 543-7474.

Northern California Garden Notebook

by **LAUREN BONAR SWEZEY**

Not long ago, as I was listening to a gardening interview on National Public Radio, I heard an interviewee exclaim how much she hated spring in the Northeast because the weather was always cold and soggy, and there were too many biting insects around. What a contrast, I thought, to spring in the West!

As the days grow longer in Northern California, new foliage emerges a lovely bright green, and flowers pop out everywhere—even on trees and shrubs. I feel such a sense of renewal. Lots of bloom, lots I can plant, and few biting insects! That's a lot to celebrate.

Speaking of celebrating the season, April is a great month for gardening events, too. Fortunately, three of the best—Park Day School's Secret Gardens of the East Bay tour, The San Francisco Landscape Garden Show, and the Visions of San Francisco Flower Show—are scheduled on different weekends, so there's no reason you can't enjoy all of them. *(Editor's note: dates and times in this article were valid for 1997; schedules will vary from year to year.)*

The Secret Gardens tour (9 to 5 April 27) is one of my favorites. This year, it features 10 private gardens, including the whimsical garden of artist Keeyla Meadows and a Piedmont garden designed by Bob Clark, whose specialty is garden color. Tickets cost $30 (call 510/653-6250). Start early to avoid the crowds; carpool if possible or ride your bike (bike-route maps are available). The gardens are not accessible to strollers or wheelchairs.

The third annual Visions of San Francisco Flower Show, April 11 and 12 at the Center for the Arts, Yerba Buena Gardens, 701 Mission Street, San Francisco (the show was formerly at Gump's), features more than 200 flower arrangements and horticulture exhibits by members of five garden clubs in Northern California—Carmel-by-the-Sea, Woodside/Atherton, Hillsborough, Piedmont, and Orinda. Inga Stone, London Tourist Board official guide, will lecture Friday morning ($40, with lunch) and afternoon ($35, with tea) on the best of the best gardens in England, Italy, and France. The free (except for Stone's lectures) flower show is 11 to 6 on Friday and 11 to 4 on Saturday.

MARINA THOMPSON

THAT'S A GOOD QUESTION

Q: In *Sunset's Western Garden Book,* there's a hybrid evergreen magnolia listed called 'Freeman'. Supposedly, it has a columnar shape [to 15 feet tall] with a 5-foot spread. Sounds like a wonderful tree for both an evergreen screen and limited space. Nurseries here haven't heard of it. Where can I find it?

— Dave Encisco, Menlo Park

A: 'Freeman' is a selection from a cross between *Magnolia virginiana australis* and Southern magnolia (*M. grandiflora*). Its leaves are similar to those of Southern magnolia, but smaller; its flowers are fragrant. The trees are available by mail from Louisiana Nursery, 5853 Highway 182, Opelousas, LA 70570; (318) 948-3696 (catalog $6).

Southern California Garden Notebook

by **SHARON COHOON**

April brings roses, and roses bring trouble. If you live along the coast, for example, your beautiful spring blooms probably come with foliage as riddled with holes as a sieve. (Inland gardeners don't seem to be plagued with this problem.) The villain is likely the sawfly, a wasplike insect that saws slits into the rose foliage to lay its eggs (hence the name). The hatched larvae, which look like tiny slugs, feed on the leaves, creating the holes. *Bacillus thuringiensis* (BT) doesn't work for this pest. Spraying with Sevin (carbaryl) or Orthene (acephate) is the solution usually recommended. However, since both of these insecticides are toxic to bees (Sevin is toxic to earthworms, too), I don't use them. I pick off and dispose of damaged leaves instead, destroying lots of larvae and keeping the sawfly population reasonably in check in the process. You can also spray with a fine-grade horticultural oil (such as Sunspray) to smother the larvae.

The other common rose problem, of course, is powdery mildew, the fungus that makes rose leaves look like they've been dusted with chalk. Fortunately there is an easy, effective organic solution for this one: baking soda. The soda kills the fungus by desiccating it. There are lots of recipes floating around. This one comes from *Potpourri of Roses,* the newsletter of the Huntington Rose Garden Volunteers: Mix 1½ tablespoons baking soda, 1 tablespoon canola oil, 1 tablespoon fungicidal/insecticidal soap, and 1 tablespoon dis-

tilled white vinegar with 1 cup warm water. Add the vinegar last—it makes the mix fizz. Stir well. If using a tank sprayer, add enough additional warm water to make a gallon. For a hose-end sprayer, pour the mixture into the container and add enough water to bring it to the 1-gallon mark. Then spray the foliage thoroughly.

NEW BOOK ON ROSES

Speaking of the Huntington, Clair Martin, curator of rose collections at the Huntington Botanical Garden, has a new book due out this month: *Smith & Hawken: 100 English Roses for the American Garden* (Workman Publishing, New York, 1997; $16.95 flexibound paper). Martin was among the first in this country to grow David Austin's English roses. The book is written like a field guide to Martin's top roses, with a page of description and a color photo for each rose. That format should prove very handy when you're rose shopping—whether from a catalog or in a nursery.

THAT'S A GOOD QUESTION

Q: Do I have to give up on roses if I don't have any full sun?

A: No. If you have an area that gets morning sun or broken light all day, you can grow many roses. 'Iceberg'—or many David Austin roses with 'Iceberg' in their heritage, such as 'Graham Thomas', 'Perdita', and 'Swan'—will do well.

Westerner's Garden Notebook

by **JIM McCAUSLAND**

The ultimate gawker, I shuffle through nurseries every April like a kid on his first visit to Disneyland. I'm usually scouting new annuals and perennials, of course, but sometimes standard nursery stock stops me in my tracks. Last season I was wowed by a red-leafed Japanese maple grafted onto an all-green variety and by the fresh green foliage on a larch. I always look in the tool section too. After finding cracks in the 47-inch ash handle on my favorite shovel, suddenly I'm more interested in fiberglass handles. They're lighter than steel handles, stronger than wood—and they don't crack.

A SKYLIGHT COMES DOWN TO EARTH

I love seeing gardeners improvise, so I was delighted with a space age–looking coldframe I spotted last year. It took me a minute to figure out where its gracefully arched top came from: it was an imperfect skylight that a big home center had sold cheap.

Skylights come in all shapes and sizes, but then so do coldframes. The owner of this one built a raised bed to fit perfectly under the skylight. When all danger of frost is past, she takes the skylight off and stores it in a garden shed. Then, when fall comes and the plants need extra heat again, she puts the skylight cover back in place and extends that bed's season an extra couple of weeks.

AS TREES GROW, SO DOES SHADE

After a struggle to get strong growth out of plants in one of my garden beds, I decided that something fundamental must be wrong with the soil. But a $40 soil test ruled that out: my soil was just fine.

I studied the bed again and finally figured out what was going on: an Austrian pine growing near the site was just getting too big, and its shade was overwhelming the sun-loving annuals.

The rule of thumb is to give sun-loving plants at least six hours of direct sun each day (more is usually better). Since that bed gets less sunlight than that now, my plant choices have to change. I can grow shade-loving flowers (begonias, impatiens, and many others) or leafy vegetables, which usually don't need as much sun as fruiting crops.

SPRING PLANTING PRIORITIES IN THE HIGH DESERT

When I have questions about desert gardening, especially in the high desert (*Sunset* climate zones 10 and 11), I often reach for my copy of *Growing Desert Plants from Windowsill to Garden,* by Theodore Hodoba (Red Crane Books, Santa Fe, 1995; $24.95). Hodoba, a nurseryman, recommends

spring planting for any high-desert plant that must be well rooted before hard freezes come the following winter. His recommendations for spring planting include desert willow (*Chilopsis linearis*), bird of paradise bush (*Caesalpinia gilliesii*), and all trees and shrubs in the beech family—palo verde, for example.

MEXICAN EVENING PRIMROSE NEEDS RESTRAINT

Some plants are just too successful. For example, Mexican evening primrose (*Oenothera berlandieri*) produces masses of pink blooms, thrives on little or no care or extra water, and covers dry ground quickly. But once it's taken over a good part of your garden, you may wish you'd never seen it. It spreads by runners and seeds all through the garden. You can enjoy its benefits while controlling its shortcoming by confining it to an island bed bordered on all sides by concrete. I've seen Mexican evening primrose hemmed in nicely between a garage and a sidewalk. Don't let your guard down: this plant may still outflank you, spreading by rogue seedlings that pop up outside their assigned area.

KEEP THE HARVEST COMING

Most annual flowers and vegetables literally live to go to seed, and when that happens, their work is done and the blooms and fruits stop coming. You can prolong production by forestalling their natural imperative to set seed. The practice works to various degrees with different plants. With flowers, some gardeners wait to deadhead until the main flush of bloom is past, then cut off all the faded heads at once with shears or a weed whip. With vegetables, just keep on picking.

THAT'S A GOOD QUESTION

Q: If I miss bare-root planting but don't want to wait another year to get some fruit trees started, can't I plant the same trees from containers?

A: Yes, but you'll need to pay more attention to watering after you transplant a containerized tree. When you plant a potted apple tree, for example, a mass of potting soil goes into the planting hole with the roots. When you irrigate, water might soak the native soil around the tree but not penetrate the potting soil around the roots. To get water where it's needed, build a 6-inch-high basin around the tree, barely outside the perimeter of its root mass. After you've filled the basin, let the water soak in, then check to make sure it penetrated the rootball. If it didn't, water again.

Planting

☐ **BEDDING PLANTS.** Zones 4–7: Nurseries will be stuffed with bedding plants—celosia, geraniums, impatiens, and sweet alyssum among them. Set them out as soon as danger of frost is past (normally mid- to late month). If you're itching for instant color, set out frost-tolerant plants like dusty miller and lobelia. In zones 1–3, wait until May.

☐ **PLANT BARE-ROOT.** Zones 1–3: There's still time to plant bare-root stock, but get going pronto. Everything from cane berries to ornamental trees will be available in nurseries. Keep the bare roots moist until you can get them in the ground.

☐ **PLANT BERRIES.** Zones 1–7: Plant blackberries, blueberries, raspberries, and strawberries.

☐ **PLANT VEGETABLES.** Zones 1–7: Plant cabbage, carrots, lettuce, parsnips, peas, potatoes, radishes, spinach, and Swiss chard.

Maintenance

☐ **AMEND SOIL.** Zones 1–7: Dig organic matter into beds whenever the soil is dry and warm enough to work. Peat moss, leaf mold, compost, and well-rotted manure are all good amendments. After you dig them in, rake the ground smooth and let it settle for a week before planting.

☐ **CHECK DAHLIA TUBERS.** In zones 4–7, gardeners can leave dahlia tubers

in the ground all winter, but if you dug yours up, get them back into the ground this month. In zones 1–3, where you must dig and store them, wait until next month to set them out. Meanwhile, check stored tubers for signs of rot or dehydration. If you find rotten spots, cut them out and dust the

wounds with sulfur. If tubers are withered, sprinkle them lightly with water to rehydrate them.

☐ **COMPOST.** As you collect garden debris this month, you can speed up decomposition by mixing new material with old compost and high-nitrogen fertilizer. Turn the compost and, if rains are light, soak the pile until it's as moist as a wrung-out sponge.

☐ **GROOM RHODODENDRONS.** Snap off flower trusses as they fade. Most will come off with a tweak of thumb and index finger.

☐ **MOVE TENDER PLANTS OUTDOORS.** Zones 4–7: Cymbidiums can go out early in the month. Begonias, fuchsias, and geraniums should go out mid- to late month.

☐ **MOW LAWNS.** For the next two to three months, you may well have to mow weekly, especially in the mild, moist climates of zones 4–7.

Pest and weed control

☐ **CONTROL TENT CATERPILLARS.** In zones 4–7, tent caterpillars will spin their fuzzy webs this month; a strong jet of water from the nozzle of the hose will usually blast them out of the trees. *Bacillus thuringiensis* is an effective biological control for these caterpillars.

☐ **WEED.** Now, before most weeds have set seed, is the best time to clear them from beds.

Planting

☐ **PLANT SUMMER FLOWERS. Zones 7–9, 14–17:** All warm-season flowering annuals can be planted now. For your best buy, purchase sixpacks; plants catch up quickly to 4-inch-size plants. If you need instant color, use 4-inch plants. Try ageratum, dwarf dahlia, globe amaranth, impatiens, lobelia, Madagascar periwinkle (vinca), marigold, petunia, phlox, portulaca, salvia, sanvitalia, statice, sunflower, sweet alyssum, verbena, and zinnia.

☐ **PLANT YOUNG CITRUS. Zones 7–9, 14–17:** Buy 5- to 7-gallon-size trees; they're likely to become established faster than older, larger ones. Plant in full sun. Dig a planting hole at least twice as wide as the rootball, but not much deeper. Water thoroughly—about twice a week for the first couple of months (check soil moisture first)—then reduce watering to once a week or so (more often in sandy soil). In cooler climates, try 'Oroblanco' grapefruit and 'Trovita' orange.

☐ **PLANT BULBS.** Plant callas, cannas, dahlias, gladiolus, and tuberous begonias.

☐ **PLANT VEGETABLES. Zones 7–9, 14–17:** Sow seeds of beans, corn, cucumbers, squash, most root crops (beets, carrots, radishes, turnips), and greens (chard, lettuce, mustard, spinach). Leave space for another planting—two to three weeks later—of

Sunset
CLIMATE ZONES
▢ Mountain (1-2)
▢ Valley (7-9)
▢ Inland (14)
▢ Coastal (15-17)

bush beans and other root crops. Set out seedlings of eggplant, peppers, and tomatoes.

☐ **SHOP FOR PERENNIALS. Zones 7–9, 14–17:** When plants are blooming, colors are easier to combine effectively. Try combining blue and yellow, purple and peach, or purple and pink. Some easy-care choices include varieties of brachycome, catmint, coreopsis, delphinium, dianthus, diascia, echinops, gaillardia, lavender, penstemon, rudbeckia, salvia, scabiosa, scaevola, sedum, verbena, and yarrow.

☐ **UNCOIL ROOTS.** When it's time to plant trees, shrubs, and vines in the ground, check their root systems when they come out of the containers. Some

plants you buy may not be in ideal condition, and roots might be starting to circle around the soil ball. Before setting plants in the ground, it's always a good idea to score the rootball with a knife and cut any circling roots (but don't do this on sensitive-root plants, such as bougainvillea).

Maintenance

☐ **CARE FOR SPRING GIFT PLANTS.** To keep plants like cineraria, Easter cactus, Easter lily, gloxinia, kalanchoe, and Rieger begonia blooming longer indoors, set them in a cool place away from drafts in bright, indirect light. Or set plants outdoors in filtered shade (in high elevations, wait until last frost has passed). Keep the soil moist but not wet (except for kalanchoe, which grows best if the soil almost dries out between waterings).

☐ **CARE FOR LAWNS.** Sow or sod new lawns; overseed damaged old lawns.

☐ **CLEAN BIRD FEEDERS.** Clean plastic feeders with a 3 percent bleach solution (1 tablespoon of bleach mixed in 2 cups hot water). Use a bottle brush to remove debris; rinse thoroughly and allow to dry completely. Clean hummingbird feeders every three to four days in warm weather. Clean feeding areas on hummingbird feeders with a pipe cleaner or bottle brush. Scrub wood feeders with hot, soapy water and a stiff brush, rinse, and allow to dry thoroughly.

Planting

☐ **PLANT SUMMER VEGETABLES.** If you live within sight of the ocean, continue planting quick-maturing cool-season crops like beets, carrots, chard, leaf lettuce, radishes, spinach, and turnips. Inland (zones 18–21), shift attention to warm-season crops such as bush and pole beans, corn, cucumbers, eggplant, peppers, pumpkins, summer squash, and tomatoes. Near the coast wait until late April to plant these crops. High-desert (zone 11) gardeners should delay summer planting for two to four weeks; frost is still a possibility until midmonth.

☐ **PLANT CONTAINER-GROWN ROSES.** Though bare-root roses are less expensive, buying roses in bloom allows you to judge flower color and form. Nurseries are well stocked with flowering plants this month. Choose roses with at least four strong canes and make sure the swollen bud joint at the base of the plant is at least an inch above soil level.

☐ **PLANT SUMMER-FLOWERING BULBS.** Calla lilies, cannas, dahlias, gladiolus, and tigridia can still go into the ground.

☐ **PLANT SUMMER ANNUALS.** Plant summer annuals such as ageratum, amaranth, celosia, cleome, bedding dahlias, marigold, nasturtium, nicotiana, petunia, phlox, annual salvia, and sunflower. For dry areas, cosmos, portulaca, sanvitalia, annual verbena, and zinnia are good choices. Bedding begonias, caladium, coleus, and lobelia

Sunset
CLIMATE ZONES

1-3 7-9 11 13 14-24

are good annuals for shade. Gardeners in the high desert (zone 11) can still plant pansies, snapdragons, stock, sweet alyssum, and violas.

☐ **PLANT SUBTROPICALS.** The best time to plant subtropicals is late spring. They'll have all summer to grow before they slow down and harden off for winter. If appropriate for your zone, plant bougainvillea, gardenia, ginger, and hibiscus now. This is also a good time to add subtropical ornamental trees—such as the Hong Kong orchid tree—as well as avocado, citrus, and other subtropical fruit trees.

Maintenance

☐ **PREPARE GARDEN BEDS.** Add organic matter to the soil before you do summer planting. Spread compost 2 to 3 inches deep over planting area. Deeply cultivate the mixture into the soil.

☐ **TREAT PLANTS FOR IRON DEFICIENCY.** If bottlebrush, camellias, citrus, gardenias, geranium (*Pelargonium*), hibiscus, pyracantha, roses, or other ornamentals have yellowing leaves with green veins, feed them with a fertilizer containing iron chelate.

☐ **DIVIDE CYMBIDIUMS.** If pots are packed with bulbs, it's time to divide plants. Knock the root mass out of the pot and separate as many clumps as you can by hand or with pruning shears. Keep at least three healthy bulbs with foliage in each division.

Pest control

☐ **MANAGE PESTS.** New spring growth attracts aphids. Blast foliage and flowers with strong streams of water or apply insecticidal soap to control. You might also want to release ladybugs—dusk is the best time to disperse them—to feast on the aphids. Or order lacewings. They feed on aphids as well, and on mealybug, scale, and other soft-bodied insects. Treat severe caterpillar damage with BT (*Bacillus thuringiensis*), sold as a liquid or powder. Trap snails and slugs under raised boards, handpick, or use bait, especially around young seedlings.

Planting

☐ **BARE-ROOT.** If they're still available where you live, set out bare-root fruit and ornamental trees early this month. They're less expensive than containerized stock, and adapt to garden soil more easily. Just don't let roots dry out before you plant.

☐ **HARDY VEGETABLES.** Plant bare-root asparagus, horseradish, and rhubarb as soon as possible. As soon as you can work the soil, sow seeds of beet, carrot, chard, endive, kohlrabi, lettuce, onion, parsley, parsnip, pea, radish, spinach, Swiss chard, and turnip. Set out transplants of broccoli, brussels sprouts, cabbage, cauliflower, and green onions; plant seed potatoes. Floating row covers help protect seedlings: they take the edge off cold nights and get plants off to a fast start.

☐ **ROTATE VEGETABLE BEDS.** Never plant the same kinds of crops in the same beds two years in a row. For example, if you planted nightshade family members (tomatoes, eggplant, or potatoes) in a bed last year, put cabbage family members there this year. Or where you had a heavy feeder like corn in a bed last season, put in legumes (peas or beans) this year to rebuild the soil.

Sunset
CLIMATE ZONES
☐ 1-3   ▨ 10-11

Maintenance

☐ **FERTILIZE LAWNS.** Apply 1 to 2 pounds of high-nitrogen fertilizer per 1,000 square feet (more on heavily used lawns and those growing in poor soil) and water it in well.

☐ **MULCH.** A 2- to 3-inch layer of mulch suppresses weeds, holds in moisture, and (after the weather heats up) keeps roots cool and growing. Put it around annuals, perennials, trees, and shrubs, especially if summers are hot and dry where you live. Keep mulch a few inches back from warm-season vegetables—their roots need the warmest soil they can get until hot weather sets in.

☐ **PRUNE.** Before new growth emerges, prune deciduous fruit and ornamental trees, vines, grapes, and roses. Prune spring-blooming trees and shrubs like forsythia, Japanese apricot, and spiraea after they bloom. Or prune them lightly after buds swell, and put the cuttings in vases indoors—they'll flower for you there.

Pest and weed control

☐ **APPLY DORMANT SPRAY.** After pruning, spray fruit trees with a mixture of oil and lime sulfur or oil and copper. If rain washes it off within 48 hours, reapply. If you use oil and copper, keep the spray off walls and fences; it can stain them.

☐ **DIG OR HOE WEEDS.** Hoe small weeds early on a dry day; sun and thirst will kill tiny roots by day's end. For larger weeds, water thoroughly, then hand-weed, taking roots out whole.

Planting

☐ **ANNUALS.** As soon as the danger of frost is past, you can plant ageratum, calliopsis, celosia, cosmos, four o'-clock, globe amaranth, gloriosa daisy, kochia, lisianthus, marigold, Mexican sunflower, portulaca, strawflower, vinca rosea, and zinnia.

☐ **BULBS.** Zones 12–13: Plant canna, crinum, dahlia, daylily, gladiolus, montbretia, and other summer-flowering bulbs. Zones 10–11: Plant these bulbs after danger of frost is past.

☐ **CITRUS.** Zones 12–13: Plant citrus in full sun. Protect trunks from sunburn with cloth or white latex paint.

☐ **LAWNS.** Zones 12–13: When average nighttime temperatures top 70°, plant hybrid Bermuda grass.

☐ **PERENNIALS.** Zones 10–11: Start chrysanthemum, columbine, coreopsis, gaillardia, gazania, geranium, gerbera, hollyhock, Michaelmas daisy, salvia, and Shasta daisy.

☐ **VEGETABLES.** Zones 10–11: Immediately set out cabbage family members, chard, lettuce, and root vegetables. Also, sow seeds of cucumber, melon, okra, pumpkin, soybean, squash, and watermelon in a protected place, and plant seedlings of eggplant, pepper, sweet potato, and tomato. Zones 12–13: Sow beans and cucumbers by mid-April; set out eggplant, okra, peanut, squash, and sweet potato any time this month.

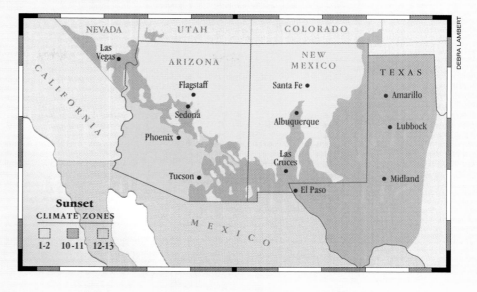

Maintenance

☐ **FEED LAWNS.** Zones 12–13: Give Bermuda grass 3 to 4 pounds of high-nitrogen fertilizer per 1,000 square feet about two weeks after the grass greens up. Water thoroughly.

☐ **FERTILIZE GARDEN PLANTS.** Apply about 1 pound of 10-10-10 per 100 square feet. Water the day before you spread the fertilizer and immediately afterward.

☐ **MULCH SOIL.** A 2- or 3-inch mulch suppresses weeds, holds in moisture, and keeps roots cool. Put it around annuals, perennials, trees, and shrubs, especially where summers are hot and dry.

☐ **STAKE TREES.** If spring winds are a problem where you live (especially in West Texas), stake new trees and thin them so wind will pass through.

Pest and weed control

☐ **CONTROL APHIDS.** Check tender new growth on plants for aphid infestations. Spray them off with a jet of water, then follow up with a dose of insecticidal soap.

☐ **DIG OR HOE WEEDS.** When weeds are small, wait until soil is dry, then hoe early in the day. Sun will kill rootlets by day's end. For larger weeds, water thoroughly, then pop weeds out with a hand weeder, roots and all. Let weeds dry and die before you compost them, or they might flower and disperse seeds.

Superstars of the summer garden

Homegrown tomatoes, corn, and melons are unbeatable for flavor. Here are the best varieties of each

Like your mom's apple pie and your dad's barbecued ribs, your garden's summer vegetables—especially sun-ripened corn, melons, and tomatoes—will always be peerless.

Sniff a sun-ripened tomato and you can tell it's homegrown by its rich tomato aroma. Bite into its baby-soft skin and the succulent, juicy flesh spurts out a rich tomato flavor that makes supermarket tomatoes seem downright bland by comparison. Homegrown corn picked at peak flavor is so delicious that you can peel back the husk and nibble on the sweet, milky kernels right in the garden. And homegrown melons are pure nectar: fragrant and fruity, with dewy flesh.

These three crops are the most flavor-packed ones you can grow. No commercially grown crops even come close to matching them for flavor and sweetness.

Which varieties are best to grow? We asked county extension agents, Master Gardeners, and vegetable specialists around the West. Their mouthwatering favorites (listed on the following pages) might become yours, too. The letters after each variety indicate the region(s) recommended for growing.

NW = Pacific Northwest
MT = Mountain and intermountain climates
NC = Northern California
CV = California's Central Valley
SC = Southern California
SW = Southwest deserts

Tomatoes

Tomatoes come in a phenomenal range of colors, sizes, and shapes. Flavors range from sweet and mild with little acid content (such as 'Lemon Boy') to sweet and sharp with a good acid-sugar balance (like 'Brandywine'). Plants can be weakly or strongly determinate or indeterminate (see definitions below). All are tasty red slicers unless noted otherwise.

D = Determinate (grow to a certain size, bear a single crop, then stop). Grow in short (4-foot-tall) tomato cages.

I = Indeterminate (grow and produce until cold stops them). Contain in 6-foot-tall cages, or tie to tall stakes or fences.

'Ace' (**D**). Medium to large fruits have thick walls and excellent color. 90 days. **CV**
'Better Boy' (**I**). Large, 10- to 16-ounce fruits are flavorful, and vines are productive. Disease-resistant. 75 days. **CV**
'Big Beef' (**I**). Large, 10- to 12-ounce juicy red tomatoes are very flavorful. Heavy producer. All-America Selections winner. 73 days. **SC**
'Brandywine' (**I**). This 1885 Amish heirloom has superior flavor. Its medium to large fruits

Freshly harvested from the garden are (clockwise from top) mouthwatering 'Ambrosia' and 'Galia' melons, 'Peaches and Cream' corn, and 'Early Girl', 'Green Grape', and 'Supersweet 100' tomatoes.

by JIM McCAUSLAND & LAUREN BONAR SWEZEY

NORMAN A. PLATE

are pinkish. 80 days. **SC**

'Carmello' (**I**). Yields large crop of heavy, juicy fruits with very fine flavor. Fruits don't split and aren't prone to blossom end rot. Produces into late fall in mild climates. 72 days. **CV, SC**

'Celebrity' (**D**). Yields heavy crops of large fruits that have superb flavor. Resists disease and cracking. 70 days. **CV, MT, SC, SW**

'Champion' (**I**). This one is a little larger and meatier than 'Early Girl', with good flavor. 65 days. **NW**

'Dona' (**I**). Vigorous plant produces big crop of tasty fruits. 65 days. **CV, SC**

'Early Girl' (**I**). This best-selling tomato's fruits weigh only 4 to 6 ounces, but flavor and production are good. 54 days. **NC, NW, SC, SW**

'Enchantment' (**I**). Bears heavy clusters of egg-shaped, 3-inch fruits that are as good for sauce as for eating fresh. Produces many fruits over a long period. Disease-resistant. 70 days. **CV, SW**

'Floramerica' (**D**). This disease-resistant plant bears its large fruits well almost everywhere. 72 days. **MT**

'Gardener's Delight' (**I**). Also sold as 'Sugar Lump'. An extra-sweet cherry tomato, this one doesn't split like 'Sweet 100'. The plant is large and extremely productive. 70 days. **NW, SC**

'Green Grape' (**D**). Yellow-green tomatoes about the size of large (1-inch-wide) grapes on compact plants. Juicy, with fabulous flavor. 70 days. **NC, SC**

'Jet Star' (**I**). Bears heavy crops of medium-size, tasty, crack-resistant fruit; compact. 72 days. **MT**

'Lemon Boy' (**I**). Yellow fruits weighing 4 to 5 ounces are firm and mild-tasting. 72 days. **CV, NW**

'Oregon Spring' (**D**). Fruits are often seedless and can come very early in warmer areas of the Pacific Northwest. 65 days. **MT, NW**

'Pearson Improved' (**D**). Disease-resistant plant with large, tasty fruit. 90 days. **SC, SW**

'Punta Banda' (**D**). An extremely prolific bush-type cherry tomato, this does well in heat. **SW**

'Small Fry' (**D**). This standard red cherry tomato is very productive and easy to grow. 60 days. **NW**

'Stupice' (**I**). Heirloom from eastern Europe produces many 1- to 2-ounce tomatoes. Very early, and a good pro-

NORMAN A. PLATE

" SPECIALISTS SAY ... "

'Supersweet 100' tomatoes can bear as many as 37 fruits per cluster.

"I like a medium-size tomato like 'Carmello' and 'Early Girl'—one I can eat in the garden and that's also good for salads. I also look for good resistance to fusarium, verticillium, and nematodes. ('Early Girl' dislikes nematodes.)"
— Vincent Lazaneo, UC Cooperative Extension, San Diego County

"'Gardener's Delight' is absolutely delicious. It's sweeter and larger than 'Sweet 100', but has a good acid balance. It also puts out tons of tomatoes."
— Yvonne Savio, Garden Education Coordinator, UC Cooperative Extension, Los Angeles County

"Without a doubt, 'Pearson Improved' is my benchmark variety. Nothing else has ever quite matched it."
— Terry Mikel, University of Arizona Cooperative Extension, Maricopa County, Phoenix

"Large and meaty, 'Super Italian Paste' is no big producer, but it has great taste (not cardboardy) and dries beautifully."
— Sandy Penner, Cooperative Extension Master Gardener, Fresno County

ducer in cool climates. Rated first in flavor and production in San Francisco Bay Area test. 52 days. **NC, SC**

'Sugar Lump' (**I**). Also sold as 'Gardener's Delight'. **NW, SC**

'Sun Gold' (**I**). This orange-fruited cherry tomato was an All-America Selections winner. Bears hundreds of fruits per plant in long trusses. 65 days. **CV**

'Super Italian Paste' (**I**). Fat, 6-inch-long orange-red heirloom tomato is very sweet, with little juice and few seeds. 73 days. **CV**

'Supersweet 100' (**I**). Produces clusters of extra-sweet 1-inch fruits that are high in vitamin C; heavy yields. Disease-resistant. 65 days. **NC**

'Yellow Pear' (**I**). Producing large clusters of yellow cherry tomatoes over a long season, this antique variety has good weather resistance. 75 days. **NW**

Corn

Every year, seed catalogs rave about outstanding new varieties of corn—primarily the extra-sweet kinds. The best varieties also have good corn flavor and tender kernels.

Corn comes in early-, mid-, and late-season varieties, and in three colors (white, yellow, and bicolor). Since the super-sweet hybrids (labeled **SH2** below), followed by the sugary-enhanced types (**SE** or **EH**), were first introduced, debates have raged over which of these extra-sweet categories is best. Many gardeners prefer the latter because the varieties are not just sweet, they also have good corn flavor. Both types retain their sweetness well after harvest. (To avoid tough, tasteless corn, isolate **SH2** types from other corn plants in the garden by at least 60 feet, or time the planting of different varieties so maturity dates are at least 10 days apart.) **SU** denotes normal sweet corn.

'Breeder's Choice' (**SE**). Medium to large, 8-inch-long ears filled with extra-sweet and creamy yellow kernels. 73 days. **CV, NC**

'Breeder's Bicolor' (**SE**). Medium to large, 8-inch-long ears with extra-sweet and tender white and yellow kernels. 73 days. **SW**

'Double Treat' (SE). Large, 9-inch-long ears filled with yellow and white kernels. 84 days. NC

'Early Sunglow' (SU). Short, (4- to 4½-feet-tall plants produce two 6- to 7-inch long ears with tender yellow kernels. 62 days. CV

'Golden Jubilee' (SU). Large, 8½-inch-long ears filled with deep, tender yellow kernels. May not mature in cooler parts of the Northwest. 85 days. CV, NW, SC, SW

'Honey and Cream' (SU). Medium-size, 7½-inch-long ears filled with white and yellow kernels. 78 days. CV, SW

'Illini Xtra-Sweet' (SH2). Large, 8½-inch-long ears filled with extra-sweet yellow kernels. 80 days. CV, SC

'Kandy Korn' (SE). Large, 8-inch-long ears filled with extra-sweet yellow kernels. 84 days. CV, NC

'Miracle' (SE). Large, 9½-inch-long ears filled with extra-sweet and tender yellow kernels. 84 days. MT, NW

'Peaches and Cream' (SU). Medium-size ears about 7 inches long filled with extra-sweet yellow and white kernels. 70 days. CV, MT, NC, NW, SW

'Phenomenal' (SH2). Large, 8½-inch-long ears filled with very sweet yellow kernels. 85 days. MT

'Sugar Buns' (SE). Medium-size, 7½-inch-long ears filled with sweet, creamy yellow kernels. 70 to 80 days. MT

'Silver Queen' (SU). Large, 8- to 9-inch-long ears filled with tender white kernels. 92 days. CV, NW, SC

'Silver Choice' (SE). Large, 8-inch-long ears filled with extra-sweet white kernels. 75 days. SW

Melons

Sweet-flavored cousins of the squash family, melons do well in the Southwest and less well as you move north, toward the coast, or up in elevation. Nonetheless, there are good melons for even short- or mild-summer climates, as long as the melons get as much heat as possible for the longest season possible. (In marginal melon areas, give plants a boost early in the season by covering the soil with black plastic; cut an "X" through the plastic and plant through it. Then cover the plants with floating row covers; remove the covers

❝ SPECIALISTS SAY ... ❞

'Peaches and Cream' corn is ready to pick when silks turn brown.

"[In California's Central Valley], we have the perfect climate for corn. With a 62- to 70-day corn, we can harvest three or four crops through the summer."
— Pam Elam, UC Cooperative Extension, Fresno County

"A lot of supersweets taste like candy. 'Golden Jubilee' tastes like good old-fashioned corn should."
— Pam Bone, UC Cooperative Extension, Sacramento County

"'Breeder's Bicolor', 'Peaches and Cream', and 'Silver Choice' are what my grandparents would have called good roastin' ears. They're more interesting-looking than yellow, and the sweetness is excellent."
— John Augustine, owner, Desert Tree Farm nursery

"'Kandy Korn' is very consistent, and it tastes great."
— Nancy Garrison, UC Cooperative Extension, Santa Clara County

"I like 'Miracle' because it's good and tasty, not syrupy."
— Larry Sagers, Utah State University Cooperative Extension, Salt Lake County

when melons begin flowering.)

Melons fall into three main groups: muskmelons (called cantaloupes), which are early and have netted skin at maturity; late melons (honeydew, casaba, and Crenshaw); and watermelons. Here are the experts' picks.

MUSKMELONS AND LATE MELONS

'Ambrosia'. Incredibly flavorful and juicy orange-fleshed cantaloupe. Very productive; vines are resistant to powdery mildew. 86 days. CV, MT, NC

'Burpee Hybrid'. Oval 4½-pound fruits are ribbed and netted; thick, deep orange flesh. 82 days. CV

'Charmel'. Hybrid French Charentais melon about 6 inches wide with smooth, gray-green rind. Flesh is deep orange and sweet, with floral undertones. Productive and resistant to powdery mildew (pick before melon slips from vine and rind color changes from grayish to cream; not orange). 78 days. SW

'Crème de la Crème'. Large (7 to 8 inches) hybrid melon with characteristics of both muskmelons and honeydews. Flesh is orangish, skin is slightly netted orange yellow. 75 days. SW

'Earligold'. Early 4-pound cantaloupe with thick orange flesh. 75 days. NW

'Flyer'. French Charentais melon the size of a grapefruit with netted, pale orange–tinted skin. The flesh is orange and sweet. Harvest like 'Charmel'. 68 days. NW

'Galia'. Bred from Israeli perfume melons. The 2- to 3-pound fruit has spicy, sweet green flesh and green-and-gold netted skin. Productive even in marginal climates. Resistant to powdery mildew. 85 days. NC, NW, SW

'Gallicum'. Round, 3-pound melons turn from green to greenish yellow when ripe. Flesh is green and intensely sweet. 80 days. NC

'Ha-Ogen'. Israeli melon with thick green spicy, sweet flesh. Green skin turns yellow at maturity. Mildew-resistant. 82 to 85 days. SC

'Minnesota Midget'. Very early, small, 4-inch-wide cantaloupe with sweet orange flesh. Grows on short, 3- to 4-foot-long vines. 65 days. NW

'Pancha'. Cross between French Charentais and American-style cantaloupe. Melons are about 6 inches wide with slightly green ribs. Intensely sweet, deep orange flesh. 80 days. **SW**

'Rocky Sweet'. Round fruit (up to 4 pounds) with moderate netting, yellowish skin, and sweet, succulent green flesh is classified as a "honeydew type." 80 days. **NC**

'St. Nick' Christmas melon. Football-shaped fruit with deep green striped rind and cream-colored flesh. Flavor is said to be like pears and honeysuckle. Keeps two months after harvest. 84 days. **CV, SW**

'Summet'. Oval, 6-inch-wide cantaloupe with distinct ribs. Tolerant to powdery mildew. 75 days. **MT**

'Sweet 'n Early'. Round to oval, 4½- to 5-inch-wide cantaloupe. Bears six to eight melons each. 75 days. **NW**

WATERMELONS

'Bush Sugar Baby'. Similar to 'Sugar Baby', but melons are a bit larger (12 pounds) and grow on compact, 3½-foot-long vines. 80 days. **CV, SC**

'Crimson Sweet'. Green-striped melon with red flesh produces large (25 pounds), sweet melons. 95 days. **MT**

'Garden Baby'. Round, 6- to 7-inch-long, dark green fruits have thin rinds and sweet, crisp red flesh. Vines are only 3 to 4 feet long. 78 days. **NC**

'Golden Crown Hybrid'. All-America Selections winner. Round, 7-pound melons have golden rind and red flesh. 75 days. **CV**

'Mickeylee'. Round, 7- to 15-pound melon with gray-green rind and sweet red flesh. 80 days. **MT**

'Moon and Stars'. Large, (25-pound) Russian heirloom with reddish pink flesh and green rind spotted with yellow moons and stars. 100 days. **SW**

'Sugar Baby'. Round, 7- to 8-pound melon with thin, greenish black rind and sweet, red flesh. Productive and very early. 68 to 75 days. **NW, SC**

'Sweet Heart Hybrid'. Round, 8- to 10-pound melons have crisp, sweet flesh. 85 days. **CV**

'Yellow Baby'. All-America Selections winner. Round, 7-pound melon with green-striped rind and yellow flesh. Very sweet with few seeds. 70 days. **CV**

'Yellow Doll'. Round, 5- to 8-pound melons have light green rind with dark green stripes and sweet yellow flesh. Shorter than average vines. Reliable. 76 days. **NC, NW**

'Rocky Sweet' melons ripen beneath rich green leaves. Fruits will be ready to pick when skin turns yellowish orange. Vines are vigorous and productive.

JERRY HOWARD/POSITIVE IMAGES

"Mildew and lack of heat are a big problem [with melons] near and on the [Southern California] coast. I always recommend mildew-resistant and small-fruited varieties, which perform much better."
— Vincent Lazaneo

"'Crème de la Crème' ... is not like a muskmelon. The flesh is softer, almost puddinglike. The flavor is distinctive and extremely sweet, but not so sweet that that's all you taste."
— John Augustine

"For the [San Francisco] South Bay, I find that 'Ambrosia', 'Galia', 'Gallicum', and 'Rocky Sweet' are really reliable year after year."
— Nancy Garrison

TIPS FROM THE PROS

- "Corn tends to ripen at the same time. If you plant a sweet variety, it gives you a wider window for harvest before the corn turns starchy." — Vincent Lazaneo

- "The best way to eat corn is ... right off the stalk. If you can't take the raw flavor, husk it, set it on a rack over water in a pressure cooker, and turn up the heat. When the petcock starts rocking, turn off the heat, release the pressure, and eat [the corn] immediately." — Yvonne Savio

- "I like to use short-season varieties and plant them early. That way, they get in and out before corn earworm hits in mid-June." — Sandy Penner

- "We grow melons commercially, but aphid-borne viruses are a severe problem in the home garden, especially on muskmelons and late melons. Use of reflective mulches [even aluminum foil] over a bed can help delay infestations so you can get a crop." — Pam Elam

Where to find plants or seed

Nurseries carry transplants of some varieties. But most corn and melons, as well as some tomatoes, must be grown from seed, which you can order from the following catalogs. Not all varieties are carried in every catalog; those that are available from only one source are noted. For a list of sources for each fruit and vegetable described in this story, send a self-addressed, stamped legal-size envelope to Superstars of Summer, *Sunset Magazine*, 80 Willow Rd., Menlo Park, CA 94025.

D. V. Burrell Seed Growers Co.: (719) 254-3318. Supplier of 'Pearson Improved' tomato.

Garden City Seeds: (406) 961-4837. Supplier of 'Minnesota Midget' melon.

Johnny's Selected Seeds: (207) 437-4301.

J. W. Jung Seed Co.: (414) 326-3121 (can send only fruit and vegetable seeds to California). Supplier of 'Rocky Sweet' melon.

Native Seeds/SEARCH: 2509 N. Campbell Ave., Suite 325, Tucson, AZ 85719 (no phone orders). Supplier of 'Punta Banda' tomato.

Nichols Garden Nursery: (541) 928-9280.

Park Seed: (800) 845-3369. Supplier of 'Sweet Heart Hybrid' melon.

Seeds of Change: (505) 438-8080. Supplier of 'Ha-Ogen' melon.

Shepherd's Garden Seeds: (860) 482-3638. Supplier of 'Carmello' tomato, 'Peaches and Cream' corn, and 'Charmel', 'Galia', and 'St. Nick' Christmas melons.

Stokes Seeds: (716) 695-6980. Supplier of 'Double Treat' corn and 'Summet' melon.

Territorial Seed Company: (541) 942-9547.

Tomato Growers Supply Company: (941) 768-1119. Supplier of 'Small Fry' and 'Super Italian Paste' tomatoes.

Totally Tomatoes: (803) 663-0016. Supplier of 'Sugar Lump' tomato.

W. Atlee Burpee & Co.: (800) 888-1447. Supplier of 'Breeder's Bicolor', 'Breeder's Choice', 'Honey and Cream', and 'Silver Choice' corn and 'Bush Sugar Baby', 'Crème de la Crème', and 'Golden Crown Hybrid' melons. ◆

Meet Joseph Howland, discoverer of 'Early Girl'

'Early Girl' is "a remarkable tomato ... dependable," says Howland.

Four years ago, 'Early Girl' was voted the most popular tomato by *Sunset* readers. This year, she wins the popularity vote again, this time with cooperative extension agents and vegetable specialists. Four regions named her a favorite. Why is 'Early Girl' so popular? Just ask her dad, Reno resident Joseph Howland. "It's a remarkable tomato. It's a good size (about 4 to 6 ounces), a nice shape, a good-looking red outside and very red inside, and dependable," says Howland, a professor emeritus of horticulture and journalism at the University of Nevada.

'Early Girl' has a rich tomatoey flavor and is early, of course—about 54 days—which means ripe tomatoes in short-season climates. It also turns out that it's one of the few tomatoes that doesn't go into shock and stop growing when nighttime temperatures dip down to 40°—a common occurrence in high-elevation Reno.

Howland never expected 'Early Girl' to be so popular. All he wanted was to find a tomato he could grow in Reno, where he retired after a career as chairman of Pan American Seed. After much convincing (some might say badgering), Howland was finally able to interest PetoSeed, the world's largest tomato seed grower, in developing a short-season variety—a venture that didn't seem commercially viable at the time (it helped that Howland was on the board of directors). They gave him some seed to test, and Howland discovered 'Early Girl' growing in that first crop. "In 1974, Burpee put her on the cover, and she became a runaway success," Howland says like a proud father. Her popularity continues. She's still the number one–selling early home-garden tomato—an unusual achievement in a market where the popularity of most new hybrids lasts four to five years.

EDDIE DANT

A garden of earthly delights

Two Los Angeles artists put
their heavenly touch
to container gardening

Giant Burmese honeysuckle vine is a fragrant backdrop for pots of red and yellow cannas and flowering sedums.

An angel made them do it. That's the explanation offered by artists Peter Dudar and Sally Marr. How else, they say, do you explain two apartment dwellers with virtually no prior gardening experience taking on the challenge of creating an Eden in pots? Before they designed the lush courtyard garden shown here, the two didn't have as much as a potted geranium between them.

Reina de Los Angeles, a monumental bronze statue the two artists created for the entrance to a West Hollywood residential complex, is the angel responsible. What happened, say the duo, is that their creation turned out to be so convincingly ethereal it made them feel a bit guilty. Surrounded entirely by stucco and concrete, she looked like an angel evicted from paradise. So Dudar and Marr convinced the building's owners to let them create an earthly paradise for their queen—in a space without an inch of dirt.

They began by visiting dozens of nurseries and soliciting advice on container gardening, their only option. "It got so they hated to see us coming," says Dudar. "We were like walking question marks." Gradually, though, the two began accumulating a collection of paradisiacal plants. For color: bougainvillea, cannas, epidendrum orchids, fuchsias, hibiscus, and hydrangea. For fragrance: jasmine, gardenia, honeysuckle, and, of course, angel's trumpet (*Brugmansia*), along with rosemary, lavender, and thyme for

their savory scents. And finally, since no Eden should be without fruit: lemon, peach, tangerine, fig, and banana trees, and 'Flame' grapevines.

Once they had collected the plants, Dudar and Marr rounded up the pots. For a Mediterranean mood, they chose mostly classical Greek and Roman shapes. To keep things light, they added a strong jolt of Mexican whimsy with pots shaped as turtles, goats, and even a kangaroo, as well as other

animals. Then, in a marathon planting session, the duo matched plants to pots. Since they started with a fair number of large specimen plants—including a 20-foot-tall floss silk tree (*Chorisia*), several 15-foot Australian tree ferns, and a 50-year-old bougainvillea with a trunk like a tree—the garden looked mature from the day they created it.

Keeping everything healthy was the next hurdle. Because Dudar and Marr

by **SHARON COHOON**

DEIDRA WALPOLE

had agreed to be the garden's caretakers as well as creators, they needed to learn how to garden quickly. They mastered drip irrigation: every plant got its own drip emitters, with misters at treetop level for additional humidity. The irrigation was set for early mornings to avoid exposing wet leaves to scorching midday sun. They added moisture-holding polymers to the soil to keep it from drying out, and to help them grow even water hogs like papyrus successfully. And they mastered plant feeding—fertilizing the plants regularly at half the recommended strength.

The success of these two amateur gardeners is a little astounding—even to two born optimists like Dudar and Marr. "It's just the sort of garden of earthly delights we'd hoped for," says Marr. "I guess," she says with a smile, "we must have an angel on our side." ◆

At right, golden daylilies shine beside a fountain guarded by a stone lion. Below right, a terra-cotta tortoise appears to bear a bouquet of hydrangeas on its back. Below left, Dudar and Marr's sculpture "Reina de Los Angeles" tiptoes through a garden pool, while orange epidendrum orchids bloom behind her and bougainvillea blazes up the wall.

The new sprinklers

They're more efficient, more adaptable, and less wasteful

Drip irrigation may have stolen the limelight during the last few years, but sprinklers are in the news now. Recent improvements have made them more efficient and adaptable than ever.

Tom Bressan knows the new sprinklers well; he runs the Urban Farmer Store in San Francisco, which specializes in designing residential irrigation systems. "In the past, sprinklers have had limitations," says Bressan. "Runoff, overspray onto buildings and fences, blockages, and uneven water distribution were common problems. When local ordinances were implemented that restricted runoff, it helped push irrigation companies to improve sprinkler designs."

Although drip irrigation is still the best way to water planting beds, sprinklers continue to be the most practical solution for most lawns—and sometimes for the entire garden, particularly for those gardeners who don't feel comfortable with drip technology.

SPRINKLER HEADS AND RISERS: SMALL IMPROVEMENTS, BIG RESULTS

Inspect a new sprinkler and you'll find it looks pretty much the same as its counterpart of 10 years ago. But a number of improvements help keep new models free of clogging, leakage, runoff, and overspray.

Built-in check valves. Check valves, more available to homeowners now, prevent water from seeping out of sprinklers when the system is turned off (a seeping sprinkler is a particular problem at the bottom of a slope, especially next to paving, where runoff might make the pavement slippery).

Filters. Internal filters (either inside the riser stem or under the nozzle), which prevent clogging, are a new feature in most sprinklers (except for some inexpensive models). Up until now, if grit entered a pop-up sprinkler, the sprinkler often didn't seat properly

Pop-up sprinkler with variable-arc nozzle waters a new lawn in a San Francisco garden designed by Janet Moyer Landscaping.

when snapping back into place. Grit caused the sprinkler to protrude from its casing, ready to trip someone or stop a lawn mower in its tracks.

Pressure-compensating device (PCD). This element, new to sprinklers, is either built-in (Toro brand) or an extra part (Rain Bird). PCDs are useful for regulating pressure in water-distribution lines, so the first head on the line won't use all of the pressure and prevent succeeding heads from popping up (or performing properly). They also prevent fogging and drift if water pressure in the system is high. By changing the size of a PCD, you can

also reduce the throw of the sprinkler (to prevent overspray), which is more effective than throttling down on the screw.

Swing joint. This nifty mechanism (by Hunter) allows you to add a taller sprinkler head to a water line even if it doesn't sit deep enough in the ground to accommodate the taller head. The joint moves up and down, making height adjustments easy. In new construction it can be used to set the sprinkler at just the right level.

Taller risers. Unlike old-fashioned lawn sprinklers, which generally had 2-inch-tall risers, new pop-ups are 4 to 6

by LAUREN BONAR SWEZEY

GARY PARKER

inches tall. The added height helps them clear even long, ready-to-mow grass. You can also buy 12-inch pop-ups for planting beds to clear tall ground covers or low shrubs.

Wiper seals. Like gaskets, wiper seals prevent water from leaking out around sprinkler shafts when they pop up. Big improvements in the rubber and plastic materials used for the seals mean little chance of leakage.

NOZZLES: A BROADER RANGE OF DESIGNS

Sprinklers now come in a wider range of nozzle designs and sizes, so there's much less chance that a system will waste water.

Variable-arc nozzles (VANs). Manufacturers such as Hunter and Rain Bird offer variable-arc nozzles ("arc" refers to the percentage of the circle being watered) that range from 0° to 360°. These allow you to water peanut-shaped or other odd-shaped lawns without overspray and runoff. Companies that don't offer VANs usually do offer a good range of arcs, including ¼-, ⅓-, ½-, ⅔-, ¾-, and full-circle nozzles.

Nozzles for small areas. A broader range of nozzles is available for small areas. Companies such as Toro offer sprinklers with a 5-, 8-, or 10-foot radius—more precise for small planting areas than the typical 12- or 15-foot radius of traditional sprinklers. The 5-foot-radius nozzle is particularly useful for rose beds and other plantings where foliage shouldn't get wet, since it has a low trajectory (the angle of spray from the ground).

Strip nozzles for watering narrow planting beds or parking strips come in more sizes, too, so you can tailor your system to cover strips measuring, say, 2 by 6, 4 by 18, 4 by 30, and 9 by 18 feet.

Sealed nozzles. New nozzles, which retract into a protective plastic casing when the system is off, are sealed from all debris and critters. Old sprinkler nozzles (particularly brass) are known to get clogged by dirt and earwigs.

WHERE TO BUY SPRINKLERS

Sprinklers are available at home improvement centers and irrigation supply stores. You shouldn't go wrong if you stay with major brands (some sprinkler manufacturers don't offer a wide range of nozzle choices or special features, such as filtration).

Some irrigation supply stores will help you design your system if you bring in a plan of your garden. You can also find design help in the yellow pages under Irrigation Systems & Equipment or Sprinklers—Garden & Lawn, Installation & Service. ◆

Riser

Filter

Swing joint

CURTIS ANDERSON

Nozzles & PCDs

8-foot-radius flat spray nozzle, ¼ circle

15-foot-radius nozzle, ⅔ circle

Variable-arc nozzle, adjusts from 0° to 360°

Four-way adjustable nozzle

Color-coded PCDs (pressure-compensating devices) fit underneath nozzles to help regulate water pressure and prevent overspray.

Ironclad rhodies scoff at the cold

A hardy band of handsome rhododendrons for the inland Northwest

Rhododendron aficionados in cold parts of the Northwest owe much to the late Ernest H. Wilson, curator of Boston's Arnold Arboretum. From 1891 into the early 1900s, a string of brutally cold winters stung New England. As a plant explorer, Wilson carefully noted which rhododendrons survived the frigid weather. His findings helped the Northwest's frontier gardeners get off to a good start.

Today, this group of rhodies is known as the Ironclad hybrids, and they provide gardeners in *Sunset* climate zones 1 through 3 with a fine selection of cold-tolerant plants in a range of flower colors. Several varieties on Wilson's original list—including 'Catawbiense Album', 'Purpureum Grandiflorum', and 'Roseum Elegans'—are still treasured by gardeners, but the ranks of Ironclad hybrids have grown extensively, thanks to breeders in the Northwest. Now, dozens of plants will survive prolonged exposure to temperatures below -20° (see the list below right).

This month, nurseries will be selling rhododendrons in containers. Set in the ground now, a plant has three seasons to get established before winter puts it to the test.

Choose a site where plants will be protected from intense sun and drying winds, such as in the shade of a north- or east-facing wall or under tall trees. Rhodies require acid soil and good drainage. In areas with alkaline soil, you'll need to supplement it with acid amendments. Dig a large planting hole (4 feet square by 2 feet deep is not too big) and replace existing soil with a blend of humus and finished compost mixed with an ample amount of peat moss or well-rotted manure (use a combination of some or all of these additives). The top of the rootball should be level with the existing soil grade. Water plants frequently through summer and fall. ◆

Early-blooming 'PJM' rhododendron bears inch-wide blossoms among leaves that take on a mahogany cast in winter.

12 choice plants

Here are a dozen of the hardiest and most popular Ironclad hybrids.

'Catawbiense Album'. White flowers with yellow blotches; plants grow 4 to 6 feet tall.

'Catawbiense Boursault'. Rose-lilac flowers with a yellow blotch; 6 feet or taller.

'English Roseum'. Rosy pink flowers; 6 feet or taller.

'Ken Janeck'. White flowers with pink shading; 3 to 4 feet.

'Lee's Dark Purple'. Royal purple flowers; 6 feet or taller.

'Minnetonka'. Lavender-pink flowers with a chartreuse blotch; 3 to 4 feet.

'Nova Zembla'. Red flowers with black spotting on the top petal; 4 to 6 feet.

'Olga Mezitt'. Deep-pink flowers; mature leaves are bronzy green; 4 to 6 feet.

'PJM'. Lavender-pink flowers (shown above); to 4 feet.

'Purpureum Elegans'. Purple flowers with brown spots; 4 to 6 feet.

'Purpureum Grandiflorum'. Violet flowers with green flecks; 4 to 6 feet.

'Roseum Elegans'. Rose-lilac flowers; 6 feet or taller.

by **STEVEN R. LORTON**

MICHAEL S. THOMPSON

Lessons from a tiny garden

It measures just 600 square feet, but this garden is filled with ideas

NORMAN A. PLATE

Angled patio and gently curving pathway make this small garden look larger than it is. A koi pond adds a swirl of motion.

A typical backyard in a new housing development is about the same size and shape as a two-car garage. And it generally receives about as much attention. Most of us look out our patio doors, see the slabs of concrete and the few yards of dirt, and shut the shades again, quickly. These uninspiring little rectangles don't exactly resonate with possibility for us.

Landscape designer Phil Snow saw things differently. When he looked at the backyard of his El Cajon, California, condo, he saw more than a roofless garage. He pictured an outdoor living room about to happen, a microenvironment with a dynamic water feature, multiple conversation areas, and tons of tropical ambience. Then he fit it all into a 600-square-foot space.

Every small garden should have a water feature, insists Snow. Tiny gardens need focal points even more than larger ones, since they have no sweeping vistas. If your water feature is going to be a pond, chalk out various shapes until you come up with one you like. Then try to find a prefabricated polyvinyl chloride (PVC) pond liner in approximately the same shape—as Snow did in his own yard—or use PVC sheeting to form it.

Take special care with the finishing touches. Camouflage pond edges with rock or split flagstone, and use plant foliage to blur boundaries. "You want the pond to look at home, not like it was just plopped down," says Snow.

Once the water feature is in place, most of the remaining area will be people space. "A few seating areas and a walkway between them is about all

you'll have room for," Snow says. In his yard, Mexican terra-cotta tiles, covering the original concrete slab, define one conversation area. Stone benches topped with flagstone, reached via a semicircular path, form a second. The curve of the path encourages visitors to venture farther into the garden. So does the see-through lattice fence and gate at the rear of the property, with their implication of more beyond.

Since the spaces remaining for plants tended to be shallow, Snow put in lots of vines—bougainvillea, violet trumpet vine, Carolina jessamine, and, in the shade, Boston ivy—and espaliered a pink powder puff and a red hibiscus against the walls. Then he balanced all the tropical heat with the verdure of palms and split-leaf philodendron.

"This little backyard has turned out to be a wonderful living space," says Snow's wife, Carolyn. ◆

by **SHARON COHOON**

What it cost

Koi pond (including PVC pond liner, pump, filter, coping, and electrical supplies, but excluding fish)	$450
Terra-cotta tile to cover concrete slab (including mastic and grouting), $2.50 a square foot, 64 square feet	$160
Flagstone walkway (flagstones over compacted decomposed granite)	$250
Stone benches (flagstone tops, stone facing)	$200
Irrigation system (automatic)	$200
Lighting (seven low-voltage fixtures plus transformer)	$310
Plants	$600
Total material costs (labor provided by owner)	$2,170

Hundreds of flower-filled baskets adorn lampposts and porches in McMinnville, Oregon. Learn how the whole town caught hanging basket fever on page 144.

ALLAN MANDELL

May

gardenguide

WILLIAM B. DEWEY

An all-white garden is a charming idea. But it's one we mentally link with England and perpetually gray skies. Can this quintessentially English notion be adapted to a Western garden with an ever-sunny Mediterranean climate? And if so, what would you plant? Come see for yourself at the International Rosarium at Descanso Gardens. A quarter-acre of the rosarium is planted entirely in white-flowering or white-variegated plants, and it is at its peak this month.

Roses—including 'Sally Holmes', 'White Delight', 'Class Act', and white Lady Banks' rose—are the anchors of the rosarium's white garden. The extensive cast of supporting players includes white forms of valerian, veronica, and scabiosa, along with calla lilies, white 'Peter Pan' agapanthus, white geraniums and pelargoniums, and tall, stately *Nicotiana sylvestris*. Low mounds of snow-in-summer (*Cerastium tomentosum*) and 'Iceberg' shrub roses frost the bed shown at left.

Though it looks gorgeous, curator Mary Brosius insists the white garden is still evolving. "We are continuing to experiment with plant material well adapted to our drier climate to make it look even more Mediterranean."

Descanso Gardens, at 1418 Descanso Drive, La Cañada Flintridge, is open 9 to 4:30 daily, except Christmas. For more information, call (818) 952-4401.

White on white

Descanso Gardens offers great lessons
for combining white-flowered plants

by SHARON COHOON

gear

CURTIS ANDERSON

Wouldn't it be a pleasure to wear gardening shoes that combine the comfort of
Birkenstock sandals with the impermeability
to water and mud of classic gardening clogs? Apparently Birkenstock thought so, too. Its Birki Clogs
have all the features of its beloved sandals: toe bars that encourage a foot's natural
flex and grip motion, strong arch supports, neutral heels for correct body align-
ment, and deep heel cups for balance and shock absorption. The slip-on clogs have
the simple-to-clean waterproof polyurethane construction so appreciated in garden clogs. Birki Clogs (about $46) come in European sizes 35 to 46 in black, white,
green, or blue polyurethane, and 36 to 43 in red and yellow. Super Birki Clogs
(about $60) come with a removable, washable cork-based foot bed and are avail-
able in sizes 35 to 48 (47 and 48 in blue only). To find a retailer near you, call (800)
761-1404. — *S. C.*

the NATURAL WAY

Squirrels like their peanuts roasted, thank you

In their zeal to keep birds well fed,
many backyard wildlife-watchers
put out raw peanuts, as was recommended in the *Sunset's* December
1996 Garden Guide ("Edible Ornaments for the Birds"). Invariably, squirrels feed on the peanuts too.

We've since learned from James
Kieswetter at Eastern Washington University that many kinds of raw legumes,
including peanuts and soybeans, as
well as sweet potatoes, can cause nutri-
tional problems for squirrels. They contain a trypsin inhibitor, a substance that
interferes with the enzyme that enables
the intestines to absorb protein.

The higher the percentage of raw
legumes in the diet, the more serious
the physical effects, ranging in severity
from a dull coat to malnutrition and
even death.

Fortunately, roasting destroys the inhibitor and makes the peanuts safe and
nutritious for squirrels. You can get
roasted, unsalted peanuts from such
outlets as Wild Birds Unlimited. Call
(800) 326-4928 for a location near you.
— *Jim McCausland*

new PERENNIALS

Twinspur's new colors

Twinspur (*Diascia*), a favorite
perennial for planting under
roses and mingling with catmint, is wearing some new colors.
Until the last year or so, nurseries
generally carried only two varieties of
twinspur: salmon pink–flowered *D.*
'Ruby Field' and light pink *D. vigilis*.
Twinspur now comes in expanded
ranges of color and plant form.

All types bloom from midspring to
fall and grow well in *Sunset* climate
zones 7–9 and 14–24. Use in containers and rock gardens or at the
front of borders. Periodically cut off
old flower spikes to encourage new
bloom. Trim plants back in fall or
late winter. Buy plants at nurseries
or mail-order them from Digging
Dog Nursery, Box 471, Albion, CA
95410; (707) 937-1130. Catalog $3.

'Blackthorn Apricot'. This 6-
inch-tall mat produces 6-inch-long
stems of apricot pink flowers.

'Hector Harrison'. This variety
develops peachy pink flowers that
rise 5 inches above 3-inch-tall mat-
ting leaves.

'Joyce's Choice'. This 10-inch-tall
variety with light salmon flowers that
fade to pink has hardy green foliage
that looks good through winter.

'Langthorn's Lavender'. This 6-
to 8-inch-tall plant has lavender
flowers and small, dark green leaves.
— *Lauren Bonar Swezey*

NORMAN A. PLATE

Border color without a bloom

There isn't a single flower in sight in the border shown below. Foliage alone carries this handsome planting that mixes the colors, leaf textures, and forms of evergreen and deciduous shrubs. Three plants make the statement: *Euphorbia characias wulfenii*, purple smoke tree (*Cotinus coggygria* 'Velvet Cloak'), and a dwarf blue spruce (*Picea pungens* 'Montgomery'). The bluish gray-green leaves of the euphorbia march up vertical stems that can reach 4 feet tall. The roundish, dark purple leaves of the smoke tree similarly line vertical stems, and the frosty blue needles of the dwarf spruce stand out in horizontal tiers.

These are low-maintenance plants. All three take full sun and will tolerate a good deal of drought. Give them loose, rich soil. The smoke tree is cut back hard each spring to keep it low and bushy and to stimulate the production of leafy shoots to fill in and around the blue plants. — *Steven R. Lorton*

Dwarf blue spruce, purple smoke tree, and euphorbia make a handsome trio.

Hard-rock mulch for desert gardens

Gravel and stone mulches are as inconspicuous in desert landscapes as leaf mulches are in northern forests. Yet both organic and mineral mulches perform the same basic jobs in the landscape: slowing evaporation, minimizing weeds, and keeping soil cooler during the day and warmer at night.

Sold as crushed granite or crusher fines, these mineral mulches are inexpensive and effective. A layer at least 2 to 3 inches deep allows water to penetrate easily and keeps the soil from crusting over after irrigation.

Even a rock mulch needs to be renewed periodically, though: foot traffic kicks it aside and grinds some of it in. And before you plant something new in a mulched bed, rake the rocks out of the way so they don't become unintended soil amendment. — *J. M.*

Sunscape for beds and baskets

The white flowers of African daisy (*Osteospermum fruticosum*) were so common along Los Angeles freeways in the late 1960s that the plant gained the nickname "freeway daisy." But good breeding has helped bring it back into favor with gardeners.

This month, the newest series—Sunscape—is being introduced. Its flowers come in yellow, pink, and purple as well as white. There are both mounding and hanging-basket types. Give plants light shade during the hottest part of the day and keep them well watered. *Osteospermum* grows remarkably quickly: one plant can cover a 3-foot circle in a single season. A tender perennial, it will live on in *Sunset* climate zones 12 and 13, blooming in spring, dying back in the heat of summer, then regrowing and reblooming in fall.

Sunscape is sold in gallon cans and hanging baskets by nurseries across the West. — *J. M.*

BEN WOOLSEY

Good-bye lawn, hello vegetables

Pressed for space to start a vegetable plot, Donna and Ken Erickson of Port Orchard, Washington, cast a covetous eye at the lawn growing on the south side of their house. Basking in full sun all day long, the site was perfect.

Using a spade, Ken stripped the sod off the 9- by 30-foot plot, then tilled the underlying soil thoroughly. The existing soil was rocky and poor, so the Ericksons overlaid the area with a mix of equal parts of peat moss, sand, and manure, then blended in a complete fertilizer. Donna raked the soil into mounds about 1 foot tall and spaced about 2½ feet apart. The mounds warm up quickly in spring, and the soil drains fast.

Donna sows vegetable seeds directly into the raised mounds. For cool-season crops, she plants cabbage, broccoli, lettuce, peas, and spinach. Next come beets, carrots, and onions. And finally a late spring planting of heat-loving plants—beans, squash, and tomatoes.

Seedlings are hand-watered at first. Then, after plants are growing well, they're watered with a hose-end sprinkler. Liquid fertilizer is applied about once a month. — *J. M.*

Azalea Festival in Brookings

Brookings, Oregon, straddles U.S. Highway 101 in the state's "Banana Belt." The Northwest's most temperate coastal climate (*Sunset* zone 17) and a meteorological phenomenon called the "Brookings Effect" create comfortable temperatures—for people and plants—even in winter. Abundant rainfall and rich soil provide ideal conditions for many varieties of flowers, shrubs, and trees. The world's largest Monterey cypress grows here, as does Oregon's only stand of coast redwoods.

Brookings is best known, though, for its native azaleas, some of which were mature shrubs when Lewis and Clark wintered on Oregon's coast in 1805-06. Nearly 1,100 azaleas are thriving again in the town's Azalea Park.

After years of neglect and budget constraints, the park entered a new phase when, in 1992, the state turned control of the 37-acre site over to the city. Then retired Hollywood filmmaker Elmo Williams and his wife, Lorraine, organized the Azalea Park Foundation to fund the park's restoration.

Thanks to the efforts and hard work of more than 1,500 volunteers, and donations of more than $85,000 in materials, Azalea Park now has sidewalks meandering through ancient azaleas as well as recently planted rhododendrons, flowering trees, and bulbs. The new KidTown is a child's fantasy kingdom of towers, walkways, bridges, and hiding places—all built by dedicated volunteers.

Although peak bloom can occur anytime between late April and early June, some azaleas and other plants are always in bloom for the Azalea Festival— a four-day celebration staged over Memorial Day weekend. Events include barbecues, bonsai and quilt shows, art and crafts fairs, and a parade that takes over U.S. 101 for two hours.

For a schedule of festival events, call the Brookings Harbor Chamber of Commerce at (800) 535-9469. To reach the park from U.S. 101, turn east on North Bank Road, then left on Old County Road. — *Kenn Oberrecht*

NORMAN A. PLATE (2)

Hang up an orchid cactus for blooms indoors and out

When a mature orchid cactus (*Epiphyllum*) blooms, it dazzles the eye and brightens the most subdued surroundings. The large plant pictured above, which grows in a hanging pot on one of *Sunset's* outdoor patios, is no exception. Its huge (10-inch-wide) flowers, which appear in mid- to late spring on the ends of arching 2-foot-long stems, blaze like fire in daylight.

Although species bloom at night and then close during the day, hybrids like this one open at night and stay open as long as two to eight days.

Flowers come in "every color but blue," says Jim Pence of Epi World, a retail nursery in Cupertino, California, that specializes in epiphyllums. Many varieties have multicolored flowers, such as golden orange trimmed in fuchsia. The spineless stems are smooth, flat, and often notched.

Unlike Christmas cactus, which are terrestrial, orchid cactus are epiphytes. "In the tropics, they grow in branch crotches where leaf mold and bird droppings collect to nourish the plant," says Pence. Plants are sold growing in a fast-draining potting soil.

Orchid cactus thrive in filtered light—or sunshine either in early morning or late afternoon. During the growing period (spring through fall), give plants a thorough drink and allow them to dry out between waterings. Apply a low-nitrogen (10-10-10) fertilizer about once a month while plants are growing.

Buy plants at nurseries or order cuttings (which take a year or two to bloom) from Epi World in Cupertino; (408) 865-0566. Catalog $2. —*L. B. S.*

NORMAN A. PLATE

PICK-*of-the*-CROP

Shelling beans

Snap beans such as 'Blue Lake' are grown for their tasty pods and are well known to Western gardeners. 'Vermont Cranberry' and other varieties harvested when beans have dried are becoming familiar, too. But shelling beans like French flageolets and Italian Borlotto (shown above), best harvested when the beans inside have fully developed but are still fresh and tender, are a treat that Americans are just beginning to discover.

In *Sunset's* test garden late last spring, we planted several varieties of shelling beans. All proved to be easy, tasty crops. Just plant seeds of these bush bean varieties in soil that has been well amended with compost, in a warm, sunny area; plant them 1 inch deep at the rate of about 10 seeds per square foot. Fertilize them once a week with diluted fish emulsion until plants set flowers, then stop. Water deeply once a week. Harvest when beans are fully formed and starting to pull away from the pod (you'll see the bulge of the developing bean through the shell) but before pods start to change color and the beans inside start to rattle.

Shell the beans, then steam or simmer until just tender. Sauté in a little olive oil with garlic, onion, and herbs of choice.

The following seed catalogs carry shelling beans: Johnny's Selected Seeds, (207) 437-4301; and Shepherd's Garden Seeds, (860) 482-3638. — *S. C.*

Hanging basket fever hits an Oregon town

Drive through the Willamette Valley town of McMinnville, Oregon, anytime from May through summer and you'll see hundreds of flower-filled baskets hanging from lampposts and porches (see photo on page 138). Remarkably, each of the baskets is individually owned and maintained.

Local gardener Fred Koch started it all as his own community beautification project in the late 1980s and early '90s by hanging 40 baskets in various spots. But Koch's spirit was infectious, and eventually the whole town caught hanging basket fever. Now the baskets are everywhere—down Baker Street past the Linfield College campus, through the heart of the historic district, and out along the residential streets.

Each season, Melissa and Joe McLaughlin, the owners of Country Garden Nursery (6275 N.W. Poverty Bend Road, McMinnville; 503/472-1351), make up several hundred baskets for both businesses and residents. The McLaughlins start with heavy wire baskets about 24 inches across and 13 inches deep. They line each basket with burlap and cut holes in the fabric to insert plants, adding soil mix as they go. This light, porous mix is made from equal parts of finely ground aged bark, peat moss, and pumice with the consistency of fine beach pebbles. The McLaughlins stir 1 to 1¼ cups of controlled-release fertilizer into the mix for each basket.

About 40 plants go into each basket. The McLaughlins use an assortment that features geraniums, marigolds, Swan River daisies (*Brachycome iberidifolia*), Dahlberg daisies (*Dyssodia tenuiloba*), verbena, and nasturtiums. Trailing multiflora petunias in assorted colors are by far the showiest performers.

Almost all the baskets in town are hooked up to irrigation systems with timers; every day these baskets get a thorough soaking for 30 minutes. —*S. R. L.*

Artful trellises

"The trellis is a simple vertical design on which to contrast a beautiful vine," writes Ferris Cook, author and illustrator of *The Garden Trellis: Designs to Build and Vines to Cultivate* (Artisan, New York, 1996; $15.95). Sorry, Ms. Cook, but your trellis designs contradict your definition. The trellis patterns you provide are so beautiful in and of themselves, it seems a shame to cover them with anything. Or if you must, then with only the most delicate and ephemeral of vines. And never with some of the rambunctious climbers you mention, such as 'Heavenly Blue' morning glory, which would completely smother a delicate trellis.

The nine gorgeous trellis blueprints, the simple building instructions, and the 50 watercolor illustrations (each handsome enough to frame) are enough to justify the book's cost. Readers may also find the historical lore woven into the text entertaining. Did you know, for instance, that Darwin clocked the rotation of a hop vine in search of a support at two hours and eight minutes? Just one caveat: The author gardens in upstate New York and writes from a cold-climate perspective. Vines will often perform differently in the West than she describes. So cross-check cultural data with a regional reference like *Sunset's Western Garden Book.* — *S. C.* ◆

Pacific Northwest Garden Notebook

by **STEVEN R. LORTON**

A branch of my family has always lived in the Deep South, so I've spent a lot of time down there. Early in my life, in the kitchen of a culinary wizard named Hallie Mae Reed, I learned to love greens. My mouth waters as I write this. Often she cooked up a pot of red beans and rice and a mess of greens. Semantics are important here: one does not cook a pot of greens; one cooks a *mess of greens.*

Hallie Mae cooked many kinds of greens: beet, chard, kale, mustard, spinach, turnip, and even dandelion and poke greens that she found in fields and woods. I learned to love them all, though collards are still my favorite.

My family grows collards in our vegetable patch in Washington's Skagit Valley. We plant collards twice a year: early in March and again in May. The earlier planting produces tender, delicious leaves until the weather gets hot, causing the plants to bolt (go to seed) and the leaves to turn bitter. Then the later planting kicks in, providing us with collards from fall through winter and into early spring. Last January, when temperatures were in the 20s, I pushed the snow away from plants to cut frozen leaves. They cooked up beautifully and tasted great.

It's easy to grow a mess of collards. A packet of seed will sow a 40-foot row. Simply make a shallow trench in the soil, drop the seeds at 1- to 2-inch intervals, cover, and water. Thin and transplant seedlings until the plants are growing 1 foot apart. Harvest the leaves from the bottom up, leaving six or more leaves at the top to keep the plants growing up.

MARINA THOMPSON

And cooking a mess of greens is as easy as growing them. Wash the leaves. Cut out damaged and tough fibrous spots (including the woody central vein). Cut the greens into strips about an inch wide. Put a couple of quarts of water in a soup pot with a ham hock. Let that boil for about an hour. Lower the heat to a simmer. Drop in the greens and let them cook until tender, 15 minutes to half an hour or more for tough leaves. Then they're ready to serve. After I polish off a mess of collards, I like to pour the pot liquor (the broth the greens cooked in) into a mug and drink it.

Collard seed may be hard to find on nursery racks. Two mail-order sources are Nichols Garden Nursery (1190 N. Pacific Highway, Albany, OR 97321; 541/928-9280) and Territorial Seed Co. (Box 157, Cottage Grove, OR 97424; 541/942-9547).

THAT'S A GOOD QUESTION

Q: Can you prune rhododendrons when they are in bloom?

— *Steve Burns, Seattle*

A: That's one of the best times to prune them—the blooming branches that you remove will make spectacular displays in vases indoors. Rhododendrons can really be pruned anytime, with the exception of marginally hardy species and hybrids. Prune these well before prolonged freezing spells to lessen the chance of dieback from cold. And always make a smooth, clean cut.

Northern California Garden Notebook

by **LAUREN BONAR SWEZEY**

Every spring, I don my trekking shoes and visit as many gardens as possible—both public and private—for inspiration. One of my favorite public gardens for new plant ideas is the Elizabeth F. Gamble Garden Center (1431 Waverley St., Palo Alto). Early in May, the garden also sponsors its annual spring tour of six Palo Alto gardens. For tickets and information, call (415) 329-1356.

SPEAKING OF GARDEN TREKKING ...

On a recent trip to Kauai, I checked out Limahuli Garden, a newly opened garden run by the National Tropical Botanical Garden. Located on the north side of the island past scenic Hanalei Bay, the garden features Hawaii's native plants and Polynesian introductions. We were greeted by Nancy Merrill of the visitor program, who offered umbrellas to shelter us from drizzle, then explained the ¾-mile, self-guided tour.

We headed off, following the trail through a system of ancient terraces constructed by Hawaiians about 1,000 years ago for growing taro. We climbed the trail past the roaring Limahuli Stream—one of the few pristine streams left in Hawaii—into a forest of trees, ferns, and flowering plants. Signs explain how introduced trees such as Brazilian pepper are choking out native plants. The short walk was enlightening: I discovered the essence of "real Hawaii" and in the process learned about the importance of preserving Hawaii's endangered plant species.

The garden is open from 9:30 to 4 Tuesdays through Fridays and Sundays. A self-guided tour costs $10; a guided tour, $15 (by reservation). For details, call (808) 826-1053.

MARINA THOMPSON

GARDEN SHOW MOVES TO CARMEL

Last year I attended the Pebble Beach Garden Show, which has now been succeeded by the Carmel Garden Show. This month (9 to 6 from May 8 through 11) the four-day event is being hosted by the Quail Lodge Resort & Golf Club in the Carmel Valley (on Rancho San Carlos Dr. off Carmel Valley Rd.). It showcases several gardens by talented landscape designers from the region, and it also includes seminars, "tablescapes" (elaborate table settings) by well-known residents of the Central Coast, and a high-quality marketplace where you can buy garden art and accessories. Advance tickets cost $15 per person per day; $18 on the day of the show. You can also purchase two- and three-day passes. For details, call (408) 625-1954. *(Editor's note: dates and times in this article were valid for 1997; schedules will vary from year to year.)*

THAT'S A GOOD QUESTION

Q: I am trying to locate *Wisteria floribunda* 'Longissima', the Japanese wisteria that produces very long, fragrant flower clusters. My local nurseries can't find it. — *Virginia J. Langford, Davis, California*

A: Greer Gardens, a mail-order supplier (800/548-0111; catalog $3) offers a number of Japanese wisteria, including 'Longissima Alba' (15-inch-long white flowers); 'Macrobotrys' (18- to 36-inch-long, reddish violet); and 'Rosea' (18-inch-long, pale rose).

Southern California Garden Notebook

by **SHARON COHOON**

"How do I get rid of the ants on my artichokes?" asked Linda Burns of Santa Barbara. That question set me off on a research trail that went on for weeks. Aphids, not ants, are the problem, Master Gardeners tell me. But to combat aphids, you need to control the ants. Argentine ants (Southern California's principal ant pests) adore sweets, and aphid honeydew is their snack of choice, say the gardeners. To protect their supply, ants scare off aphid enemies. The ant-aphid dilemma is never-ending, it seems, and there is no simple solution.

Let's attack ants first. The best way to reduce the population is to trace the ants back to their nest(s) and pour a big pot of boiling water into it. "Ignore the tiny screams," one wit joked. If this method would damage nearby vegetation, try sprinkling a few tablespoons of Epsom salts in the hole instead. If you can't locate nests, set boric-acid traps under affected plants. Use a product like Victor or make your own bait. Mix 1 part boric acid with 9 parts clear corn syrup. Set the mixture out in small jar lids. If you have pets or young children, secure the bait in lidded jars with holes punched in the lids so ants can get in. (Boric acid is a kidney and liver toxin.)

To knock back aphids, try any or all of the following: Blast aphids off plants with a strong stream of water. (Dislodged aphids can't return.) Put down an aluminum foil mulch. (Reflecting sun disorients aphids.) Spray plants with insecticidal soap spray. Set out yellow sticky traps. Plant flowers such as feverfew and chamomile, which attract aphid-eating insects like ladybugs and lacewings.

MARINA THOMPSON

NEED HELP WITH GARDEN PROBLEMS?

Master Gardeners are an underutilized resource. Since that seems a pity, let me share some phone numbers. In San Diego, call (619) 694-2860; in Ventura, (805) 645-1455; in Los Angeles, (213) 744-4863; in San Bernardino, (909) 387-2182. The ant bait recipe ("feeds thousands") is courtesy of Loren Nancarrow, weather and environmental reporter for San Diego's KFMB TV (Channel 8). For more of his tips, see the Organic Gardening story on page 154.

THAT'S A GOOD QUESTION

Q: Hasn't someone discovered a solution for combating giant whitefly yet? plead readers from San Diego and Orange counties facing unsightly beards of honeydew on their hibiscus and other subtropicals.

A: Try Dr. Bronner's Peppermint Pure-Castile Soap (yes, the same all-purpose liquid soap beloved of backpackers since the hippie era). Donald Trotter, consulting horticulturist at Anderson's La Costa Nursery in Encinitas, came up with the solution. Regular soap sprays, he'd noticed, were ineffective in stripping away the waxy cuticle left by tropical whitefly. Maybe the soap's peppermint oil, which made his skin tingle when he used it, would make the soap a superior plant cleaner, Trotter speculated. Tests proved it did. Mix 5 tablespoons of Dr. Bronner's soap (available at health food stores) in 1 gallon of water. Spray plants thoroughly. Follow immediately with a spray of ultra-fine horticultural oil. (Apply mornings or evenings to minimize chance of burning foliage.) Repeat both sprays four times at four-day intervals.

Westerner's Garden Notebook

by JIM McCAUSLAND

Several plants that recently grabbed my attention have earned a place in my garden. I learned about them from fellow gardeners, from scouting nurseries that cater to plant collectors, and from studying this year's crop of catalogs.

With no common name and a botanical moniker that doesn't exactly roll off the tongue, *Zaluzianskya ovata* was brought back from South Africa in 1994 by Panayoti Kelaidis, curator of the Denver Botanic Garden's Rock Alpine Garden, where it grows very well. Its quarter-size, single white flowers have magenta backs and petals with the cutout look of paper dolls; they rise thickly above the 5-inch-tall, 18-inch-wide plant's sticky green leaves in spring. It's worth trying even in the desert. You can buy it from Siskiyou Rare Plant Nursery (2825 Cummings Rd., Medford, OR 97501; catalog $3).

Paraguayan sweet grass (*Stevia rebaudiana*) has grassy leaves and insignificant daisy flowers, but you grow it for something else: its super-sweet flavor (hundreds of times as sweet as sugar, with 1/300 the calories). This is a novelty for sure, but a compelling one. You can order plants from Nichols Garden Nursery, 1190 N. Pacific Highway, Albany, OR 97321; (541) 928-9280.

Native to Europe, annual honeywort (*Cerinthe major purpurascens*) grows 1 to 2 feet tall and bears all-blue flowers above heart-shaped leaves in midsummer. (The blue flowers of its more common form, *C. major,* have yellow bases.) It's available from Thompson & Morgan (800/274-7333).

BERRIES BY MAIL

The small fruits make quite a list: blueberries, caneberries (like blackberries and raspberries), cranberries, currants, elderberries, gooseberries, grapes, huckleberries, lingonberries, and strawberries. Most don't take up much room in the garden, yet they're productive and easy to eat—you don't have a peel or core to throw away. A new mail-order source, WBN Berry Patch, sells all of these. If you want bare-root stock for planting this month, order before May 10 through its Internet site: http://www.navicom.com/~wbnberry. You can also order its free spring catalog on-line, or send your request to WBN Berry Patch, Box 21116, Keizer, OR 97307.

THAT'S A GOOD QUESTION

Q: Why shouldn't different kinds of corn be planted next to one another?

A: Something called xenia gets in the way. Simply defined, xenia is pollen's power to alter the seed it fertilizes. For example, when you plant popcorn next to sweet corn, pollen from the popcorn can fertilize the sweet corn. Since each kernel of the sweet corn is a seed, with the blended characteristics of both parents, the cross-pollinated kernels will be tough like popcorn and not so sweet. If you must grow popcorn, plant it in another part of the garden so that only sweet corn pollinates sweet corn.

Planting

□ ANNUALS. Zones 4–7: All summer annuals can go outside in beds and containers: lobelia, petunias, and snapdragons are the most well known. In zones 1–3, you really aren't safe from frost until after Memorial Day. Direct-sow seeds for bachelor's buttons, calendula, clarkia, cosmos, impatiens, marigold, nasturtium, nicotiana, pansy, salvia, and sunflower.

□ BEGONIAS, FUCHSIAS, GERANIUMS. Zones 4–7: You can put these plants into the ground or outdoor containers early this month. In zones 1–3, wait until the end of the month to do this.

□ DAHLIAS. Zones 1–3: Set out dahlia tubers, staking tall varieties as you go.

□ PERENNIALS. Throughout the Northwest, nurseries will be well stocked with plants in 4-inch pots and 1-gallon containers. Buy now and plant immediately.

□ VEGETABLES. As soon as the soil warms, set out seedlings of basil, cucumber, eggplant, pepper, and tomato. Sow seeds of melon, squash, and pumpkin. Beans, corn, and New Zealand spinach can go into the ground.

Maintenance

□ REMOVE FADED BLOOMS. Deadheading makes plants look neater and stops faded blooms from turning into seed pods, thus channeling the plant's energy into active growth.

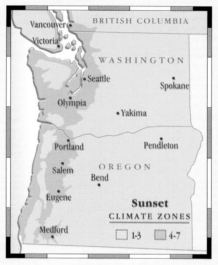

□ FERTILIZE ANNUALS. Feed annuals in beds and pots early in the month and again at midmonth. A liquid plant food such as fish emulsion works well, since the dissolved nutrients go directly to the plants' roots.

□ FEED FLOWERING SHRUBS. Apply a balanced or high-nitrogen fertilizer to these plants this month. A granular fertilizer scattered around the bases of the shrubs encourages strong growth and good bud set.

□ FEED LAWNS. Throughout the Northwest, mid-May is an excellent time to give lawns a generous feeding. Apply ½ to 1 pound of actual nitrogen per 1,000 square feet of turf to keep grass green and vigorous.

□ DIVIDE PERENNIALS. All Northwest climate zones: Divide perennials once plants have finished blooming. You can also dig and divide late-summer- and fall-flowering perennials without sacrificing bloom. A clump the size of a dinner plate will divide neatly into four pieces. Replant divisions at once and water them well.

□ TEND COMPOST. Grass clippings, prunings, and spent flowers should all be turned into the compost pile.

Pest and weed control

□ COMBAT SLUGS. Whatever your war strategy (handpicking, bait, traps), get them now before they grow, only to eat more and lay eggs. If you use bait, be careful to keep it away from children and pets.

□ WEED. Pull weeds now while they're young and most have not yet formed seeds.

Planting

☐ **PLANT FLOWERS FOR CUTTING.** Long-blooming perennials provide a good source of cut flowers. Try alstroemeria, coreopsis, gaillardia, gloriosa daisy, lavender, *Limonium perezii,* purple coneflower, scabiosa, Shasta daisy, and yarrow.

☐ **PLANT FOR PERMANENCE.** Almost any container-grown ground cover, perennial, shrub, tree, and vine can be planted now. In zones 1 and 2, wait until after the last frost to set out tender plants. Dig planting holes no deeper than the rootball, but at least twice as wide. If you live in a windy area, stake young trees. Otherwise leave them unstaked; they'll develop a stronger trunk if allowed to rock gently. Use ties that won't strangle trunks, and secure them loosely so trees can sway; remove them after one growing season.

☐ **SHOP FOR SPECIALTY VEGETABLES.** Thanks to several growers who offer European and specialty vegetable varieties through local nurseries or by mail, you now have a much wider selection of vegetable seedlings from which to choose. Check availability at nurseries or order from the Natural Gardening Company (707/766-9303) or Santa Barbara Heirloom Seedling Nursery (805/968-5444).

Maintenance

☐ **APPLY IRON CHELATE.** If azalea, camellia, citrus, and gardenia foliage is

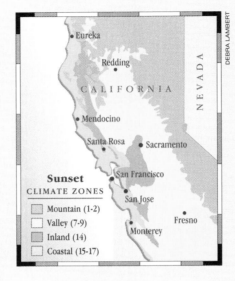

Sunset
CLIMATE ZONES

☐ Mountain (1-2)
☐ Valley (7-9)
☐ Inland (14)
☐ Coastal (15-17)

yellowish with green veins, the plants need iron. Apply a fertilizer containing iron chelate if the plants haven't been fertilized in a while. Otherwise, use iron chelate (according to label directions).

☐ **MULCH.** To maintain soil moisture and keep weeds down, spread a 1- to 3-inch layer of organic material around plants (use the deeper layer for larger plants), leaving a small circle of bare soil around the trunk or stem of each plant. Use bark chips, compost, straw, or other material that won't blow away.

☐ **AERATE LAWNS.** To help improve air and water movement in the soil around roots, aerate the lawn. You can rent an

aerator from an equipment supply store (look in the yellow pages under Rental Service Stores & Yards). Rake up the cores and top-dress with mulch. If you haven't fertilized recently, apply a lawn fertilizer and water in well.

☐ **PRUNE LARGE SHRUBS INTO TREES.** You can train overgrown shrubs into handsome single or multitrunked trees by thinning out excess growth from their interiors and then pruning up lower branches to raise the canopy. Good subjects for pruning include oleander, pineapple guava, pittosporum, strawberry tree, and xylosma.

☐ **STAKE PERENNIALS.** If you use either hoop or enclosed square stakes, install them when plants are small, so foliage can grow up through the openings. Once plants are bushy, these stakes are almost impossible to install.

☐ **THIN FRUIT.** Zones 7–9, 14–17: On apples, nectarines, peaches, and Asian pears, gently twist off enough immature fruit to leave 4 to 6 inches between remaining fruit. This allows the remaining fruit to grow larger and may also reduce problems with insects (such as codling moth) and diseases (apple mildew and apple scab) because there's more room for air circulation around the fruit and they aren't touching each other. Zones 1 and 2: Thinning should be done in early summer.

Planting

☐ **SUMMER ANNUALS.** In sunny areas plant summer annuals such as ageratum, amaranth, celosia, cleome, marigold, nasturtium, nicotiana, petunia, phlox, salvia, salpiglossis, scabiosa, strawflower, sunflower, and zinnia. For shady areas try begonia, browallia, caladium, coleus, impatiens, and lobelia.

☐ **SUMMER VEGETABLES.** In inland and coastal gardens (zones 18–24), set out plants of basil, cucumber, eggplant, melon, pepper, squash, and tomato. Sow seeds of snap and lima beans, corn, cucumber, dill, melon, and okra. For a Halloween harvest, plant pumpkins by midmonth. In the low desert (zone 13), plant Jerusalem artichoke, okra, and peppers.

☐ **LATE-BLOOMING PERENNIALS.** Selection at nurseries is at its peak. To extend your bloom period, look for varieties that will continue blooming through the summer into fall. These include aster, chrysanthemum, gaillardia, gayfeather, helianthus, lion's tail, penstemon, pentas, reblooming daylily, salvia, and yarrow.

☐ **SUBTROPICALS.** Late spring is the best time to plant subtropicals. They'll have all summer to grow before they slow down and harden off for winter. If appropriate for your zone, plant bougainvillea, gardenia, ginger, hibiscus, and palm. This is also a good time to add subtropical ornamental trees—such as the Hong Kong orchid tree—as well as avocado, banana, citrus, and other subtropical fruit trees.

Sunset
CLIMATE ZONES

1-3 7-9 11 13 14-24

Maintenance

☐ **FEED AZALEAS AND CAMELLIAS.** Fertilize azaleas and camellias after they finish blooming to support strong growth and a heavy set of flower buds for next year. Use an acid-type fertilizer formulated for these plants, at half-strength. Feed camellias two or three times more at six- to eight-week intervals during this growth period. Feed azaleas one more time in late September.

☐ **STEP UP WATERING.** As temperatures warm, plants will need to be watered more often. Monitor new plantings closely to be sure soil around them doesn't dry out. Also check container plants frequently. To rejuvenate a dry rootball, set entire pot in a bucket or tub of water. When the soil is thoroughly wet, lift out pot and drain.

☐ **THIN FRUIT.** On apple, nectarine, peach, and other deciduous fruit trees, each fruiting spur should be reduced to a single fruit on heavy-bearing trees, and a pair of fruit on lighter-bearing trees. Remaining fruit should be no closer than 6 inches apart.

☐ **TEND TOMATOES AND PEPPERS.** To prevent blossom-end rot, mulch to maintain uniform soil moisture, water deeply, and don't overfertilize with nitrogen. In the low desert, cover plants with shadecloth or screen to prevent sunburn.

☐ **PINCH BACK MUMS.** For an ample supply of flowers and an attractive bushy plant, pinch back the growing tips of chrysanthemum plants.

Pest control

☐ **MANAGE PESTS.** Spray or dust *Bacillus thuringiensis* (BT) on tomato, petunia, nicotiana, and geranium leaves at first sign of caterpillar damage. Watch for grape leaf skeletonizer in desert areas (zones 11 and 13). Remove leaves that have worms. Spray underside of leaves with BT if damage is severe. To keep aphids, spider mites, and whiteflies in check, spray affected foliage with a strong stream of water. Follow up with insecticidal soap or horticultural oil if necessary.

Planting

☐ **FLOWERS.** Nurseries are filled with annuals and perennials this month. Shop early to get the best selection.

☐ **LAWNS.** Sow bluegrass, fescue, ryegrass, or, better yet, a combination of the three. New plantings should go into tilled, raked, fertilized, and relatively rock-free soil. To overseed worn or bare spots in an old lawn, rough up the soil surface with a steel bow rake, scatter seed, cover with compost or peat, and don't let the soil surface become completely dry until the grass is tall enough to mow.

☐ **PERMANENT PLANTS.** You can plant trees, shrubs, vines, and ground covers from containers this month. They'll have the summer to get roots established before they have to face fall freezes and winter snow.

☐ **VEGETABLES.** Plant cool-season crops from nursery seedlings, or sow warm-season crops (corn, cucumbers, eggplant, melons, peppers, squash, tomatoes) right away for transplanting into the garden after danger of frost is past. If frost is past where you live, you can sow these—and beans—right away.

Maintenance

☐ **CARE FOR TOMATOES.** Indeterminate varieties (vinelike types, which keep growing all season) need to be staked or caged early or they'll flop over. Keep soil moisture even (mulch and drip irrigation help) to minimize blossom end rot.

Sunset
CLIMATE ZONES

☐ 1-3   ☐ 10-11

☐ **FERTILIZE.** Dig in 1 to 2 pounds of complete fertilizer per 100 square feet before planting vegetables or flowers. Feed flowering shrubs after they bloom, and start a monthly fertilizing program for long-blooming perennials, annuals, and especially container plants.

☐ **HARDEN OFF TRANSPLANTS.** Take seedlings to a lath house, patio, or partly shaded cold frame, exposing them gradually to more sun and nighttime cold. After 7 to 10 days, they'll be tough enough to be transplanted into the garden—as long as the danger of frost has past.

☐ **MAKE COMPOST.** Alternate 4-inch-thick layers of grass clippings and fresh weeds with layers of dead leaves and straw, watering the pile between layers. Turn the pile weekly and you'll have compost within two months.

☐ **MULCH PLANTS.** Use ground bark, compost, grass clippings, rotted leaves, or even sawdust to keep down weeds and hold in moisture.

☐ **PINCH BACK FLOWERING PLANTS.** Encourage branching and compact growth by pinching or tip-pruning plants such as azaleas, fuchsias, and geraniums.

☐ **PROTECT COOL-SEASON CROPS.** Suspend laths or row covers above vegetables such as broccoli, cauliflower, lettuce, and spinach to keep them from bolting (going to seed) and becoming bitter when the weather warms up.

☐ **PRUNE FLOWERING SHRUBS.** After spring bloom ends, prune lilac, mock orange, and spiraea.

Pest and weed control

☐ **PROTECT CROPS FROM BIRDS.** Bird netting can protect all kinds of small fruits from hungry birds. Fasten edges shut (clothespins are good for this) so birds can't get in.

☐ **WEED.** Hoe weed seedlings on a warm morning, and the afternoon sun will finish them off. Pull larger weeds out by the roots a few hours after you've watered deeply.

Planting

☐ **VEGETABLES.** Zones 12–13: Plant eggplant, okra, peanuts, peppers, summer squash, and sweet potatoes. Zones 10–11: Plant all the crops above, plus beans, corn, cucumbers, melons, pumpkins, radishes, Southern peas, and tomatoes. Put most in early in the month; okra, Southern peas, and sweet potatoes can be planted through midmonth. Zones 1–2: Plant cool-season crops outdoors; start seeds of warm-season crops (corn, peppers, squash, tomatoes) indoors right away for transplanting into the garden after danger of frost has past.

☐ **BLOOMS IN THE SUN.** Zones 10–13: As early in the month as possible, set out ageratum, celosia, coreopsis, cosmos, firebush (*Hamelia patens*), four o'clock, gaillardia, globe amaranth, gloriosa daisy, kochia, lantana, lisianthus, nicotiana, portulaca, salvia, strawflower, tithonia, vinca rosea (Madagascar periwinkle), and zinnia. Zones 1–2 (Flagstaff, Santa Fe): Set out all of the above after danger of frost is past.

☐ **COLOR IN THE SHADE.** Good choices include begonia, caladium, coleus, gerbera, impatiens, lobelia, oxalis, pentas, and spider plant.

☐ **LAWNS.** Zones 12–13: Plant Bermuda or improved buffalo grass when nighttime temperatures rise above 70°. Zones 1–2, 10–11: Plant or overseed with bluegrass, fescue, ryegrass, or a combination of these early in the month.

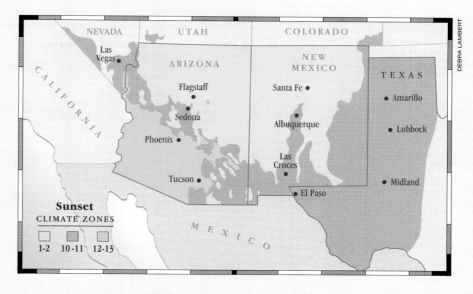

Sunset
CLIMATE ZONES
☐ 1-2   ◼ 10-11   ◻ 12-13

☐ **PERMANENT PLANTS.** Zones 1–2, 10–11: Plant trees, shrubs, vines, and ground covers this month.

☐ **SUMMER BULBS.** In most Southwest zones: Plant acidanthera (*Gladiolus callianthus*), canna, dahlia, daylily, gladiolus, Mexican shell flower (*Tigridia*), montbretia, and zephyranthes (except in zones 10–11). Zones 12–13: Also plant agapanthus, caladium, and crinum.

Maintenance

☐ **CARE FOR CITRUS.** Zones 12–13: Fertilize trees whose leaves aren't dark green. First water the tree well, then spread 1 cup ammonium sulfate per inch of trunk diameter. Water it in well. If the tree still doesn't green up, apply chelated iron, zinc, and manganese to take care of chlorosis. Also give mature

trees a two- to three-hour sprinkler soaking every two to three weeks. Soak young trees one to two hours every 5 to 10 days.

☐ **FERTILIZE.** Feed flowering shrubs after they bloom, and start monthly feedings of long-blooming perennials, annuals, and container plants.

☐ **INCREASE WATERING.** When daytime temperatures start hitting 100°, check plants—especially any new growth—twice a day for wilting. Most plants need extra water, even cactus and succulents.

GLENN CORMIER (6)

THE NEW
Organic

Expert gardeners share tips for growing gorgeous crops without chemicals

A mere 20 years ago, when the 1950s chemical mentality still dominated the agricultural scene, organically grown vegetables were found only in a few backyards and natural-food stores, and organic gardeners were thought of as antiestablishment types who flavored their macrobiotic meals with bean sprouts.

But in recent years scare after scare over pesticide-contaminated foods has prompted many farmers and home gardeners to begin using alternative controls for pesticide-resistant insects and diseases. As we've discovered in *Sunset's* editorial test garden, a healthy, chemical-free garden—filled with colorful and diverse plants—is always rich in wildlife.

FAR LEFT: NORMAN A. PLATE. LEFT: WENDY FOSTER

Garden

On the following pages, organic-gardening pros Joe Queirolo, Loren Nancarrow, and the Foster family reveal the secrets of their gardens' success. Although they live in different climates and garden for different reasons, all of them agree on this basic principle: Take care of the earth and it will reward you well.

Clockwise from top left: Onions grow in rich, mulched soil. Hand tools are fine for cultivating small areas. Disease-resistant varieties like 'Prima' apples don't need chemicals to stay healthy. Loren Nancarrow spreads mulch around squash. Post holes are homes to solitary bees. A replica of an antique wheelbarrow displays flowers. Green lacewing will produce larvae that prey on pests. Topping the seedbed with compost keeps the soil from crusting. Fennel flowers attract bees and other beneficial insects. These organically grown vegetables are picture-perfect.

MICHAEL S. THOMPSON

NORMAN A. PLATE

Good garden, good food at Crow Canyon Garden

Joe Queirolo's life changed 20 years ago when he read a book called *How to Grow More Vegetables,* by organic-gardening guru John Jeavons (Ten Speed Press, Berkeley, 1995; $16.95). The book advocated chemical-free gardening and other methods that, when combined, build soil fertility and produce higher yields—using a fraction of the resources consumed by crops produced by conventional methods. "It made so much sense to work with the natural world rather than trying to dominate it," Queirolo explains. "And

I just didn't trust chemicals."

Jeavons's book prompted Queirolo to study horticulture at the local college. One day his class visited the garden next to Mudd's Restaurant in San Ramon, California (then owned and run by the restaurant, now owned by the city and managed by the nonprofit Crow Canyon Institute). And there, Queirolo saw 2 beautiful acres carpeted with lush vegetables and herbs and edged with fruit trees. "Their basil was huge—mine was puny. They were growing all of the herbs, vegetables, and

fruits that I like to grow, and the garden was so alive and vibrant," he says.

Queirolo took a job as a gardener at Mudd's, and has been there ever since. "When I started, everything was done by hand, including weeding," says Queirolo. "You become synchronized with the garden when you pay such close attention to it—you can almost feel when something has to be done." Since then, the staff has moved up the "ladder of technology" (they use hoes). But, says Queirolo, "we're always in the garden and always watching."

by **LAUREN BONAR SWEZEY**

Queirolo's gardening tips

Start with healthy soil. It'll provide naturally stronger plants, and strong plants are more resistant to diseases and insects. Each spring, gardeners at Crow Canyon Garden work 1 to 2 inches of composted horse manure into each bed. During the growing season, if the soil in a heavily used bed is hard—not crumbly and friable—they add additional horse manure or homemade compost (from their three-bin system).

Horse manure from nearby stables is composted in two weeks in summer by being kept moist with a sprinkler and turned three times a week. The gardeners turn it when the thermometer indicates that the temperature has started dropping from its highest point.

Rotate your crops every year. They should never grow in the same

bed two years in a row. Potatoes shouldn't grow in the same bed for at least four years.

Choose friendly fertilizers. Fishmeal, organic cottonseed meal, and alfalfa meal (when he can find it) are Queirolo's favorites; he alternates these. For trace minerals, he mixes azomite (also called rock dust) into the soil (from Peaceful Valley Farm Supply; 916/272-4769).

Use cover crops. Legumes add nitrogen back to the soil. If you can leave a planting bed open for five to six weeks in summer, plant cowpeas. In fall, plant fenugreek, which is easy to work into the soil. Fava beans are difficult to chop into the soil without a rotary tiller; cut them down and compost them instead.

GLENN CORMIER

An urban cowboy's dream garden

Loren Nancarrow, you could argue, became an organic farmer because he always wanted to be a cowboy. "Growing up in Connecticut, being a cowboy seemed like the most exotic life imaginable," says the San Diego County resident. But when Nancarrow got the opportunity to observe ranching firsthand while attending college in New Mexico during the '70s he was appalled at the amount of chemicals used to sustain that lifestyle. "Basically, they treated everything as a pest. I found it very troubling," he says.

Surely the self-sustaining lifestyle didn't require annihilating so many other living things. But it wasn't until 1991, when Nancarrow took the position of broadcaster of weather, wildlife, and gardening news on KFMB TV Channel 8 and bought a 3-acre property in the still predominantly agrarian community of Olivenhain, California, that he was able to put that theory to the test.

He put in a 1,000-square-foot vegetable garden and a citrus and stone fruit orchard. Turkeys and either a cow or a pig are usually on hand, too. With all the animals on the premises—and access to neighbors' horse stables—Nancarrow has no shortage of manure. He also maintains a huge compost pile. Naturally, his soil is wonderful.

Pest management is Nancarrow's biggest problem. Gophers, snails, tomato hornworms, and aphids all like his crops, too. "Being an organic gardener is a lot like being a hunter," says Nancarrow. "You learn your prey's life cycles, habits, and needs. Then you use that knowledge to do them in."

by **SHARON COHOON**

Nancarrow's gardening tips

Replenish beds before putting in new crops. Nancarrow adds at least 4 inches of compost supplemented with fishmeal, bonemeal, kelp meal, cottonseed meal, and soft rock phosphate.

Attract pollinators. Cosmos is an excellent magnet for bumblebees and other solitary bees. Take a piece of cut wood, drill a few holes in it, and hang it in a tree and the bees may nest on your property.

Use wheat bran to kill snails. The roughage, Nancarrow speculates, destroys their digestive systems. Buy a 50-pound bag for about $5 from a feed store and sprinkle it around crops that snails like.

Use blood meal to scare off rabbits. It smells like death and makes rabbits think predators are around. Sprinkle the fertilizer around

susceptible crops and water it in well so the plants don't burn.

Toss banana peels under the base of a plant to kill aphids. Nancarrow doesn't know why it works, only that it does. He's had good luck with this method with roses, butterfly weed, and artichokes.

Catch gophers first thing in the morning. They dig all night long and cover up their airholes first thing in the morning, before sleeping the rest of the day. Flush them out with a hose, grab them with long-handled barbecue tongs, drop them in a bucket, and dispatch them.

Provide water for birds. Birds drill holes in ripening tomatoes because they're thirsty, says Nancarrow. Keep a birdbath full of fresh water and they'll leave them alone.

MICHAEL S. THOMPSON

Fresh produce for a family of four

Rick and Wendy Foster are committed to a simple and healthful lifestyle. Organic gardening doesn't drive that—it fits into it.

The Fosters grow most of what they and their two daughters eat, including tree fruits, vegetables, berries, and grapes, on their hillside in timber country above the south fork of the Umpqua River in Days Creek, Oregon. Their fenced, 1-acre garden grows in tilled rows. About three-quarters of the space is planted with fruits (apples, pears, plums, all kinds of berries, grapes, and kiwis), and a quarter is in vegetables. Their crops are healthy and abundant.

The results of their efforts over the past 13 years show in every part of their lives. In the Fosters' annual budget, food accounts for only about $1,000, mostly for grains, nuts, oils, and other ingredients that won't grow efficiently (or at all) in southern Oregon. They grow what pays. Plants that give a high return for little work get priority: lettuce, for example, and zucchini, cantaloupes, plums, berries, and grapes.

Gardening also fits into their home-school curriculum. "Our girls really know where food comes from," says Rick. "Growing, tending, and harvesting get them back to the basics of life— and that whole concept is very important to why we garden."

The Fosters raise all their food from April to October. On concert tour from January through March most years (Rick is a classical guitarist), they're back by spring planting time.

by **JIM McCAUSLAND**

The Fosters' gardening tips

Compost all garden waste. Sift it through a ½-inch screen when it's finished, stretch it with rotted horse manure, then dig it back into the garden before planting.

Mulch. To keep weeds out from under the fruit trees and to keep ripe apples and plums from bruising when they fall, the Fosters cover the ground in the orchard with straw mulch from a pasture.

Start a manure pile. The Fosters bring in several truckloads of horse manure every fall and let it rot. Then they use it to amend soil and side-dress plants as needed.

Start seedlings with care. The Fosters start theirs in a 3- by 6-foot outdoor seedbed. It's amended with 3 inches of well-aged manure, then topped with a mixture of one part sand and three parts sifted compost. This top-dressing sharply increases germination and won't crust over after it's watered, so seedlings can push through easily.

Space plants properly. Transplants from the seedbed are easy to space properly, but seedlings that have been sown directly into garden rows are often moved to fill gaps or picked and eaten when they're too close together. The Fosters successfully transplant some crops that aren't typically moved, like beets and kohlrabi. The trick to success: plant the seedlings' roots straight, not coiled or bent.

Plant cover crops. In early November plant crimson clover, annual rye, buckwheat, Austrian field peas, and hairy vetch. A couple of weeks before spring planting, till these crops into garden beds.

Use disease-resistant varieties. The Fosters plant disease-resistant fruit trees, for example, so they won't have to spray them. For scab-resistant apples, they grow 'Freedom', 'Liberty', 'Prima', and 'Redfree'.

Pest control:

More tips from the pros

Pests, diseases, and weeds are easier to control when they're caught early. Grow plants that beneficial insects—which feed on the pests—like. When allowed to flower, bronze fennel, carrots, celery, and parsley attract lacewings and syrphid flies. Pink clover and yarrow attract other beneficial insects.

If asparagus or cucumber beetles get out of hand on squash, melon, or bean plants, or if flea beetles invade cabbage, broccoli, and tomato seedlings, dust plants with rotenone.

Aphids: Wait two weeks after you first notice them to see whether lacewings, ladybird beetles, or syrphid flies arrive to control them. They usually do. Otherwise, hose them off with water.

Asparagus beetles: Spray these beetles off plants with water, or shake them off, then squish them.

Birds: Cover rows of seedlings or tender plants such as baby lettuce with bird netting over hoops. String reflective tape across vulnerable parts of the garden (while beets are small or tree

Reflective tape (left) shimmers in the breeze, keeping marauding quails from eating broccoli transplants. Bird netting (right) covers hoops to protect tender lettuce.

fruit is ripe, for example). As breezes twist the shiny tape, it flashes in the sunlight, keeping birds away long enough to save the crop. To keep crows from eating corn seed, plant kernels extra-deep.

Codling moths: To keep these insects from traveling among fruits, thin small (1-inch-wide) apples to 4 to 6 inches apart before they grow large and begin to touch. Or use pheromone traps to catch moths and help prevent egg-laying on or near apples.

Cucumber beetles: Catch and dispose of them. Queirolo uses calendula flowers as a trap crop. When the gardeners harvest petals for salads, they collect 50 to 60 beetles a day and "squish as we go."

Damping-off fungus: This soilborne fungus is a problem on greenhouse-grown plants. Use a well-drained planting medium, avoid overwatering, and thin seedlings early.

Deer: If all else fails, build an 8-foot-tall fence to keep them out.

Root aphids on lettuce: These insects are a sign that the lettuce is stressed—it's either not being watered enough or is growing out of season when the weather is too hot.

Snails: Queirolo used to collect and squish them. Now he feeds them grain so they can be served at the restaurant.

Squash bugs: Set boards near plants so the bugs will congregate underneath them at night, then collect and destroy the bugs in the morning.

Weeds: Hoe between plants. Hand-weed everything that's too close to vegetables to hoe. Till lightly between the rows. ◆

What does "organic" mean?

To commercial farmers, "organic" is a set of federal guidelines—spelled out in the Organic Foods Production Act passed by Congress in 1990—that sets standards for organic food production. Many state agriculture departments also have their own specific guidelines. The California Department of Food and Agriculture, for example, states that "Organic agriculture ... promotes and enhances biodiversity, biological cycles, and soil biological activity. It is based on ... management practices that restore, maintain, and enhance ecological harmony...." The guidelines prohibit the use of such materials as certain chemical fertilizers, insecticides, and herbicides, excluding low-toxicity oil sprays, insecticidal soaps, biological insecticides such as *Bacillus thuringiensis* (BT), and natural, plant-based insecticides such as pyrethrum and rotenone.

To home gardeners, organic means pretty much the same thing—"chemical-free" gardening—although the guidelines are interpreted more loosely according to their needs.

All-seasoning gardens

Starting an herb garden? Try growing—and cooking with—
the flavors favored by Western gardeners and chefs

estern cooks in ever-increasing numbers are pushing aside the dried,
crushed herbs that sit in dusty little jars
on shelves in favor of fresh, more flavorful herbs from their own gardens.
And they're growing herbs everywhere:
in front yards of country inns, in raised-
bed kitchen gardens, and even in containers. Why? "Herbs have a season, just
like vegetables," says Jerry Traunfeld,
chef at the Herbfarm in Fall City, Washington. "It's best to use them fresh, instead of drying or freezing them." Once
you've tasted fresh herbs, nothing else
measures up. And growing your own
can become a passion.

For the beginning gardener-cook,
though, growing and using fresh herbs
can seem intimidating. Which ones
are the easiest to grow and essential
for kitchen use? And when do you harvest them?

On the following pages, discover
which herbs are indispensable for professional herb gardeners around the
West, and learn how to grow and use
them—with special suggestions from
cooking professionals. Once you master the essentials, you can try growing
culinary herbs that aren't as commonly

*Purple perilla is surrounded by
creeping silver variegated oregano.
At right, Sycamore Herb Farm's
demonstration garden contains
culinary herbs, such as rosemary
(in lower border).*

used. At special herb farms, listed on
page 165, you can see herbs growing in
attractive garden settings and buy
plants to take home.

by JIM McCAUSLAND & LAUREN BONAR SWEZEY

The essentials:

14 culinary herbs for every garden

A good cook simply can't live without certain herbs. Here are the ones that specialists from across the West consider essential garden and cooking ingredients. "We call the basic herbs 'kitchen herbs,'" says V. J. Billings of Mountain Valley Growers in Squaw Valley, California. "These are the ones recipes call for."

French tarragon

Basil (*Ocimum basilicum*). This fragrant warm-season herb bears tender green leaves on 2-foot-tall stems. Start with seeds or seedlings. Basil needs full sun and warm nights to grow well.

Pinch plants for bushiness and keep flowers constantly picked off. To harvest for pesto, cut plants back halfway and allow to regrow. Or plant basil seedlings in succession every month or so and harvest entire plants for pesto. Grow four to six plants (if you plan to make pesto). ANNUAL. ALL ZONES.

'Berggarten' sage (*Salvia officinalis* 'Berggarten'). This pungent, musky herb is the first choice of herb professionals for culinary sage. It grows about 2 feet tall, has round, grayish leaves, and doesn't usually blossom like other sages. Grow one or two plants. PERENNIAL. ALL ZONES.

Chives (*Allium schoenoprasum*). Plants form 12- to 24-inch-long grasslike spears in clumps. Rose-purple flowers appear on top of thin stems in spring. Harvest chives by snipping the spears to the ground. Otherwise you'll have unsightly brown foliage mixed in with the green. Increase the number of plants by dividing every two years. Grow three or four plants. PERENNIAL. ALL ZONES.

Cilantro (*Coriandrum sativum*). Fragrant, bright green leaves grow on

'Berggarten' sage

foot-tall stems. Cilantro refers to the leaves; the seeds are called coriander. When cilantro goes to seed, the flavor of the leaves changes—it becomes more like coriander. Start cilantro from a bolt-resistant variety of seed. It does best in cool weather. Grow two or three plants. ANNUAL. ALL ZONES.

Common thyme (*Thymus vulgaris*; sometimes also called English thyme). Tiny, sweetly pungent leaves grow on upright stems about 12 inches tall. Plants tend to flop over onto the ground. Harvest before blossoms appear. To harvest, hold the foliage like a

Chives

ponytail and shear it to about 6 inches tall. Grow three or four plants. PERENNIAL. ALL ZONES.

Fennel (*Foeniculum vulgare*). Finely cut green leaves taste like anise. Flower stalks grow to 4 feet tall but foliage is low. Seeds are also used as a flavoring. To save the seeds, Billings suggests covering the seed heads with brown bags just as the seeds start turning brown. Allow seeds to finish ripening, then shake loose. Grow two plants. PERENNIAL. ALL ZONES.

French tarragon (*Artemisia dracunculus sativa*). Shiny, narrow dark

NORMAN A. PLATE

CULINARY *uses*

BASIL: Marinades, meats, pastas, salads, soups, and stews. "This is the best herb to add to tomato, mushroom, and Italian dishes," says executive chef James Boyce of Loews Coronado Bay Resort in Coronado, California.

CHIVES: Butters, eggs, mayonnaise, potatoes, sauces, seafood, soups, sour cream, stews, and vegetables.

CILANTRO: Beans, curries, fish, fowl, lamb, Mexican dishes, salads, sauces, and stir-frys. "I mix it into bean soup, serve it with lime juice as a green salsa, and put it in yogurt,"

says *Sunset's* senior food editor Jerry Anne Di Vecchio.

FENNEL: Use foliage to flavor fish and vegetables, and as a garnish. Use seeds in baked goods, fish, meats, poultry, sauces, sausages, and soups.

MARJORAM: Cheeses, eggs, fish, meats, pastas, poultry, rice, sauces, soups, stews, and vegetables.

MINT: Baked goods, beverages, desserts, fish, fruits, ice cream, jellies, sauces, soups, tea, and vegetables. Mint has a cooling effect on powerful aromatics, such as basil and cilantro, and on chilies and salsas.

OREGANO: Beans, cheeses, meats, pastas, salsas, and

ALLAN MANDEL

Two-tiered herb bed contains basil and chives (top), and rosemary, fennel, common thyme, and sage.

green leaves have a spicy anise flavor. Woody stems on the 1- to 2-foot-tall plant should be cut to the ground in June and August to encourage new growth. Divide plants every four years. Grow four plants. PERENNIAL. ALL ZONES.

Mint (*Mentha*). Spearmint (*M. spicata*), with bright green shiny leaves, is the preferred mint for cooking. It grows 1½ to 2 feet tall. Peppermint (*M. piperita*), with narrow, dark green leaves, is best for tea. Plant grows to 3 feet tall. Cut back plants to about 2 inches tall twice a year—in late spring and fall—before flowers form. Plant one or two kinds in (separate) containers to control vigorous underground stems. PERENNIAL. ALL ZONES.

Oregano. All herb professionals agree that Greek oregano (*Origanum vulgare hirtum*) is one of the best oreganos for cooking. The shrubby plant with slightly fuzzy, pungent leaves grows 3 feet tall. For something milder, Virginia Saso of Saso Herb Gardens in Saratoga, California, suggests Italian oregano (*O. majoricum*), which has bright green foliage and grows 2½ feet tall. The "oil is strongest when the plant is in bud but before flowers open," says Saso. Cut plant back to 4 inches tall in late spring, summer, and fall. Grow two plants of Greek or one of each. PERENNIAL. ALL ZONES.

Parsley (*Petroselenium*). Chefs prefer Italian flat-leafed parsley (*P. crispum neapolitanum*), but curly-leafed types (*P. crispum*) are good for garnishes. Plants grow 6 to 12 inches tall. Set out parsley any time of year (except winter in cold climates). In hot climates, plants may bolt when set out in summer, so plant in partial shade. Grow three plants of each. BIENNIAL. ALL ZONES.

Rosemary (*Rosmarinus officinalis*). Short, narrow green leaves with gray undersides grow on woody stems. Varieties have a similar intense, peppery flavor but different habits (upright or trailing) and flower colors (blue, pink,

---

vegetables; use sparingly in sauces, soups, and stews.

PARSLEY: Bouquets garnis, casseroles, fish, meats, omelets, poultry, sauces, soups, stews, vegetables, and as a garnish. "Add parsley to fresh vegetables at the end of cooking [to avoid overcooking it]," says Boyce.

ROSEMARY: Breads, cheeses, dressings, eggs, fish, game, legumes, marinades, oils, potatoes, poultry, roast game, soups, stews, stuffings, and vegetables.

SAGE: Apples, beans, breads, cheeses, game stuffings, marinades, pork, poultry, soups, and stews. "Since sage helps digest fatty foods," says Boyce, "it works well with duck."

SWEET BAY: Bouquets garnis, breads, fish, fowl, marinades, meats, puddings, and stuffings. "Fresh bay leaves have a nutmeg and vanilla quality," says Traunfeld.

TARRAGON: Chicken, dressings, eggs, fish, meats, pickles, sauces, vegetables, and vinegars.

THYME: Bouquets garnis, breads, casseroles, cheeses, eggs, fish, grains, marinades, meats, mushrooms, poultry, soups, stews, tomato-based sauces, and vegetables.

WINTER SAVORY: Beans, marinades, meats, poultry, and vegetables. "Strong-flavored winter savory is considered a bean herb—that's its best use," says Traunfeld.

May 163

Nine kinds of traditional and flavored basil grow in this bed at the Elizabeth F. Gamble Garden Center in Palo Alto.

NORMAN A. PLATE

or white). 'Arp' is hardy to -15°, but it's not as bushy as other types of rosemary. Plants take sun or partial shade. Prune to shape. Grow one or two plants. PERENNIAL. ZONES 4–24.

Sweet bay (*Laurus nobilis*). This is the bay (also referred to as Grecian laurel) used for cooking. The evergreen shrub or tree grows 12 to 40 feet tall and is best when used as a background shrub. Leathery, 2- to 4-inch-long dark green leaves are very aromatic. Because it's slow-growing, it does well in containers. ZONES 5–9, 12–24.

Sweet marjoram (*Origanum majorana*). Tiny gray-green leaves have a sweet, floral scent and a milder flavor than Greek oregano. Grows 1 to 2 feet tall. Follow harvest suggestions for oregano. Grow three plants. PERENNIAL IN ZONES 4–24; ANNUAL ELSEWHERE.

Winter savory (*Satureja montana*). Low-growing, 12- to 15-inch-tall mounding plant with pungent, peppery-tasting ½- to 1-inch-long dark green leaves that are more intensely flavored than those of summer savory. A good substitute for salt. Harvest leaves as needed before flowers appear, or shear back twice a year. Grow two or three plants. PERENNIAL. ALL ZONES.

HOW *to*

Grow and maintain herbs

Herbs are easy to grow if the soil drains well (if not, amend it with plenty of organic matter, or plant in raised beds). Choose a site that gets six to eight hours of full sun.

Water perennial herbs to get them established, then taper off to occasional supplemental irrigations. Annual herbs such as basil and chives prefer evenly moist soil.

To keep foliage fresh and at peak quality for cooking, herbs must be cut back regularly. Follow the pruning guidelines under individual herb descriptions.

In early spring, feed herbs with a nitrogen fertilizer or spread compost around the base of plants. After chopping back basil and chives, feed the plants with fish emulsion.

Beyond the basics:

11 "gourmet herbs" that are easy to grow

Once you've grown and experimented with basic kitchen herbs and are familiar with their flavors, try growing herbs with more complex flavors. "Gourmet herbs are not more difficult to grow," says Billings. "They challenge the palate instead of your gardening skills."

Bronze fennel (*Foeniculum vulgare purpureum*). Like green fennel, it has an aniselike taste, but foliage is bronze. PERENNIAL. ALL ZONES.

Caraway-scented thyme (*Thymus herba-barona*). Caraway-flavored leaves. Creeping plant to 4 inches tall. PERENNIAL. ALL ZONES.

Culantro (*Eryngium foetidum*). Flowers and leaves have the intense flavor of cilantro. Produces all season, even in hot climates. Grows 8 to 12 inches tall. TENDER PERENNIAL. ALL ZONES.

Garlic chives (*Allium tuberosum*). Similar to chives, but leaves are slightly larger, and they have a mild garlic flavor. PERENNIAL. ALL ZONES.

Lemon grass (*Cymbopogon citratus*). The blanched white ribs (used in Thai cooking) are spicy and lemony. Use the sweet, lemony leaves at the base of "pups" (young plants) for tea. PERENNIAL IN ZONES 16–17, 23–24; ELSEWHERE, OVERWINTER A DIVISION IN A POT INDOORS.

Lemon thyme (*Thymus citriodorus*). Dark green foliage has lemon flavor. Grows 1 foot tall. PERENNIAL. ALL ZONES.

Lemon verbena (*Aloysia triphylla*). Long (3 inches), narrow leaves have intense lemon scent. Use for lemon flavoring or tea. Gangly shrub 3 to 6 feet tall. PERENNIAL. ZONES 9–10, 12–24.

Mexican tarragon (*Tagetes lucida*). The narrow, dark green leaves of this 3- to 4-foot-tall marigold species have a sweet licorice flavor similar to tarragon. PERENNIAL IN ZONES 8–9, 12–24; ANNUAL ELSEWHERE.

Pine-scented rosemary (*Rosmarinus angustifolia*). Similar to rosemary, but leaves have a pine fragrance. PERENNIAL. ALL ZONES.

Sorrel (*Rumex acetosa*). Tangy, lemony, bright green leaves perk up soups and salads. Harvest during cool weather. PERENNIAL. ALL ZONES.

Vietnamese cilantro (*Polygonum odoratum*). A perennial that has the flavor of cilantro, but doesn't go to seed. TENDER PERENNIAL. ALL ZONES.

ALLAN MANDELL

Various thymes soften edges of raised beds in the culinary section of the Thyme Garden in Alsea, Oregon. Most are at peak bloom in June.

Herbal outings:

Five great farms to visit, south to north

Herb nurseries, restaurants, and farms are abundant in the West. Most let you sniff, taste, and buy herbs—usually by the sprig, often in teas, and sometimes in food, when the farm has an on-site restaurant. Many also offer classes on gardening and cooking with herbs.

Loews Coronado Bay Resort, Coronado, California. This is a chef's garden, no mistake: you can taste the results in any of the resort's three restaurants.

Pick up a brochure for a self-guided walking tour from the concierge and spend some time in the garden—built in a square pattern between buildings—before lunch or dinner.

Loews is on the strand, just south of the Naval Air Station, at 4000 Coronado Bay Road. For restaurant reservations, call (619) 424-4444.

Sycamore Herb Farm, Paso Robles, California. With all the laid-back charm of an old California ranch, Sycamore Herb Farm & Vineyard is well ordered and beautiful, with stone-lined dirt paths winding among raised herb beds. You can buy plants or shop for herbal gifts. Classes show how to grow and cook with herbs.

From U.S. Highway 101, take State 46 west 3 miles. Open 10:30 to 5:30 daily; (800) 576-5288.

Meadowview Farm, Grants Pass, Oregon. Just a 10-minute drive off Interstate 5, this is a great place to break for lunch or high tea, and to see and buy herbs at their spring prime. The formal herb garden, along with vegetables and fruits, lies behind a rambling rose arbor. The restaurant and gift shop are in a historic converted barn.

Open from 11 to 4 Tuesdays through Saturdays. Call for directions; (541) 476-6882.

Thyme Garden, Alsea, Oregon. Tucked back into Oregon's coastal mountains, the Thyme Garden is the Northwest's newest herb garden. Herbs of every color, texture, and fragrance thrive in dozens of raised beds. Here you can buy seeds, plants, and herbal products.

The Thyme Garden, at 20546 Highway 34 just 4½ miles east of Alsea, is open 10 to 5 daily through June (10 to 5 Fridays through Mondays July to mid-August); (541) 487-8671.

Herbfarm, Fall City, Washington. The crème de la crème of herb farms, this one takes the culinary side of its business as seriously as the nursery side. Indeed, its restaurant was booked six months in advance when it burned not long after Christmas. But the nursery is intact, and both restaurant and cooking classes will likely be back, perhaps by this fall.

The Herbfarm's nursery benches are set out under old fruit trees. A gift store, greenhouses, aviaries, and animals complete the picture. The Herbfarm is at 32804 S.E. Issaquah–Fall City Rd. Open 9 to 5 weekdays, 9 to 6 weekends. Call for directions; (206) 784-2222. ◆

The ultimate cutting garden

Choice perennials yield a succession of blooms all season long

Trained in biointensive gardening at the University of California at Santa Cruz in the 1970s, Paul Sansone and Sue Vosburg wondered whether the organic principles they'd learned could be harnessed to grow flowers commercially. The cutflower business is unforgiving—each blossom must be absolutely unblemished to sell—and it demands a steady stream of blooms over a long season.

Sansone and Vosburg decided to try it, and they succeeded mightily in their Here and Now Garden in northwest Oregon. They grow mostly old-fashioned perennials, from peonies to asters, harvesting cut flowers from April through October. Planting the right varieties is important—the tried-and-true plants that do best for Sansone and Vosburg are charted at right (bloom times may vary in your garden climate). Growing methods they use guarantee big harvests of robust cut flowers.

PERFECT BLOOMS, ORGANICALLY

Sansone and Vosburg have studied several methods of gardening. The Rudolph Steiner system of organic farming (called biodynamics), which they learned at UC Santa Cruz, is a mainstay, but they also draw on lessons learned from Dutch horticulture. Here are the principles that underlie their success.

Soil preparation. Healthy, fertile soil grows strong, disease-resistant plants. Before new ground is ever planted with flowers, it's used to grow cover crops for a year to clear the soil of weeds. "I do two rotations of buckwheat the summer before I plant," Sansone says. "I like buckwheat because it just takes six weeks to go from seed to flower. Tilled in, it equals an inch of manure. Then in winter, I grow rye and vetch to choke out bindweed."

Other cover crops Sansone and Vosburg use are alfalfa, crimson clover, fava beans, and oats. Once those crops have done their work, the soil is enriched with ½ inch of compost and a balanced organic fertilizer before planting.

Planting. Perennials are planted in deeply tilled, 3-foot-wide beds through holes in a woven polypropylene weed barrier. When the plants are two years old and growing densely enough to

Flower farmers Paul Sansone and Sue Vosburg wade through a knee-high sea of coppery rose 'Autumn Joy' sedum.

MICHAEL S. THOMPSON

by **JIM McCAUSLAND**

The harvest of blooms includes red crocosmia and Chinese lantern, pink sedum, white delphinium and phlox, and blue delphinium and gentian.

crowd out most weeds, the barrier is carefully removed and reused.

Watering. All plants are watered by drip irrigation. Since the water doesn't get on leaves and flowers, they're less prone to disease.

Composting. Every fall, the perennials are mowed to the ground. Then ¼ to ½ inch of compost is applied as top dressing, followed by a 1- to 2-inch layer of mulch (Sansone and Vosburg use straw recycled from horse barns).

The mowings are mixed with dairy-cow manure and piled in windrows where they decompose over the course of a year.

Fertilizing. Compost provides plants with most of the nutrients they require, but they receive extra organic fertilizer as needed through the drip-irrigation system. Sansone and Vosburg try not to overfeed plants with nitrogen, since the soft leafy growth that results is especially vulnerable to diseases and predatory insects.

Insect control. Beneficial insects do most of the control work, but when pests like cucumber beetles or flea beetles start to take hold, they're dispatched by spot spraying of botanical insecticides—pyrethrum or rotenone.

Harvesting. As flowers are cut in the field, the stems are plunged into a bucket of water mixed with a commercial floral preservative. Then, still in a bucket, the flowers go into a refrigerator for 8 to 12 hours. After chilling (called "conditioning" in the floral trade), they're ready for display or shipment. ◆

Garden Color CALENDAR

Bloom Colors	Common Name	Botanical Name	Apr.	May	June	July	Aug.	Sept.	Oct.
	Peony—single-flowered	*Paeonia*		▬					
	Firetail	*Polygonum amplexicaule*	▬				▬		
	Fleece flower 'Superbum'	*Polygonum bistorta*		▬				▬	
	Siberian iris	*Iris sibirica*		▬					
	Peach-leaf bellflower	*Campanula persicifolia*			▬				
	Peony—mid- and late-season	*Paeonia*			▬				
	Checkerbloom	*Sidalcea*			▬				
	Yarrow	*Achillea millefolium*			▬	▬			
	Yarrow 'Moonshine'	*Achillea*				▬	▬	▬	
	Lady's-mantle	*Alchemilla mollis*			▬				
	Campanula	*C. glomerata*				▬			
	Monkshood	*Aconitum*				▬			
	Helenium	*H. kanaria*				▬			
	Helenium 'Bronzed Beauty'	*H. magnificum*				▬			
	Balloon flower	*Platycodon*				▬	▬		
	Gooseneck flower	*Lysimachia clethroides*				▬			
	Penstemon 'Husker Red'	*P. digitalis*				▬			
	Veronica 'Sweet Sue'	*V. spicata*				▬	▬	▬	
	Summer phlox	*P. paniculata*				▬	▬	▬	
	Summer phlox—Bartels Stek series	*P. paniculata*				▬	▬	▬	
	Crocosmia 'Lucifer'	*C. masonorum*				▬			
	Butterfly weed	*Asclepias incarnata*				▬			
	Lysimachia	*L. vulgaris*				▬			
	Obedient plant 'Summer Spires'	*Physostegia virginiana*				▬			
	Oregano 'Hopley's Purple'	*Origanum*				▬			
	Turtlehead	*Chelone obliqua*				▬			
	Veronica 'Blaureisen'	*V. longifolia*					▬	▬	
	Veronica 'Lila Karina'	*V. longifolia*					▬	▬	
	Delphinium—Barba series	*D. elatum*					▬	▬	▬
	Delphinium 'Volkenfrieden'	*D. belladonna*					▬	▬	
	Solidaster 'Tara'	*Solidago*					▬	▬	
	Solidaster 'Yellow Submarine'	*Solidago*					▬	▬	
	Gentian	*Gentiana makinoi*					▬	▬	
	Joe Pye weed	*Eupatorium maculatum*					▬	▬	
	Sedum 'Autumn Joy'	*S. spectabile*					▬	▬	
	Sunflower	*Helianthus*						▬	
	Monkshood	*Aconitum arendsii*						▬	
	Aster—Master series	*A. ericoides*						▬	▬
	Aster 'Monte Cassino'	*A. ericoides*						▬	▬

PHOTOGRAPH BY MICHAEL S. THOMPSON   CHART BY DEBRA LAMBERT

The cordless mow-off

We tested rechargeable mowers for cutting quality and ease of use

GARY PARKER

Resembling sleek go-carts, cordless electric mowers get a workout on Sunset's lawn. These 24-volt models are by (from top to bottom) Ryobi, Makita, Toro, and Black & Decker.

Y ank-start an older gasoline-powered lawn mower and you may find yourself grabbing for a gas mask and a pair of earplugs.

Push a button or flick a switch, and then gently pull the tension bar of a new battery-powered mower and you'll hear not a roar but an electric *hum,* and you won't smell anything but fresh-cut grass.

Plug-in electric mowers have been around for decades, and they've earned a reputation as efficient, nonpolluting workhorses. But they were limited by their short tethers. Now even the electric cords have disappeared, thanks to the latest in battery technology. The new cordless mowers draw energy from powerful 24- and 36-volt batteries that

store enough juice to easily cut most Western-size lawns on a single charge. In most cases, these machines also offer wider cutting paths (usually 18 or 19 inches) than older models.

How much lawn can they actually cut on a single charge? That depends on both the mower and the lawn conditions. Some manufacturers' brochures claim a 24-volt machine can cut as much as ½ acre per charge. But in reality, "run time is variable; it all depends on the outside temperature, condition of the grass, and the amount of load," says Frank Coots of Ryobi North America. The wetter and heavier the grass, the shorter the run time. On average, most 24-volt mowers can cut ¼ to ⅓ acre of lawn (or run 1 to 1½ hours); a

36-volt mower can cut up to ½ acre (or run up to 3 hours).

All of the machines *Sunset* tested are mulching mowers, with blades that leave finely shredded grass in place so nutrients can be recycled back into the lawn. No raking or bagging is necessary, although some models offer an optional bag for occasions when the grass gets too long to cut and mulch. The cordless mulching mowers cost about the same as high-quality gas mulching mowers.

Maintenance is a breeze. The batteries recharge in 8 to 16 hours, plugged by extension cord into a 120-volt outlet. The batteries last five to seven years (replacements are available from dealers for $80 to $150). The blades cut best

by LAUREN BONAR SWEZEY

when they are sharpened twice a year.

With batteries, the cordless mowers weigh 5 to 10 pounds more than equivalent gas models, making them hard to push over hilly terrain—a self-propelled electric model may be a better choice in this case.

A MOW-OFF COMPARES BRANDS

Last summer, we held a mow-off at *Sunset's* headquarters in Menlo Park, California, putting five brands of 24-volt electric mulching mowers through their paces on a fescue lawn. Each machine was analyzed for ease of starting and pushing, cutting and mulching quality, and ease of cutting-height adjustment and battery recharging.

There was no runaway winner—each of the machines cut the grass well, and most had one or two features with which they excelled. When it came time for our test-drivers to select a favorite, weight became the decisive factor for a simple reason: the lighter the machine, the easier it was to push.

Run time for the machines is 1½ hours unless noted. For the names of local dealers, call the numbers listed.

Black & Decker's 24-volt mulching/bagging CMM1000 (about $370) was, at 76 pounds, the heaviest to push. A single-lever cutting-height adjustment was a favorite feature. Handle folds for storage. *(800) 544-6986.*

Lawn-Boy's 24-volt mulching/bagging mower (about $350) was the lightest machine—at only 58 pounds—and the easiest to push, making it a favorite. On the downside, it posted one of the shortest run times—about one hour. A 36-volt model (about $390) weighs 68 pounds. Both models have a steel undercarriage (most others are plastic). *(800) 526-6937.*

Makita's mulching/bagging 24-volt UM401DW cordless mower (about $400) had the narrowest cutting width (only 16 inches), which means more mowing is required. But testers appreciated the single-lever cutting-height adjustment that indicates mowing height in inches. Run time was 75 minutes. The mower weighs about 70 pounds. Handle folds for storage. *(800) 462-5482.*

Ryobi's BMM 2400 24-volt Mulchinator ($350) was, at 75 pounds, one of the heaviest to push. But testers liked the single-lever wheel adjustment and the handle that folds down for storage. The BMP 2418 self-propelled Mulchinator ($450) weighs 80 pounds; run time is about one hour. Both are made for mulching only. *(800) 345-8746.*

Toro's mulching/bagging 24-volt mower (about $370) came in a close second for sturdiness of design and best cutting quality. And our long, moist grass didn't bog down the motor, because of Toro's unique body design. The 24-volt model weighs 70 pounds. A 36-volt model (about $470) weighs 85 pounds and runs about three hours. Both models have steel undercarriages. *(800) 348-2424.*

Clean mowers, clean air

Besides their attributes on the lawn, electric mowers leave the air cleaner than their gasoline-powered counterparts, which release hydrocarbon emissions into the atmosphere.

This source of pollution came under regulation in 1995 when state and federal environmental agencies began targeting small "nonroad" engines, of which gas mowers represent the largest portion. In California alone (before 1995), these engines spewed 70 tons of hydrocarbons into the air each day, according to the California Air Resources Board. That's a significant amount when compared with the 990 tons emitted by the millions of cars on the state's highways.

By 1999, manufacturers must reduce the emissions of their nonroad gas engines by 90 percent (of the pre-1995 figures) in order to have their machines approved for sale in California. Electric mowers, which do not burn gas or oil and have no direct emissions (they have only indirect emissions from the generation of electric power), already meet the requirements.

The Electric Power Research Institute of Palo Alto claims that replacing half of the nearly 1.3 million walk-behind gas mowers used in the United States by electric mowers would eliminate the equivalent hydrocarbon emissions of 2 million cars. ◆

Lightweight and easy to push, Lawn-Boy's 24-volt mulching/bagging mower was a favorite with test-drivers.

NORMAN A. PLATE

'Elizabeth', a hybrid variety, wears a crown of curly filaments.

The mystique of passion flowers

When Patrick Worley was 8 years old, his grandmother invited him to view a passion flower she had grown from seed. That moment marked the beginning of his fascination with passion flowers. Worley, who lives in northern Monterey County, has since selected and developed nearly 60 varieties.

The exotic flowers and fruits of passion vines (*Passiflora*) have been prized for centuries. The flower has religious significance for Christians: parts symbolize the crown of thorns worn by Jesus Christ and the nails that secured him to the cross.

The flowers are borne on mostly vigorous vines suitable for covering fences, trellises, and walls. Some plants prefer cool, coastal climates; others thrive in the warmth of Southern California. Most don't like desert conditions, says Worley. The flowering varieties listed on page 85 tolerate temperatures down to 20° to 30°. The vines may freeze to the ground, but the plants spring back from the roots.

Plant in full sun and well-drained soil amended with organic matter. The vines don't need much, if any, fertilizer. Water regularly to get plants established. Mature plants can get by on low to moderate water.

Train the vine onto supports. Trim off wayward branches occasionally. At the end of a plant's second year, prune out excess branches, cutting them back to the base or another branch.

CHOICE PLANTS FOR CALIFORNIA

Worley, who has gardened in both Southern and Northern California, has discovered which passion flowers do best in warmer areas and which ones thrive in cooler climates. Following are some of his favorites (all except 'Coral Seas' are Worley's creations or selections). Flowers range from 3 to 4 inches wide unless noted. These evergreen or semideciduous vines grow 20 to 30 feet long.

'Coral Glow'. Fuchsia-pink flowers are nearly everblooming in coastal areas of Southern California. Glossy, three-lobed leaves are broad. Very vigorous plant. Hardy to 30°. (Similar **'Coral Seas'** thrives in cooler, coastal areas of Northern California and is hardy to about 25°.)

'Elizabeth'. Spectacular lavender flowers (shown on page 83) appear spring through fall. Big, 4-inch-wide leaves are a glossy yellow-green. An extremely vigorous plant, it prefers some warmth, yet it performed well in *Sunset's* test garden in Northern California. Hardy to about 25°.

'Lavender Lady'. Lavender-purple flowers have delicate violet filaments. Dark green leaves are 2 to 3 inches wide. Grows well in the north and south. Hardy to about 20°.

Passiflora sanguinolenta 'Maria Rosa'. Lovely deep rose, bell-shaped flowers measure 1½ to 2 inches across. Medium-green leaves are crescent shaped. Hardy to about 25°.

'Purple Tiger'. Spectacular purple-red flowers, with banded dark purple and blue filaments, appear all summer in Northern California, almost year-round in Southern California. Hardy to 25°. (Similar **'Ruby Glow'** does best in Southern California and is hardy to about 30°.)

'Scarlet Flame'. One of the showiest, it bears red flowers with reflexed petals all summer. Prefers warm climates. Hardy to 25°. (May be sold incorrectly as *Passiflora manicata*, whose flowers do not reflex.)

SOURCES

Nurseries may sell a few of these passion flowers, but all the listed varieties are available by mail from Wild Ridge Nursery (17561 Vierra Canyon Rd., Box 37, Prunedale, CA 93907), which sells about 50 flowering and fruiting kinds; send $1 for a list. ◆

by **LAUREN BONAR SWEZEY**

NORMAN A. PLATE

Pieris japonica 'Mountain Fire' sports vivid red new growth.

You'll love Pieris in the springtime

Lily-of-the-valley shrub is a stellar landscape plant

Like movie stars, certain plants suffer from public overexposure or from being cast in the wrong part too often. Among landscape plants, few stars have shone brighter than *Pieris japonica* (*Andromeda japonica*), lily-of-the-valley shrub. From the 1940s to the '60s, hardly a garden was without this evergreen. And year after year, the plant turned in a respectable performance, demonstrating its stage presence most vividly each spring by showing off flashy new foliage and clusters of lily-of-the-valley-like flowers. Then the spotlight went out.

This plant's fall from horticultural favor can be attributed to both its ubiquitous presence and overzealous pruning. Early on, gardeners tended to use *P. japonica* as a foundation planting around the base of a house, often pruning plants into rectangles or balls and shearing them back after bloom. This only encouraged the plants to send up vigorous new growth, so that over the years they grew into a snarl of twigs.

In recent years, however, *P. japonica* has made a comeback, as a new generation of garden designers has discovered its virtues—statuesque form, rugged bark, and a crown of dense branches growing in tiers. The species eventually reaches 10 feet tall; compact forms grow to 3 to 6 feet.

There are dozens of named varieties. Probably the most widely sold is *P. j.* 'Mountain Fire', whose leaves—vivid red when new—turn lustrous dark green when mature. *P. j.* 'Valley Rose' has upright clusters of rosy pink flowers; *P. j.* 'Valley Valentine' has deep red flower buds and blooms. *P. j.* 'Variegata' has white flowers and green leaves with white margins; the foliage has a pink tinge in spring. *P. j.* 'Spring Snow' bears cream-colored flowers in clusters.

P. japonica is hardy in *Sunset* climate zones 1 through 9 and 14 through 17. Provide plants with light shade and shelter from drying winds. They also need rich, loose soil with ample water. Fertilize these plants as you do other flowering broad-leafed evergreens, such as azaleas and rhododendrons.

Because *P. japonica* has a penchant for producing lots of side growth, you'll need to keep the suckers clipped off to develop handsome upright trunks and a graceful branch structure. Young plants should be selectively pruned so that trunks grow in the form you want the adult shrubs to take. If you have a big, overgrown bush in your garden, judicious pruning can often restore the plant's naturally elegant form. Working from the bottom up and from the inside out, prune off the small twiggy growth, opening up the trunk and major branches. ◆

Pieris japonica 'Valley Valentine' bears clusters of tiny blossoms.

by STEVEN R. LORTON

Inspired by the cottage gardens of England, this casual, colorful corner looks right at home in Northern California. For details on these pretty perennials, see page 176.

GARY PARKER

June

gardenguide

NORMAN A. PLATE

A country border

Herbs and tough Mediterranean plants never had it so good

Moving from a tiny yard with a few annuals to a 5-acre country spread is quite a gardening leap. It's like vaulting from elementary to graduate school. Karel Wigand took that giant step when she and her husband, Bill, bought property in rural Rainbow in northern San Diego County.

Since her husband and his brother were building a log house on the land with their own hands, it never occurred to Karel not to tackle the landscaping on her own. So what if the land was covered with scrub and she'd be starting from scratch? Or if she wasn't used to temperatures of 100°-plus between June and October, commonplace in Rainbow? Wigand just plunged in.

"Oh, I just started in the back, where my mistakes wouldn't show too much, and moved to the front when I got more confident," she says, shrugging off praise. She is equally nonchalant about her crowning achievement—a huge perennial border hugging her grassy hillside midslope, 20 feet across at its widest point and at least 125 feet long. "I just followed the contours of the land and put in a few herbs," says Wigand modestly.

Herbs never had it so good. The combination of sandy loam, sharply draining slope, full sun, and a long, hot summer would melt delicate English garden plants. But salvia, lavender, and artemisia thrive in this demanding location. "They seem to like it here," she says. So, it would appear, does Wigand.

by **SHARON COHOON**

gear

CURTIS ANDERSON

Screens make great drainage-hole covers for pots. The fine grid keeps dirt from seeping out of holes but doesn't block water. A screen is also an effective barrier against ants, sow bugs, earwigs, and cutworms.

In fact, until now there has been only one reason not to use screening routinely when potting: not having any on hand when you're ready to plant. Screen Between is small enough to store. It's precut into one-size-fits-all-pots (3⅞-in.) circles and sold in packets of six. A single pot screen is as easy to use and keep on hand as a coffee filter. Why didn't someone think of this sooner?

Screen Between sells for $1.29 per packet and is widely available at retail nurseries and garden supply centers. If you can't find it, call (714) 970-5107 to order. — *S. C.*

TIPS, TRICKS & SECRETS

What vegetables need at 8,000 feet

When home gardener Shirley Blumberg moved to Mammoth Lakes, California, at 8,000 feet, she found that high-elevation gardens have consistently lower yields of smaller vegetables than lowland gardens. Blumberg wondered why vegetables struggle at high altitudes even when they are raised in rich, well-irrigated soil: Was it low soil temperature, low humidity, or excessive ultraviolet light? She decided to find out by testing different combinations of plastic mulch, row covers, and glass over a variety of salad greens, basil, potatoes, and tomatoes. Here's what she learned.

• It was most important to keep the soil temperature and humidity relatively high around vegetables, and to block moisture-robbing wind. To do that, she planted through perforated clear-plastic mulch and covered the vegetables with summer-weight row covers (she used a spunbonded fabric that allows 90 percent of the light to pass through). With this system Blumberg was able to raise daytime soil temperatures by 9° and humidity by 10 percent. Her plants thrived.

• The intensity of ultraviolet light, controlled with single- and double-pane glass suspended over plants for the entire growing season, wasn't much of a factor in overall plant growth, but reducing the amount did help young plants get off to a faster start.

• Potatoes and miner's lettuce, which are adapted to high elevations by nature, did fine without row covers.

• Tomatoes, which eventually grew too tall for row covers, did best inside a water-filled commercial cloche called Wall-O-Water.

You can reach Blumberg by e-mail at sjblumberg@qnet.com if you have specific questions. —*Jim McCausland*

CONTAINER GARDENING

Secrets of a prize-winning hanging basket

Two years ago, Kerry Zerr of San Diego won the grand prize—$100 worth of seeds annually for the rest of her life—in Thompson & Morgan's hanging basket competition. We asked Zerr to plant another basket for *Sunset*. We think her latest creation (pictured below) is pretty spectacular, too.

Laurentia axillaris 'Blue Stars', spilling out of the basket, has a starring role. The rest of the cast, balanced for texture, shape, and color, includes three shades of impatiens, pink-leafed polka dot plant, lime green coleus, and needlepoint ivy. Zerr propagated the white heliotrope from stem cuttings, since it's not typically sold small enough to insert into a hanging basket. (She starts hard-to-find favorites like *Lobelia pendula* from seed.)

Zerr lined a wire basket about 18 inches in diameter with sphagnum moss and soil, then planted through the sides and across the top.

"I put in a lot of different things, and I plant quite close," says Zerr. "I want my baskets to look like living balls of color." — *S. C.*

PAUL BOWERS

ROB PROCTOR

SUMMER COLOR

Mini zinnias take the heat

Small, strong, and colorful, *Zinnia angustifolia* (also sold as *Z. linearis*) is winning new respect, as evidenced by the variety 'Crystal White' earning an All-America Selections award for 1997. In addition to 'Crystal White', orange and yellow versions of *Z. angustifolia* have been on the market for years. All produce abundant quarter-size blooms over a long season. The plants stay compact and they have greater resistance to heat and disease than the larger garden zinnia (*Z. elegans*).

In *Sunset's* garden in Menlo Park, California, head gardener Rick LaFrentz has been growing these mini zinnias in beds and terra-cotta pots. LaFrentz likes them "because they're so easy to start from seed, they never need deadheading—they just drop faded flower petals—and they never get mildew."

Nurseries often sell *Z. angustifolia* as a bedding plant or in hanging baskets, but you can also order seed for planting next spring. —*J. M.*

Cottage corner of colorful perennials

Inspired by some of the best cottage gardens in England, San Francisco landscape architect Richard William Wogisch transformed a corner of Sky and Jerry Hill's San Mateo garden into a floral extravaganza of cottage-garden perennials (see photo on page 172).

There are no boundaries here: gravel and unstructured beds flow together to give the garden its casual style. "I wanted a relaxed feel around the potting shed [which sits behind the wood fence]," says Wogisch. "And a path that's safe to walk on when your hands are full. With gravel, you don't have to look where you're going like you do with steppingstones."

Gravel is also good for the plants, he explains. It keeps the soil cool and holds in moisture. During winter, when some plants are dormant, the gravel keeps the area looking neat.

Before planting the garden, Wogisch amended the soil with organic matter. Then, instead of following a defined planting plan, he and Sky selected plants together right at the nursery. "Sky picked plants she liked, and I grouped them according to color, height, and growing conditions," says Wogisch. The garden's basic color scheme was yellow, blue, and peach, with touches of deep coral.

For a focal point, Wogisch placed an Adirondack chair in one corner of the garden. Visually, the chair suggests a retreat, and practically, it offers a respite from potting chores. To the right of the chair is *Lavandula pinnata buchii* and peach *Nicotiana alata*. At left is a yellow 'John Innes Petra' foxglove. Blooming in front is salvia mixed with blue-flowered ground morning glory, Santa Barbara daisy, and 'Sweet Vivien' rose.

Below the potting-bench window is a planter filled with a rose, an ivy geranium, ivy, and Johnny-jump-ups. A purple clematis twines over the window frame. —*Lauren Bonar Swezey*

'Phasion' canna

Plant breeding and marketing have become global industries, so maybe it's not surprising that a plant bred in South Africa should come to North America by way of Australia, then excel in the Southwest. That's the case with 'Phasion', a new orange-flowered canna that should thrive here.

'Phasion' has leaves that open green with burgundy stripes. Each leaf's center vein is chartreuse, and it stays that way as the burgundy stripes gradually change to red, pink, yellow, gold, and then deep green. The foliage develops its full range of colors only when nighttime temperatures remain above 58°, so 'Phasion' is at its best in the low and intermediate desert.

Look for plants in nurseries and mail-order catalogs this month. Nursery stock of 'Phasion' (usually sold under the name Canna Tropicanna) is available in containers. You can transplant it directly into good garden soil, but give it filtered sun (full sun in the hot exposures of low and intermediate deserts can burn its leaves). Or repot the plant in a large container—16 to 20 inches in diameter—and move it indoors or out as needed.

Canna Tropicanna grows to about 3 feet in containers and about 4 feet the first year in the ground. Eventually, garden-grown plants can reach 6 feet.—*J. M.*

NORMAN A. PLATE

A new book on water-wise landscaping

Chamisa, or rubber rabbitbrush (*Chrysothamnus nauseosus*), native to the Southwest's high desert and the Rocky Mountains, drops its leaves in August as bloom begins—a showy mass of fluffy, golden yellow flowers that are a magnet to bees and butterflies. New gray-green leaves emerge in the following spring.

Planted this month in mountain and high-desert gardens (*Sunset* zones 1 through 3, 10, and 11), chamisa can make a striking contribution to a late-summer flower border of low water-use plants. This shrub reaches 6 feet without pruning, but you can keep it compact by shearing it back to 1 or 2 feet in early spring. In this garden (shown in the photo at right), designed by Julia Berman of Eden Landscapes in Santa Fe, New Mexico, chamisa plays off blue grama grass, blue-flowered Russian sage, and piñon pines.

Chamisa is just one of more than 100 unthirsty plants in the new *Xeriscape Plant Guide,* by Denver Water and the American Water Works Association (Fulcrum Publishing, Golden, CO, 1996; $34.95). As garden writer Rob Proctor notes in the book's introduction: "Call it what you will—xeriscaping, water-smart gardening, environmentally friendly planting—it is based on common sense....Why squander precious water on exotic plants that stand a slim chance of survival or that never fulfill their promise? The answer is simple. Grow plants that thrive in our specific regions."

Arranged in encyclopedic style, the 184-page hardbound volume has sections on shade plants, trees and shrubs, perennials and vines, and ground covers and grasses. Each plant is illustrated with a botanical drawing and several color photographs.

Look for the *Xeriscape Plant Guide* in bookstores, or order by calling (800) 992-2908. Look for chamisa in nurseries that sell native plants, or order seed or plants from Agua Viva Seed Ranch (800/248-9080) or Plants of the Southwest (505/438-8888). —*J. M.*

CHARLES MANN

Select plants for mountain gardens

As mountain gardeners know well, some plants just love high altitudes, cold winters, and continental weather extremes. But *which* plants? Colorado State University and Denver Botanic Gardens have been working to find out, running promising plants through trials at a variety of locations and awarding the best of them the Plant Select designation. This year when you shop at nurseries, look for the Plant Select label (with the sun logo) on several outstanding plants for mountain and high-plains gardens.

One of the most promising plants is *Agastache rupestris,* a mint that's related to anise hyssop, with a habit like lavender, and burnt orange, red, yellow, and brown flowers that look good close up or at a distance. It flowers August to frost.

Other Plant Select winners you'll find this year include silver sage (*Salvia argentea*), *Daphne burkwoodii* 'Carol Mackie', *Viburnum rhytidophylloides* 'Alleghany', and *Veronica liwanensis*. —*J. M.*

'Sensation' is a show-off

Long a favorite house plant, *Spathiphyllum* flourishes in low light, bearing attractive leaves and tiny flowers that resemble calla lilies. Now, you can grow an offspring called *Spathiphyllum* 'Sensation', which has much showier leaves than its parent.

The glossy, deep green leaves of 'Sensation' can easily reach 2½ feet long and 9 inches wide. The flowers of 'Sensation' are also larger and brighter white than those of its parent, although the blooms are not as profuse.

Expect to pay about $20 for a 2½-foot-tall specimen in a 10-inch pot. This plant should be grown in rich potting soil in a container that provides excellent drainage.

Place the plant where its big, tender leaves won't be frayed by passersby. Feed 'Sensation' as you do other house plants, on a monthly basis from April through October with a liquid fertilizer such as 12-12-12— *Steven R. Lorton* ◆

Homestead garden

The concepts of the *country* garden and the *cottage* garden are familiar to readers who have perused the many books devoted to those landscaping styles. In the Northwest, another style merits study: the *homestead* garden. And there's hardly a better example of this genre than Kathy Hirdler's 1½ acres in Mount Vernon, Washington. When Kathy and her husband, David, started the garden, she drew on gardening lore she had learned from her grandmother who settled in the Northwest early in this century. Hirdler's gardening concepts are as straightforward as a row of corn.

Work with the land. In pioneer gardens, level ground was reserved for growing food; flowers and ornamental shrubs were consigned to sloping areas, where plants were grown in shallow terraces. In Hirdler's garden, a mixed border (shown below) was planted on a gentle slope between an entry drive and the house.

Use indigenous materials. Frontier gardeners built rock walls from stones they found on their land, and they formed steps from cast-off lumber or saw logs. Arbors (like the one pictured), trellises, fences, and gates were often built of saplings. Hirdler used old railroad ties to frame the earthen steps in her garden. And to keep deer at bay, she enclosed her vegetable garden with a fence of 4-foot saplings.

Use plants that come your way. The pioneers' plant palette was a big-hearted mix of whatever came along in the form of seeds or "slips"—cuttings.

Hirdler's thyme was started from her grandmother's plant.

Showcase favorite objects. On early homesteads, a sunlit pocket garden was often a gallery of mismatched pots filled with annual flowers. Hirdler's favorite piece of garden art is a chunk of basalt upon which a friend carved a stylized petroglyph. —*S. R. L.*

Bucking the trend in Jamul

Retail nurseries, like most businesses, are scurrying to cross the electronic bridge to the 21st century. They're putting customers on computer databases, setting up Web sites, and accepting ATM cards. Simpson's Garden Town Nursery in Jamul (about 20 miles east of San Diego), on the other hand, still refuses to get a telephone.

Lee and Cathy Smith's reluctance to get with the times hasn't doomed their nursery to failure, though. Their roster of fans grows steadily by word of mouth, and the nursery's parking lot is rarely empty.

Maybe customers find the Smiths' low-key, soft-sell approach refreshing. Or maybe they like the huge selection. (With 15 acres to browse, customers drive rather than walk through the aisles here.) Or perhaps they like the fact that Simpson's grows 90 percent of its own stock, chemical-free, or that it has one of the best selections of landscaping trees around. Or maybe, just maybe, they like pulling up to the white wood fence, seeing the 1954 fire truck and old Burma Shave signs, being handed an ice-cold red apple, and stepping back in time.

Shopping at Simpson's is like a cruise in the country. So allow time for visiting Homer, the potbellied pig, admiring the Smiths' collection of vintage vehicles, and picnicking under the pepper trees, as well as shopping. The nursery also has an extensive cycad collection.

Simpson's Garden Nursery is open 9 to 5 every day except Thanksgiving, Christmas, and New Year's Day; 13925 Campo Road (State Highway 94), Jamul. — *S. C.*

BEN WOOLSEY

'Ruby Slippers' dogwood

No matter how familiar you are with kousa dogwood (*Cornus kousa*), it's always a pleasant surprise to see one explode into bloom from mid-May through early July, when the spring dogwood season is long past. It's even more surprising to see one with bright red blossoms. For the last several decades, growers have been working to perfect varieties with rich pink, rose, and red flowers. Wells Nurseries in Mount Vernon, Washington, has succeeded in breeding one that bears rich, rosy red blossoms in abundance—*C. k.* 'Ruby Slippers' (pictured below). The flowers are unusually large, often 3½ inches across, sometimes more.

'Ruby Slippers' should grow to 20 feet, as other kousa dogwoods do, with a single trunk. Its glossy green leaves are ribbed, pointed, and 2 to 3 inches long. On mature plants the flowers turn into bright red fruits that hang on the tree from midfall into early winter. In autumn, the foliage puts on a good show in shades of scarlet and dark, port-wine red. The plant has handsome winter form.

'Ruby Slippers' in 1-gallon cans sell for $50 each; 6-foot plants balled and burlapped, start at $125. For more information, call Wells Nurseries at (360) 336-6544. — *S. R. L.*

PHIL SCHOFIELD

Monkey flowers with spotless faces

Like magicians, plant breeders can make things disappear. Take the monkey flower (*Mimulus hybridus*), for instance. This short-lived perennial (usually grown as an annual) bears velvety, two-lipped flowers that are often flecked with spots, giving the impression of a smiling monkey face. A new line of these flowers called the Mystic series, developed by Sakata Seed America in Morgan Hill, California, is available without spots. The flower colors are clear and intense: scarlet, wine, orange, yellow, and ivory. Look for plants in single shades and mixtures in nursery sixpacks and flats.

These plants stay compact, topping out at about 10 to 12 inches, with bright green, toothed leaves. They tolerate full sun but prefer par-

NORMAN A. PLATE

tial shade, and they like rich, moist soil. Use them in beds where their massed color can stand out, or tuck them into containers or hanging baskets in spring and early summer. In *Sunset's* gardens, we filled several big terra-cotta pots with Mystic and enjoyed two rounds of bloom: from spring to midsummer (after which we sheared back the plants), then again in late summer.

We also combined the sizzling orange monkey flowers in big pots with cool, sky blue lobelia tumbling over the edges. The effect was stunning.
— *Dick Bushnell*

Meet the forgotten pollinators

With honeybees declining throughout North America, which creatures will do their job? Stephen Buchmann at the Arizona-Sonora Desert Museum in Tucson says, "Within 100 miles of here, you can find more than 1,000 kinds of pollinating birds, bats, and insects, including a huge variety of leafcutter, mason, carpenter, cactus, and digger bees." These are the forgotten pollinators: essential creatures whose work often goes unnoticed.

To see them at work and learn how to attract them to your garden, visit the museum's pollination gardens. The yucca garden, butterfly garden, and hummingbird garden-aviary are open during regular hours. The new nocturnal garden, open Saturday evenings, is where hawkmoths do their work; see them after mid-June. Bee and bat gardens should be finished by year's end. The museum (2021 N. Kinney Rd.;

520/883-1380) is open 7:30 to 6 Sunday through Friday, 7:30 A.M. to 10 P.M. Saturdays (June through October). Admission costs $8.95.

Even if you aren't able to visit the museum, you can follow Buchmann's advice to attract pollinators to your own garden.

• Install bee nests.

• Stop using all pesticides, especially acephate, carbaryl, diazinon, malathion, and synthetic pyrethroids.

• Plant part of your landscape with native wildflowers, shrubs, and trees that bloom throughout the year.

• Make a puddle that insects can visit to draw water and salt. Overhead watering or row irrigation normally provides this; if you have drip irrigation, aim one emitter or spray head at open ground.

• Read *The Forgotten Pollinators,* by Stephen Buchmann and Gary Nabhan (Island Press, Washington, D.C., 1996; $24.95; 800/828-1302), a fascinating series of essays covering the state of pollinators worldwide.

• Visit the forgotten pollinators' Web site at http://www.desert.net/museum/fp/.
— *J. M.*

A red-hot mandevilla

'Ruby Star' mandevilla will give 'Alice du Pont' some competition this summer. This new hybrid of *M. splendens* shares the glossy green foliage, vigorous growth habit, and readiness to bloom of 'Alice du Pont'. But instead of hot pink trumpets, 'Ruby Star', as you would guess from its name, has dark red blooms. They don't start out that way, though. When the buds open, the flowers are a pinwheel swirl of pink and white. Then they gradually darken to a deep, velvety red. You can see flowers at all stages on the plant when it's in bloom.

Tender 'Ruby Star' can't take frost. It will overwinter only in frost-free areas in *Sunset* climate zones 21 through 24. Elsewhere, just enjoy it for the summer. Or move plants indoors or to a greenhouse when temperatures drop. Like her sister, 'Ruby Star' appreciates rich soil, ample moisture, frequent feeding, and full sun or partial shade in hot, inland locations. Aphids and whiteflies can be problems.

'Ruby Star' should be widely available at retail nurseries and garden centers this summer. — *S. C.*

Watch out for puncture vine

During the past 16 years, Phil Bunnelle of Santa Clara, California, has waged war against puncture vine (*Tribulus terrestris*), a noxious, ground-hugging weed that grows below 5,000-foot elevations. This annual weed, which forms a low mat of tiny leaves, bears hard, thorny seed pods (burrs) that poke into bare feet, paws, and tires. (Bunnelle's war began after one too many burrs punctured his bicycle tires, and he has since been removing the weed wherever he sees it.)

Puncture vine is common along lawn edges and in open areas, and is so vigorous that within a couple of weeks one plant can grow several feet wide. The burrs contain seeds that spread the plant.

This weed emerges around early May. If possible, remove it before the burrs start forming in mid-June. Use a trowel to dig out larger plants; taproots make older plants harder to pull. If burrs have formed, place harvested weeds in a plastic bag, tie it closed, and toss it into the garbage.

Puncture vine can also be controlled with a herbicide made from the potassium salts of fatty acids (Safer Superfast Weed and Grass Killer). — *L. B. S.*

A tomato tuck-in

A rambunctious tomato vine needs a sturdy cage to contain it. The one pictured below, designed and built by *Sunset* writer Bill Crosby and test garden coordinator Bud Stuckey comes apart easily for storage at the end of the season. Its materials cost only $25.

Crosby and Stuckey built the cage using four 8-foot-tall rough-cut redwood 2-by-2s and about fifty 3-foot-long bamboo stakes (packages of about 18 are available at nurseries).

First they painted the bottom 2 feet of each 2-by-2 with wood preservative. Then, using a drill with a ¾-inch bit and starting 2½ feet up from the bottom of each post, they drilled 12 ¾-inch-wide holes through the wood 6 inches apart. Starting 33 inches up from the bottom on the adjacent side of each post, they drilled 12 holes 6 inches apart.

To form the cage, they set the posts 2½ feet apart in a square and sunk them 2 feet into the ground.

Stuckey sets a tomato plant in the middle of the posts, then inserts two or three levels of bamboo stakes through the posts to steady them. As the plant grows, he inserts additional stakes.

— *L. B. S.* ◆

NORMAN A. PLATE (3)

Pacific Northwest Garden Notebook

by **STEVEN R. LORTON**

Recently I returned from a two-week visit to the East Coast. As always when I go there, I talked to lots of gardeners and I saw lots of gardens. I admire those Easterners, but I can't count the number of formal boxwood hedges, geometric flower beds, parterres, topiaries, walls, and obelisks made of trellis I saw back East. When I landed at Sea-Tac, I felt the urge to kiss the ground. Give me our Northwest gardening style any day.

Here, art imitates nature. Vine maples lean out over walkways, underplanted with a lush carpet of ferns and other ground covers. Vines scramble up walls following their whims. Annuals and perennials don't march in rows or grow in smugly isolated cliques, but range all around the garden, tucked next to rocks or shrubs as they might grow in the wild.

Our best design inspirations come from nature. In my garden in Washington's upper Skagit Valley, for example, I draw inspiration from the nearby forest floor, using native sword ferns to form a green understory that weaves my borders together. Where sunlight and space permit in this ferny carpet, I sprinkle some color: the mahogany, burgundy, and puce leaves of the heucheras; the blue bells of balloon flower or campanula; the pink spires of astilbe or foxglove.

Don't get me wrong: this Northwest style—a look of controlled wildness—is not easy to achieve or maintenance-free.

MARINA THOMPSON

You have to match plants with the proper microclimates and light conditions, and prune (almost constantly), dig, divide, transplant, and edit.

So Northwest gardeners, let us pursue our own vigorous style and stand fast against the monkey-see, monkey-do impulse that seizes us when we look at those glossy books filled with formal Eastern gardens. Who knows? In a few years, the East may look to Bellingham—rather than Buckingham—for its inspiration.

THAT'S A GOOD QUESTION

Q: I love melons. What's the best way to grow good ones here?
— *Mary Johnson, Sedro-Woolley, Washington*

A: The cool, moist summers on the west side of the Cascades, where you live, are not as conducive to melon culture as the warm, dry summers on the east side. Territorial Seed Company (541/942-9547) sells 'Earligold' cantaloupe, a 75-day variety. I've seen it grow successfully in Vancouver, B.C., in raised beds covered with black plastic to hold in warmth. The melon seedlings, sprouted indoors at the first of this month, are planted through slits cut in the plastic.

Northern California Garden Notebook

by **LAUREN BONAR SWEZEY**

Open Garden Day, a one-day event in early June during which community and school gardens in the San Francisco Bay Area are open to the public, has lots to offer families interested in gardening and farming—workshops, activities for children, walking tours, and plant sales, for instance.

One weekday afternoon, my 3-year-old son, Drake, and I visited Loma Vista Farm and Garden Center in Vallejo, a learning farm. The visit was memorable for both of us.

We arrived on a Winnie-the-Pooh kind of blustery day when kids were just getting out of school. Thom Arcadi, the teacher in charge, greeted us and showed us around. He explained that the site—adjacent to Loma Vista Elementary School and operated by the Vallejo City Unified School District—is a hands-on educational center where students of all ages and abilities "learn by doing."

"We began with a few sheep and rabbits and a pony," says Arcadi. "Then we started collecting and building things." The 5-acre farm, which took three years to get going, now has livestock (Drake particularly enjoyed feeding leaves to the hungry goats), poultry, rabbits, waterfowl, a 1-acre vegetable garden, a pond, greenhouse, barns, and a classroom. "Everything was built by children," explains Arcadi. "The barns were built at the high schools and then disassembled and rebuilt on the site."

Classes from Vallejo schools visit the center as often as once a week. The farm is also open to classes from outside

MARINA THOMPSON

the school district. Projects include cooking with the produce children grow in the garden, feeding and observing the animals, weighing baby animals, graphing the animals' growth, and compiling scientific notebooks, to name a few.

Once students are back in the classroom, the farm experience continues to help them in math (students learn how to count seeds in multiples of 10, for instance), science, social studies, and a variety of other subjects. For more information about Loma Vista Farm and Garden Center, call (707) 556-8765.

THAT'S A GOOD QUESTION

Q: The August 1992 issue of *Sunset* (page 48) mentioned a garden mail-order company for kids. I called the number, but it has been changed. Is this company still in business? — *Vinh Pham, Stockton*

A: Yes, ***Gardens for Growing People,*** which specializes in children's gardening supplies and backyard nature study, has changed its phone number. The company's current address and number are Box 630, Point Reyes Station, CA 94956; (415) 663-9433 (catalog is free). Besides the tools, games, and storybooks they've always carried, they now offer gardening curricula for teachers developed by organizations such as Seattle Tilth and Growlab, and a free newsletter available by e-mail. To subscribe to the newsletter, send a request to growpepl@nbn.com.

Southern California Garden Notebook

by **SHARON COHOON**

My husband must be piping his old Martin Denny albums into my dreams. Otherwise, why would my Mediterranean garden be migrating to Maui? For a long time, we had an ideal arrangement. He'd lobby for tropicals, and I'd ignore him and plant Mediterraneans. Then I started a story on banana trees, and he saw a perfect opportunity to infiltrate. "You really ought to grow a banana yourself for research purposes," he said, and I let him plant one.

Darn if that banana didn't look good, too. The sun glowing through its broad, translucent leaves added a lushness to the garden that was positively seductive. Before I knew it, I'd spent the whole summer buying things to complement its tropical foliage—coleus, variegated cannas, crotons, copper leaf plants, and red-leafed hibiscus. Finally, cold weather stopped me—but only temporarily.

Hey, why fight it, I've decided. There are few places in the country that can grow these plants, so why not celebrate the fact that Southern California can? A few broad leaves really *are* a nice contrast to the classical austerity of Mediterranean plants. And if you plant them near the house where the soil stays moist and they're in semishade, many tropicals don't need *that* much water.

So, maybe I'll go back for that variegated 'Ae Ae' banana my husband wanted last summer, and perhaps I'll try those gingers that tempted me. But that, my dear, is the end of it, do you hear? (Is it my imagination, or is the Martin Denny getting louder?)

MARINA THOMPSON

TROPICAL DREAMS ...

If you've been looking in vain for a good reference book on tropicals, you're now in luck. *Tropical Gardening,* a volume in the American Garden Guidesseries, is an excellent reference book. It profiles 200 tropical plants, giving thorough growing instructions and cultivar recommendations. The 223-page book has a chapter on garden design so you can put everything together tastefully, and a chapter on technique to keep plants flourishing. And it has 300 gorgeous color photos. I'm hiding it from my husband. *Tropical Gardening,* Fairchild Tropical Garden/David Bar-Zvi, Pantheon Books, New York, 1996; $25, hardbound.

THAT'S A GOOD QUESTION

Q: I love pink and lavender, and I hate yellow and orange. What can I plant for summer in my colors?

A: Lots of things. Dwarf pentas comes in lavender and pink, for starters. Pentas (*P. lanceolata*) loves the heat, attracts butterflies, and blooms nearly year-round along the coast. Ivy geraniums are almost as tough as zinnias and come in pink and lavender shades. Yarrow is another sun-lover: 'Apple Blossom' is a pale pink variety; 'Heidi' is a darker, clear pink. And Swan River daisy comes in mauve pink. If you prefer annuals, try some pastel petunias, and the new rosy pink vincas (Madagascar periwinkle) and lavender and lilac-blue impatiens. Fill in any gaps with rose-pink or lavender sweet alyssum.

Westerner's Garden Notebook

by **JIM McCAUSLAND**

While interviewing pollination biologist Stephen Buchmann for this month's report on the forgotten pollinators (see page 179), I learned a fascinating bit of trivia. About 8 percent of the world's flowering plants, including blueberries, eggplants, kiwis, some peppers, and tomatoes, are buzz pollinated. Buchmann explains how it works: native bees land on the flowers, push up under the anthers, then vibrate their bodies at about 525 cycles per second. The buzz—close to middle C on the musical scale—vibrates pollen grains out of the holes in the ends of the anthers onto the insect, which carries them to the next plant.

MARINA THOMPSON

FLOWER CARPET ROSE GOES WHITE

One of the best landscape roses I've ever grown is Flower Carpet Pink, which blooms long and heavily and has almost no trouble in my garden with insects or diseases. My experience with the pink variety has whetted my appetite for Flower Carpet White, new this year. It bears dense clusters of fragrant, camellia-shaped flowers whose petals drop cleanly when they die. The plants grow about 2 feet tall and 3 feet wide. A gold-medal winner in Europe, this plant has excellent disease resistance for a white rose. If you can't find plants, call the growers' toll-free number (800/580-5930) for help locating a retail source.

MATH FOR BAGGED MANURE

Like most gardeners, I buy potting soil, peat moss, and manure in bags rather than in bulk quantities. The bagged amendments are sometimes measured in quarts and sometimes in cubic feet, so it's tough to compare prices. Suddenly, it dawned on me that there are 25.7 quarts per cubic foot, and comparison shopping became easier. For example, when you compare a 1-cubic-foot (round it off to 25 quarts) bag of manure selling for $2 (less than 8 cents per quart) with a 17-quart bag selling for 69 cents (just 4 cents per quart), you don't need to be a rocket scientist to figure out which is the better deal.

THAT'S A GOOD QUESTION

Q: Why, when, and how do you thin fruit?

A: Apples, apricots, Asian pears, pears, and plums frequently set too much fruit. By thinning some of it out, you'll ease the strain on tree limbs, reducing the risk of breaks, and the fruit that's left will grow larger. Thin after so-called June drop—the time when trees naturally abort unpollinated, imperfect, or excess fruit. Don't bother thinning trees with light crops (apples like 'Gravenstein', for example, are alternate bearers, producing a heavy crop one year and a light crop the next; you needn't thin during the off years). Thin apricots, Asian pears, and most plums 4 to 5 inches apart, apples and pears 6 to 8 inches apart. If you want a little more fruit, just thin triple clusters to doubles and doubles to singles. Many kinds of fruit, including apples and pears, are borne on thornlike spurs; take care not to break off these spurs as you thin the fruit.

Planting

☐ **ANNUALS.** Zones 1–7: You can freely set out all annuals. Before you plant, it's a good idea to soak plants overnight in their nursery containers so they take up as much water as possible before they go into the ground. Fill a bucket or washtub with water and set plants in it so the soil is immersed.

☐ **DAHLIAS.** Last call to get tubers into the ground for blooms this summer and early fall.

☐ **PERENNIALS.** Zones 1–7: Shop for plants in 1-gallon cans, and thoroughly soak the soil before planting. Don't fertilize plants until after flowers have faded.

☐ **VEGETABLES.** Zones 1–7: Set out seedlings of basil, cucumber, eggplant, peppers, and squash, if you haven't done so already. Sow bush beans, turnips, and rutabagas.

Maintenance

☐ **CLIP HEDGES.** If you shear hedges twice a year, do it early this month and again in late summer or early fall. If you are a once-a-year trimmer, do the job in early July. Trim so the hedge is slightly wider at the base than at the top—this way sunlight and rain can reach the entire hedge surface.

☐ **CUT ROSES.** Harvest roses so the cut is just above a leaflet with five, not three, leaves. New growth will start just

Sunset
CLIMATE ZONES
☐ 1-3

ALASKA
Fairbanks •
YUKON
TERRITORY
Anchorage •
• Kodiak   Juneau •

DEBRA LAMBERT

Sunset
CLIMATE ZONES

Vancouver •   BRITISH COLUMBIA
Victoria •
WASHINGTON
• Seattle   Spokane •
Olympia •
• Yakima
Portland •   Pendleton •
OREGON
Salem •
Bend •
Eugene •
Sunset
CLIMATE ZONES
Medford •
☐ 1-3   ☐ 4-7

below the cut. If you cut above a three-leaf leaflet, you won't get new growth.

☐ **DIVIDE PERENNIALS.** You can dig and divide early-blooming plants as soon as flowers fade. Cut back flower stalks and slice around the plant with a spade or

shovel. Pop the clump out of the ground. A clump 12 inches across will divide nicely into four equal parts. Set divisions into the planting hole and water them well from now through the end of summer. Don't fertilize until early next spring.

☐ **THIN FRUITS.** After trees drop their infertile fruit naturally, thin clusters so the remaining fruit develops to full size. On trees with heavy crops, thin doubles and triples to one or two, then thin remaining fruit to 6-inch intervals along the branch. You'll get fewer but larger fruits and you'll ease the strain on tree limbs.

Pest and weed control

☐ **BATTLE SLUGS.** Set out traps or bait in the late afternoon before a string of dry days. Slugs are most active between dusk and dawn. Keep children and pets away from poison bait.

☐ **BEFRIEND GARTER SNAKES.** On the west side of the Cascades, a 4- by 8-foot piece of plywood or a pile of large rocks at one end of the vegetable garden makes a great hideout for garter snakes. These nonpoisonous reptiles gobble slugs and help control other pests.

☐ **WEED.** Pull weeds before seeds can form and scatter. Shake dirt from roots, allow the plants to wither atop the soil or pavement, then toss them onto the compost pile.

Planting

☐ **PLANT BULBS, CORMS, TUBERS.**
Zones 1–2: For late-summer color (except in highest elevations), plant begonias, dahlias, gladiolus, montbretia (*Crocosmia*), and Mexican shell flower (*Tigridia*).

☐ **PLANT DWARF CRAPE MYRTLES.**
Zones 7–9, 14: These heat-loving shrubs thrive in areas where days are long and hot. Use dwarf varieties in small gardens. For 3- to 4-foot-tall types, try 'Chica Pink' or 'Chica Red'. For slightly larger varieties that generally grow 5 feet tall and 4 feet wide, try rose red 'Petite Embers', dark pink 'Petite Orchid', clear pink 'Petite Pinkie', deep purple 'Petite Plum', deep crimson 'Petite Red Imp', or white 'Petite Snow'. Near the coast, crape myrtles often mildew.

☐ **PLANT LOW-MAINTENANCE SHRUBS.**
Zones 7–9, 14–17: Try blue hibiscus, Cape mallow (*Anisodontea*), Cape plumbago, ceanothus, euphorbia, feathery cassia, flax, Jerusalem sage, lavender, plumbago, rockrose, Russian sage (*Perovskia* 'Blue Spire'), and tree mallow (*Lavatera*).

☐ **SET OUT SUMMER COLOR.** For best value and a long season of performance, start with sixpacks. For instant color, look for blooming plants in 4-inch pots or 1-gallon cans. Good choices include catmint, coreopsis, dahlia, diascia, gaillardia, globe amaranth, Madagascar periwinkle (vinca), penstemon, perennial statice, portulaca, salvia, sanvitalia, sunflower, verbena, and zinnia.

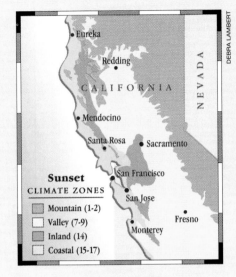

Sunset
CLIMATE ZONES

Mountain (1-2)
Valley (7-9)
Inland (14)
Coastal (15-17)

Maintenance

☐ **CARE FOR HOUSE PLANTS.** Fertilize them once a month or every time you water (diluted to half-strength). To prevent sunburn, move house plants away from hot south- or west-facing windows, or cover the windows with translucent curtains. Wash dust off leaves periodically and check plants for insects, such as mealybugs and spider mites.

☐ **PROTECT FRUIT CROPS.** To keep birds from raiding fruit trees, such as sweet cherries, cover trees with plastic bird netting or row cover fabric (available at nurseries). To keep it from blowing off trees, fasten it to the branches and around the trunk with wire or twine.

☐ **REMOVE FIRE HAZARDS.** In fire-prone areas, clean up brush and debris to reduce the fuel volume. When grasses turn brown, mow them down to about 4 inches. Prune dead and diseased wood from trees and shrubs. Prune tree limbs lower than 20 feet off the ground. Cut branches back at least 15 feet from the house. Clean off any plant debris that may have accumulated on the roof.

☐ **STAKE TALL, FLOPPY FLOWERS.** To hold up sprawlers like bachelor's buttons, carnations, and yarrow, insert four stakes at least 2 feet tall (depending on height of flowers) into the soil around the plant; wrap the outside with two layers of twine, one toward the top and one toward the bottom of the stakes. Or purchase Y-Stakes that wrap around plants, available at nurseries and by calling (206) 455-0568.

Pest control

☐ **SPRAY ROSES.** Aphids, black spot, powdery mildew, rust, and whiteflies can all cause severe damage to roses. Now they can all be controlled with one biodegradable, organic pesticide derived from neem-tree seed (and sold under names such as Green Light Rose Defense). Spray according to label directions when pests build up to damaging numbers or when diseases first appear.

Planting

□ **ADD FRAGRANCE.** Summer evenings and sweet flowers were made for each other. Double your sundown pleasure by adding one of the following to your garden: Arabian jasmine (*Jasminum sambac*), common heliotrope, gardenia, Madagascar jasmine (*Stephanotis floribunda*), night jessamine (*Cestrum nocturnum*), sweet olive (*Osmanthus fragrans*), or tuberose.

□ **ADD LATE-BLOOMING COLOR.** It's not too late to plant summer annuals, especially heat-loving *Catharanthus roseus,* marigolds, verbena, and zinnias. Also look for summer-to-fall-blooming perennials such as lion's tail, rudbeckia, and salvias.

□ **PLANT SUBTROPICALS.** Tropical and subtropical plants grow quickly when planted during summer's warmth, and they have plenty of time to harden off before winter. Nurseries have their best selections now. Choices include banana, bird of paradise, bougainvillea, ginger, hibiscus, palms, and tree ferns.

□ **PLANT VEGETABLES.** Sow seeds of beans, beets, carrots, corn, cucumbers, pumpkins, and summer squash. Set out seedlings of cucumbers, eggplant, peppers, and tomatoes. Coastal gardeners can squeeze in another harvest of leaf lettuce from seed or seedlings. High-desert gardeners (zone 11) can plant short-season varieties of beans, corn, cucumbers, melons, pumpkins, squash, and tomatoes.

DEBRA LAMBERT

Bishop

NEVADA

CALIFORNIA

San Luis Obispo

Bakersfield

Santa Barbara

Tehachapi

Lancaster

Los Angeles

Palm Springs

Sunset
CLIMATE ZONES

1-3 7-9 11 13 14-24

San Diego

MEXICO

Maintenance

□ **SPREAD MULCH.** To conserve water, suppress weeds, and enrich the soil, spread a 2- to 3-inch layer of organic mulch around vegetables, trees, shrubs, and flowers; keep mulch away from the stems and trunks of plants. Use compost, ground bark, weed-free straw, or dry grass clippings.

□ **STOP WATERING NATIVE PLANTS.** Native plants, having adapted to dry summers, are especially vulnerable to disease when subjected to warm, wet soil. Water them infrequently or not at all. Newly planted natives will need to be irrigated, however, because they are not yet established. Water them in the evening when the soil is cooler to reduce risk of root rot, and allow the water to drip slowly over the rootball several inches away from the trunk.

□ **STAKE TOMATOES.** For easy picking and to prevent fruit rot, support tomatoes off the ground with a cage, stakes, or a trellis. It's best to provide the support when you plant. As plants grow, tie vines to supports with plastic ties or strips of old nylon.

Pest and disease control

□ **WATCH FOR PESTS.** Spray or dust plants that have pest caterpillars (such as cabbageworm, corn earworm, geranium budworm, and tomato hornworm) with *Bacillus thuringiensis* (BT). Apply sparingly, starting when caterpillars are small. Keep spider mite, thrip, and whitefly populations in check by spraying affected foliage with a strong stream of water and/or insecticidal soap.

□ **TREAT POWDERY MILDEW.** As long as fog brings "June gloom" to coastal gardens, mildew on roses remains a problem. Washing off leaves during early-morning hours helps keep mildew in check. Or try spraying roses with this mixture: 1½ tablespoons baking soda, 1½ tablespoons canola oil, 1 tablespoon vinegar, and 1 tablespoon mild dishwashing detergent (without ammonia) to 1 gallon of water.

Planting

□ **ANNUALS.** Scatter seed of cosmos, marigold, portulaca, sunflower, and zinnia. Or plant seedlings of any of these plants, as well as African daisy, baby snapdragon, bachelor's button, calendula, clarkia, forget-me-not, gaillardia, globe amaranth, lobelia, pansy, snapdragon, spider flower, sweet alyssum, sweet William, and viola. After the last frost, set out coleus, geranium, impatiens, Madagascar periwinkle, marigold, nasturtium, and petunia.

□ **BULBS.** Plant canna, dahlia, gladiolus, Mexican shell flower (*Tigridia*), montbretia, and tuberous begonia.

□ **PERENNIALS.** Sow aster, basket-of-gold, campanula, columbine, delphinium, erigeron, gaillardia, gilia, heuchera, penstemon, perennial sweet pea, potentilla, and purple coneflower. Or buy seedlings of all the above, and blanket flower, coreopsis, and salvia.

□ **PERMANENT PLANTS.** At lower elevations, transplant container plants. At highest elevations, plant either balled-and-burlapped stock or container-grown shrubs and trees. Plant ground covers from flats or cans.

□ **STRAWBERRIES.** Plant strawberries from nursery sixpacks or pots. Choose a sunny place and provide coarse soil mix with lots of organic matter.

□ **VEGETABLES.** Sow cucumber and squash, as well as successive crops of

Sunset
CLIMATE ZONES

□ 1-3   ■ 10-11

beets, bush beans, carrots, chard, kohlrabi, lettuce, onions, parsnips, peas, radishes, spinach, Swiss chard, and turnips. If the season is long and warm enough in your area, sow corn, pumpkin, and watermelon, and plant nursery seedlings of eggplant, peppers, and tomatoes. Plant seedlings of warm-season crops such as melons, peppers, squash, and tomatoes through perforated plastic sheets to increase warmth around plants.

Maintenance

□ **CARE FOR ROSES.** Cut off faded flowers, fertilize, then build a basin around each plant to concentrate water around the root zone.

□ **FERTILIZE.** Feed lawns with nitrogen fertilizer; repeat in four to six weeks. If

you haven't already done so, apply fertilizer to flower beds and vegetable gardens.

□ **MOW LAWNS.** Cut bluegrass, fescue, and ryegrass to about 2 inches, bent grass to 1 inch or less.

□ **MULCH.** Spread a 3-inch layer of organic mulch (compost, ground bark, leaves, or pine needles) around permanent plants.

□ **PRUNE SPRING-FLOWERING SHRUBS.** After bloom, remove dead, injured, diseased, crossing, and closely parallel branches.

□ **WATER.** Beyond periodic deep watering of permanent plants, focus your irrigation efforts on seedbeds, new plantings, container plants, and any plants sheltered from the rain.

Pest control

□ **CONTROL SOD WEBWORMS.** If brown spots appear in lawns, and leaf blades pull out easily, suspect webworms (look for them feeding on grass blades at night). Treat the infested area and the perimeter with a specific insecticide.

□ **PROTECT FRUIT CROPS.** Cover strawberries and ripening cherries with bird netting or row covers until fruit is ready to pick.

Planting and harvest

☐ **PLANT PALMS.** Zones 12–13: Plant or transplant them into holes as deep as their rootballs and twice as wide. Tie the fronds up over the buds to protect them. After new growth begins, cut the twine.

☐ **PLANT SUMMER COLOR.** Plant cockscomb, globe amaranth, Madagascar periwinkle, portulaca, purslane, salvia, starflower, and zinnia early in the month in a place that gets only filtered sun in the hottest part of the day.

☐ **PLANT SUMMER CROPS.** Zones 10–11: Plant corn in the first days of the month, cucumbers, melons, and summer squash by midmonth. Zones 12–13: You can still plant black-eyed peas, corn, melons, okra, peanuts, sweet potatoes, and yard-long beans.

☐ **SOW FALL CROPS.** Zones 10–11: Sow brussels sprouts, cabbage, and carrots any time this month; wait until midmonth to sow broccoli and cauliflower. Zones 12–13: Sow tomato seeds indoors for transplanting into the garden in late July; some good varieties include 'Champion', 'Early Girl', 'Heatwave', 'Solar Set', 'Sunmaster', and 'Surefire'.

☐ **HARVEST CROPS.** Pick cantaloupe when the skin is well netted and fruit slips from the vine with little pressure; corn after tassels turn brown and milk comes from nicked kernels; eggplant when the skin turns glossy; peppers after they turn color; new potatoes just after plants flower, and full-size spuds when tops start to die; watermelon when the tendrils closest to the fruit begin to turn brown.

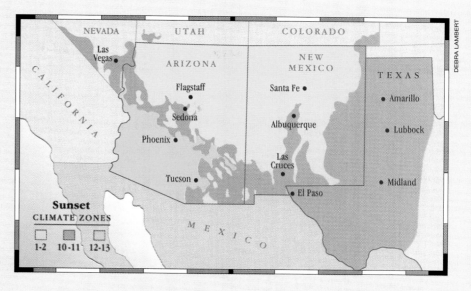

Maintenance

☐ **MOW.** Mow Bermuda, St. Augustine, and zoysia grass 1 to 1½ inches tall. Keep hybrid Bermuda at about 1 inch.

☐ **MULCH TREES, SHRUBS.** Spread a 2- to 4-inch layer of organic or gravel mulch over the root zones of trees and shrubs.

☐ **TREAT CHLOROSIS.** Plants that grow in alkaline soil are subject to chlorosis, an iron deficiency whose telltale sign is yellow leaves with contrasting green veins. Treat the condition with iron chelate.

☐ **WATER.** Deep-water with flooding or drip irrigation; if you use drip, also flood-irrigate monthly to wash salts down out of the root zone.

Pest control

☐ **CHECK FOR SQUASH VINE BORER.** Look for tiny eggs on squash vines. Rub them off before the borers hatch out, drill into the vine, and weaken the plant.

☐ **CONTROL BEET LEAF HOPPERS.** These greenish yellow, inch-long insects spread curly top virus to cucumber, melon, and tomato plants. Protect your crops by covering them with shadecloth. Remove infested plants from your garden.

A BIT OF
England in Napa

*Every inch of this lush California garden
is filled with flowers and foliage*

by LAUREN BONAR SWEZEY

photographs by SAXON HOLT

■ For Sabrina and Freeland Tanner, owners of Proscape Landscape Design, gardening means "no bare earth." Every plant in the Tanners' ½-acre garden grows shoulder to shoulder with the next one. And in a valley well known for its hot, dry summers, such abundance of foliage and flowers—which comes so naturally in more temperate climates—is truly inspiring. Though the Tanners' garden is surrounded by suburban homes and streets, it exudes lushness and romance typical of a garden in England.

Trees around the periphery provide privacy and shade. In wide borders, shrubs and grasses of varied textures, shapes, and colors form the garden's backbone. Flamboyant flowering perennials and roses are vivid accents. A low boxwood hedge defines the borders and the lawn and unifies all plantings. "Without the hedge, the garden would be too chaotic," says Freeland. "Now it's a controlled chaos."

Throughout the garden, plants play off each other handsomely. Arbors, a gazebo, and fanciful sculptures add to the garden's charm.

Towering Pacific strain delphinium, pink 'Marjorie Fair' rose, dark red 'Crimson Pygmy' barberry, 'Great Western' rose (right), and 'Apricot Queen' New Zealand flax surround the Summer House. A maple provides shade.

Far left: A formal rose arbor, covered with 'Climbing Souvenir de la Malmaison' and flanked by 'Sexy Rexy', defines the front entry.

Top center: Birdhouses hang from curly willow branches sunk in concrete, behind pink 'Baronne Prévost' rose, purple Erysimum 'Bowles Mauve', 'Marjorie Fair' rose, and silvery blue Picea pungens 'Globosa'.

Bottom center: Gently curving boxwood hedges edge the lawn. In the foreground are 'Rose Glow' barberry, 'Yellow Wave' New Zealand flax, and yellow 'Moonshine' yarrow.

Above: Iris pallida 'Aurea Variegata' makes a stunning accent behind Helichrysum petiolare 'Limelight' and blackish red Anthriscus sylvestris 'Ravenswing'. Above it, the sun lights up giant feather grass. ◆

A BACKYARD
fantasy

One family's oceanfront garden sets the stage for great gatherings

by SHARON COHOON

photographs by JIM BROWN

■ Casa del Mar, Max and Ana Negri's home and garden overlooking the blue Pacific in Rancho Palos Verdes, California, is a perfect setting for a party. Thanks to the house's open layout and lavish use of glass, indoors and outdoors flow together seamlessly. Guests—whether lingering in the front courtyard near the pool or sipping wine in the living room—are all visible to one another.

But it's curiosity about the view through all those windows that inevitably leads guests out onto the back patio and across the lawn to the edge of the bluff. There, to their surprise, they find stairs to the sea and catch their first glimpse of Max's secret, cliff-hugging garden. After ambling down the switchback path past jungle plantings, they arrive at the beach. Here, they might see the youngest family members exploring

A round stone table and encircling benches made from beach boulders and concrete provide the Negri family with a place to congregate for twilight suppers. Farther down the beach are a firepit and additional seating.

Switchback path (top left) passes ferns and other plants. Pepper and other trees are pruned to reveal—not obscure—the view. The "trailhead" (above) offers grand views of the coast. Max and Ana Negri (top right) relax on a trail bench.

tidepools while their parents or grandparents ready the firepit for the evening's barbecue.

If there ever was a backyard heaven for a big family, this is it. A "jungle" to explore, surf to wade in, firepit to cozy up to: all the pleasures of a summer camp are right here. This perfect site makes it hard to believe that the Negris' children and grandchildren were once disappointed by Casa del Mar. When they first saw the Negris' new but much smaller home—with no guest bedrooms and a lawn too small for team

sports—they felt excluded. "Our reaction," said their son Guy, "was, 'Where are we all going to play now?'"

Casa del Mar isn't as big as Casa Feliz, the Negris' former home. Casa Feliz had housed Dr. Max and Gloria Negri and their seven children easily, and later, when the widowed Max married Ana Doran (also a doctor), who had 10 children, it accommodated even more at various times. If that house was ever crowded, it was only with happy memories. How could tiny Casa del Mar possibly replace it?

The Negri and Doran children, it turns out, should have known their parents better. Before the senior Negris were even fully moved into their new house, Ana was mentally knocking out walls, converting the garage to a family room, and taking out the wall facing the pool. The result, says their daughter Kathy Doran-Hasey, is "the biggest little house in the West."

THE GARDEN TAKES SHAPE

Meanwhile, Max was out contemplating the seashore at the base of the cliff—so tantalizingly near, yet so inaccessible. He trampled out a path to the bottom, then widened and stabilized it and set out steps (134 in all), with help from his children and grandchildren (24 at last count). "Max has a way of making these things seem like fun," laughs Ana.

Once the path was in place, he put in retaining walls and planted trees, shrubs, ground covers, and vines. If a plant didn't slide off the slope or perish in the salt spray, he put in more.

At first the eclectic nature of the garden bothered daughter Kathy. A landscape designer, she felt duty-bound to suggest that Max stick to a theme. But now, she says, she just enjoys it. "Max's slope garden reflects his nature," she says. "It shows his spirit of adventure, his willingness to experiment, and his love of virtually every living thing."

And it fits Max's definition of paradise. "Happiness," he says, "is being in a garden with the people you love." ◆

By the bunch or by the sprig: Properly stored cilantro lasts up to two weeks.

NOEL BARNHURST

Keeping the fresh in herbs

Tender perishables last longer if you act like a florist

Fresh flavor is just a snip away if you keep a bouquet of tender green herbs in the kitchen. Basil, especially, thrives in a container of water on the kitchen counter, and the stems may even develop roots in several weeks.

But other delicate green-stemmed herbs, such as cilantro, parsley, and watercress, need more coddling. For their well-being, you need to control air, light, and temperature, says George K. York, extension food technologist at the University of California at Davis.

Oxygen in the air reacts with cut plants and creates brown or black spots on leaves. Spots first appear where the leaves are bruised.

Light breaks down the chlorophyll in herbs and makes yellow spots that often turn white. Chervil is quite sus-ceptible to this damage because its leaves are so thin.

Temperature that's warm enough to keep us comfortable will release the volatile oils in tender herb leaves. The room gets the fragrance that the herbs lose—unless they begin to grow, as basil does. All tender herbs except basil keep their flavor best in the refrigerator (basil leaves are susceptible to cold and turn black).

How herbs are grown also affects how long they last. Commercially pro-duced herbs and garden herbs may have different flavor and durability. Wendy Krupnick, former garden man-ager for Shepherd's Garden Seeds, ex-plains that many commercially pro-duced herbs are given high-nitrogen fertilizer to yield a quick crop. These herbs often contain more water, mak-ing them more perishable, and are less flavorful because they have fewer es-sential oils.

How well commercially grown cut herbs will keep also depends on when they were cut and how they have been handled since then. Wilted leaves often perk up if you cut off the damaged part of the stem and put it in water.

Although rinsed herbs (except basil), wrapped in towels and enclosed in a plastic bag, keep well enough for a day or two, their life is greatly extended when you store as follows.

FOUR STEPS TO FRESHNESS

1. Untie herbs and immerse in cool wa-ter, shaking gently to dislodge any soil or insects. Discard decayed stalks and leaves. Snip off stems just above a break or a bruise. Gently shake excess water from leaves (don't use a lettuce spinner; it bruises leaves).
2. Place stems in a container of water (a vase or canning jar) that holds them snugly, leaves above the rim.
3. Cover leaves loosely with a plastic bag, such as a produce bag.
4. Refrigerate, changing water when it looks murky. Snip off any parts of stems that show signs of decay. If you're stor-ing several jars, group them on a close-fitting rimmed tray to protect them from being knocked over. ◆

How to keep tender herbs fresh

Prepare herbs as described above, then use this chart as a storage guide. Their quality when stored af-fects how well they keep.

Herb	Storage	Days
Basil	countertop	up to 31
Chervil	refrigerator	up to 8
Chives	refrigerator	up to 9
Cilantro	refrigerator	up to 14
Dill	refrigerator	up to 9
Parsley	refrigerator	up to 21
Tarragon	refrigerator	up to 17
Watercress	refrigerator	up to 8

by **ANDREW BAKER**

Flame-colored fruits of the fiery 'Habanero' pepper fill a hanging basket. A plastic-lined polyester pouch keeps the rootball from drying out too quickly.

VEGETABLES *aloft*

*A Southern California gardener shares tips
for growing tomatoes and other tasty
crops in hanging baskets*

by SHARON COHOON

photographs by NORMAN A. PLATE

■ You know how it is. When your tomatoes start to color up,
you're out in your garden every morning to monitor their
progress. Finally, when you're sure they're ready, you go out to
pick them, taste buds aquiver, only to discover that someone else
got to them first.

That happened to Grace Mayeda once too often. The villains in
her garden in Orange, California, were her four Shetland sheep-
dogs: Hanako, Markie, Tanoki, and Cammie. "The dogs seemed to
have a sixth sense about when things were ripe," says Mayeda. "They
always got there before I did. Even to the beans and watermelon."
So Mayeda did something about it. She raised her crops. Off the
ground, that is, in hanging baskets well above the dogs' reach.

First she planted bush beans. When they proved successful, she
tried bush tomatoes, sweet and hot peppers, eggplant, zucchini,
even watermelon. She found compact varieties of each that were
good producers within the confines of a hanging basket. "If they
produce 70 percent of what a standard variety does, I consider
them a success," she says. Mayeda was so sold on vegetable baskets
that she introduced the idea at her family's nursery, M & M Nursery

in Orange. They've been popular with summer customers ever since.

Growing vegetables in hanging baskets has its drawbacks, admits Mayeda. Because their root development is limited, vegetables in hanging baskets need to be fed and watered frequently. But, she says, there are compensations. Space savings, for one thing. Stagger your baskets so they're at different levels, she says, and you can get a lot of crop into a little space. Monitoring and treating pests is easier, too. "It's hard to overlook a hornworm when it's at eye-level," says Mayeda. "And you don't have to stoop when you spray with BT [*Bacillus thuringiensis*]."

Crop protection, in fact, is the baskets' strongest selling point. Raise your crops and they're safe from snails, slugs, and rabbits. And, yes, even dogs. ◆

The best varieties for containers are compact growers. Here are some of Mayeda's favorites:

Bush beans: 'Blue Lake' and 'Burgundy'.

Eggplant: 'Bambino'.

Peppers: 'Yolo Wonder' and 'Habanero'.

Tomatoes: Red or yellow bush cherry and bush 'Roma'.

Watermelon: 'Garden Baby' and 'Yellow Doll'.

Zucchini: 'Black Beauty'.

Seeds for these varieties, as well as wire baskets and liners, are available by mail from M & M Nursery. To order, call (800) 644-8042 or visit the nursery's Web site, http://www.mmnursery.com.

Top left: 'Yellow Doll' is small but sweet—a perfect one-meal watermelon. Top right: 'Roma', still one of the best paste tomatoes, is just starting to ripen. Bottom: 'Blue Lake', the classic bush bean, grows surprisingly well in the confines of a basket.

VEGETABLE BASKET : PLANTING & CARE

Wire hanging baskets are best; they hold more soil than comparable redwood or plastic hanging baskets. Use 14-inch-diameter baskets for most vegetables; 16-inch or larger for watermelon and zucchini.

PLANTING. Line the baskets with sphagnum moss, or use handy pop-in liners. Fill the lined baskets with a good potting soil and 2 tablespoons of a controlled-release, all-purpose granular fertilizer per basket. A teaspoon of soil polymer at the bottom of the basket helps plants retain moisture in roots. Start beans from seed, if desired, but otherwise use seedlings.

Hang baskets from rafters, patio structures, or balconies in full sun, or where they'll get four hours or more of full afternoon sun. To promote uniform growth, rotate baskets every two or three days. Swivel hooks make this easy.

WATERING. Avoid overwatering newly planted seedlings so you don't stunt plant growth. Once seedlings become established, don't let them dry out. On hottest days, watering twice a day may be necessary. During hot, windy weather, move baskets out of direct wind and water immediately. If you didn't add soil polymers when planting, you can add them later by making as many as six small holes at least 6 inches deep around perimeter of plant and dropping a few crystals in each.

FERTILIZING. After seedlings are several weeks old, feed them with all-purpose soluble fertilizer at three- to four-week intervals, according to directions. Never fertilize a dry plant.

White flowers and silver foliage, the main ingredients of a moon garden, shine on a moonlit night and look cool by day. This pot is filled with 'Snowflake' candytuft (front), silver-leafed Artemisia 'Valerie Finnis' (center) and dusty miller (right), and Chrysanthemum paludosum.

NORMAN A. PLATE

Gardens made for moonlight

Creating a garden to be seen by the light of the moon might sound like an endeavor for insomniacs. But if you stroll through such a garden on a night when the moon shines bright, you'll understand its magical attraction.

The basic concept is simple: plant enough white flowers together to form a reflective surface for moonlight. The trick is to choose plants that complement one another and produce flowers throughout a long period. Plants with silver foliage also make handsome moonlight mirrors, and they mix well with white-flowered plants.

A moon garden can be any size and shape: a long border works well, but you might prefer a square, a crescent, or a lunar circle. You can even capture moonshine in a big terra-cotta pot.

You'll enjoy a moon garden most when you can linger and watch the subtle spectacle unfold: a cloud passing across the face of the moon, changing the mood of the garden, or the stroboscopic movement of a moth when moonlight strikes its wings.

When you shop for plants, remember that the best candidates for moon gardens are, ironically, sun-loving types, since they must be planted out in the open, away from trees and other objects that would otherwise obstruct moonlight. You'll probably need to visit several nurseries to get all the whites and silvers you need. Feel free to mix perennials and flowering shrubs, and tuck annuals into the bare spots. ◆

Plants that shine in the moonlight

TALL WHITE FLOWERS
- Azalea
- Cosmos
- Delphinium
- Foxglove (*Digitalis purpurea* 'Alba')
- Hollyhock
- Hydrangea
- Irises (bearded and Japanese)
- Lilies (daylily and Oriental lily)
- Phlox
- Rose
- Shasta daisy (tall types)

MEDIUM & LOW-GROWING WHITES
- Candytuft (*Iberis*)
- *Centranthus ruber* 'Albus'
- Chrysanthemum
- Lupine ('Noble Maiden')
- Nicotiana
- Peony
- Petunia
- Shasta daisy (low types like 'Little Princess')

SILVER FOLIAGE
- Artemisia ('Powis Castle', 'Silver King', 'Valerie Finnis')
- Dusty miller (*Senecio cineraria*)
- Lamb's ears (*Stachys byzantina*)
- Russian sage (*Perovskia atriplicifolia*)
- Santolina (*S. chamae-cyparissus*)
- Snow-in-summer (*Cerastium tomentosum*)

by STEVEN R. LORTON

NORMAN A. PLATE

Narrow side yard provides interest at every step. Rosy gazing globe echoes pink flowers of Leptospermum scoparium at left.

Heaven in a hard place

A Southern California designer transforms a "bowling alley" side yard into a showplace

Think like a plant for a minute. Your mission, should you decide to accept it, is this: Infiltrate a skinny, 18-inch strip of dirt and try to establish some roots. And, oh yes, try to look pretty while you're at it. The site will be as dark and dank as a cellar all winter, and your feet will never dry out. Then, come summer, it will feel like a furnace as the sun beats down and the reflected heat of walls on either side of you sucks any remaining moisture from your already desiccated leaves. Would *you* take this assignment if you were a plant? If it were forced upon you, would you survive?

Unfortunately, such a scenario is typical in cities and subdivisions where houses are packed together. About the only spaces left for a garden on some lots are the narrow strips of dirt between the walls. The canyon effect the walls create is hardly an ideal environment for plants; it shades them in winter and holds in heat during summer. No wonder most homeowners faced with such a garden space quickly throw in the trowel. This is landscaping hell.

Ross Holmquist faced this problem when he moved into his house in Lake Forest, California. Two narrow strips of earth bordering a concrete walkway the length of a bowling alley made up his main gardening space. His house walled the corridor on one side; his neighbor's walled the other side, just a few feet away. Holmquist, a landscape designer, initially thought of the site primarily as a design challenge. How

by **SHARON COHOON**

NORMAN A. PLATE

One way to make a long, narrow border more interesting is to force the eye to see it in segments. Ross Holmquist has used garden ornaments as the focal points of several of his vignettes. These include a gazing globe (left), which reflects the golden daylilies and other nearby flowers, and a stone greeting with mondo grass.

could he make the space seem less elongated? What could he do to create a view from indoors? But the longer he lived there, the more he let the plant survivors dictate the design. "I learned to love anything that lived," he laughs.

European white birch, the first thing Holmquist planted, not only survived but also solved a multitude of problems. The handsome white trunks of these trees and the graceful shadows they cast created the attractive view from indoors that he was seeking. The way the treetops gracefully canopied the walkway was another asset. The birches' deciduous habit also happened to be perfect for this space: When fully leafed out in summer, the trees provide pockets of shade perfect for sheltering seasonal annuals. But by conveniently dropping their leaves in winter, they allow more permanent plants full access to that season's limited light.

Finding understory plants that worked was largely trial and error. "The ones that survived . . . tolerate a wide range of conditions," says Holmquist. "They're real toughies." These include star jasmine, pink powder puff, and liriope. If they don't produce as many flowers as they do in other gardens, he forgives them. "You've got to remember that they only have half the growing season under these harsh conditions that they would in an ideal situation."

The site has taught Holmquist a valuable landscaping lesson: overreliance on color is always a temptation in our mild climate. This site has made him a connoisseur of textures.

"Lots of textural interest with just a few exclamations of color here and there is actually pretty restful," he says. "It may not be the garden I set out to create, but I've come to like it very much. I'm pretty happy in this space." ◆

TOUGH PLANTS FOR URBAN CANYONS

TREES
- Cajeput tree (*Melaleuca quinquenervia*)
- European white birch (*Betula pendula*)
- Fern pine (*Podocarpus gracilior*)
- Guava (*Psidium guajava*)
- Weeping Chinese banyan (*Ficus benjamina*)

SHRUBS
- Chinese lantern (*Abutilon hybridum*)
- Garden hydrangea (*Hydrangea macrophylla*)
- Heavenly bamboo (*Nandina*)
- Holly (*Ilex* species)
- Lavender starflower (*Grewia occidentalis*)
- New Zealand tea tree (*Leptospermum scoparium*)
- Pink breath of heaven (*Coleonema pulchrum*)
- Pink powder puff (*Calliandra haematocephala*)
- Star jasmine (*Trachelospermum jasminoides*)

PERENNIALS
- Calla lily (*Zantedeschia aethiopica*)
- Canna (*Canna*)
- Daylilies (*Hemerocallis* hybrids)
- Kaffir lily (*Clivia miniata*)
- Statice or sea lavender (*Limonium*)
- Sun begonia (*Begonia* 'Richmondensis')

GROUND COVERS
- Bellflower (*Campanula* species)
- Big blue lily turf (*Liriope muscari*)
- Blue fescue (*Festuca ovina* 'Glauca')
- Blue star creeper (*Laurentia fluviatilis*)
- Mondo grass (*Ophiopogon*)

GRASSES & GRASSLIKE PLANTS
- New Zealand flax (*Phormium tenax*)
- Papyrus (*Cyperus papyrus*)
- Purple fountain grass (*Pennisetum* 'Rubrum')

FERNS
- Holly fern (*Cyrtomium falcatum*)
- Lace fern (*Microlepia strigosa*)
- Mother fern (*Asplenium bulbiferum*)
- Sword fern (*Nephrolepsis exaltata*)

A LITTLE
water
music

*This small fountain can fill a garden with
the soothing sounds of trickling water*

by LAUREN BONAR SWEZEY

photographs by NORMAN A. PLATE

■ "A garden without water is like a theater without a stage,"
says English garden designer Rosemary Verey. But you don't
need a huge pond to bring water to your garden. The fountain shown here is elegant enough to enhance a formal patio
or leafy garden corner. It's easy to make from readily available materials. It's also a bath for birds.

To landscape architect Richard William Wogisch, who designed the fountain, the sight of falling water "adds motion
and life to a garden." And when that water is just a quiet
trickle, its melodious sound is also very soothing. Quiet
trickles don't splash either—a plus on a wood deck or patio.

A low terra-cotta bowl forms the fountain's base and
catches the falling water. A terra-cotta azalea pot (a container
that's wider than it is tall) is inverted in the bottom of the
bowl to support a strawberry pot and hide the recirculating
pump. Water is pumped up through clear tubing inside the
strawberry pot, gurgles out into a saucer on its top, and
drips lightly over the saucer's rim into the low bowl.

TIME: About four hours (excluding two-day drying time)

COST: About $225

TOOLS: Drill with ⅝-inch masonry bit, ¼-inch round file, paintbrush, shears (sharp), bucket

WHAT YOU NEED

• Tapered terra-cotta bowl, 24 inches wide and about 8¼ inches deep

• Terra-cotta azalea pot, 10½ inches wide and about 7½ inches deep

• Terra-cotta strawberry pot, 14 inches wide (at widest point) and about 13 inches tall

• Terra-cotta saucer, 9½ inches wide (sized to sit in your strawberry pot's top)

• Terra-cotta-colored plastic saucer, 12½ inches wide

• Submersible pump, with a flow adjustable to 2 feet

• Cubic-foot bag of ¾-inch river rock

• 2 feet of ½-inch clear vinyl tubing

• ½-inch barbed to ½-inch male brass pipe thread adapter

• ½-inch female to ¼-inch female brass bell reducer

• ¼-inch brass close nipple

• Terra-cotta vinyl latex sealer (such as Universal Terra Cotta Sealer)

• Waterproof adhesive (such as Liquid Nails)

• Silicone sealer

• Six 1-gallon water plants (available in many nurseries)

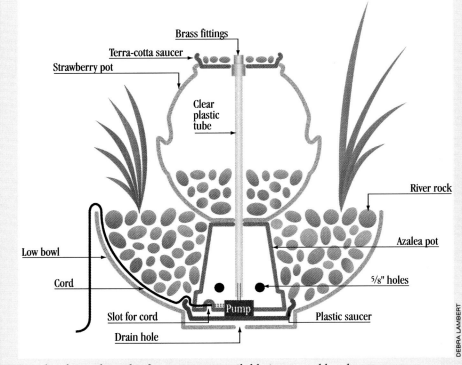

Supplies for making this fountain are available in general hardware stores. Pots are sold at nurseries.

1. Seal terra-cotta pots. Brush sealer on the inside of the low terra-cotta bowl, and on the inside and outside of the strawberry pot and the terra-cotta saucer. Allow to dry for 24 hours.

2. Drill holes, file slit. Drill four to six evenly spaced holes around and just below the 2-inch lip of the azalea pot. Also drill a hole in the center of the terra-cotta saucer. Using the round file, file a small notch in the lip of the azalea pot (for the submersible-pump cord).

3. Install brass fittings. Attach the barbed hose fitting to the vinyl tubing, and insert the threaded end through the hole in the terra-cotta saucer. Screw the bell reducer to the threaded end protruding through the saucer and attach the nipple to the bell reducer. Trim the hose to 14 inches.

4. Install saucers. Apply a band of waterproof adhesive to the bottom outside edge of the plastic saucer. Place the saucer in the bottom of the low bowl (it will fit snugly), level it, and weight it down with the bag of river rock.

Set the terra-cotta saucer in the strawberry pot's top, and insert the vinyl tubing through the bottom of the strawberry pot. Lift the saucer up slightly and apply adhesive to the base of the outer rim of the saucer; reset it in the strawberry pot opening. Allow both saucers to dry overnight.

5. Assemble the fountain. The next day, move all of the materials to the area where the fountain will be permanently positioned. Apply a bead of silicone sealer between the strawberry pot and the terra-cotta saucer to ensure that water doesn't seep through the crack. Allow to dry for two hours.

Set the pump on the plastic saucer inside the low bowl. Turn the azalea pot upside down over it. Position the strawberry pot on top of the azalea pot. At the same time, insert the vinyl tubing through the hole in the bottom of the azalea pot (the fit will be snug).

While supporting the pots, carefully tip the azalea pot and attach the tubing to the pump outlet (if it's too much of a juggling act, find someone to hold the pots while you attach the tubing). Thread the electrical cord through the notch in the pot lip and up over the edge of the low bowl. Level the pots by adjusting the azalea pot in the saucer.

6. Add the plants. Fill a bucket with water. Dip plants in it to wash off loose soil. Set aside temporarily.

Arrange the plants in the low bowl, interspersing low ones with taller ones. Fill in the bowl and bottom of the strawberry pot with river rock. Add decorative rock or river rock to the top saucer to camouflage the brass fittings.

Fill the low bowl with water until it just begins to overflow. Plug in the pump. The water will be a bit dirty until it reaches equilibrium after a few hours. As water evaporates, add more water; never let the pump run dry. ◆

It takes Susanna Gamble only minutes to arrange a bouquet of freshly cut roses from her farm.

ACEY HARPER

Garden-shopping in Carmel Valley

Browse for horticultural treasures on the pastoral outskirts of Carmel-by-the-Sea

Carmel's crescent of silver sand and the deep-sea wonders of Monterey's aquarium draw hordes of visitors year-round to the California coast. But a less crowded part of this tourist mecca beckons traveling gardeners. On a horticultural detour from Carmel or Monterey, you can drive into the rural heart of Carmel Valley and return laden with a choice plant or per-

fect pot, a bouquet of fragrant roses, and a wealth of gardening ideas.

The route is about a 25-mile round trip from State Highway 1. Along the way and in Carmel Valley Village, there are restaurants where you can dine and delis and farm stands where you can pick up supplies for a picnic in Garland Ranch Regional Park.

Barnyard. More than an acre of ter-

raced flower beds surround the barn-like buildings at this rustic shopping center, built by John and May Waldroup 21 years ago on the site of the old Hatton Ranch. Wander among the alstroemerias and roses and quiz longtime gardener John Lyons about his plantings. At noon on any Sunday through September, join a free garden tour led by a horticulturist; at other times arrange a

by **LINDA JOAN SMITH**

Bucketfuls of blooms are cut fresh daily at Gamble's Flower Farm; you can also cut your own cosmos (below) in the field.

tour by calling (800) 833-2276.

At the north end of the Barnyard, explore the outdoor nooks and crannies of **Succulent Gardens & Gifts.** Owner Robin Stockwell offers up a symphony of wind chimes, along with birdhouses, fountains, garden sculptures, gazing globes, steppingstones, bonsai pots, and more. Stockwell's specialty is succulents—more than 200 varieties are for sale in 2- to 6-inch pots—and he willingly shares tips for incorporating these plants into a landscape.

•*Where:* At the end of Carmel Rancho Lane. From State 1, turn east onto Carmel Valley Rd. (G16) and take the first right, Carmel Rancho Blvd.; then turn right again on Carmel Rancho Lane. Look for the Barnyard's hallmark windmill.

•*Hours:* The gardens at the Barnyard are always open; the shops are open 10–5:30 daily.

Pot Farm. Even many local gardeners have yet to discover the ceramic treasures stacked in the side yard of Hacienda Hay & Feed: more than 5,000 stoneware pots, tubs, urns, and oil

ACEY HARPER

jars—some richly glazed and all for sale at wholesale prices. Roosters, turkeys, and guinea hens strut among the imported wares, which range in color from cobalt to ocher, and in size from cup to cauldron. Owner Dave Nelson began selling pots three years ago when he bought the feed store; manager Gail Ludwig plans to start a cut-your-own herb garden this spring. A donkey, goats, and other animals stabled on the property will keep your kids entertained while you shop.

• *Where:* 7180 Carmel Valley Rd., just past Quail Lodge on the right.

• *Hours:* 9–5:30 Mon-Fri, 10–4:30 Sat-Sun.

Valley Hills Nursery. You won't find regimented rows of plants at this 1-acre nursery. Instead, you'll stroll along pathways that wind past ever-changing islands of cottage-garden perennials and California natives, through groves of boxed coast live oak and magnolia trees, and into a pair of color-filled greenhouses. Dick and Kazue Tanaka, who have owned the nursery for 22 years, estimate they tend more than 5,000 plant varieties. Look for unusual perennials such as 'Chiapensis' salvia with fuchsia pink blooms and 'Chameleon' euphorbia with wine red foliage. Or choose from an extensive array of standbys, from cyclamen to cypress.

• *Where:* 7440 Carmel Valley Rd., ½ mile east of Quail Lodge.

• *Hours:* 8–5 Mon-Sat.

Gamble's Flower Farm. Down a dusty drive, past olive, apple, and apricot trees, Carl and Susanna Gamble cultivate a flower lover's heaven on earth: nearly 2 acres of annuals, perennials, and 200 varieties of roses. Pick your own bouquet of bachelor's buttons, cosmos, snapdragons, stock, or sunflowers in season ($7) or have Susanna cut you a custom bouquet of roses—'Double Delight', 'Just Joey', or 'Mr. Lincoln'. A select stock of nursery plants and potted roses is also available.

• *Where:* 9000 Carmel Valley Rd. Immediately after you pass the Chateau Julien Winery (watch for the château's medieval-looking turret), make a sharp right at the Flower Farm sign.

• *Hours:* 9–6 Wed-Sat, 10–5 Sun.

Ornamental grasses shine at Valley Hills Nursery.

Griggs Nursery. Ask some local landscapers why they favor this new 2-acre nursery and they'll say, "Color"— from annual bedding plants to standout perennials. But owners Dean and Barbara Griggs, whose original nursery has been a Pacific Grove mainstay for 17 years, also specialize in uncommon indoor plants. Don't overlook the perennials in 4-inch containers, the terra-cotta pots, or the gifts, from birdhouses to topiaries.

• *Where:* 9220 Carmel Valley Rd., just around the curve from Gamble's Flower Farm.

• *Hours:* 8–5 Mon-Sat, 10–4 Sun.

Village Garden. Surrounded by Carmel Valley Village, which still reflects its ranching heritage and flower-child days, this nursery opens onto a decades-old display garden of California and Mediterranean native plants.

Gene and Lynne Iantorno bought the 1-acre nursery and adjoining garden on a whim six years ago; now they offer an extensive array of landscaping plants that run from shrub roses to Western natives like wild mock orange (*Philadelphus lewisii*). If you visit in summer, search out the Persian mulberry (*Morus nigra*), one of many mature trees on the property; after sampling its succulent black fruit, you might end up taking a sapling home.

• *Where:* 8 Pilot Rd. When you reach Carmel Valley Village on Carmel Valley Rd., turn left (north) on Pilot and look on your left for the cheerful trompe l'oeil cutouts of the Iantornos and their grandkids.

• *Hours:* 8–4 Tue-Sat, 9–4 Sun. ◆

Pairing the formal with the informal, the refined with the rustic, and the ornamental with the utilitarian gives this Northwest garden plenty of visual impact. For details on the plants and the structural elements, see page 216.

NORMAN A. PLATE

July

gardenguide

ROB PROCTOR

Wheelbarrow bouquet

Rolling planters made from carts or wagons
carry loads of summer color

by **ROB PROCTOR**

Any number of small garden or farm vehicles can be employed as vessels to hold a movable feast of flowers. In my Denver garden, a rusty old wheelbarrow has found new life as a portable container. Not only is it wide and deep enough to stuff with both annuals and perennials, but it also leaks, providing perfect drainage. I roll the flower-filled wheelbarrow to any spot in the garden that needs a lift.

My plant selections vary from year to year. One summer, daylilies might star with a sunny supporting cast of coreopsis, liatris, and sedums, as in the planting shown at left. Another summer, I might try a planting for partial shade, grouping 'Stargazer' Oriental lilies with coleus, nicotiana, and trailing ivy.

I've also put an old Radio Flyer wagon (much like the one I played with as a kid) to use as a portable planter. The wagon once served as a carrier for hauling nursery purchases from the alley to the garden. Then one day I noticed how great a load of bronze-leafed cannas and scarlet dahlias looked with the wagon's fading coat of red paint. Now my wagonload of tropical beauties adds a touch of whimsy to the garden.

Flowers planted in the same vehicle, such as those in my wheelbarrow, must share similar cultural requirements for sun or shade, soil, and water. But the vehicles don't necessarily need to be filled with soil (my wagon isn't deep enough); they can simply serve to hold a variety of conventional pots.

Beware of the slug-buster's troublesome cousin

Diatomaceous earth (DE) is a fine white powder made from diatoms, the ground fossilized shells of tiny water-dwelling organisms. One type, insecticidal DE, is an effective natural pesticide for controlling slugs, snails, and earwigs. When the powder is sprinkled around plants to form a barrier, its microscopically fine, sharp edges desiccate pests that crawl through it.

The trouble is, some gardeners confuse this type of DE with another type of DE used in swimming pool filters. The latter should *never* be used in the garden because it's a hazard to human health. The DE used in swimming pool filters is heat-treated, a process that converts the silica in DE to crystalline silica. According to the Environmental Protection Agency, crystalline silica has long been associated with silicosis, a progressive lung disease that may result in lung cancer in humans. Insecticidal DE is amorphous silica dioxide and has not been associated with lung cancer.

When shopping for DE to use in the garden, look for a product labeled insecticidal DE. If you can't find insecticidal DE locally, you can order it from Peaceful Valley Farm Supply, Box 2209, Grass Valley, CA 95945; (916) 272-4769.
— *Lauren Bonar Swezey*

BEN WOOLSEY

The boldest sea holly of all

The stars that burst in the sky this month are usually of the pyrotechnic type, in celebration of Independence Day. But in the beds of gardeners who grow *Eryngium giganteum*, stars will be exploding closer to the ground as this plant—the largest species of sea holly—bursts into bloom. The 3- to 6-inch-wide flower heads are composed of faint blue to silvery gray cones 2½ inches tall encircled by spiny bracts. The blooms last for many weeks on the plant; if cut, they dry beautifully without water.

One of the earliest plants to emerge in the spring, *Eryngium giganteum* develops flower spikes that resemble thistles. Plants eventually reach 3 feet.

E. giganteum, which is also known as Miss Willmott's ghost, is hardy enough to grow in all *Sunset* climate zones. Generally considered a biennial, sea holly is readily grown from seed.

Plants in 4-inch pots and 1-gallon cans are often available in nurseries from early spring until bloom time—July through September. Set out plants in quick-draining soil in a spot that gets full sun. Seeds of *E. giganteum* are sold by J. L. Hudson, Seedsman (Star Route 2, Box 337, La Honda, CA 94020). Plants are sold by Heronswood Nursery (360/297-4172). — *Steven R. Lorton*

gear

The Gardena multipurpose trigger nozzle ($16.99) does so many jobs well that you may never have to take it off the hose. Twist its rotating spray head to one of four settings and squeeze the trigger. Depending on the setting, you'll get a powerful jet, a gentle shower, a flat jet that's almost a mist, or an aerated stream that can serve as a bubbler. This deluxe unit comes with a trigger lock and a flow-control valve. There's also a quick-release collar for detaching the spray head from the hose coupling (caution: do not remove it while the hose is filled with water or the head will go blasting off). Many garden and home supply centers carry this nozzle. You can also order it by calling (800) 426-8419. — *Jim McCausland*

CURTIS ANDERSON

Try this sun-loving coleus

Rich colors and intricate details give these new coleus the look of miniature Persian rugs. But complex foliage patterns are only part of the news. These jazzed-up versions are also more sun-tolerant than most kinds of coleus. Sold as the Solar and Sunlovers series, these coleus have successfully grown in sun in San Gabriel, San Bernardino, and the San Fernando Valley—in the same sunny spots where *Catharanthus roseus* might grow.

The bright coleus in the photo below thrive in hanging baskets at M & M Nursery in Orange. Heat doesn't seem to bother them, either. In Southern California's desert areas, however, their sun tolerance is untested, and the traditional advice of "thin shade" is still safest.

Like their predecessors, these new coleus appreciate rich, loose soil,

ample water, and regular fertilizing. For best appearance, pinch stems often to encourage branching and compact growth and to remove flower buds. — *Sharon Cohoon*

EDDIE DANT

NORMAN A. PLATE

An artful illusion extends the garden

Only one of the pots pictured below needs water. And the worn-looking trowel—despite the mud on its blade—has never seen dirt. Even the window and the garden reflection in it are fakes. The whole scene, with the exception of the pot of pink begonias in the foreground, was produced with paint.

The trompe l'oeil was a solution to a long-standing dilemma at the Fullerton, California, residence of Sue and Steve Dutcher. A long stretch of garage wall faced their garden. "You had to look at that boring thing every single day," says Sue. But an overhang, which kept the area in perpetual shade, and a cement walkway that abutted the garage precluded shrouding the wall in vines and shrubs. It was a perplexing problem.

When the Dutchers saw a fake arch painted on a patio wall at a garden benefit show, they recognized their solution. So they commissioned Fullerton artist Tony Trafport to paint the scene shown. The 6- by 4-foot mural cost approximately $1,000.

Contrary to popular belief, paint readily takes to stucco. "The texture actually helps," Trafport says. And modern acrylics endure well. "I have 15-year-old paintings in full sun that still look great," he says. "But with all the protection this mural gets, it will probably outlast the Dutchers." — *S. C.*

Jungle magic

The long, sturdy limbs of the Florida figs that shade this tropical patio in San Diego make you think they were installed decades ago. But in truth, almost everything in this cool, green scene has been planted within the last four years. When Scott Sandel and Jim Marich bought this property in 1991, landscape architect Sandel decided to clear away the hodgepodge of existing vegetation and start over.

Sandel wanted the garden to look like "an outdoor living room that had been hacked out of the jungle." To create that effect, he started with two Florida figs (*Ficus rubiginosa*) in 36-inch boxes, which had to be craned in over an existing block wall, and four floss silk (*Chorisia speciosa*) trees in 24-inch boxes.

"I wanted an instant canopy," says Sandel. "I was too impatient to wait for shade to grow in." Once he had his shade umbrellas, Sandel put in his understory plants: Australian tree ferns, bird's nest ferns, bromeliads, ginger, Japanese aralia, and ligularia.

For a focal point and soothing sound, he added a 1,000-gallon koi pond with a small waterfall. The low red brick walls that retain the jungle on two sides also provide extra seating for parties. The red flagstone around the koi pond is echoed in the hardscaping of the large central patio.

As lush as this garden is, it fits into a total water-conserving landscape plan. The front yard of this property is planted with drought-tolerant natives, and the thirstier backyard plantings are efficiently irrigated with separate drip systems for sunny and shady areas, as well as a separate spray system for seasonal color. This "jungle" actually requires a lot less water to maintain than a comparable-size fescue lawn, says Sandel. And living under its shady canopy is a lot more inviting on hot summer days. — *S. C.*

Mature trees, planted from large boxes, create a tropical garden almost instantly

Pan's Garden

Garden objets d'art that deserve the label "art" are rare—but not at Pan's Garden. If you're looking for the perfect piece to adorn your garden or a garden room, this small retail nursery in Summerland, just south of Santa Barbara, has an extraordinary collection from which to choose. Douglas White, the proprietor responsible for the collection, was an art history major and has an educated, discerning eye. Sample booty includes statues of Pan, Artemis, and other members of the Greek pantheon molded from a mix of ground marble and polymers—a semitranslucent composite material with the grainy smoothness of stone; handmade furniture; small, freestanding water elements; painted wood figurines from Indonesia of roosters, monkeys, and other animals; Tibetan prayer flags; Mexican-made gargoyles; elaborate stepping stones that you see in mail-order catalogs (but at a fraction of the price); and pots, pots, and more pots. There are plants at Pan's, too, though it may take you awhile to get to them— the nursery is small, but there's a lot to browse through. Allow yourself time.

Pan's Garden is at 2360 Lillie Ave., just off U.S. Highway 101, Summerland. Open 9 to 6 daily; (805) 969-6859. — *S. C.*

PAUL BOWERS

GARY PARKER

GREAT DESTINATION

Flowers forever

Late summer is showtime at Goldsmith Seeds, one of the world's largest wholesale breeders of annual garden color. The acres of brightly colored marigolds, petunias, salvias, and other popular garden annuals light up the company's fields and display beds in Gilroy, California, just 30 miles south of San Jose.

A new 2-acre public display garden features Goldsmith's most recent introductions, available at retail nurseries. A wheelchair-accessible pathway meanders past rich green lawns and brightly colored flower beds filled with gems such as Maverick geraniums in red, pink, and salmon; miniature Fantasy petunias in carmine, light salmon, and sky blue; and bicolor Salsa salvias in light purple, purple, and rose. Arbors and benches provide cool spots to take a break.

In the adjacent 6-acre trial grounds, more than 5,000 experimental varieties grow beside older varieties. (Goldsmith staffers compare the two for performance.) Some of the experimental flowers are eventually released into the nursery trade. The area is also an official trial site for Fleuroselect of Europe and All-America Selections.

Goldsmith Seeds is at 2280 Hecker Pass Highway (State 152). From U.S. 101 in Gilroy, take State 152 west about 5 miles. For details, call (408) 847-7333. The gardens are open daily during daylight hours; admission is free.

— L. B. S.

NATIVE PLANTS

Bubble gum for hummingbirds

The mint family includes a huge array of plants with fragrances and flowers that hummingbirds love. One of the more unusual of these is *Agastache cana*, an herbaceous perennial that bears bubble gum–scented flowers. Hummingbirds hone in on the tubular magenta blooms, which appear in late summer on bushy 2- to 3-foot-tall plants. As you would expect of a native to New Mexico and West Texas, *A. cana* takes heat and drought in stride.

Look for *A. cana* (sometimes called double bubble mint or hummingbird's mint) at nurseries that specialize in native plants. Planted this month from

CHARLES MANN

nursery stock, *A. cana* will start flowering before the end of summer. Set out plants in well-drained soil in a spot that gets full sun. But even though established *A. cana* plants tolerate drought, it's best to water new transplants weekly until the weather cools off in autumn.

If you can't find *A. cana* in local nurseries, you can order plants from A High Country Garden (800/925-9387) and plants or seed from Plants of the Southwest (800/788-7333).

— J. M.

DESIGN TIPS

A quick study in contrasts

Contrasting elements are commonly used to enhance the visual impact of a garden. Gary Craig of Yelm, Washington, is a master of contrasts, using plant materials and garden structures to add interest at several levels. Even in a small slice of his garden pictured on page 210, you can easily see the pairing of the formal with the informal, the refined with the rustic, and the ornamental with the utilitarian.

Consider Craig's use of plants. The formal geometric shapes of globe arborvitae (*Thuja occidentalis* 'Globosa') and dwarf Alberta spruce (*Picea glauca* 'Conica') contrast with the freewheeling vines overhead—a flowery cloud of honeysuckle and a leafy cascade of hops—and the loose, open form of daylilies.

Craig also makes good use of contrasting structural elements. An ornate teak bench plays off a raised bed made of unstained redwood. At the end of the bed, a decorative finial points with Victorian dignity to the rustic arbor, which in turn supports a birdhouse with classic architectural lines.

The raised bed is one of 12 such planters Craig built to perform both ornamental and utilitarian functions in a 40- by 50-foot space. The 2-foot-tall beds, which vary in width and shape, are made from 2-by-12s stacked two on edge. The 2-by-12s are joined at the corners to 4-by-4 posts with screws. Craig fills the beds with a rich planting mix consisting of 2 parts humus, 2 parts mushroom compost, 1 part aged steer manure, and 1 part peat moss. In addition to conifers and assorted seasonal flowers, the beds support a variety of herbs and vegetables for Craig's kitchen table. — S. R. L.

Pacific Northwest Garden Notebook

by **STEVEN R. LORTON**

As predictable as our weather is, it always seems to befuddle Northwesterners. When the rest of the country is donning linen jackets, we're still wearing our woollies. I can't remember a Fourth of July that wasn't cold and wet. Then July 15 rolls around and all the fussing we've done about the soggy weather for the last eight months turns into the annual hysteria about the lack of rain. Summer drought is a perfectly natural condition in the Northwest, and you can cope with it in one of two ways: either turn on the sprinklers (if local water-use ordinances permit) or embrace the thousands of unthirsty plants that stand up to our seasonal drought. Frankly, I prefer the latter approach.

Take a tip from Richard Hartlage of Seattle. He loves to grow big plants in pots but never worries about watering. Richard recommends staghorn sumac (*Rhus typhina* 'Laciniata') as a very dramatic container plant (to 15 feet) with big, ferny leaves and velvety stems. Conical red fruit clusters appear in autumn and stay on the plant through winter. Even in a pot, it takes hot, dry weather in stride as long as you soak it thoroughly once a week.

You'll find many more unthirsty plants growing in the 150-foot-long drought demonstration border at Joy Creek Nursery in Scappoose, Oregon. This border brims with good ideas for handsome, heat-beating combinations, including butterfly bushes, lavenders, penstemons, sedums, daisy-flowered

MARINA THOMPSON

Inula royleana, and ornamental grasses. The nursery, at 20300 N.W. Watson Rd., is open 9 to 5 daily through the end of November. If you can't visit, call the nursery at (503) 543-7474 for a copy of its catalog ($2), which lists nearly 1,000 varieties.

Of course, no plants are better equipped to deal with the Northwest's climatic swings than our natives. And if you want to know which are worth growing, check out *Gardening with Native Plants of the Pacific Northwest,* by Arthur R. Kruckeberg (University of Washington Press, Seattle, 1996; $35). I've consulted the first edition so often that my copy is tattered—and cherished. Now there's a revised and enlarged second edition filled with complete information about everything from the stately silver fir (*Abies amabilis*) to the cream-colored death camas (*Zigadenus elegans*).

THAT'S A GOOD QUESTION

Q: I was recently amazed to hear a speaker refer to roses as drought tolerant. Is this true? — *Willa Trask, Woodway, Washington*

A: Yes and no. To develop the big, flouncy flowers they're famous for, hybrid tea roses must have plenty of water. But the old-timers—shrub roses (like *Rosa rugosa*), ramblers, and species roses—sail through hot, dry summers. Old roses growing along fencerows in the country and shrub roses thriving in highway medians depend on rain alone.

Northern California Garden Notebook

by **L A U R E N   B O N A R   S W E Z E Y**

About 25 years ago, when my brother-in-law was just a boy, he planted a redwood seedling (*Sequoia sempervirens*) in his parents' small backyard. For the first dozen years, it was a charming little tree with lovely deep-green foliage and an elegant, pyramidal shape. Then, like Jack's beanstalk, it grew and grew. Soon, it towered over the house's second-story roof. It was a handsome tree, but it robbed the soil of moisture, so the surrounding plants had difficulty surviving. And with every storm, it dropped many branchlets, smothering the plants below.

Now, I garden under this 40-foot-tall memento to a child's whim. Though still beautiful, this tree is at the root of all of my gardening woes. To compensate for severe soil-moisture loss in summer, I irrigate the plants below the tree with drip, so water is distributed directly to the roots of each one. But some of the plants still struggle.

If you're thinking about planting a redwood tree, here's some advice. Don't plant one in a small garden. In larger gardens, plant the tree well away from the house foundation; its trunk grows very big. If you want to grow plants beneath the tree, try native woodland plants that thrive in dry shade—*Dichelostemma* (*Brodiaea*), evergreen

MARINA THOMPSON

currant, *Heuchera micrantha,* and Pacific Coast iris.

THAT'S A GOOD QUESTION

Q: Is sewage sludge safe to use on food crops? I understand that it may contain heavy metals. — *Sacramento*

A: Sewage sludge that has been processed to make a high-quality soil amendment is usually referred to as a biosolid—and as such is exhaustively tested and regulated. Biosolids are tested for 10 heavy metals. If the amount of heavy metals in these products falls below certain levels, the amendments are deemed safe for land applications (including potting soil). Still, possible safety issues surround biosolids. "[Researchers] determine a particular material is bad for you, then they allow a certain intake," says Jim West of the Soil and Plant Laboratory in Santa Clara. "Some leafy vegetables tend to accumulate heavy metals in their leaves. If leafy vegetables are a major part of someone's diet, it could create a problem." Gardeners who grow lots of leafy vegetables to eat should probably avoid mixing biosolids into the soil around them.

Southern California Garden Notebook

by **SHARON COHOON**

You'd never call me a tool freak. I usually make do with whatever rusty old thing happens to be lying around. But after a visit to Denman & Company, a store in Placentia that specializes in quality garden tools, I'm getting hooked. Bob Denman is pretty eloquent in his arguments for "investing in the right tool for the job."

Take the Pest Blaster—a nozzle that adjusts down to a stream that's almost as fine as a laser beam. You can dispatch aphids with surgical precision using this weapon. Attach the Blaster to Denman's long-reach watering wand, adjust the nozzle to a narrow, high-pressure cone of water, and blast away the spider mites hiding out under your rose leaves—without getting your jeans as wet as the roses in the process. The whole assembly costs $40.

Another nifty tool is the Screen Aire nozzle ($23). So soft is the water stream from this commercial-grade nozzle that you can water dozens of pots in seconds without displacing a speck of dirt.

Denman & Company sells products by mail; for a brochure, call (714) 524-0668. But since the brochure lists only a fraction of the store's inventory, consider a visit (1202 E. Pine St.) even if Placentia isn't in your neighborhood. You could make a day of it. The Fullerton Arboretum on the Cal State Fullerton campus is nearby and has great plant sales on weekends. The arboretum is at the inter-

MARINA THOMPSON

section of Yorba Linda Boulevard and Associated Road, one block west of State Highway 57. Pixie Treasures, a Yorba Linda retail nursery specializing in miniature roses, isn't far away (4121 Prospect Ave.) and is always fun to visit. Also in Yorba Linda is the Richard Nixon Library & Birthplace (18001 Yorba Linda Blvd.), which has gorgeous rose gardens.

THAT'S A GOOD QUESTION

Q: "I'm still getting blossom-end rot on my tomatoes [dark, sunken areas at the bottom of fruits] despite the fact that I'm watering more often and mulching. What now?" — *Linda Burns, Santa Barbara*

A: Inconsistent levels of soil moisture are the major cause of blossom-end rot. First, make sure you really *are* watering thoroughly enough. Saturate the soil a couple of feet all around the plant so the whole rootball takes up moisture, says Vincent Lazaneo, horticultural adviser at the UC Cooperative Extension in San Diego. Avoid high-nitrogen fertilizers. You might try applying a calcium supplement. (Blossom-end rot is a calcium uptake disorder.) Mike Hirsch, manager at Anderson's La Costa in Encinitas, likes Kelzyme (fossilized kelp). Apply ¼ cup suspended in two quarts of water per plant, or gypsum (calcium sulfate) in the same proportions. Foli-Cal, a foliar form of calcium, is another possibility, says Lazaneo.

Westerner's Garden Notebook

by **JIM McCAUSLAND**

Now, as summer irrigation begins in earnest, is when I judge how successful I've been at grouping plants according to water use. When I see one wilted-looking plant surrounded by robust, turgid neighbors, I know the wilted one is in the wrong place. It will do better in a community of plants that need more frequent irrigation. In nature, plants live with neighbors having similar needs, so it's no surprise that they want the same thing in the garden. Identify problem plants now, and move them in fall.

TWO FERTILE WEB SITES

It's 9 on Saturday morning and you've decided to start your first compost pile. But how? If you've got an Internet connection, the Colorado State and New Mexico State University Cooperative Extension sites on the World Wide Web can give you instant help with that and innumerable other gardening problems.

For Colorado, just visit http://www.colostate.edu/Depts/CoopExt/. From there you can download extension publications or transfer to a related site with more localized information. A great example is CSU's Tri River Area Gardening & Horticulture site, which lists workshops you can attend and offers local pointers on everything from pest control to pruning.

For New Mexico, visit http://www.cahe.nmsu.edu/cahe/ces/Welcome.html. From there you can find extension publications or transfer to NMSU's Yard and Garden site (http://www.cahe.nmsu.edu/cahe/ces/yard/), where you'll find answers to gardening questions you probably haven't even thought of yet.

BONING UP ON POISONOUS PLANTS

A young friend asked for help in identifying edible plants, but his parents were afraid he'd eat the wrong ones and be poisoned. It occurred to me that if he studied poisonous plants first, he'd have a healthy respect for them when he started studying edible ones. Two books will help my friend in his quest.

Medical Botany, by Walter Lewis and Memory Elvin-Lewis (John Wiley & Sons, New York, 1977; $59.95), has a wealth of information about plants—including their poisonous and medicinal properties—and offers some engrossing bits of folklore. Written by two professors at Washington University in St. Louis, this book makes fascinating reading for anybody from a casual gardener to a botanist.

Common Poisonous Plants and Mushrooms of North America, by Nancy Turner and Adam Szczawinski (Timber Press, Portland, 1995; $24.95), is an excellent reference for identifying poisonous plants, learning about their toxicity, and getting treatment information quickly.

THAT'S A GOOD QUESTION

Q: After a walk through my summer garden, I invariably come inside with my jeans streaked with lily pollen. How do I get it off my clothes?
A: Don't try to brush it off with your hand; the oil from your skin will mix with the pollen and smear it into the fabric. Instead, try to get it off with a hairbrush. If that doesn't work, apply a clothing stain remover like Shout or a concentrated detergent like Wisk. As a last resort, hang the clothes in the sun. After about three days, the sun will have bleached the pollen out. If you're still fed up with pollen stains, but don't want to give up on lilies, switch to pollen-free double-flowered varieties.

Planting

☐ **ANNUALS.** It's a long way to frost, so if you get annuals into the ground or containers quickly, you have a long season of summer flowers ahead. Buy plants in sixpacks and 4-inch pots. Put them in tubs or buckets of water (so that the top of the soil is covered) and let them soak overnight. Remove them from their containers, loosen the rootballs, and plant.

☐ **CROPS.** Seed for beets, broccoli, bush beans, carrots, chard, Chinese cabbage, kohlrabi, lettuce, peas, radishes, scallions, spinach, and turnips can all be sown directly into the ground.

☐ **SHRUBS.** If you succumb to the urge to buy a shrub, be careful of the heat for the next three months. Plants are probably safer in the ground than in pots. Dig a generous hole, enrich it with plenty of organic matter, fill it, and let it soak down several times to thoroughly wet the surrounding soil. Plant, water well again, mulch, and continue to water until fall rains start. Do not fertilize until next spring.

Maintenance

☐ **CARE FOR GROUND COVERS.** To keep them neat and compact, shear ground covers back after they've bloomed. Scatter a complete dry fertilizer around beds and water in well.

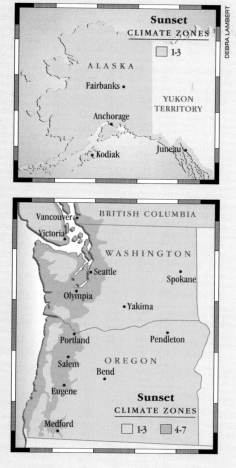

☐ **FEED CHRYSANTHEMUMS.** For best bloom this autumn, feed plants every three weeks until buds start to show color. When the first bloom opens, feed weekly.

☐ **FUSS WITH FUCHSIAS.** Snip off blooms as they fade to keep flowers coming. Feed plants monthly with a complete liquid plant fertilizer.

☐ **IRRIGATE WISELY.** Beds of annuals, perennials, and shrubs should be watered early in the morning to minimize the loss from evaporation and to allow plants time to dry off so that mildew won't get going. Lawns can be watered in the evening.

☐ **MANAGE THE COMPOST PILE.** Keep adding organic matter and turn the pile. If it's dry, give it a good soaking.

☐ **MONITOR HOUSE PLANTS.** If plants are summering outdoors, watch for aphids and other critters. Check daily to make sure plants have enough water. Hose off dusty leaves. If normally green leaves take on a bronzy cast, shelter them from the sun.

☐ **MULCH SHRUBS.** A 3- to 4-inch layer of mulch under shrubs is a great way to conserve moisture.

☐ **TEND STRAWBERRIES.** Clean up beds. Remove dead leaves and stems. Fertilize and water plants thoroughly.

Pest and weed control

☐ **ATTACK THISTLES.** Cut them to the ground before the flowers become seed heads. If you do this consistently for several years, your thistle population will shrink dramatically, if not die out altogether.

☐ **BATTLE SLUGS.** The heat may chase them into hiding, but they're there. A little bait in the cool spots will go a long way right now. Set out bait under stones, along the edges of walks, and near foundations.

Planting

☐ **PLANT A PATRIOTIC POT.** Nurseries sell many plants in full bloom right now. For a Fourth of July display, fill a pot with red-, white-, and blue-flowered plants. For red, try annual phlox, celosia, flowering tobacco (*Nicotiana*), geranium, petunia, *Salvia coccinea*, and scarlet sage. For white, try alyssum, annual phlox, dahlia, dwarf cosmos, flowering tobacco (*Nicotiana*), geranium, heliotrope, petunia, and a white variety of scarlet sage. For blue, choose from gentian sage, lobelia, mealy-cup sage, petunia, and verbena.

☐ **PLANT FALL VEGETABLES.** Zones 1–2: For harvest in fall (except in highest altitudes), plant beets, broccoli, bush beans, cabbage, carrots, cauliflower, green onions, peas, spinach, and turnips. Below 5,000 feet, plant winter squash among spinach; the spinach will be ready to harvest before the squash takes over.

☐ **SET OUT MUMS.** To add rich and bright colors to the fall garden, plant garden chrysanthemums now. If plants haven't formed flower buds, pinch growing tips to keep plants compact.

Maintenance

☐ **CARE FOR CONTAINER PLANTS.** Flowers and shrubs growing in containers dry out quickly in summer, and constant watering drains the soil of nutrients. Water pots often enough to keep the soil moist. Every time you water, fertilize with a half-strength dilution of

Eureka
Redding
CALIFORNIA
NEVADA
Mendocino
Santa Rosa
Sacramento
San Francisco
San Jose
Sunset
CLIMATE ZONES
Monterey
Fresno
☐ Mountain (1-2)
☐ Valley (7-9)
☐ Inland (14)
☐ Coastal (15-17)

DEBRA LAMBERT

liquid fertilizer or use the dosage recommended on the label every couple of weeks. If soil dries out and water rolls off the top of it, use a wetting agent (available at nurseries) diluted with water to rewet the soil.

☐ **CARE FOR LAWNS.** Keep the mowing height high during summer's heat; mow when the grass is about a third taller than the recommended height. For bluegrass and fescue, mow when the grass is 3 to 4 inches tall, with your mower set at 2 to 3 inches. Cut Bermuda grass when it's not quite 2 inches tall, with the mower set at 1 inch. If your lawn is full of crabgrass (broad-spreading weed with blue-green foliage) and it has set seed, collect the clippings after mowing to keep the weed from spreading.

☐ **DIVIDE IRISES.** Dig up old clumps with a spading fork, then cut the rhizomes apart with a sharp knife. Be sure to include a leaf with each division. Replant the younger, more vigorous sections of rhizome.

☐ **LET ROSES REST.** Zone 17: Heat-stressed roses will give a much more spectacular bloom in fall if you allow them to rest a bit now. Let rose hips form, and stop fertilizing the plants. Water often enough to keep roses healthy, but don't water heavily. In late summer, trim off hips and apply fertilizer to encourage a magnificent fall flush of bloom.

☐ **POLLINATE MELONS, SQUASH.** When the weather is hot, high temperatures may inhibit fruit set. To aid pollination, use an artist's brush to gather yellow pollen from freshly opened male flowers and dust it onto the stigma of female flowers, which have slightly enlarged bases. You can also pull off male flowers, gently remove petals, and shake flowers directly over the female flowers.

Pest control

☐ **CONTROL TOMATO HORNWORMS.** Look for chewed leaves and black droppings, then hunt through foliage for these fat green worms. Handpick the worms and destroy them. If they're still small, spray with BT (*Bacillus thuringiensis*).

Planting

☐ **ADD SUMMER COLOR.** It's too hot and too late in the season to plant masses of color, but not to tuck a few annuals into bare spots. Try *Catharanthus roseus* or petunias in the sun and impatiens in the shade. New color choices this year make these old standbys look fresh again.

☐ **PLANT VEGETABLES.** In coastal and inland gardens (zones 22–24 and 18–21, respectively), you can still plant vegetables for a late-summer harvest. Plant seeds of bush beans, carrots, corn, cucumbers, and summer squash. Set out seedlings of cucumbers, eggplant, melons, peppers, pumpkins, squash, and tomatoes. In the low desert (zone 13), plant pumpkins and winter squash.

☐ **SOW FLOWERS.** Plan ahead for color next spring. Sow seeds of Canterbury bells, foxglove, hollyhocks, verbascum, and other biennials in flats or pots now. In September, transplant to the garden when seedlings are 4 to 5 inches tall. July is a good month to start spring perennials and annuals from seed, too.

Maintenance

☐ **CARE FOR FRUIT TREES.** Prune fire blight damage from apple, loquat, pear, and quince trees. Make cuts 12 inches below infected tissue on large branches, 4 to 6 inches below on smaller ones. Wash foliage periodically to remove dust and honeydew secretions and to dislodge aphids, spider mites, whiteflies, and other pests.

Clean foliage also encourages beneficial insects like parasitic wasps.

☐ **CARE FOR LAWNS.** Cool-season grasses are slowing down. Leave ryegrass 1½ to 2 inches tall, and fescues 2 to 2½ inches tall so there will be enough foliage left for the lawn to produce food. Warm-season grasses like Bermuda, St. Augustine, and zoysia, on the other hand, are growing rapidly. Keep them shorter than 1 inch to lessen thatch buildup.

☐ **FERTILIZE SELECTIVELY.** Warm-season annuals benefit from a monthly feeding. So do most summer vegetables. (Tomatoes are an exception—too much nitrogen produces lots of leaves and little fruit.) Also this month, feed warm-season lawns and subtropicals such as ba-

nanas and hibiscus and anything container-grown. Give camellias and azaleas their last feeding of the year to promote next year's flowers. Water plants thoroughly a day or two before feeding; then deep-water again immediately afterward.

☐ **CARE FOR CYMBIDIUMS.** Next year's flower spikes are developing now. To ensure proper development, water weekly and feed plants with a high-nitrogen fertilizer this month and next. Follow label directions.

☐ **DIVIDE IRISES.** Remove old, overgrown clumps of bearded irises. Cut off healthy new rhizomes at the outer edge of the mother clump with a sharp knife and discard the woody center. Dust ends of cut rhizomes with soil sulfur and plant 1 to 2 feet apart. Barely cover with soil.

Pest control

☐ **CATERPILLARS.** Geraniums, nicotiana, and petunias are favorites of geranium budworm (alias tobacco budworm). At first signs of the green larvae, spray with *Bacillus thuringiensis*. Inspect tomato plants for tomato hornworms. Treat small worms with BT; pick off larger ones.

☐ **SPIDER MITES.** Spray the foliage of roses and other plants plagued by spider mites with a strong stream of water, directed especially at the underside of the leaves.

Planting and harvest

□ **PLANT FALL VEGETABLES. In all but** the highest elevations, plant beets, broccoli, bush beans, cabbage, cauliflower, carrots, green onions, peas, spinach, and turnips. Below 5,000 feet, plant winter squash among spinach plants; it will cover the ground when you harvest the spinach. Above 7,000 feet, plant warm-season vegetables in large pots; if temperatures are predicted to drop below 60°, move them under cover.

□ **PLANT IRISES. Dig** overcrowded clumps of bearded irises three weeks after flowers fade. Discard any dried-out or mushy rhizomes; cut apart healthy ones, trim the leaves back to 6 inches, and replant in fast-draining soil in full sun. Plant new rhizomes in the same way.

□ **HARVEST VEGETABLES, FLOWERS. As** vegetables mature, pick them often to keep new ones coming and to keep ripe ones from becoming overmature (cucumbers and zucchini) or downright rotten (tomatoes). Also pick flowers before they go to seed to encourage continued bloom.

Maintenance

□ **CARE FOR BULBS. In** coldest climates, pluck faded flowers and seed heads from daffodils, tulips, and other spring-flowering bulbs. Let leaves remain until they brown. When bloom is finished, feed plants with high-phosphorus fertilizer.

Sunset
CLIMATE ZONES

☐ 1-3 ■ 10-11

□ **COMPOST. Add** leafy garden debris, grass clippings, and annual weeds to the compost pile. Turn and water it regularly to keep it working.

□ **FERTILIZE. Feed** annuals and vegetables with high-nitrogen fertilizer, watering it in well.

□ **MULCH. To** conserve moisture and reduce weeds, apply organic material around and under plants.

□ **MAINTAIN ROSES. After** each bloom cycle, remove any faded flowers, cutting them off just above a leaf node that has five leaflets (the nodes closest to the flower have three leaflets). Then fertilize and water the plants deeply in preparation for the next round of bloom.

□ **POLLINATE MELONS, SQUASH. In** hot-summer areas, high temperatures inhibit fruit set on melons and squash. You can improve matters by daubing pollen-bearing male flowers with a small artist's brush, then "painting" the pollen onto female flowers (they have swollen bases).

□ **PRUNE CANE BERRIES. After** harvest, remove old raspberry canes as they begin to die. This encourages air circulation, which helps prevent mildew. (In coldest climates, wait until August.)

□ **STAKE TALL PLANTS. If** you haven't already done so, stake beans, delphiniums, peas, peonies, and tomatoes against high winds. Drive stakes at least 1 foot into the ground and tie plants securely to the stakes.

□ **THIN FRUIT TREES. On** trees with heavy fruit set, thin plums 2 inches apart, and apples, nectarines, and peaches at least 4 inches apart.

□ **WATER. Continue** a regular deep-watering program for ground covers, lawns, shrubs, and trees.

Pest control

□ **CONTROL SPIDER MITES. Mottled** leaves and fine webs indicate the presence of spider mites; spray with insecticidal soap or a stronger miticide. Keep foliage free of dust by rinsing with water.

Planting and harvest

☐ **PLANT FALL CROPS.** Zones 1–2 and 10–11: Plant beets, broccoli, cabbage, carrots, cauliflower, green onions, leaf lettuce, peas, spinach, and turnips for fall harvest. In zone 10 (Sedona, Albuquerque, El Paso), also plant cantaloupe, eggplant, okra, peppers, pumpkins, tomatoes, watermelons, and winter squash. Plant potatoes at month's end.

☐ **HARVEST SUMMER VEGETABLES, FLOWERS.** As crops mature, pick them often to keep new ones coming and to keep ripe ones from becoming overmature (cucumbers, zucchini) or downright rotten (tomatoes). Pick flowers before they go to seed to encourage continued bloom.

Maintenance

☐ **CARE FOR ROSES.** After each bloom cycle, remove faded flowers, cutting them off just above a leaf node with five leaflets. Then fertilize and water plants deeply in preparation for the next round of bloom.

☐ **COMPOST.** Add leafy garden debris, grass clippings, and annual weeds to the compost pile. Turn and water it regularly to keep it working.

☐ **FERTILIZE.** Zones 1–2 and 10–11: Feed annuals and vegetables with a complete fertilizer.

☐ **STAKE TALL PLANTS.** Stake beans, delphiniums, peas, peonies, and tomatoes against high winds.

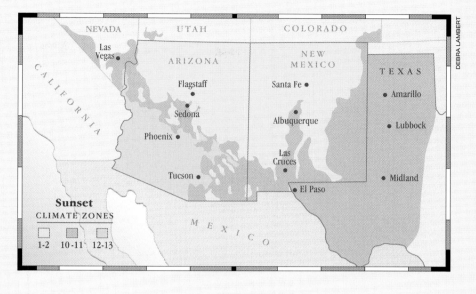

☐ **MULCH.** Apply a 3-inch layer of organic mulch around the bases of permanent plants to conserve the moisture in the soil and give plants a cool root run.

☐ **TEND CYMBIDIUMS.** To help build buds for next year's bloom, apply a quarter-strength dose of liquid fertilizer every time you water.

☐ **THIN TREES.** Open up top-heavy trees like acacia, Brazilian pepper, mesquite, and olive to protect them from strong winds. Take out suckers; dead, diseased, or injured wood; and branches that run closely parallel to each other.

☐ **WATER.** Water annual vegetables and flowers only after the top inch of soil has dried out. Basins and furrows help direct water to the roots. Deep-rooted permanent plants can be watered less often, but water them deeply whenever you do irrigate.

Pest and weed control

☐ **BUDWORMS.** When budworms eat through the buds of geraniums, nicotiana, penstemons, and petunias, preventing flowering, spray plants every 7 to 10 days with *Bacillus thuringiensis*.

☐ **SOLARIZE SOIL.** To clean soil of weeds, cultivate and water the soil, then cover with a sheet of clear plastic for two to three weeks. The sun will heat the soil under the plastic and kill the weed seedlings.

No time to garden?

Take a few tips on low-maintenance care from two busy Westerners

English country gardens overspilling with flowers may make us weak-kneed with envy. But they only *look* carefree. It's work maintaining that fine line between insouciance and seediness. Someone's out there in Wellingtons every day, tending all those flowers. And forget about owning one of those classical French gardens with their neatly scissored hedges. It takes an army of pruners to keep those shrubs in line.

Most of us already juggle career, family, and community obligations. If we manage to squeeze in an hour of gardening on weekends, we consider ourselves lucky. But we don't have to throw in the trowel and roll out the AstroTurf. We just need to toss aside those fantasies of inherently high-maintenance gardens and follow new role models.

Take Scott Spencer in Fallbrook, California, and Rami Courtney in Santa Barbara, for example. Both homeowners have attractive gardens that take little time. Spencer's island beds filled with undemanding plants require minimal care, while Courtney's front yard of easygoing shrubs needs even less. These are gardens we can realistically achieve.

One hour per week

■ Scott Spencer's backyard—a series of ornamental borders separated by broad pathways of decomposed granite—looks like a full-time job. Each island bed is a complex tapestry of textures and colors. But Spencer is too busy creating new gardens at Buena Creek Gardens nursery in San Marcos, California, to spend much time on his own garden. The large (75 ft. by 16 ft.) border shown at right and two others like it manage fine with only an hour a week of Spencer's labor.

One reason for the garden's easy-care design is its plants: large flowering shrubs such as salvias, ornamental grasses like *Miscanthus sinensis*, and evergreen subshrubs like santolina are Spencer's mainstays. Perennials play a secondary role in his borders.

These plants all take temperatures topping 90° in stride—common during summer in Fallbrook, where Spencer lives—and they're plagued by few diseases. Other than regular irrigation and light feeding, all they need is to be cut back sharply once a year. "Grasses are the easiest," he says. "You just tie a rope around them and cut them like a sheaf of wheat."

Another way to reduce labor in a border, he says, is not to overplant. Not only do most of us crowd plants, we also plant too many things. "Try to use a lot of different shapes and forms, but not a lot of different plants," he advises. "It's time-consuming to keep track of a lot of [different] cultural requirements. Besides, 'drifts of one' never make an impact."

Selecting plants that self-clean or have attractive seed heads, and developing a tolerance for a little imperfection, are other ways to cut down gardening time. "I've never been compulsive about deadheading," says Spencer. "I don't cut off individual dead flowers. I wait until about two-thirds are brown, and then I cut back the whole plant."

With good planning, a little restraint, and a dose of tolerance, Spencer has proved that you can have an ornamental border that looks good year-round without creating another full-time job.

by **SHARON COHOON** *photographs by* **NORMAN A. PLATE**

Tough but colorful perennials in Scott Spencer's garden include Salvia superba (purplish blue flower spikes), catmint (blue flowers), pink 'Apple Blossom' penstemon, and golden 'Moonshine' yarrow. Westringia fruticosa 'Wynyabbie Gem', with bluish lavender flowers, grows at top left, beside 'Graham Thomas' rose (yellow flowers). Sedums (front) and grasses provide textural contrast throughout.

SCOTT SPENCER'S MOST CAREFREE BORDER PLANTS

CATMINT (*Nepeta faassenii*). Perennial with mounding growth habit, aromatic gray-green leaves, and lavender flower spikes. All zones. "Blooms from April through December here," says Spencer.

MAIDEN GRASS (*Miscanthus sinensis 'Gracillimus'*). A tall, urn-shaped ornamental grass. All zones. "Wonderful backdrop, great texture, sounds great in the wind, looks beautiful both green and dormant," says Spencer. "And all you have to do is cut it back once in early spring."

SALVIA SUPERBA. Neat, clumping perennial, 2 to 3 feet tall. All zones. Blooms April through December if sheared regularly. "'East Friesland' is my favorite."

SISYRINCHIUM STRIATUM. Perennial with irislike gray-green foliage and small, pale yellow flowers in spring. *Sunset* climate zones 8 through 24. "Great plant; I don't know why it's not used more often."

YARROW (*Achillea* 'Moonshine'). Short, tough, Mediterranean perennial with gray-green leaves and soft yellow flowers. All zones. "Neat habit, long bloom period, not fussy—my kind of flower."

On-the-go Rami Courtney (inset) lets his front garden practically take care of itself.

One hour per month

■ Rami and Cindy Courtney have full-time jobs (he's an attorney; she's a personnel specialist) as well as two active young daughters to keep up with. "That doesn't leave much time for yard work," says Rami, the gardener in the family. So he concentrates his energy on the area where his family spends most of their time—the backyard—and lets the landscaping in the front pretty much take care of itself.

The fact that the front yard is so carefree is, of course, no accident. Landscape architect Owen Dell, its designer, specializes in low-maintenance, "sustainable" landscape design. To keep the Courtneys' front yard as carefree as possible, Dell relied exclusively on "bulletproof plants" (right) which don't require a lot of water or fertilizer to look good, have few pests or diseases, and tolerate a wide range of microclimates and soils. They also grow to a certain size, then stop. Dell didn't leave much for Rami to do except turn on the drip irrigation system when the garden needs it—about once a month from April through October—and prune lightly a few times a year.

Color may be subtle—French lavender is the showiest bloomer—but there are ample compensations, including interesting texture and aromatic foliage. ◆

OWEN DELL'S TOP SIX BULLETPROOF PLANTS

FRENCH LAVENDER (*Lavandula dentata*). Short shrubs with gray-green, aromatic, narrow leaves and lavender flower spikes. *Sunset* climate zones 8, 9, and 12 through 24. Blooms nearly year-round in mild climates. "The most reliable of all lavenders," says Dell, "as long as you don't overwater."

LAVENDER STARFLOWER (*Grewia occidentalis*). Fast-growing, rather sprawling shrub often trained as an espalier or shaped into a hedge or screen. Zones 8, 9, and 12 through 24. Lavender-pink, starlike flowers occur nearly year-round.

MEXICAN BUSH SAGE (*Salvia leucantha*). Evergreen shrub with gray-green foliage and fuzzy purple flowers over a long bloom period. Zones 10 through 24.

ROSEMARY (*Rosmarinus officinalis*). Upright and prostrate versions of this Mediterranean shrub endure a wide range of growing conditions, including blazing sun, cool ocean spray, and temperatures down to 15°. Zones 4 through 24. "A classic plant," says Dell. "Looks great cascading over a wall or massed under olive trees."

CALIFORNIA GRAY RUSH (*Juncus patens*). Stiff-stemmed, grasslike plant. Zones 8 through 24. "This beautiful native rush demands nothing and tolerates everything," says Dell. "I don't understand why it's not more popular. It's great in mass or as an accent plant."

WESTRINGIA (*W. fruticosa* and *W. 'Wynyabbie Gem'*). Tall, informal shrubs with fine-textured silvery foliage and small white or lavender flowers. Zones 8, 9, and 14 through 24. "Great for screening," says Dell.

GOLDEN RULES OF LOW-MAINTENANCE GARDENING

Use the toughest plants in your region. They aren't the hottest, trendiest varieties on the market. They're the plants you keep seeing over and over again in city median strips, county parks, and older neighborhoods. There's a reason these plants are common. They never fail.

Match the plant to the site. Plant sun lovers in sun, shade lovers in shade, bog plants in wet spots, and hillside plants on slopes. "A happy plant is a healthy plant is a low-care plant," Dell sums it up.

Give plants space. An instant garden means eternal pruning thereafter. Allow each plant enough room to develop to its full size at the start.

Keep it simple. The more different things you plant, the more you have to keep track of. Tasks get forgotten and plants get overlooked. Fewer is usually better visually, too. A row of blue agapanthus backed by a bank of 'Bonica' roses is perfectly simple, and simply perfect.

Mulch, mulch, mulch. A thick layer of wood chips reduces your work load in many ways. It prevents weeds from forming; it helps the soil retain moisture; and it adds organic material to the soil as it slowly decomposes. Mulch also makes the garden look so neat people will think you spend hours a week caring for it.

Banish perfectionism. A dry, brown flower might turn into an interesting seed head, or a rose into hips, if you don't get around to deadheading. Is that so bad? And a few bug-chewed leaves aren't the end of the world.

Room with a view

A window wall keeps this enclosed Arizona patio open

by **LAUREN BONAR SWEZEY**

Ann Liebert wanted her garden in Tucson to be a private, enclosed space surrounded by native vegetation. Landscape designer Jeffrey Trent wanted enclosure for the semi-rural garden, too, but in the least intrusive way possible.

First, he designed a solid 6-foot wall. But soon he realized the wall would create a dead-end view from the kitchen, and render the patio cold and cheerless. Trent wanted it to be light and airy. Then, during what he calls a "eureka moment," he came up with a

A painted metal gecko looks down on a potted Cereus peruvianus 'Monstrosus' and octopus agave, underplanted with purple heart.

solution: emphasize the various garden rooms with changes in elevation, and sink part of the patio to help reduce the wall's height and profile. A window in the wall edging this lower dining patio frames a view of the existing vegetation and is fronted with raised planters. (See photo below.)

"Now [the garden] is very roomlike, and … intimate," says Trent. (For comfort, Liebert often tops the seat walls with cushions.) A trickling gargoyle fountain supplies the soothing sound of water, and mesquite trees provide shade.

The upper patio provides not only a transition from the house and space for entertaining but also a pleasant setting to view the city lights on summer nights.

Burnt adobe brick wall screens views of a nearby house and street, and encloses the sunken outdoor dining area. The low seat wall defines the foreground patio without blocking the desert scene.

TERRENCE MOORE

WHAT YOU NEED (to paint at least four pots)

- Four pots (various sizes)
- 1 quart water sealer (such as Jasco)
- 1 quart cream-colored exterior latex paint (such as Benjamin Moore MoorGlo Latex House and Trim 183) to use as base coat
- 1 quart latex paint in *each* of two different colors (such as apricot MoorGlo 1228 and green Moor-Glo HC 130)
- 1 quart low-luster paint sealer (such as Benwood Stays Clear Acrylic Polyurethane for Floors and Trim)
- 2-ounce tube of burnt-umber acrylic paint (such as Golden Acrylics burnt umber) or 1 quart similar color latex paint

TOOLS
Paintbrushes • 5 yards cheesecloth • Scissors • Watercolor paper (optional) • Hair dryer (optional) • Drop cloth • Latex gloves (optional) • Masking tape • Two 1-pint plastic containers • Plate

The art of "faux" pots

An artist shares her elegant painting techniques for containers

One day, visual artist Io Bonini of Kensington, California, needed some attractive plant containers for a client who was having a party. "I didn't have time to shop," says Bonini, "so I applied what I knew about faux-finishing walls to decorating pots."

Faux-painting is a centuries-old art that has been recently popularized by designers. "Faux simply means fake," says Bonini. "To faux-finish something means to make it look like what it's not. You can make a terra-cotta pot look like a plaster pot with moss growing on it or make a cement pot look like aged terra-cotta."

Bonini found that applying faux-painting techniques to pots is a lot easier than using them on walls, especially for beginners. "Designs on a large, flat wall have to look consistent. But on a pot [whose sides aren't seen all at once], the layers don't have to be perfect," she explains. In fact, you can enhance the effect by letting some of the drips show on the final coat.

Almost any kind of unglazed pot can be faux-painted. Sometimes Bonini uses plain, inexpensive clay pots. She's also worked with ornate concrete or clay pots.

When selecting colors for pots, Bonini takes her cues from fabrics and colors around her. She even suggests taking a favorite fabric or piece of tile to the paint store and having the clerk match the colors in paints. For this project, Bonini chose an apricot-and-green color scheme overlaid with burnt umber.

After you've selected your colors, if you're a beginning faux-finisher, Bonini suggests that you experiment with them on watercolor paper first until you get the look you want. This is especially important if you're using colors other than the ones described here.

Once you've gathered the materials and the pots have been sealed, the painting process goes quickly, but you'll need to allow time for each coat to dry (at least two hours per layer).

The total cost of the paint and materials listed above is about $75. Paint stores stock everything you'll need except the acrylic paint, which you can buy at an art supply store.

by **LAUREN BONAR SWEZEY** *photographs by* **NORMAN A. PLATE**

Step-by-step faux-painting

DO-AHEAD CHORES

Brush on water sealer. Coat the inside of each pot with water sealer. Allow to dry three to four days.

Prepare cheesecloth. Cut cheesecloth into 1½-foot lengths. Wash the cloth with dishwashing soap, rinse, and hang to dry (do not use a clothes dryer).

Practice on paper. Io Bonini recommends that you practice on watercolor paper first. Follow the steps for painting pots; to speed up the process, blow-dry the paper with a hair dryer. Once you're happy with the test results, you're ready to work on the containers.

When selecting colors for pots, Bonini takes her cues from fabrics and colors around her.

PAINTING THE POTS

Instructions are for Bonini's apricot-and-green color scheme. If you choose another scheme, substitute those colors for the ones mentioned here.

Photo 1: Apply the base coat. Spread a drop cloth over your work area and slip on latex gloves if desired. Using a brush, apply the cream-colored exterior latex paint to the sides and about 1½ inches down the inside of the pot. (To paint a straight line inside, apply a circle of masking tape 1½ inches down on the inside of the pot.) Allow to dry thoroughly, at least two hours.

Photos 2 and 3: Apply the first color. Set the pot on a can so you can rotate the pot without touching it. In a pint container, mix 1 part (¼ cup) apricot-colored paint and 1 part (¼ cup) low-luster sealer with 2 parts (½ cup) water. The slurry should have the consistency of milk. Dip a clean brush in the slurry and allow some to drain off. Starting at the top, paint the pot, working on a small section at a time and blotting off drips with a scrunched-up piece of cheesecloth, until the base coat is covered inside and out. For a less uniform look, blot paint lightly in some areas so the color is darker, and more heavily in other areas so it's a bit lighter. For a more solid appearance, brush on more color and blot the entire pot lightly. Allow to dry at least two hours.

Photos 4 and 5: Apply the second color. Mix the green paint (using the same ratio as for the first color) and apply it as you did the first color. Remove more or less of the color as you go, depending on how dense you want the green. Allow to dry at least two hours.

Photos 6 and 7: Apply the third color. Squeeze the burnt-umber acrylic paint onto a plate, dip a clean brush into the paint, then dip it in water. Apply the paint to the pot and let it drip down. Blot the drips to spread the color, or let some of the drips remain. Allow to dry thoroughly. Then the pot is ready to plant. ◆

In this organic garden in Washington's San Juan Islands, vegetables and flowers are gathered almost daily. For details on the nonstop cornucopia, see page 238.

MICHAEL SKOTT

August

gardenguide

tools

If you think all trowels are pretty much alike, try out one of the four English specialty trowels sold by the Kinsman Company ($12.95 each). The **Transplanting Trowel (1),** with a curved 2½-inch-wide blade, is handy for digging small holes in which to set sixpack-size plants. The **Large Trowel (2),** with a 3¼-inch-wide blade, is an all-around tool suitable for a variety of garden chores. The **Crevice Trowel (3),** with a 1¼-inch-wide pointed blade, is designed for planting in cracks in flagstone paths and rock gardens. And avid container gardeners will appreciate the **Potting Trowel (4),** whose 1¾-inch-wide blade slips neatly into tight spaces without disturbing other plants. The trowels have wood handles and blades made of high-carbon, hot-rolled, tempered steel; each has inch and centimeter markings for measuring planting depth. Kinsman Company, Box 357, Point Pleasant, PA 18950; (800) 733-4146. (The mosaic pot is from Smith & Hawken; (800/776-3336.) — *Lauren Bonar Swezey*

LEFT: LEIGH BEISCH   RIGHT: CHARLES MANN   BELOW: ACEY HARPER

QUICK TIP

Harvesting herbs such as basil, oregano, rosemary, or thyme this month? If so, bunch them together and pop them into a water-filled pitcher. You can snip from this fragrant kitchen bouquet as needed.

THE NATURAL WAY

Easy potpourri

■ "I have a lot of rose petals," says Susanna Gamble, who grows nearly 1,700 of the plants at Gamble's Flower Farm in Carmel Valley, California. Faced with the task of continually removing faded blooms, Gamble found an easy way to recycle the petals—into potpourri.

As the blossoms get droopy, she gathers their petals and pours them, in a layer no more than 1 inch deep, into an open basket and air-dries them for two days.

"Dark pinks keep their color," she says. "Orange turns the best red. Reds tend to darken, but I like that. Yellows and light pinks tend to turn yucky brown." — *Dick Bushnell*

Air-dried for a couple of days, rose petals make fragrant potpourri.

Grassy beauty in Santa Fe

by PAMELA CORNELISON

■ Landscape architects David Lovro and Tina Rousselot of LandDesign/Southwest in Santa Fe responded to that city's recent water-use restrictions by replacing an ever-thirsty lawn and perennial garden with water-thrifty ornamental grasses and plants and a "stream" of adobe-colored gravel.

Rousselot, an experienced oil painter, wanted to create "a tactile garden you want to reach out and stroke," she says. The garden is alive with texture and color, from the exuberant clumps of eulalia grass (*Miscanthus sinensis* 'Morning Light', right rear) and ravenna grass (*Erianthus raven-*

nae, center rear) to the rigid red blades of Japanese blood grass (*Imperata cylindrica* 'Rubra', foreground).

The lavender flowers of blue mist (*Caryopteris clandonensis,* left rear) enhance the garden's cool tones, while the blood grass punctuates it with fiery color. Low-growing conifers give structure to the garden, and borders of artemisia and sedum add movement as they meander along the banks of the dry streambed.

Maintenance is minimal. The beds are irrigated with a drip system and mulched with compost for moisture retention. Irrigation is usually required

Fiery tufts of Japanese blood grass grow 1 to 2 feet tall.

only during drought periods. Plants are given a complete fertilizer twice a year: in the fall before the big grasses are cut back, and in the spring before new growth. The Japanese blood grass also gets a trim in the fall to keep it compact.

The grasses were planted on the garden's west side so they could also be enjoyed with the evening view. "That's when magic happens," Rousselot says, referring to the sunsets that cast the eulalia grass in glowing pastels and the ravenna grass in spidery silhouette.

Spidery tufts of Acorus gramineus 'Ogon' spill over colorful border of bedding begonia and lobelia.

LANDSCAPING SOLUTIONS
Leaves that light up the garden

■ Want to see how foliage can brighten up a border? Try this: Put your hands across the middle of the photograph above so that you block out the chartreuse tufts. Without the foliage, the red semperflorens begonia and blue lobelia still make a handsome combination. Now take your hands away. See how those fountaining mounds of foliage set the whole scene aglow?

A number of plants with grassy foliage can do this. In this scenario, the bright-foliaged plant is *Acorus gramineus* 'Ogon'. Hardy in all *Sunset* climate zones, this plant bears tufts of golden yellow leaves. It's a perfect candidate for soggy but sunny spots, or for pool edges. In a mixed border, the spidery leaves creep through the other plantings as the season progresses.

Other plants with bright foliage include spider plant (*Chlorophytum co-* *mosum* 'Variegatum'), which has cream-striped leaves, and golden sedge (*Carex elata* 'Bowles Golden'), with bright yellow leaves.

A. g. 'Ogon' is not readily available in nurseries. One good mail-order source is Siskiyou Rare Plant Nursery (2825 Cummings Rd., Medford, OR 97501; 541/772-6846), which sells plants for $4.95 each or three for $13.95, plus shipping. —*Steven R. Lorton*

Summer lawn care: The kindest cut

Soft enough to lie on, tough enough to play on: a lawn is a remarkably versatile part of the landscape. But it does make demands, the most frequent of which is "Cut me!" Here's how to do the job right.

• Cut the grass at least weekly, never taking more than a third of the blade off each time; if you do, the loss of food-producing leaf blade temporarily checks root growth.

• Use a sharp blade. A dull blade leaves the grass ragged and brown on the tips. A sharp blade cuts fast and clean, leaving the grass healthy.

• Cut at the right height. Set your mower's cutting height to ½ inch for Bermuda and creeping bent grass (the kind used on putting greens); about ¾ inch for colonial bent grass and zoysia; and about 1 inch for St. Augustine. During the warm months, mow the taller cool-season grasses about a third higher than in spring and fall—about 2 inches for bluegrass, fescue, and ryegrass.

• Let clippings stay on the lawn. Grass contains nitrogen. Cut grass with a mulching mower (it chops blades into tinier pieces than a conventional mower) and let clippings fall; they will dry up, decompose, and eventually recycle nitrogen into the lawn, so you use less fertilizer. — *Jim McCausland*

Fragrant gingers for mild-climate gardens

■ Landscape consultant Benjamin Goetz loves tropical plants and grows lots of them in his Santa Cruz garden.

Among his favorites are white ginger lily (*Hedychium coronarium*), kahili ginger (*H. gardneranum*), and shell ginger (*Alpinia speciosa*). All are fragrant. Like many tropicals, they are also frost-tender, so although Goetz's mild coastal climate (*Sunset* climate zone 17) rarely sees freezing temperatures, he positions the plants in his garden's warmest microclimates: under the eaves, under large trees, and in a narrow side yard bordered by two houses.

For added protection he also sprays his plants with an anti-transpirant (available at nurseries) on days or nights when the temperature is expected to plunge. If a severe frost is predicted, he covers the plants with blankets and tarps.

Gardeners in other mild-winter locations who want to try growing tropical plants can order them from Brudy's Exotics (800/926-7333). — *L. B. S.*

Kahili ginger has intensely fragrant yellow flowers with red stamens.

This crocus springs up in autumn

■ It always shocks new gardeners: the sight of a crocus blooming away furiously in a bulb box on a nursery shelf in late August or September. "Aren't crocus supposed to flower in spring?" they ask. Not autumn crocus (*Colchicum*). It produces flowers in shades of white, lavender, or rose during a period of several weeks in late summer or early fall. Then the plant goes dormant until spring, when it sprouts strapping foot-long leaves. During summer, the leaves die back, and all is quiet until the flowers pop out again.

Autumn crocus does well in *Sunset* climate zones 1 through 9 and 14 through 24; in zones 10 through 13, treat it as a living bouquet and discard the bulbs after flowering.

Look for bulbs in nurseries. Plant them immediately in soil with good drainage, in full sun or partial shade, and water them in well. Cluster autumn crocus along the edges of shrub beds where they won't compete with other low-growing plants.

— *J. M.*

Tall, narrow beds allow easy access

■ Most raised beds are only as tall as the timbers that frame them—usually just 4 or 6 inches above the ground—and not all gardeners have an easy time stooping that low. Many beds are also rather wide, with plants in the middle beyond arm's reach. It's essential to scale a bed's height and width to fit its gardeners' comfort zone, especially when it's going to be tended by youngsters or people with limited mobility.

Dorothy McMahon's garden in Tacoma, Washington, was designed to provide her with comfortable access to two beds with a total of about 140 square feet of growing space. Built of pressure-treated 4-by-6s, the beds are 18 inches high, 3½ feet wide, and 20 feet long. They are filled with a soil mix rich in compost. A 4-foot-wide path of gravel over hard-packed soil runs around and between the beds, allowing McMahon to maneuver her power wheelchair directly up to them.

McMahon grows bush beans, cucumbers, lettuce, peas, tomatoes, and herbs, as well as flowers. To pick crops or blooms, she never has to bend down or reach more than 21 inches from either side of the beds. The plants are irrigated by soaker hoses that run down the middle of each bed.

— *Peggy McMahon*

She reaps what she grows

■ You've probably heard a version of these three proverbs: You reap what you sow. You make your bed, then you lie in it. And all that you give comes back tenfold. Jan Helsell puts this collective wisdom to work in her organic garden in Washington's San Juan Islands (pictured on page 232). The garden produces crops and flowers almost faster than she can pick them, all from transplants, seeds, or self-sowing volunteers that grow in beds of organically enriched soil. Helsell gathers vegetables and flowers almost daily, sharing the bounty with her friends, and her generosity just keeps the harvest coming.

The nonstop cornucopia includes asparagus and rhubarb, beets and carrots, lettuce and spinach, beans and sweet corn, squash and pumpkins, and potatoes. As for flowers, Helsell's plantings run from bachelor's buttons to zinnias, and she allows self-sowing calendulas, cosmos, and nasturtiums to pop up all over the garden.

The beds the crops lie in benefit from the family farm. The chickens, cows, horses, and sheep they raise generate plenty of manure, and the Helsells shovel the stuff on a big pile to decompose. Then around mid-April, Jan and her daughter Mary Jane spread a 4- to 6-inch layer of well-aged manure over the planting beds and till it in until the soil has the texture of coffee grounds. — *S. R. L.*

NORMAN A. PLATE

Autumn crocus burst into bloom on leafless stems.

Pacific Northwest Garden Notebook

by STEVEN R. LORTON

When I think about the plants that best represent the horticultural bounty of the Northwest in August, dozens come to mind—and many of them are shown throughout this issue. But the single most vivid image is of baskets hanging from the rafters of my porch—and dripping with fuchsias. Summer without fuchsias would be like April without daffodils and tulips, or May without rhododendrons.

There are hundreds of hybrid fuchsias with spectacular and exotic-looking blooms. But my favorite is still the hardy old species *Fuchsia magellanica*. It grows well in *Sunset* climate zones 2 through 7 and is hardy enough to handle all but our coldest weather. In milder climates, it can reach 20 feet. It bears delicate bicolored flowers (rosy red and deep, regal violet) about 1½ inches long from July until frost. *F. m.* 'Riccartonii', a particularly robust variety, makes a wonderful, feathery filler for any shady corner of the garden. If you cut it to the ground early each spring, it sends up arching stems that reach 3 to 5 feet around bloom time.

To celebrate the species, fuchsia societies throughout the Northwest will be staging their annual shows this month. And many nurseries will offer fuchsias for sale this month.

MARINA THOMPSON

But if you want to see some unusual plants, make an appointment to visit Fellows Family Flowers (206/588-4541) in Steilacoom, Washington. Ken and Donna Fellows began growing fuchsias as a hobby, and now it's their life's work. Their small backyard bulges with fuchsias, and more than 800 varieties are crowded into their greenhouse. If you see something you like but it's sold out, ask the Fellowses to put it on their propagation list and you can pick it up next spring.

that's a good question...

Q: I once saw a trailing plant in a pot, with bright red fruits like small cherries. The owner said it was a fuchsia. Is there such a thing? — *Susan Thomson, Spokane*

A: Indeed: *Fuchsia procumbens*. It has apple-green leaves (about the size of the tip of your little finger) on trailing stems sporting tiny yellow and purple flowers that ripen into ornamental fruits. Grow it in a pot in the shade outdoors, and bring it inside to a sunny window through the winter. Nip back stems to keep plants bushy. Stems root easily in water.

Northern California Garden Notebook

by LAUREN BONAR SWEZEY

*a*round midsummer, when the long days are sunny and warm, the traveling bug strikes me. That's when I find any excuse to hit the road and see the sights. Of course, I make many of my journeys a horticultural experience.

One of my favorite jaunts is to the Half Moon Bay Coastal Flower Market, from 9 to 3 on the third Saturday of the month, May through September. At this open-air market, you can shop for plants, cut flowers, and herbs cultivated by 15 to 25 coastside growers, and also enjoy performances by dancers and musicians. To get to the market, take State Highway 92 to Main Street, turn left, and drive a few blocks to Kelly Avenue.

On your way to or from the flower market, stop along State 92 at Half Moon Bay Nursery (11691 San Mateo Rd.) on the eastern outskirts of town. The nursery's grounds and greenhouses are always filled with blooming plants in containers of all sizes. And you can choose from an excellent selection of landscape plants.

SPEAKING OF TRAVELING …

If you're driving north on U.S. 101, drop by the Luther Burbank Home & Gardens at the corner of Santa Rosa and Sonoma avenues in Santa Rosa.

The 1.6-acre historic site features much of the famous plant hybridizer's work in perennial borders, orchard plant-

ings, and demonstration gardens (a butterfly garden, a wildlife garden, a rose garden, and a Victorian garden).

Operated by the city, this public garden just garnered an award from the California Parks and Recreation Society for high-quality maintenance of the facility, which incorporates innovation, creativity, and ecological consciousness.

The gardens are open 8 to 7 daily. House tours are given and a museum and gift shop are open 10 to 4 Wednesdays through Sundays from April through October. For more information, call (707) 524-5445.

that's a good question...

Q: I would like to plant two trees in our backyard when our twins are born. I was thinking of chestnut trees, but have no idea if they are suitable. — *Patrick McEvoy, Palo Alto*

A: They're not. They're large and cast dense shade. For a deciduous tree, try Chinese tallow, a small tree with poplarlike leaves and gorgeous fall color, or 'Rosemary Clarke' Japanese flowering apricot, a picturesque 20-foot tree with spicy-sweet, double white and red flowers in winter. For an evergreen (in *Sunset* climate zones 15–24), try *Tristania laurina* 'Elegant', a small tree with lush, glossy foliage.

MARINA THOMPSON (2)

Southern California Garden Notebook

by SHARON COHOON

Late summer, when my garden is past its peak but not yet at rest, has become my favorite season. But I wasn't sure why. Was it the garden's lusty exuberance or its mellowed, mature beauty that appealed? Then I read an essay by Louise Erdrich from the *New York Times Magazine,* reprinted in the "Potpourri of Roses" newsletter. "Gardens are lovely according to their season, as are men and women," wrote Erdrich. "July reminds me of the textured sensuality of Helen Mirren ... August, the sexy spirituality of Susan Sarandon." Suddenly, I knew why I like late summer! And I look forward to "September, the powerful arc of Tina Turner's voice," in Erdrich's words, and to "October, the delicate carnality of Jeanne Moreau." Now, if I can just learn to age as gracefully.

The other good thing about the late-summer garden is that, except for watering, I can just let it slide and spend some quality time in my hammock. My lounging companion this month will be *California Gardens,* by Winifred Starr Dobyns (Allen A. Knoll Publishers, Santa Barbara, 1996; $55). This limited-edition reprint of the 1931 original may be the ultimate picture book. After a brief foreword, it's solid photos: gorgeous black-and-white shots of the estate gardens of the 1910s and 1920s—the golden age of California gardening. Many of these gardens, with exceptions like Lotusland and Filoli, no longer exist. So these seductive portraits are as close as we'll come to visiting them. It's almost enough.

WATCH FOR THE SWEET POTATO BEETLE

If you grow sweet potatoes or morning glories, watch out for a new pest—the sweet potato weevil. This colorful, ¼-inch-long beetle has a dark blue body and a red waist and legs, so it should be easy to spot. Adult beetles eat holes in leaves and roots, and lay eggs around the bases of the plants; larvae tunnel into the sweet potatoes. The sweet potato weevil is a serious threat to California's home and commercial sweet potato production. So far, however, it has been found only in San Diego County. Report any evidence of infestation to your county department of agriculture; in San Diego, call (619) 694-2739.

that's a good question...

Q: I love the flowers of blue hibiscus (*Alyogyne huegelii*), but not the way it grows. Can I prune it, and if so, how much?

A. You can't shear blue hibiscus, but you can encourage it to branch more freely. I follow garden writer Pat Welsh's suggestion: cut back two or three of the longest branches by one-half to two-thirds of their length every month from spring to fall.

MARINA THOMPSON (2)

Westerner's Garden Notebook

by JIM McCAUSLAND

My Irish ancestors, I'm told, grew crops in ground made up of "two rocks for every dirt." I garden in similarly rocky ground, and it makes things difficult but not impossible.

To break virgin ground, I use a rear-tined tiller. As it kicks up potato-size rocks, I throw them onto a stone path or areas beneath hose bibbs where I have mulched with rocks to keep the hoses out of the mud.

Once the heavy tilling is done and the soil is amended, I pick out the larger rocks as I encounter them. But I leave any stone smaller than a table-tennis ball, just to be true to my Irish roots.

WATER LILY LOVERS GATHER IN DENVER

With their big floating blooms, water lilies have a naturally tropical look wherever they grow. To celebrate these irresistible flowers, the International Water Lily Society Symposium will be held in Denver August 10 through 13. You can attend the full conference, which features speakers, garden tours, and a banquet or two, for $400 plus lodging (call 303/671-7964 for a registration brochure). If your time and budget are limited, come on Sunday between 9 and 12 or 1 and 5. Visit the free trade show and book signing at the Tech Center Marriott Hotel, 4900 S. Syracuse St. Then head over to the Denver Botanical Garden, 1005 York St., to see the results of the water lily variety trials. Many of the lilies that succeed here will eventually be registered and sold commercially.

A CUT FLOWER THAT ROOTS ITSELF

Sedum telephium 'Autumn Joy' has wormed its way into my affections with its coppery-rose flowers that last for a long time, either on the plant or in a vase. As cut flowers, they will root in the vase. You can pot them up to set out later in fall or next spring.

that's a good question...

Q: It's hard enough choosing ripe watermelons at the market. How do you know when they're ripe on the vine?

A: A melon farmer recently disabused me of the notion that watermelons are ripe when the tendrils on the stem ends start to dry out. "Some years that's true," he mused, "but some years it's not. It's better to watch the melon's skin: when it goes from shiny to dull, pick the melon." He also advised me to back off on watering during the last three weeks the watermelons are maturing. "It makes them sweeter," he said—and after 25 years of growing melons, he should know.

MARINA THOMPSON

Pacific Northwest Checklist

PLANTING

☑ **Annuals.** Zones 4–7: There's still enough frost-free weather ahead to give annuals a good long run (75 days or more). Perk up beds and make new container plantings with annuals that are still for sale in some nurseries.

☑ **Fall crops.** Zones 4–7: Early in the month, you can still set out seedlings of cole crops and sow beets, Chinese cabbage, mustard, onions, radishes, spinach, and turnips.

☑ **Perennials, shrubs.** This is the worst time to put new plants in the ground, especially in full sun. But if you see a plant you can't resist, you have two choices. Keep it in the container out of direct sun and water it religiously until October, when you can plant it in the ground. Or put it in the ground now and water it super-religiously until the weather cools and fall rains begin.

MAINTENANCE

☑ **Harvest herbs.** For maximum flavor and freshness, harvest herbs in the morning just after dew has dried. One way to preserve them is to lay them out on a clean window screen in a shady but dry and dust-free place. When all plant parts are perfectly dry, you can store them in jars.

☑ **Compost.** As you prune and harvest, put the organic waste matter on

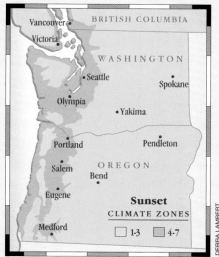

the compost pile. If you chop it up, it will decompose more quickly. Keep the pile moist and turn it monthly.

☑ **Fertilize annuals.** There is enough summer left that annuals will benefit from a feeding with a liquid plant food that is low in nitrogen and high in phosphorus and potassium.

☑ **Propagate shrubs.** Broad-leafed evergreens like azaleas, camellias, daphne, euonymus, holly, rhododendrons, and viburnum and deciduous plants like hydrangeas and magnolias can all be propagated this month from semihardwood cuttings.

Take 4- to 6-inch cuttings in the morning. Strip leaves from the bottom, dip the cut ends into rooting hormone powder, and set the cuttings into 4-inch pots filled with sterile soil. Water well. Put them in a spot out of direct sunlight and keep them thoroughly moist. Before cold weather hits, move them into a greenhouse or a sunny room. By next spring, you'll have rooted plants to set out.

☑ **Prune cane berries.** On June-bearing plants, remove all canes that produced fruit this summer. On everbearing plants, cut back by half any canes that have already borne fruit.

☑ **Water wisely.** August can be one of the most stressful months for plants. Rhododendrons and other moisture-loving plants are especially vulnerable; spray their foliage with water and irrigate deeply to reach their roots. ◆

Northern California Checklist

PLANTING

☑ **Plant for extended bloom.** Zones 7–9, 14–17: Perennials that bloom now into fall include achillea, asters, begonias, coreopsis, dahlias, daylilies (some), fortnight lilies, geraniums (pelargoniums), lantana, *Limonium perezii,* Mexican bush sage, scabiosa, and verbena. (In zones 1–2, check hardiness; a few plants, including *Limonium perezii* and Mexican bush sage, aren't suitable for cold-winter climates.) For long-blooming annuals, choose celosia, cosmos, Madagascar periwinkle, marigolds, sweet alyssum, and zinnias. To make an instant color bowl, use blooming plants in 4-inch pots or 1-gallon cans.

☑ **Sow cool-season annuals.** Zones 7–9, 14–17: Start seeds of fall- and winter-blooming annuals, including calendula, Iceland poppy, pansy, primrose, stock, and viola.

☑ **Select plants carefully.** Most nurseries provide meticulous care for their plants. But a missed watering during the summer months can stress plants severely. When shopping, check plants carefully. Unless a particular variety is going through summer dormancy, foliage should look perky and lush, without burned leaf edges. Avoid leggy plants or ones that are overgrown and rootbound.

☑ **Sow perennials.** Zones 7–9, 14–17: For bloom next spring and summer, sow seeds of carnations, columbine, coreopsis, feverfew, gaillardia, hardy asters, hollyhock, lupine, penstemon, phlox, purple coneflower, Shasta daisy, statice, and yarrow. Plant seeds in flats or small pots filled with a peat-based potting mix.

☑ **Sow sweet peas.** Zones 7–9, 14–17: To get a crop of early flowers, sow an early-flowering variety such as 'Winter Elegance' (available from Shepherd's Garden Seeds, 408/335-6910) this month. Color choices include salmon/cream/pink, lavender, and white. This type will bloom when days are short. Protect new growth from slugs and snails and provide support for the tall vines.

MAINTENANCE

☑ **Care for flowers.** To keep warm-season annuals blooming through the end of summer and into fall, water and feed plants regularly with fish emulsion or another fertilizer. Remove spent flowers before they go to seed.

☑ **Irrigate trees, shrubs.** Large trees and shrubs may need a deep soaking now, even if they're watered by an irrigation system (some systems don't run long enough for water to penetrate the soil deeply). Use a soaker hose or a deep-root irrigator, or build a berm of soil around the plant and slowly soak the area inside with a hose. Let the water run until the soil beneath the drip line of the plant is soaked to a depth of 12 to 18 inches (use the deeper amount for larger shrubs and trees). Check moisture penetration by digging down with a trowel.

☑ **Treat nutrient deficiencies.** Inspect foliage for signs of nutrient deficiencies. Pale yellow leaves indicate that plants need nitrogen. Yellow leaves with prominent green veins indicate an iron deficiency; apply chelated iron according to the package directions. ◆

Southern California Checklist

PLANTING

☑ **Cool-season crops.** In coastal, inland, and high-desert gardens (zones 11, 18–24), sow cool-season vegetables in flats at midmonth for transplanting into the garden in six to eight weeks. Good candidates include broccoli, brussels sprouts, cabbage, cauliflower, kale, mustard; root vegetables such as beets and carrots; celery; head and leaf lettuces; and edible-pod peas.

☑ **Spring bulbs.** Freesias, sparaxis, and other South African bulbs that naturalize easily in Southern California appear in nurseries this month. Plant them immediately after purchase.

☑ **Sweet peas.** Sow seeds now for blooms by December. To speed germination, soak seeds overnight before planting. Provide a trellis or several 6-foot poles for vines to climb, or plant along a wall.

☑ **Biennials.** Start seeds of Canterbury bells, foxglove, hollyhocks, lunaria, and other biennials now. When seedlings are about 3 inches tall, transplant them into the garden. Plants will become established during fall and bloom next spring.

MAINTENANCE

☑ **Prepare for fire season.** If you live near native chaparral (including in ur-

Sunset
CLIMATE ZONES

1-3 7-9 11 13 14-24

DEBRA LAMBERT

ban canyons), reduce fire risk to your property by pruning dead vegetation from trees and shrubs, especially near structures. Cut tall grasses and weeds down to stubble. Remove clippings or prunings from your property or recycle them as compost or mulch. For more information on fire-safe landscape practices, contact your local fire department.

☑ **Feed annuals, vegetables.** Continue to fertilize warm-season flowers and crops every two to four weeks, especially those in containers.

☑ **Feed turf.** Give warm-season turf grasses such as Bermuda and St. Augustine a light feeding with a high-nitrogen fertilizer.

☑ **Water adequately.** Shallow-rooted plants and container plants, especially those in hanging baskets, are particularly vulnerable during hot spells; daily watering may be necessary. Large shade trees need deep irrigation on a monthly basis. Deciduous fruit trees should be watered every 10 to 14 days near the coast, weekly in inland areas.

PEST CONTROL

☑ **Combat lawn grubs.** Irregular brown patches in summer lawns may be caused by beetle larvae that feed on grass roots. Pull up sections of dead turf to expose them. If grubs are a problem, treat with parasitic nematodes. Following label instructions, spray the nematode-water mixture in late afternoon after watering.

☑ **Control fireblight.** This bacterial disease makes affected plants look as if they have been scorched by fire. Cotoneaster, evergreen pear, pyracantha, toyon, and members of the rose family are susceptible. Prune out diseased twigs and branches: cut small branches 4 to 6 inches below the infection, large branches at least 12 inches below the infected part. ◆

Mountain Garden Checklist

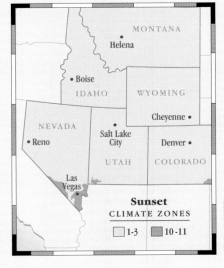

Sunset
CLIMATE ZONES

☐ 1-3   ▨ 10-11

DEBRA LAMBERT

PLANTING AND HARVEST

☑ **Plant fall crops.** Where frosts aren't expected until late October, sow beets, carrots, radishes, and spinach for fall harvest. In mildest climates, set out transplants of broccoli, cabbage, and cauliflower.

☑ **Start greenhouse vegetables.** Sow eggplant, peppers, and short-season tomatoes in early August. When seedlings have two sets of true leaves, transplant them into pots at least 8 inches deep (12 inches for tomatoes). Grow them outside, then transfer to the greenhouse before nighttime temperatures fall below 55°. Keep the greenhouse between 60° and 80° during the day, 60° and 70° at night.

☑ **Sow wildflowers.** Sow seeds of annual and perennial wildflowers now for bloom next spring. Try bachelor's buttons, coreopsis, Mexican hat, perennial blue flax, poppies, prairie aster, Rocky Mountain penstemon, and rudbeckia. (In coldest areas, do this in September.) Cultivate the soil lightly, spread seeds, then mulch with ¼ to ½ inch of ground bark or other organic matter.

☑ **Harvest flowers for drying.** Pick them with long stems, strip off the leaves, bundle them together, and hang them upside down in a garage or basement.

☑ **Harvest crops.** Pick early apples, beets, broccoli, bush beans, cauliflower, new potatoes, peaches, raspberries, strawberries, summer squash, sweet corn, tomatoes, and zucchini. Pick herbs in the morning just after dew has dried.

MAINTENANCE

☑ **Check for chlorosis.** If leaves are yellowish but their veins are green, apply chelated iron to correct iron deficiency (chlorosis). If leaves are yellowish overall and you can spot no insect or cultural problems, apply a complete fertilizer.

☑ **Divide perennials.** After delphiniums, German iris, Oriental poppies, and Shasta daisies bloom, divide large clumps. Dig up and cut the root mass into several sections. Add organic matter to soil and replant. (In shortest-season areas, wait until spring to dig and replant.)

☑ **Protect vegetables.** In high-elevation gardens, use cardboard boxes, floating row covers, or plastic cloches to protect vegetables if cold temperatures come early. Set the covers in place by late afternoon and remove them before midmorning.

☑ **Prune water sprouts, suckers.** Water sprouts are vigorous shoots growing from trunks or branches of birch, crabapple, hawthorn, lilac, Russian olive, and willow. Suckers grow from a plant's rootstock. Prune off both.

PEST CONTROL

☑ **Treat powdery mildew.** Dahlias, peas, squash, and zinnias are particularly susceptible to powdery mildew—a white, dusty-looking fungus. Rake up and destroy fallen leaves; remove diseased stems and leaves. Treat severe infestations with a fungicide such as benomyl or karathane. ◆

Southwest Garden Checklist

PLANTING

☑ **Plant vegetables.** Zone 10 (Sedona, Albuquerque, El Paso): Sow beans, cabbage family members, collards, corn, cucumbers, potatoes, spinach, squash, and Swiss chard early in the month, or set out nursery transplants at month's end. Zone 11 (Las Vegas): Sow beets, carrots, radishes, and spinach, and set out transplants of broccoli, cabbage, and cauliflower for fall harvest. Zones 12–13: Late in August, sow beans, cabbage family members, carrots, collards, corn, cucumbers, green onions, leeks, lettuce, and squash for a late harvest.

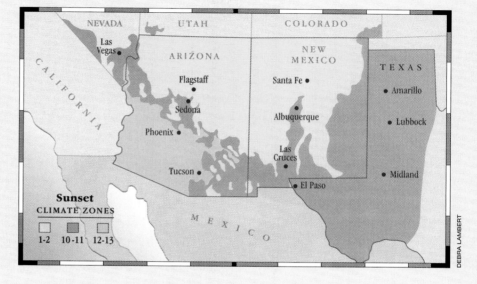

☑ **Sow wildflowers.** Sow seeds of annual and perennial wildflowers now for bloom next spring. Try bachelor's buttons, coreopsis, globemallow, goldfields, Mexican hat, penstemon, perennial blue flax, and poppies. Cultivate the soil lightly, spread seeds, then mulch with ¼ to ½ inch of finely ground bark or other organic material.

MAINTENANCE

☑ **Care for roses.** To get roses ready for strong fall bloom, acidify soil with soluble sulfur (such as Disper-Sul), fortify it with a complete fertilizer, and apply iron chelate to correct chlorosis. Water in all amendments thoroughly.

☑ **Feed shrubs.** Give them a half-strength application of a complete fertilizer, watering it in well, to help them recover from heat stress.

☑ **Make compost.** Haul garden waste to the compost pile, mixing weeds, lawn clippings, and nonmeat kitchen waste. Keep the pile evenly moist and turn it regularly.

☑ **Water.** Container plants, nursery stock, recently planted seedlings, and anything growing under house eaves need extra attention this time of year. Thoroughly drench the roots of permanent landscape plants with a soaker hose, a deep-root irrigator, or a hose running slowly into a watering basin built around the plant.

PEST CONTROL

☑ **Lawn pests.** Just as chinch bugs can cause St. Augustine grass to dry out and die back, microscopic Bermuda mites can do the same to Bermuda grass, giving it a scraggly, shaving-brush look. The treatment for both pests is the same: an application of chlorpyrifos (such as Dursban) or diazinon.

☑ **Spider mites.** Mottled leaves and fine webs signal the mites' presence. Control infestations by spraying with a miticide.

☑ **Whiteflies.** Yellow sticky traps are the best control measure. ◆

Heavenly nurseries in the Willamette Valley

Dream plants, from perennials to antique roses

■ Welcome to horticultural paradise, where the beds are lined with gold and jewels, rose blossoms perfume the air, and perennials approach floral perfection. As Dorothy said to Toto, "I've a feeling we're not in Kansas anymore." Sure enough. But this Landscape of Oz is easy to find—in Oregon's Willamette Valley, where specialty nurseries grow the sorts of plants most gardeners dream about.

Follow our yellow brick road to *Sunset's* favorite nurseries between Scappoose and Cottage Grove. Many have inspiring display gardens, and each offers plants or seeds you're not likely to find anywhere else. If you're traveling on Interstate 5, it's easy to swing off to one or more of them. The nurseries are listed from north to south and numbered on the map at right. Call for directions or an appointment if needed.

A note to visitors from California: You can take home most Oregon-grown plants without certification, but persimmon trees are prohibited, and all cherries need treatment certificates from the Oregon Department of Agriculture. Pines, many nuts, and oaks may be admitted with origin certificates. Check with the nursery.

1. Joy Creek Nursery, Scappoose. A very strong collection of clematis sets the tone here, with lots of dianthus, hydrangeas,

Northwest Garden Nursery. *From saffron-yellow kniphofia to snow-white delphinium, this display bed blends perennials into a summer tapestry.*

by JIM McCAUSLAND

hostas, penstemons, and other perennials to complete the garden. See them all in 3½ acres of display gardens, at their peak in August. *Open 9–5 daily. 20300 N.W. Watson Rd.; (503) 543-7474.*

*2. **Bovees Nursery,*** Portland. Bovees offers a fine collection of woodland perennials, with an emphasis on tropical Vireya rhododendrons (some bear warm-colored flowers this month). *Open by appointment. 1737 S.W. Coronado St.; (503) 244-9341.*

*3. **The Bamboo Gardens,*** Milwaukie. If it's bamboo and grows in the Northwest, you'll probably find it here. *By appointment. 13822 S.E. Oatfield Rd.; (503) 654-0024.*

*4. **Porterhouse Farms,*** Sandy. Dwarf conifers (850 varieties) and a large selection of companion plants are offered by Lloyd Porter and Don Howse. *By appointment. 41370 S.E. Thomas Rd.; (503) 668-5834.*

*5. **Caprice Farm Nursery,*** Sherwood. Though Dot and Al Rogers specialize in peonies, this time of year you'll most

appreciate their collection of daylilies and hostas. *10–4 Mon-Sat. 15425 S.W. Pleasant Hill Rd.; (503) 625-7241.*

*6. **Hedgerows Nursery,*** McMinnville. Focusing on unusual ornamentals, owners David Mason and Susie Grimm are developing a demonstration garden and importing many plants from England. This month, the Cape fuchsias and salvias should be at their peak. *10–5 Wed-Sun, April-September. 20165 S.W. Christensen Rd.; (503) 843-7522.*

*7. **Heirloom Old Garden Roses,*** St. Paul. With 1,500 varieties in three test gardens, John and Louise Clements have wide experience in growing roses. They offer everything from centuries-old varieties to brand-new ones. This month, the hybrid perpetuals and English roses put on an especially good show. *8–4 Mon-Fri, 9–4 Sat-Sun. 24062 Riverside Dr. N.E.; (503) 538-1576.*

*8. **Nichols Garden Nursery,*** Albany. Known for her mail-order vegetable, flower, and herb seeds, Rosemarie Nichols McGee has also developed a

Joy Creek Nursery. *Purple delphinium and scarlet Maltese cross (Lychnis chalcedonica) are standouts in this mixed perennial border.*

JANET LOUGHREY

Heirloom Old Garden Roses. *Awash with antique rose varieties, this nursery also stocks the modern line of David Austin English roses, including fragrant 'Sweet Juliet' (right).*

large trial garden that's at its prime in late summer. *9–5 Mon-Sat. 1190 Old Salem Rd.; (541) 928-9280.*

9. Gossler Farms Nursery, Springfield. You'll find 120 kinds of magnolias here, but the Gosslers are also very strong on plants that produce great fall color and winter flowers, including 30 varieties of witch hazel. *By appointment. 1200 Weaver Rd.; (541) 746-3922.*

10. Greer Gardens, Eugene. Though Harold Greer's nursery is built on its outstanding collection of rhododendrons, it has expanded to include a wide array of unusual ornamentals, from perennials to trees. *8:30–5:30 Mon-Sat, 11–5 Sun. 1280 Goodpasture Island Rd.; (541) 686-8266.*

11. Northwest Garden Nursery, Eugene. The display garden here beautifully reflects the owners' love of hard-to-find perennials. They grow and sell more kinds of *Astrantia, Corydalis, Heuchera, Pulmonaria,* and *Tiarella*

than you're likely to find in one place anywhere else. *10–6 Thu-Fri, 10–5 Sat. 86813 Central Rd.; (541) 935-3915.*

12. Baltzer's Specialized Nursery, Pleasant Hill. Through the years Bob Baltzer has assembled a wonderful array of dwarf conifers, Japanese maples, and probably the Willamette Valley's best assortment of bonsai tools and containers. *9–6 Thu-Sat and Mon, 10–5 Sun.*

36011 Highway 58; (541) 747-5604.

13. Territorial Seed Company, Cottage Grove. Tom Johns picks his vegetable and flower seeds for their adaptability to the mild Northwest climate. First stop at his store in Cottage Grove, then take the 20-minute drive to the trial gardens near London. *Store 8–5:30 Mon-Sat, 9–4 Sun. 20 Palmer Ave.; (541) 942-9547. Trial grounds 10–2 Sat.* ◆

Fiery petals of 'Orange Julius' dahlias are golden yellow brushed with bright orange.

STEPHEN CRIDLAND

fields of fire

The Northwest produces more dahlias than any other region in the West. This is the month to pay its farms a visit

by STEVEN R. LORTON

■ Radiant colors may make dahlias seem more at home in sunny southern climates. But these fiesta-hued beauties—native to the highlands of Mexico—grow prolifically in the Pacific Northwest, where they are among the major commercial flower crops. The mild, moist climate and rich, acid soil combine to produce vibrant flowers that are beautifully formed and long-lived. ■ From August until the first frost, dahlias set growing fields ablaze with bright flamenco colors as they open up to bask in the end-of-summer sun. At one of the Northwest's biggest farms, Swan Island Dahlias in Canby, Oregon, you can walk the grass paths between rows of flowers that stretch out in every direction, and celebrate the bloom peak at Swan Island's annual Dahlia Festival and Indoor Show. This is a grand time to see these gorgeous blooms in arrangements, too, or to take a field tour. Some visitors bring cameras to capture the dazzling scene on film; others set up easels to paint. ■ If the dahlia bug bites, you can order tubers for planting next spring. Dahlias grow well throughout the West if you plant tubers after soil warms and frosts are over. In hottest climates, plant them in light, filtered shade and give them ample water.

JANET LOUGHREY

'Purple Gem' dahlia has bright scarlet blooms made up of neatly rolled petals.

7 DAHLIA FARMS TO VISIT

The following dahlia farms are as friendly as they are colorful. Owners and staff are usually on hand to answer questions. Most offer price lists or catalogs so you can order tubers for delivery by mail once you're home. Flower stands in many of the fields sell dahlias by the bunch. Seasoned visitors often travel with a water-filled plastic bucket sitting in a box (so it won't tip over in the car) to transport flowers home.

Connell's Dahlias. 10616 Waller Rd. E., Tacoma, WA 98446; (253) 531-0292. Show gardens fill 5 acres. Open daily August 15–October 1. Catalog $2.

Ferncliff Gardens. 8394 McTaggart St., Mission, BC V2V 6S6; (604) 826-2447. This 77-year-old family business has a show garden and 3 acres of dahlia fields. Look for the dahlias that never need staking. Peak bloom from mid-August through early October. Open 9–4:30 daily August 10–October 10. Catalog free to visitors, $2 by mail.

La Conner Dahlias. At junction of Chilberg Rd. and La Conner–Whitney Rd. (Box 329), La Conner, WA 98257; (360) 466-3977. More than 125 varieties in 2 acres of field and display gardens. Owner David Rothrock got hooked on dahlias while living in France, where the plants grew in vegetable gardens. Open during daylight hours daily July 19 until frost. Price list free to visitors, $1 by mail.

Pioneer Dahlias. 1606 Hwy. 20, Burlington, WA 98233; (360) 855-1357.

More than 850 varieties grow in 3 acres of fields. Look for the flame red 'Lady Darlene' with 6- to 8-inch flowers (several photographers are usually clustered around it, trying to get a close-up). Open dawn to dusk daily August 1–September. Price list free to visitors, $1 by mail.

Sea-Tac Dahlia Gardens. 20020 Des Moines Memorial Dr., Seattle, WA 98198; (206) 824-3846. Owners Louis and Patti Eckhoff grow close to 7,000 plants in a 1-acre field. The Eckhoffs favor small and medium-size flowers that are good for cutting. Open during daylight hours daily mid-August until frost. Price list free to visitors, or send a self-addressed, stamped envelope.

Skagit Heights Dahlia Farm. 576 Hobson Rd., Bow, WA 98232; (360) 766-6612. This charming Skagit Valley farm is home to more than 600 varieties. Open 9–dusk Mon-Sat, 12–dusk Sun, August-September. Catalog free to visitors, $1 by mail.

Swan Island Dahlias. 995 N.W. 22nd Ave. (Box 700), Canby, OR 97013; (503) 266-7711. About one-third of the plants on these 40 acres were hybridized here, where the family has been in business for 35 years. Open daylight till dark daily August 1 until frost. The Dahlia Festival takes place August 23–25 and August 30–September 1; food and drink are sold, and picnic tables provided. Price list free, catalog $3. ◆

Catalogs in hand, shoppers at Swan Island Dahlias choose varieties to order for planting out next spring. All plants are clearly labeled.

Vibrant bouquet shows off the flaming-hued varieties listed at right.

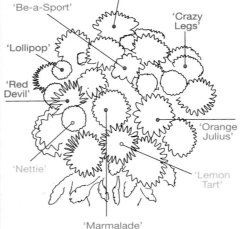

'Serenade'
'Be-a-Sport'
'Crazy Legs'
'Lollipop'
'Red Devil'
'Orange Julius'
'Nettie'
'Lemon Tart'
'Marmalade'

DAHLIAS FOR BOUQUETS

Flowers 4 inches and smaller are best.

Anemones. Single anemone-shaped flowers with nearly flat petals.

Ball and pompom. Petals tightly arranged in a globe shape.

Cactus and semicactus. Spiky, tightly curled petals resemble cactus flowers.

Collarettes. Wide, roundish petals with a ruffle of smaller petals around the centers.

Formal decorative. Uniform, rounded petals are evenly spaced.

Informal decorative. Flowers often have ruffly or gently twisted petals.

Water lily. Open clusters of flat, broad petals resemble water lilies.

STEPHEN CRIDLAND

STEPHEN SIMPSON

Rows of mature oleanders flank a brick path at Rancho Los Alamitos in Long Beach.

Destination: the garden

Four of the West's great estate gardens are in Southern California.
Visit them and they may inspire gardening greatness in you

L et's be honest. Sometimes the pleasure we derive from our backyards is diminished by the guilt we feel as we take in the scene. The unpruned peach tree, the weeds along the back fence, the bedding plants past their prime—all bear silent witness to a decided lack of gardening initiative. Instead of donning gloves and grabbing shears, we daydream about a glorious self-maintaining garden where weed-pulling is supervised from a hammock.

Though few of us will ever actually live in such an Eden, we can at least give substance to our fantasies by visit-

ing one of the West's great estate gardens. As difficult as it may be to believe today, every one of these historic gardens was once someone's backyard. And because of their residential (albeit often palatial) scale, there is no shortage of landscaping and planting ideas that could work in our own pieces of paradise. Inspired, we return home with intentions of hard work—that is, if we can get past the hammock.

The gardens at *Rancho Los Alamitos* could well roust you from your slumber. They took their final shape during the 1920s, the glory years of California gardening. It was the era of grand es-

tate gardens, complete with sweeping vistas and rare plant collections.

Florence Bixby, the woman behind the rancho's gardens, had the funds and the land to garden in the same style. But instead she opted for a garden more in keeping with her adobe ranch house and the land's rancho heritage. Rather than taking her inspiration from the built-to-impress palace gardens of England and France, she turned instead to the simple, elegant courtyards of Spain. And rather than amassing a connoisseur's collection of plants, she relied on sturdy Mediterranean staples such as oleanders, wisteria, olive trees, and potted geraniums.

Bixby encircled her home with two bands of outdoor rooms. The inner circle of sunny terraces and shady patios provided options for intimate conversation, alfresco dining, and family entertaining. The outer circle, farther away from the house, was devoted to horticultural themes (cutting and rose gardens, for example). Together, the two bands make up a 360° backyard as well suited for outdoor living now as when it was created.

- *Where:* 6400 Bixby Hill Rd., Long Beach.
- *Hours:* 1–5 Wed-Sun.
- *Cost:* Free.
- *FYI:* Attend the citrus fair on June 29.
- *Contact:* (562) 431-3541.

MORE ESTATE GARDENS

Corona del Mar. Sherman Gardens: Hands-on programs for visitors are emphasized at this Orange County horticultural display garden, with demonstrations in the rose garden, fern grotto, tropical conservatory, and fuchsia garden; (714) 673-2261.

La Cañada Flintridge. Descanso Gardens: This rare woodland garden of native live oaks underplanted with tree-size camellias also features a large rose collection and a tranquil Japanese garden; (818) 952-4400.

San Marino. Huntington Botanical Gardens: There's something for everyone on this 207-acre estate. The grounds boast 15 thematic collections ranging from a desert garden of cactus and succulents to Japanese and tropical rain forest gardens; (818) 405-2141. ◆

by **JEFF PHILLIPS** *and* **SHARON COHOON**

In the demonstration garden of Tohono Chul Park in Tucson, quirky octopus cactus spreads under a littleleaf palo verde. For tips on landscaping with these native desert plants, see page 260.

CHARLES MANN

September

gardenguide

tools

Some flowers bloom in the most inconvenient places: at the top of an arbor or among thorny branches. And if you grow grapes, you know how tricky it can be to cut a ripe cluster with one hand. That's why cut-and-hold shears were invented: they snip the flower or fruit cluster and continue grasping it firmly until you can transfer it to your free hand.

The shears shown here have 2-inch-long, stainless-steel blades, which are strong enough to cut through soft or woody stems up to about ⅜ inch in diameter. They're manufactured by Victorinox, a company famous for its Swiss Army knives. You can order a pair for $21 (including shipping) from the Wildflower Seed Company, Box 406, St. Helena, CA 94574; (800) 456-3359. — *Jim McCausland*

CURTIS ANDERSON

QUICK TIP
Shredded fall leaves compost much faster than whole leaves that you rake up. The best way to shred them? Vacuum them up with a power lawn mower that has a bagger attached (or rent a shredder), then mix the bits into your compost pile.

NORMAN A. PLATE

HEIRLOOM SWEET PEAS

From monks to painted ladies

■ Although sweet peas have been an American favorite for years, the colorful and spicy-sweet-scented harbingers of spring date back to an Italian monk, Father Francis Cupani, who discovered wild sweet peas growing in Sicily. This first species (introduced in 1699 and now sold as 'Cupani') had small, intensely perfumed flowers colored deep purplish maroon and a light violet.

Almost 40 years later, the first named cultivar—a rose-and-pastel-pink or rose-and-cream mutation from the original species known as 'Painted Lady'—was

introduced. And by 1896 European gardeners could also choose a stippled red-and-white sweet pea called 'America'.

These dainty sweet peas have been rediscovered and are available by mail from Shepherd's Garden Seeds (30 Irene St., Torrington, CT 06790; 860/482-3638). All three have superior fragrance and some heat-tolerance. Cost is $2.45 per packet for a single variety. Or you can buy a collection of three packets (all three varieties) for $7.35 (includes information on their historical background).

For the best spring show, sow seeds now so plants get established before cool weather sets in. To extend bloom in spring, pick off flowers before they set seed.

— *Lauren Bonar Swezey*

'Irene' is true blue

Plant this rosemary where it can trail

by SHARON COHOON

■ *Rosmarinus officinalis* 'Prostratus' is the West's great cascader. Nothing looks more natural spilling over our stucco ledges and rock walls. This rugged Mediterranean native also suits California climates. It weathers long, hot summers, poor alkaline soils, salt spray, and temperatures down to 15°. Its aromatic foliage deters pests, including deer and rabbits, and its flowers attract birds and bees. Unfortunately, its flowers have always lacked the rich violet-blue color of some of its upright cousins.

But *R. o.* 'Irene'—a chance seedling discovered by Phil Johnson, a Walnut Creek, California, landscape contractor—has much larger flowers than other types of trailing rosemary, and yes, they're a deep violet-blue. Its foliage is also larger and less gray. Though 'Irene' drapes beautifully, its habit is slightly more hummocky than that of 'Prostratus', which makes it useful in narrow planting strips or spots where plants meet edges.

If you can't find 'Irene', ask your retail nursery to order it. Or mail-order it from Wayside Gardens (800/845-1124; $7.95 for a 3-inch pot) or Jackson & Perkins (800/292-4769; three for $12.95).

PHIL JOHNSON

SEED NEWS
Fact-packed packaging

■ Too bad Botanical Interests had to allow room for a bar code. Otherwise it might have figured out a way to print a botanical encyclopedia on its seed packets. An impressive amount of data has been squeezed on as it is. On the front are both common and botanical names; whether annual or perennial, sun-loving or shade-seeking; bloom period; and size at maturity. On the back are suggested uses, a detailed plant description, and recommended planting time. There's also a removable plant tag listing seed depth, spacing, germination period, and thinning requirements—just the right size to staple to a juice-bar stick or nursery plant stake and use as a row marker. Neat idea.

Peel back the packets' flaps and there's more: soil and water requirements, cultivation tips, plant family, and origin—maybe even a line of poetry or a recipe. The line of seeds has also been well thought out, with lots of heirloom and gourmet edibles, for instance. Botanical Interests seeds are widely available at independent retail nurseries. — *S. C.*

DESERT CURIOSITY
A quirky native

■ The bold, sculptural forms of cactus say "Southwest" as does no other plant. Saguaro, barrel cactus, and prickly pear are the mainstays of many unthirsty yet highly ornamental landscapes. But what if you want something a little different, even a bit strange? Consider the octopus cactus (*Stenocereus alamosensis*). Its slender, upright stems grow about 4 feet tall, before their weight causes them to arch over and eventually touch the ground, where they resume their upright growth.

Let octopus cactus do its own thing—whether scrambling up a tree, sprawling on the ground, or spilling from a pot—and it will reward you with its quirky beauty. In spring and summer, its tubular scarlet flowers attract hummingbirds. You can soften the spiny look and bring out the plant's red highlights by planting red-flowering perennials such as firecracker penstemon (*Penstemon eatonii*), as shown in the photo on page 256. Place the perennials several feet away from the cactus, so you won't get poked as you clip off spent flower stalks and also so the cactus doesn't take up too much water when you irrigate the flowers.

In the demonstration garden of Tohono Chul Park in Tucson, the finely textured foliage of littleleaf palo verde (*Cercidium microphyllum*) creates an interesting backdrop—and support—for the wandering stems of octopus cactus. Native to southern Arizona and Mexico, littleleaf palo verde grows in *Sunset* climate zones 10 through 13. The tree reaches 12 feet tall, and its lime-green canopy spreads to 15 feet.

You'll find other ideas for landscaping with native plants in the demonstration garden of Tohono Chul Park. The park, at 7366 N. Paseo del Norte, is open from 7 A.M. to sunset daily.
— *Judy Mielke*

MAINTENANCE TIP
Taming bamboo

■ A ground cover bamboo from Japan called *Sasa veitchii* has recently caught on with gardeners. Hardy to 0°, *S. veitchii* grows 2 to 3 feet tall and forms a dense canopy of dark green leaves whose edges turn a whitish buff in autumn, creating an elegant variegated effect.

Before you rush out and buy *S. veitchii*, however, be forewarned: it is rampantly invasive, spreading by roots that run in every direction, quickly taking over entire beds. There are two ways to tame it: grow it in a large container (a half-barrel works well), or inside a containment bed in the ground. Luckily, the roots don't grow deep, and you can prevent them from spreading by erecting a barrier made from a 24-inch-deep strip of plastic, fiberglass, or sheet metal. You can also use this technique to keep other running types of bamboo in bounds.

First, dig out the bed where you intend to plant the bamboo, then completely cover the edges of the bed with the material so that the top of the barrier projects slightly above ground level. Then plant the bamboo in the center of the bed and fill in with soil. When the bamboo's running rhizomes eventually hit the barrier, they'll try to jump over it—just snip them off about once a year.

If you can't find *S. veitchii* in local nurseries, you can mail-order it from Tradewinds Bamboo Nursery (28446 Hunter Creek Loop, Gold Beach, OR 97444; 541/247-0835), which sells the plants in 1-gallon cans for $12 each. The firm's catalog ($2) also lists many other kinds of bamboo.
— *Steven R. Lorton*

DAVID McDONALD

MARK WHITELEY

Spiky yucca (far left) and purple Dutch irises rise over flowering perennials.

CHARLES MANN

CURTIS ANDERSON

Hillside tapestry of unthirsty natives

■ The tapestry of plants cloaking this hillside grows on a site that many gardeners would never touch. The heavy clay soil was bad enough, but the former property owners made matters worse by covering it with a foot-deep layer of crushed rock to control weeds. The only vegetation growing here was a thin line of junipers and a scattering of aspen seedlings. But Mary Ellen Keskimaki of Golden, Colorado, wouldn't be deterred: she wanted a landscape that would be attractive, drought-tolerant, and tough enough to stand up to harsh winters.

Keskimaki arranged to have the crushed rock hauled away. Then she set a few well-chosen rocks in place and covered the clay with a 12-inch layer of sand—15 tons spread over the 4,800-square-foot site. She spent a whole summer hand-digging the sand, plus 14 truckloads of manure, into the top 6 inches of clay. By the time Keskimaki was done, "I was in really great shape," she says. The ground was in great shape, too: 18 inches of loose soil with perfect drainage.

Then she started planting—unthirsty natives such as yuccas and lots of perennials for color. In the foreground of this photo, yellow ice plant (*Delosperma nubigenum*) surrounds a pair of yuccas; to its right, a clump of 'Professor Blaauw' Dutch iris rises above an island of pink *Saponaria ocymoides*. Pink *Armeria maritima* is growing in the center of the scene, with 'Munstead' lavender spreading behind it and tall bearded iris standing to the right and rear.

During summer hot spells, Keskimaki irrigates the garden every 10 days or so until either the weather cools down or it rains.

— *J. M.*

Watering vs. spritzing

■ A little water does plants little good. That's because soil is hierarchical. Particles in the upper layers have to be coated with a film of water before any excess is released to lower levels. Sandy soil, made up of large particles, is saturated quickly. But finer-textured clay soil, with many more surfaces to coat, takes much longer.

Most gardeners turn off the water too soon. They moisten the top inch of soil and let the lower levels go thirsty, discouraging plants from developing deeper, drought-protecting roots. To wet a 4- by 5-foot flower bed to a depth of 2 feet (the average root depth of perennials) in clay soil, with a hose delivering 2 to 3 gallons per minute, for instance, requires at least 30 minutes of steady sprinkling. Watering the same area with a soaker hose, which delivers water much more slowly, requires at least two hours. — *S. C.*

Pacific Northwest Garden Notebook

by STEVEN R. LORTON

*e*very September, I hear somebody complain that "summer went by too quickly." In fact, September is one of the summeriest months in the Northwest. And I can assure you that if you stock your garden with plants that bloom in September, your garden can be as floriferous this month as it is in May or June.

First on my list of late-summer bloomers are the big sedums. With their dome-shaped clusters of flowers in autumn shades, sedums light up the garden, and the blooms often host an operatic chorus of honeybees who buzz bee-Puccini from dawn to dusk. The bright coppery-rose flowers of *Sedum telephium* 'Autumn Joy' have made it a favorite. I've also come to admire two cousin species: *S. spectabile* 'Brilliant' with deep-rose flow-

ers, and *S. s.* 'Stardust' with white flowers. I have them all planted in a sunny bed backed by the silvery foliage of artichokes.

Recently, I discovered another great late-summer bloomer in Victoria, British Columbia, while prowling through a nursery with my friend Rosemary Verey, British landscape designer and author. She introduced me to *Lobelia syphilitica,* a plant native to the eastern United States. The long-lasting electric-blue flowers, which are borne on 2- to 3-foot-tall spikes, attract hummingbirds. Supposedly, this lobelia is a short-lived perennial (mine came back strong in the second year); it's hardy in *Sunset* climate zones 2 through 7. Give it rich, moist soil and partial shade. Two mail-order sources for *L. syphilitica* are Lamb Nurseries (15208 Pacific Way, Long Beach, WA 98631; 360/642-4856), which sells plants for $3.75 each, plus shipping; and Forestfarm (990 Tetherow Rd., Williams, OR 97544; 541/846-7269), which sells plants in 1-gallon cans for $7 each, plus shipping.

Many plants that bloom during Indian summers also make fine cut flowers. If you want vivid proof, visit the Tacoma Garden Club Flower Show. This year's show promises to be on the cutting edge—its theme is "Surfing the Net." The show runs September 5 and 6 at Lakewood Library, 6300 Wildaire Road S.W. in Tacoma. Hours are 10 to 5 both days. Admission is free. For more information, call (253) 588-6946.

that's a good question ...

Q: What is your favorite rose—not for flowers but for hips?
— *Stephen Puddister, Vancouver, B.C.*

A: Nothing matches the beauty of our native wild *Rosa gymnocarpa,* whose hips vary in shape (from round to pear-shaped) and in color (deep red to pale orange). *R. rubrifolia* (formerly *R. glauca*) is a knockout in September with its deep red, often pear-shaped hips and ruby-red leaf stems. And, of course, *R. rugosa* is widely grown for its bright red, tomato-shaped hips.

MARINA THOMPSON

Northern California Garden Notebook

by **LAUREN BONAR SWEZEY**

fuchsia triphylla 'Gartenmeister Bonstedt' has always been a favorite of mine. I love its gorgeous clusters of reddish-orange flowers and its neat green leaves with purplish undersides. And it has always been resistant to fuchsia mite in my garden—until now. What a disappointment to discover distorted foliage on my plant—the work of this minuscule mite, which sucks juices from the growing tips and prevents bloom.

But I'm not alone in this discovery.

that's a good question ...

Q: I have been looking high and low for gazing balls and am not having much luck. I did find a source for silver ones when I searched the Internet, but I would like a choice of colored ones.

A. Gazing balls, also called gazing globes, are shiny and opaque glass globes 12 to 14 inches in diameter used as ornaments in the garden. They have recently seen a resurgence in popularity, and many nurseries sell a few kinds. But for a wider selection, you can order by mail from Milaeger's Gardens (4838 Douglas Ave., Racine, WI 53402; 800/669-9956). The catalog ($1) offers old-fashioned hand-blown globes in six colors, swirl globes in five colors, and miniature (6 and 8 inches in diameter) globes in three and four colors, respectively. Frog globes (6 inches in diameter), which have the amphibian perched on their tops, come in three colors.

Jeff and Lisa Rosendale of Rosendale Nursery in Watsonville also recently found the mite on their 'Gartenmeister Bonstedt' plants. The Rosendales don't know why their plants suddenly succumbed, but they've stopped growing them in favor of other species and hybrids that are mite-resistant. Most of these fuchsias are medium to large background plants for borders that have tiny to medium-size flowers. Roots are hardy down to the mid-20s, but leaves start dropping when temperatures hit 30°.

One of my favorites is graceful-looking *F. thymifolia,* which grows 3 to 9 feet tall and has ½- to 1-inch-long leaves and tiny pink flowers that dangle from the stems. Other mite-resistant fuchsias you might look for are 'Coral Baby' (tiny coral-pink flowers, 3 feet tall), 'Fanfare' (2-inch-long, hot-pink-and-orange flowers, 6 to 10 feet tall), *F. fulgens* (long, narrow coral flowers, 5 to 7 feet tall), *F. glazioviana* (small, bright-pink-and-purple flowers, 4 to 5 feet tall), and *F. procumbens* (small, pale orange or yellow flowers, 6 inches tall by 3 feet wide).

If you can't find these mite-resistant fuchsias at your local nursery, ask the staff to order one or more plants for you from Rosendale Nursery (wholesale only). Berkeley Horticultural Nursery (retail 1310 McGee Ave.; 510/526-4704) sells mite-resistant fuchsias. Several kinds are also available at Emerisa Gardens (wholesale, retail) at 555 Irwin Ln., Santa Rosa (707/525-9644).

MARINA THOMPSON

Southern California Garden Notebook

by **SHARON COHOON**

Cocoa mulch from Mirana International claims many virtues. Its acidic pH (5.4) is said to be good for our alkaline soils. The gum it releases when it's watered is supposed to bind the cocoa bean shells together to form a weed-suppressing mat. And its texture is said to deter slugs, snails, and even most cats. And this may all be true. But that's not why I buy the mulch. I like it because it makes my whole garden smell like chocolate for weeks. If I inhale deeply enough, sometimes I can even convince myself I've already had dessert. Its refined texture gives the garden a nice finished look, too.

A cautionary note, however: Theobromine, a chemical found in cocoa beans, can be toxic to dogs. Even

though 100 percent of the fat and the moisture have been processed out of Mirana's cocoa mulch, theobromine has not been. And canines attracted to chocolate may try to eat it because of its yummy smell. Cats, on the other hand, not only won't eat this material, but won't even scratch in it. I use this to my advantage against my own two determined felines. Freshly planted beds are usually their favorite places to dig. But a top dressing of the cocoa mulch keeps them out.

SPEAKING OF MULCH ...

A nurseryman in Pago Pago sent us a small sample of crushed coconut shells that he's promoting as a mulch alternative. Too bad it's not available yet. I'd like to use it under my bananas and gingers. It would also lend a tropical touch to hibiscus and gardenias. Regrettably, the shells retain no lingering smell of coconut. If they did, I could get my yard to smell like my favorite candy, Mounds bars, and save a few more calories.

WHILE WE'RE TALKING TROPICS ...

Let me pass on a Hawaiian orchid trick suggested by the late Grace Mayeda of M & M Nursery in Orange. Put a teaspoon of used coffee grounds in your cymbidium and cattleya pots this month, next, and in November. The caffeine is supposed to push the plants to produce bigger flowers. Grace's grandfathers did this, and both regularly took home prizes at orchid shows.

that's a good question ...

Q: "I love beets but have no luck with them," a reader complains. "I get great tops but no roots."

A: Beets fail to establish roots if they lack water at any time before they mature, says veteran vegetable grower Charles Ledgerwood of Ledgerwood Seeds in Carlsbad. For tender, sweet roots, stimulate fast growth by providing a steady, uniform water supply and an ample supply of organic and inorganic fertilizers. Well-grown beets mature in 55 to 60 days, he says.

MARINA THOMPSON

Mountain Garden Notebook

by JIM McCAUSLAND

More than most months, September carries with it a change that both gardeners—and plants—can feel. The weather may not be truly cold yet (unless you live at a higher elevation), but it is certainly cooler, and plants whose growth was stifled by the heat in August start growing again now. In fact, the cooler air and soil temperatures make September one of the best months for planting many perennials and landscape plants. The plants you get in the ground now have all fall to establish their root systems, which gives them a long head start on spring-planted stock.

THE PEPPERMINT CANDY ROSE

Many roses produce a flush of bloom in September—one last fling before plants head into dormancy for winter. The roses aren't picky about where they put on this grand finale, performing in the garden or in a nursery container. In fact, it's a good time to buy roses since you can see exactly what you're getting. My current favorite is the lusciously fragrant 'Scentimental', a 1997 All-America Rose Selection, with red-and-white-striped flowers that look like peppermint candy. Early reports from New England give it high marks for winter hardiness, making it a candidate for colder parts of the West.

PREPPING YOUNG TREES FOR WINTER

Young trees have thin bark that burns when low winter sun cuts through cold air. You can protect the tree by painting its trunk with white exterior latex paint, which reflects enough sun to keep the bark from scorching. Dick Rifkind, who owns Bumble Bee Nursery in Kingston, Idaho, suggests adding Diazinon to the paint mix to keep borers at bay. He mixes the insecticide with the paint, using the strongest dilution rate (for water) recommended on the Diazinon label.

that's a good question ...

Q: I understand why you wouldn't compost diseased material, but why not weeds or grass clippings?

A: If you keep your compost pile evenly moist and well aerated by mixing it with a pitchfork every week, the pile will develop internal temperatures hot enough to kill most diseases, seeds, and living plant parts. But in the real world, most gardeners aren't that faithful about tending the pile, so weeds, seeds, and disease organisms that live around the fringes stay alive even when the material in the center of the pile is cooked. When this matter is mixed back into the garden, weeds (especially those of running grasses) and diseases can be reintroduced. The best solution may be to compost most things, from grass clippings and leaves to nonrunning weeds without seed heads, in one pile. Put suspect material (bent grass, dandelions gone to seed) in a covered black-plastic trash can (with drain holes punched around the bottom), where the darkness and the heat should eventually kill any viable seeds or harmful organisms. Then move this material into your main pile.

MARINA THOMPSON

Southwest Garden Notebook

by **JIM McCAUSLAND**

More than most months, September carries with it a change that both gardeners—and plants—can feel. The weather may not be truly cold yet (unless you live at a higher elevation), but it is certainly cooler, and plants whose growth was stifled by the heat in August start growing again. In fact, the cooler air and soil temperatures make September one of the best months for planting many perennials and landscape plants. The plants you get in the ground now have all fall to establish their root systems, which gives them a long head start on spring-planted stock.

that's a good question ...

Q: I need a plant that can take over a 45° slope, which is 10 feet high and 60 feet wide. I'd like it to root as it grows, and I don't want it to die away in the winter. Flowers are optional—I just want it green. The slope gets full sun. Any suggestions? — *Kevin Spence, Las Vegas*

A: Two excellent plants come to mind: *Acacia redolens* 'Desert Carpet' and *Baccharis pilularis* 'Centennial'. Both will spread, though neither is a particularly vigorous rooter. The acacia is the more vigorous of the two, but the *Baccharis* is thicker and greener.

SHOPPING FOR DESERT NATIVES IN LAS VEGAS

It's no surprise that desert plants do great things in desert gardens. If you've had trouble finding a good selection of them, try CCSN Desert Garden Center in Las Vegas, which specializes in natives. This nursery is partially supplied with plants grown in the horticulture program at the Community College of Southern Nevada, and is staffed by horticulture students and trainees from the Nevada Association for the Handicapped. The nursery also operates an orchid greenhouse and offers vegetables and fresh flowers in season. The garden center (at 6221 W. Charleston Blvd.) is open from 8 to 4 Tuesdays through Sundays. For more information, call (702) 651-5050.

WEED PROOF SKIRTS FOR TREES

Like cracks in the sidewalk, the soil at the base of a tree just seems to attract weeds. But weed whips and lawn mowers risk damaging the tree bark, and cultivating the soil can injure surface roots. For these reasons, landscape fabrics are becoming popular—so much so that at least one company is making spun-bonded polypropylene weed barriers specifically to cover the soil around trees. This circular "skirt" is 36 inches across with an 8-inch hole in the center to fit around the trunk. Typar TreeCircle (made by Reemay, 800/367-9556) is sold at garden centers and nurseries.

MARSHA THOMPSON

Pacific Northwest Checklist

PLANTING

☑ **Permanent plants.** Shop for perennials, ground covers, trees, and shrubs, including those that bear ornamental berries and fruits. Get the plants into the ground soon and keep them well watered until fall rains come.

☑ **Spring bulbs.** Daffodils, tulips, and other spring-blooming bulbs show up in nurseries around Labor Day. Shop early to get the best selection, choosing bulbs that are plump and firm. For strong growth and early flowers, plant immediately.

MAINTENANCE

☑ **Care for lawns.** Apply about 1 pound of actual nitrogen per 1,000 square feet of turf. If lawns have bare spots, remove all weeds, rake the ground, scatter and cover seed with a thin layer of soil, then water well. The grass should be up and robust by next spring.

☑ **Care for annuals, perennials.** Snip spent flowers from annuals and perennials, and water as needed to keep plants looking their best. You can squeeze another few rounds of blooms from summer annuals by feeding the plants with a liquid fertilizer early in the month and again at midmonth.

☑ **Clean greenhouses.** Before cold weather arrives, clean out the greenhouse. Empty the old soil from flats and seedbeds. Hose down the inside. Replace broken glass and cracked weather-stripping. Check the vents and heating and watering systems.

☑ **Groom roses.** Cut flowers to bring indoors, shaping plants as you cut. Later in the month, allow a few of the flowers to form hips. This encourages plants to head into dormancy. Hips also brighten the garden in fall and winter, and serve as a food source for birds.

☑ **Make compost.** Use spent annuals, prunings, and vegetable waste to start a new compost pile, alternating green with brown materials. Keep the pile as moist as a wrung-out sponge and turn it weekly.

☑ **Mulch.** Zones 1–3: Before freezing weather arrives, remove weeds around plants, then spread a 2- to 3-inch layer of organic mulch such as compost or pine needles to insulate roots and minimize soil erosion.

☑ **Tend fuchsias.** Pinch off spent flowers to keep seed pods from forming. Keep plants evenly moist and continue your feeding program.

☑ **Water.** September can be one of the hottest, driest months. Water deeply so plants won't be drought-stressed as they enter fall and winter. ◆

Northern California Checklist

PLANTING

☑ **Plant annuals.** Zones 7–9, 14–17: To get cool-season annuals off to a good start, plant after midmonth in cool areas, and at the end of the month in warm, inland areas. If the weather is hot, shade new seedlings temporarily. Keep the soil moist. Set out calendulas, forget-me-nots, larkspur, Iceland and Shirley poppies, ornamental cabbage and kale, pansies, primroses, snapdragons, stock, sweet peas, toadflax, and violas. In coastal areas, plant cineraria, nemesia, and schizanthus.

☑ **Plant mesclun salad mix.** Zones 7–9, 14–17: Instead of purchasing expensive salad mixes at the store, sow seeds now in the ground or in a wide, low container (seeds can be purchased from the Cook's Garden, 800/457-9703). Moisten the soil or potting mix, sow seed thinly, and cover with ¼ inch soil; sprinkle lightly with water. When seedlings are 1 to 2 inches tall, thin them out (use in salads). Thin again once or twice to allow room for the seedlings to develop.

☑ **Plant new lawns.** Zones 1–2, 7–9, 14–17: Toward the end of the month, sow seed or lay sod over soil that's been rotary-tilled and amended with plenty of organic matter. Zones 1–2: Plant new lawns early in September (at highest elevations, wait to plant

Eureka

Redding

CALIFORNIA

NEVADA

Mendocino

Santa Rosa • Sacramento

Sunset
CLIMATE ZONES

San Francisco

San Jose

☐ Mountain (1-2)
☐ Valley (7-9)
☐ Inland (14)
☐ Coastal (15-17)

Monterey

Fresno

DEBRA LAMBERT

seed until October; it will germinate in spring when snow melts).

☑ **Set out fall-blooming perennials.** Zones 7–9, 14–17: Some good choices include asters, chrysanthemums, gaillardia, gloriosa daisies, purple coneflower, Japanese anemones, lion's tail, and salvias.

MAINTENANCE

☑ **Divide perennials.** Now through October (zones 1–2: early this month) is the time to divide many perennials—such as agapanthus, candytuft, coreopsis, daylily, and penstemon—that are either overgrown or not flowering well. Perennials can also be divided to increase the number of plants for your garden. Use a spading

fork or shovel to lift and loosen clumps. With the shovel, a sharp knife, or pruning shears, cut clumps into sections through soil and roots. Replant sections.

☑ **Fertilize.** Zones 7–9, 14–17: To get annuals, perennials, and fall-planted vegetables off to a strong start, mix compost into the bed before planting. Follow up with fish emulsion or a fish-kelp mixture every two to four weeks, or use a commercial fertilizer.

☑ **Prepare wildflower beds.** Weeds are the nemesis of wildflower beds. To help control them, soak the soil thoroughly to germinate the seeds, then hoe down or spray with a contact herbicide, such as a nontoxic kind derived from fatty acids (Safer SuperFast) or more toxic glyphosate. If time permits, repeat the process.

PEST CONTROL

☑ **Check for spider mites.** Zones 7–9, 14–17: This tiny pest sucks juices from plant leaves, causing stippling; tiny white eggs on the undersides of leaves and fine webbing may also be noticeable. Control by spraying the tops and bottoms of the leaves thoroughly with a lightweight summer (horticultural) oil. ◆

Southern California Checklist

PLANTING

☑ **Add cool-season color.** Coastal and low-desert gardeners (zones 22–24 and 13, respectively) can set out winter-spring-blooming annuals starting midmonth, including calendulas, English daisies, Iceland poppies, linaria, snapdragons, nemesia, pansies, and stock. Wait until October to plant inland (zones 18–21). This is also a good month to set out foxgloves, Canterbury bells, and other biennials started from seed earlier or found in small pots at the nursery.

☑ **Plant sweet peas.** For flowers by December, plant seeds now. To speed germination, soak seeds overnight before planting. Provide a wall, trellis, or 6-foot poles for vines to climb.

☑ **Buy bulbs.** Nurseries are well stocked with spring-flowering bulbs now. Choices include anemone, babiana, chasmanthe, daffodil, freesia, hyacinth, iris, leucojum, ranunculus, sparaxis, tulip, and watsonia. In the high desert (zone 11), plant immediately. In all other zones, wait until the soil cools in October before planting (except for South African bulbs like babiana and freesia, which should be planted immediately).

☑ **Plant or sow cool-weather crops.** Coastal and inland gardeners can set out seedlings of broccoli, brussels

Sunset
CLIMATE ZONES

1-3 7-9 11 13 14-24

sprouts, cabbage, cauliflower, and celery after midmonth. Sow seeds for beets, chard, collard, kale, peas, radishes, spinach, and turnips. Plant sets of garlic, onions, and shallots. In the high desert, plant lettuce, radishes, and spinach.

☑ **Chill bulbs.** Chill crocus, hyacinth, and tulip bulbs for six to eight weeks before planting. Store in a paper bag in the crisper section of your refrigerator. (Don't store with ethylene-producing fruit like apples.) Plant after Thanksgiving. In the high desert, prechilling isn't necessary.

☑ **Try a fall tomato crop.** Gardeners in frost-free areas (except close to the beach) are reporting success with

tomato seedlings planted in late summer, especially when planted near a south-facing wall. 'Champion', 'Celebrity', and 'Sweet 100' work best.

MAINTENANCE

☑ **Feed permanent plants.** Feed established trees, shrubs, ground covers, and warm-season grasses, such as Bermuda, now. Repeat in a month. Coastal gardeners can also fertilize tropical plants with a fast-acting product one last time if needed. Don't feed California natives or drought-tolerant Mediterranean plants.

☑ **Protect against brushfires.** Dead vegetation adds fuel to flames. If you live in a fire-prone area, cut and remove all dead leaves and limbs from trees and shrubs, especially those that grow near the house, before the onset of Santa Ana winds. Clear leaves from gutters and remove woody vegetation growing against structures.

PEST CONTROL

☑ **Protect cabbage crops.** Those little white butterflies flitting around your cole crops are laying eggs that will turn into hungry caterpillars. Cover crops with row covers or dust with *Bacillus thuringiensis* to kill the young larvae. ◆

Mountain Checklist

PLANTING AND HARVEST

☑ **Harvest crops.** Cantaloupes are ready to pick when the skin is well netted and the fruit slips easily from the vine. Pick watermelons when tendrils near the fruit start to brown, and winter squash when the rind colors up and hardens. Pick cucumbers and summer squash any time: they're excellent when young and tender. Ripe kernels of corn should be milky inside—if the liquid is watery, the corn is immature; if pasty, the corn is past its prime. Harvest raspberries when the sun is high and berries are warm to the touch. If a light frost threatens, protect eggplants, peppers, and tomatoes under floating row covers.

☑ **Plant lawns.** Early fall is ideal for seeding a lawn or laying sod. Keep the turf well watered until cold weather stops its growth.

☑ **Plant bulbs.** Set out bulbs of crocus, daffodils, hyacinth, *Iris reticulata*, scilla, and tulips. To protect them from soil temperature fluctuations, plant large daffodil and tulip bulbs 10 to 12 inches deep; small bulbs 5 inches deep. If daffodils and tulips were crowded last spring, lift, divide, and replant them.

☑ **Plant perennials.** Set out perennials like campanula, candytuft, cat-

MONTANA
Helena

Boise
IDAHO   WYOMING

Cheyenne

NEVADA
Reno   Salt Lake City   Denver

UTAH   COLORADO

Las Vegas

Sunset
CLIMATE ZONES
☐ 1-3   ▨ 10-11

DEBRA LAMBERT

mint, coreopsis, delphinium, dianthus, foxglove, gaillardia, geum, penstemon, phlox, salvia, and yarrow. Water them well. If the ground in your garden freezes hard every winter, spread organic mulch around plants to insulate the roots and keep the freezing soil from heaving plants out of the ground.

MAINTENANCE

☑ **Clean the greenhouse.** Scrub out seedbeds and flats with a weak solution of bleach and water. Then check and replace weather-stripping, broken glass, and torn plastic. Finally, check vents, filters, and heaters, replacing or repairing broken components before winter comes.

☑ **Divide perennials.** In all but the very highest elevations, lift and divide crowded clumps of bleeding heart, daylilies, hostas, peonies, and Shasta daisies. Mulch after replanting.

☑ **Fertilize lawns.** Apply about 10 pounds of 10-10-10 fertilizer per 1,000 square feet of turf.

☑ **Lift and store summer bulbs.** When foliage dies down, lift cannas, dahlias, and gladiolus. Let the bulbs or tubers dry for a few days, then store in sand, peat moss, or vermiculite at 35° to 50° in a well-ventilated space. Leave potted begonia tubers in containers.

☑ **Make compost.** Build a pile about 4 feet in diameter, alternating layers of green (grass clippings) with brown matter (dried leaves). Keep the pile as moist as a wrung-out sponge, and turn it weekly.

☑ **Water.** Don't forget to water plants growing under eaves and in containers.

PEST CONTROL

☑ **Prevent snow mold.** If your lawn is subject to snow mold (a fungus), rake the thatch, then spray the turf with a fungicide. ◆

Southwest Checklist

PLANTING

✔ **Plant or prechill bulbs.** Zones 1–2, 10–11: Plant spring-flowering bulbs, including crocus, daffodil, grape hyacinth, hyacinth, and tulip. Zone 11 (Las Vegas): Also plant iris rhizomes. Zones 12–13: Buy crocus, hyacinth, and tulip bulbs. Place them in paper bags and store in the refrigerator for several weeks to chill before planting in the ground around Thanksgiving.

✔ **Sow cool-season crops.** Zones 10–13: As soon as temperatures drop below 100°, sow beets, carrots, celery, chard, endive, green onions, kale, kohlrabi, leeks, parsley, parsnips, peas, potatoes, radishes, spinach, and turnips. Sow lettuce and cabbage-family members (such as broccoli, cauliflower, and brussels sprouts) in flats now for transplanting in October.

✔ **Plant fall beans, corn.** Zones 12–13: If you plant beans and corn in the low and intermediate deserts around Labor Day, you'll be harvesting both crops by Thanksgiving.

✔ **Plant lawns.** Zones 1–2, 10–11: Seed a lawn or lay sod; continue to water well until grass is established.

✔ **Plant perennials.** Zones 1–2, 10–11: Plant most perennials, including campanula, candytuft, catmint,

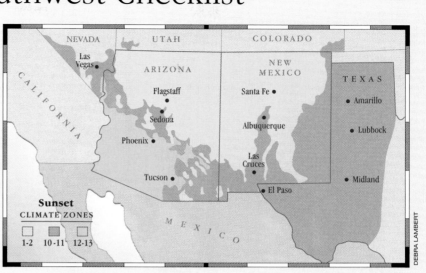

coreopsis, delphinium, dianthus, diascia, foxglove, gaillardia, geum, penstemon, phlox, salvia, and yarrow. Zones 10–13: Start seeds of carnation, columbine, coreopsis, feverfew, gaillardia, hardy aster, hollyhock, lupine, penstemon, phlox, Shasta daisy, statice, and yarrow for transplanting outside in about eight weeks.

✔ **Plant for permanence.** Zones 10–11: Set out hardy trees, shrubs, and ground covers from nursery containers.

MAINTENANCE

✔ **Care for lawns.** If you plan to overseed your Bermuda lawn, stop feeding it. If you don't plan to overseed, apply 1 pound of actual nitro-

gen per 1,000 square feet of turf and water it in well.

✔ **Feed roses.** Water plants deeply, fertilize, water again, and then apply a 3-inch layer of organic mulch around the root zone.

✔ **Water citrus.** Irrigate citrus deeply every 10 to 14 days; it will help reduce fruit split.

PEST CONTROL

✔ **Spray cabbage loopers.** To kill the little green worms that eat the leaves of cabbage-family members, spray plants with *Bacillus thuringiensis.* ◆

Country garden bouquets

California designer Linda Arietta shares her secrets for painting with flowers

■ As you travel the country lane through farmland east of Watsonville, California, nothing prepares you for the surprises at road's end. Not the green patchwork of strawberry or lettuce fields, or the chocolate squares of freshly churned soil between them, or even the distant golden hills. Nothing, except maybe a sign near the gate that modestly announces Country Essences Flowers, the 10-acre ranch that floral designer Linda Arietta calls home.

Along the driveway, a ribbon of spring wildflowers and a rambling 'Queen Elizabeth' rose cloaked with huge pink blooms hint at Arietta's fascination with flowers. Then a bright burst of blue delphiniums and a shocking-scarlet bougainvillea scrambling against blue window trim reveal her love of color.

But on the patio behind the 100-year-old farmhouse, just past the barbecue area where guests gather for yet another of Arietta's memorable Saturday evening parties, the palette ignites. Brilliant blooms are everywhere: in pots, in beds, in vases, even on exterior walls. Arietta's bouquets for the party

Top: Linda Arietta harvests a handful of dahlias beside her farmhouse.
Right: Like freshly dipped paintbrushes, bunches of larkspur hang to dry.

by KATHLEEN NORRIS BRENZEL

photographs by NORMAN A. PLATE

"We all need color in our lives, and it comes from nature."

Floral artistry starts at Arietta's doorstep, with colorful brush strokes bursting from pots, hanging baskets, and beds full of annuals and perennials.

Field notes: Growing great cut flowers

• Grow lots of different kinds of flowers together. Diversity helps control pests.

• Feed plants regularly. Arietta sprinkles granular balanced fertilizer into the soil before planting in winter (so rains can water it in). During the growing season, her plants get a diluted liquid fertilizer with each watering.

• Use drip irrigation (or soaker hoses) to avoid wetting flowers and foliage and to help prevent mildew.

• Plant in succession. When something's finished, pull it out, prep the soil, and replant with something else.

• Amend the soil with compost between plantings. Arietta uses mushroom compost from nearby farms.

are floral fireworks, color-matched to vases and dishes, and as vividly rendered as still-life paintings. On one table, an arrangement of blue larkspur, bright salmon-pink godetias, and white lilies echoes the colors of watermelon slices on a cobalt blue platter. On another table, asters in pink, rose, white, and lavender play off the Caribbean beach colors of the striped umbrella above them.

Arietta's flower beds, like her bouquets, are joyful expressions of color and fantasy. An old watering can and a fruit crate filled with magenta petunias are among the many personal touches that embellish her garden.

"We all need color in our lives, and it comes from nature," says Arietta. "I paint with flowers."

A BUDDING PASSION

Arietta's first brush with the flower business came after she'd graduated with a degree in art from Lone Mountain College in San Francisco and set-

tled on a ranch next door to her parents. She planted an acre of sweet peas ("enough to cover the whole world," she laughs) and wound up sharing the harvest with every florist in Santa Cruz County. "For years, I was known as the 'Sweet Pea Lady.'"

Gradually she branched out, adding other flowers to her palette and to her fields. She began selling flowers at farmers' markets throughout the San Francisco Bay Area, and creating bouquets for weddings, restaurants, and hotels.

Now, Arietta's ranch produces more than 50 kinds of flowers per season. Her long list of clients includes Smith & Hawken, Crate & Barrel, and Neiman Marcus. And she recently opened a shop, Country Essences Flowers, in nearby Capitola Village, where—against a cheerful backdrop of white lattice-covered walls—she sells her flowers fresh, freeze-dried, and in arrangements that she creates with help from her staff of four designers.

The secrets to Arietta's great bouquets? "I like to grow things commercial growers don't touch," she says. "I order seed mixes. And I choose flowers for their exquisite colors and shapes that combine well in natural-looking bouquets."

This month she'll be planting for next spring's bouquets. She'll sow seeds of godetia, larkspur, sweet pea, and stock, and set out delphinium seedlings. But Arietta's always looking for something new to try. "Flowers are my passion, my life," she says. "I love sharing that beauty with others." ◆

INSTANT POTPOURRI

•When dried flowers such as larkspur crumble, scoop up the petals and put them in an airtight jar with orrisroot scented with oil (orrisroot and scented, or essential, oils are sold in health food stores). Use citrus scents for yellow flowers, rose scents for pinks and blues.

•Delphinium, rose, and sunflower petals that drop from fresh bouquets as they age can be air-dried (they'll keep some color). Lay them face down on a paper towel for two to four days to dry, then toss them in a low glass bowl for display.

Secrets for sensual arrangements

•Let your decor inspire your flower choices. Walls, furniture, a great painting, or objects on the table can suggest bouquet colors.

•Prepare delicate flowers before arranging them. Delphiniums and sweet peas last longer if you soak them in floral preservative and water in a cool place overnight.

•Add fillers to give a bouquet an "airy, fieldsy, country look." Six favorites: corn cockle (*Agrostemma*), fern asparagus (*A. setaceus*), ivy, Queen Anne's lace, saponaria (*S. ocymoides*), and statice (*Limonium bellidifolium*).

•Use small-leafed foliage, such as grasses, myrtle, and salal, as accents.

•Tuck snippets of scented geranium leaves, especially rose-scented kinds, among the flowers to add wonderful fragrance to bouquets.

•For a great springtime show, fill aluminum buckets with bunches of sweet peas and cluster them under a blooming apple tree.

•Freshen bouquets daily. Flowers dry out more quickly in floral foam than in water-filled vases. Keep the foam moist. If possible, also remove the flowers from the foam daily, clip about an inch off their stems, and return to foam.

•Revive wilted flowers by cutting their stems in warm water.

•Don't waste anything. If petals drop from the bouquet, gather them up to make potpourri. *(See box at left.)*

CHOICE PLANTS FOR COUNTRY-STYLE BOUQUETS

Spring (plant in fall except where noted): Anemone, delphinium*, Dutch iris, foxglove, freesia, godetia (plant in spring in cold climates), larkspur*, lavender, lilac, narcissus, ranunculus, rose (late winter), stock, sweet pea.

Fall (plant in spring): Amaranth, aster*, dahlia*, hydrangea, sunflower*, zinnia.*

* = *Arietta's "success" flowers, popular and easiest to grow. "I plant every variety and color of these I can get my hands on."*

Left: On a buffet table, delphiniums are color-matched with a vase, candlesticks, and—behind the table—a painting of delphiniums by Katherine Myers. **Center:** *Sunflowers, zinnias, and dahlias (anchored in florist's foam) fill two half-moon-shaped terra-cotta bowls that fit around an umbrella pole. The tallest blooms are tied to the pole with raffia.* **Right:** *Puffy hydrangeas (in various stages of bloom) share a crystal vase with 'Hopley's' oregano and ivy.*

Growing your own antiques

■ Scattered throughout the West's apple country are growers who specialize in antique apples—varieties introduced before the turn of the century. Altogether, they sell nearly 100 varieties as nursery stock.

Which are the most flavorful antiques to grow? For recommendations, we turned to four growers—Carolyn and Terry Harrison, who offer 94 varieties, bare-root, by mail through **Sonoma Antique Apple Nursery** in the rolling hills of Healdsburg, California, and Catherine and Joe Brocard, who grow 189 apple varieties in the Sweet Home, Oregon, orchard they planted in 1979. After years in the business, all have well-honed apple-tasting skills—although, as in the case of 'Nonesuch', they don't always agree.

NORMAN A. PLATE (16)

Carolyn Harrison

This month at the Brocards' **Antique Apple Orchard,** you can taste antique apples to help you decide which varieties to grow. It's at 28095 Santiam Highway in Sweet Home (541/367-4840) and open 10 to 5 Tuesdays through Saturdays. The mail-order suppliers listed at right (including the Harrisons' nursery) sell bare-root stock; place your orders this fall for delivery before spring.

HARVEST TIPS

• "When you harvest an apple plays a big part in how it tastes," says Carolyn Harrison. To determine whether the crop is ripe enough to start picking, pluck an apple from the tree, cut it in half, and look at the seeds. If the seeds are dark, the apples should be ready to harvest (tasting always confirms it). If the weather is cool, you have a wider window for harvest—up to two weeks for optimum flavor (but just a matter of days for early apples). If it's hot, you should harvest right away.

• Early and midseason apples generally don't keep well. Late apples are good keepers.

BARE-ROOT SOURCES

• **In the Northwest**
Bear Creek Nursery, Box 411, Northport, WA 99157. Bear Creek has perhaps the best selection of antique bare-root in the state, and specializes in apples for cold climate zones. For a free catalog, send a fax to (509) 732-4417 or e-mail your request to BearCreekin@plix.com.

• **In California**
Sonoma Antique Apple Nursery, 4395 Westside Rd., Healdsburg, CA 95448; (707) 433-6420.

best for eating fresh

'Cox Orange Pippin' (1830). ▶
Small to medium-size green fruit has red-orange overlay. Crisp, sweet-tart flavor. Expect some apples to crack on the blossom end. Late midseason. *"It would be a good pie apple for flavor, but it's small. We put lots of these in our cider."* — Catherine Brocard

'Golden Russet' (1845). ▶
Medium-size, rust-colored fruit. Late midseason. *"I'd put its flavor just behind 'Ashmead's Kernel'. 'Golden Russet' is such a firm apple that it holds up too well in cooking, staying chunky even in pies. Eat it fresh."* — C. B.

◀ **'Nonesuch', or 'Hubbardston' (1830).** Large, with reddish skin. Moderately firm flesh. Crisp, rich, and sweet. Midseason to late. *"Not enough acid to cook with. A sweet, crisp apple that fills a gap between 'Gravenstein' and 'Spitzenburg'."* — Carolyn Harrison

◀ **'Seek-No-Further', or 'Westfield' (1796).** Medium-large apple with yellow-green flesh and tough green skin. Late. *"When you eat this apple fresh, its aroma flavors the fruit in the same way that the 'McIntosh' fragrance affects the taste of the flesh."* — C. B.

CURTIS ANDERSON

'Ashmead's Kernel' (1700). ▶
A late, medium-size russet with golden-brown skin and crisp, aromatic flesh. Tart but sugary flavor. *"Good fresh, if you like a dense, chewy apple. Someone once told me this apple has too much taste. I'd call it a gutsy apple."* — *C. H.*

'Belle de Boskoop' (1856). ▶
Large, greenish-yellow fruit with a dark red blush and rough skin. Partial russet. Hard, dense flesh. Crisp, tangy, and aromatic. Harvest midseason. — *C. H.*

◀ **'McIntosh' (1870).** Red skin tinged with yellow; fragrant white flesh. Fruit is medium-size, and doesn't store well. Midseason. *"'McIntosh' cooks down fast into great, smooth applesauce that doesn't need a lot of sugar. But it also turns to sauce when you try to bake it into pies."* — *C. B.*

◀ **'Northern Spy' (1800).** Large, attractive red-and-yellow fruit with thin skin and firm, tender flesh. Fruity, juicy, and tart. Use in applesauce, cider, or pie, or eat it fresh. Similar to 'Gravenstein', but ripens later. Mid- to late season. *"Classic old-fashioned apple taste."* — *C. H.*

'Roxbury Russet' (before 1649). ▶
Medium-size apple, on the squat side. Dense, light-green fruit with a sweet, almost nutty flavor. Late midseason to late. *"Not as highly fruity as 'Ashmead's Kernel'. Bears an amazingly huge crop every year. Don't pick too early or sugars won't develop."* — *C. H.*

'Sierra Beauty' (about 1900). ▶
Large apples with green-and-yellow skin, striped or blushed red. Juicy and crisp, with a sweet-tart flavor. A great keeper. Late. *"It won't develop overlying sweetness until really ripe (it may not ripen in a cool climate)."* — *C. H.*

◀ **'Spitzenburg' (before 1800).** Medium to large, firm fruit with red-and-yellow skin and russet dots. A shy bearer. Late. *"The Gewürztraminer of apples. Its spiciness and fruitiness really come through. It's the flavor king of apples. My mother-in-law's childhood favorite."* — *C. H.*

◀ **'White Permain' (before 1858).** Medium to large, pale green fruit with one side blushed red. Firm, crisp flesh with sweet but slightly tart flavor; pear undertones when allowed to mellow after picking. Best keeper. Late. — *C. H.*

'Bramley's Seedling' (1813). ▶
Large green apple, very high in vitamin C. Sharp, very acid. Early to midseason. *"Not for pies; it doesn't hold its shape."* — *C. H.*

'Calville Blanc d'Hiver' (1598). ▶
Medium to large green fruit tinged pink and yellow. Tart flavor. Late midseason. *"You'll pucker if you eat this fresh, but the fruit mellows in storage. Some overtones of pear or pineapple make it one of the best pie apples you can grow."* — *C. B.*

◀ **'Nonesuch', or 'Hubbardston' (1830).** This antique variety was selected as both a good eating and a good cooking apple. *"Not an especially pretty apple, but it cooks up well and makes fine cider."* — *C. B.*

◀ **'Pink Pearl' (about 1945).** A firm-fleshed, pearly-skinned apple that holds its shape. Sweet-tart flavor. Use in applesauce, cider, pies. Early. *"This apple has everything: good flavor and special color."* — *C. H.*

Sourwood fires up this Seattle garden in October. For more on this deciduous beauty, see page 284.

CLAIRE CURRAN

October

gardenguide

gear

Once, everyone from prospectors to pioneer gardeners used wheelbarrows made of wood. Then came barrows of steel, plastic, and fiberglass. Now wood is back. The Janesville No. 3 Wheelbarrow ($195–$210) is patterned after a design that was common early this century. It comes with oak sides and bottom and maple handles, and rolls along on a steel wheel. Though it can haul just about any dry material, manure to mulch, its sides are easily removable, so it doubles as a rolling platform for toting nursery plants from car to garden. Container plants look so good in this barrow, you may want to display them in it. Order from Wisconsin Wagon Co., 507 Laurel Ave., Janesville, WI 53545; (608) 754-0026. — *Jim McCausland*

HEIRLOOM FLOWERS

A poppy with panache

■ *Eschscholzia californica* 'Apricot Flambeau' looks like a California poppy decked out for a party. Its creamy yellow petals have ruffled edges and intense orange highlights.

This old favorite was first offered for sale in the 1930s, then it faded from the scene. Thompson & Morgan rediscovered it several years ago and reintroduced it.

At *Sunset's* headquarters in Menlo Park, we started seeds of 'Apricot Flambeau' in containers in the fall, then set the seedlings in the ground in full sun when they were several inches tall. (You can also sow seeds directly in the ground.) In early spring, the plants put on a show for about two months (they were given supplemental water to keep the soil moist). The plants grew 8 to 10 inches tall.

To grow your own 'Apricot Flambeau' poppies, order seeds from Thompson & Morgan, Box 1308, Jackson, NJ 08527; (800) 274-7333. Cost: $1.99 per packet, plus shipping.
— *Lauren Bonar Swezey*

NORMAN A. PLATE (2)

Magnificent monsters

For a really big show, plant a late-blooming salvia

by SHARON COHOON

■ ***Salvia madrensis*** is not a plant for the faint of heart, nor is it a wise choice for cubicle-size gardens. In the spring, it seems tame enough. Then in summer, it shoots out big, square stems, letting you know that it won't stay small for long. And sure enough, by bloom time in fall, it's taken on Amazonian proportions—7 feet tall and nearly as wide. But every inch is gorgeous, from its long spikes of large primrose-yellow flowers to its big, heart-shaped, crinkly leaves.

If you have room in your garden, this and several other big but beautiful late-blooming salvias (listed below) are worth planting for the drama they bring to garden beds.

S. wagneriana. Nearly as big as *S. madrensis* but sporting even larger flowers in a bright rose-pink, striking against lime-green, scalloped leaves. Hardy to -20°. (*S. madrensis* is hardy to -10°.)

S. guaranitica. Showy indigo blue flowers against textured green leaves. To 5 feet. Hardy to -10°.

S. azurea grandiflora. As tall as the above salvias but not as bushy. Needs staking or propping. But its flowers are that rare thing—true blue. Hardy to -30°.

S. splendens 'Van Houttei'. Very tender salvia (hardy to only 30°), but so striking—burgundy bracts and carmine flowers against light green leaves—that it's often grown as an annual. As annual, to 3 feet; perennial, 5 feet or more.

Top: Pastel yellow flowers are unexpected in the autumn garden. Salvia madrensis provides them in abundance.
Left: Showy flowers of S. splendens 'Van Houttei' light up a border in fall.

WILLIAM B. DEWEY (2)

CHARLES MANN

INNOVATIVE LANDSCAPE

A prize garden

■ One autumn day after Bruce de Cameron moved into his new house in Denver, he cut the front lawn for the first and last time. The 12- by 25-foot site—on a 45° slope—was too steep to mow easily. But the slope had the same allure for de Cameron that an easel has for a painter, and he could hardly have chosen a better angle for showing off plant colors and textures.

A garden designer by trade, de Cameron knew that October was a great time to plant. He started by killing the lawn with the herbicide glyphosate and tilling the sod into the heavy soil along with some compost. Then he planted a blend of annuals, perennials, and shrubs, including junipers, heleniums, penstemons, blue oat grass, poppies, and violas. Many of the plants are drought-tolerant Western natives, but some, like Iceland poppies, are exotics that he plugs in for seasonal color.

The resulting garden (shown here in its second year) has all the best features of a wild landscape, and it won de Cameron's firm, Great Gardens of Den-ver, an award in a recent landscape design contest. The garden changes constantly, as a wild garden should. The poppies and violas, for example, reseed freely; de Cameron lets them grow where he wants them and pulls them up elsewhere.

A thick pine-needle mulch keeps weeds down and prevents erosion. The garden needs water about once a week during the hottest days of summer. To feed plants, de Cameron scatters pellets of dehydrated chicken manure over the site every spring. —*J. M.*

NEW PLANT
A shapelier strawberry tree

■ Gardeners who appreciate the attractive foliage and berries of a strawberry tree (*Arbutus unedo*) but prefer a plant with the habit of a tree rather than a shapeless, bushy shrub will be pleased to learn about a new strawberry tree relative called *A.* 'Marina'.

'Marina', which has the growth habit and red bark of madrone (*A. menziesii*), eventually reaches a height of 40 feet. Clusters of rosy pink flowers appear along with red berries in fall. It was developed for the nursery trade by Victor Reiter, who offered cuttings to the Saratoga Horticultural Research Foundation in San Martin, California.

Plant 'Marina' in full sun or partial shade and, preferably, well-drained soil. Once established, the plant can handle regular to little water.

Trees are available with a single trunk or multiple trunks. If you can't find one, ask your nursery to order it from Monterey Bay Nursery in Watsonville (wholesale only) or Saratoga Horticultural Research Foundation. — *L. B. S.*

BRIAN HUNTOON

BULB CULTURE
Tulips with colorful foliage

■ When you're shopping for tulip bulbs in catalogs and nurseries, look for the tulips that also put on a good display of foliage before they bloom. With these kinds, you'll get a longer show for your investment.

Two tulips with attractive foliage are *Tulipa tarda* (*T. dasystemon*) and *T. greigii* 'Red Riding Hood'. *T. tarda*, the earlier of the two, has bright orange-and-yellow rosettes of young leaves that deepen to green, followed by star-shaped flowers with rich yellow centers and creamy yellow edges on 5-inch stems. 'Red Riding Hood' bears green leaves with deep burgundy stripes, and vivid scarlet blooms atop 6-inch stems. Both these tulips do well in pots and also naturalize well in the ground.

T. tarda and 'Red Riding Hood' aren't commonly sold in nurseries. Order them by mail from Van Dyck's Flower Farms, Box 430, Brightwaters, NY 11718; (800) 248-2852.

— *Steven R. Lorton*

BACK TO BASICS
Unraveling roots of container-grown plants

■ Before you set out container-grown plants in the fall, inspect their root systems and unravel any tangles that might have resulted from being in the container too long.

If a plant is only lightly rootbound, gently loosen the roots at the bottom of the root mass and tease apart. If the root mass still seems too dense, carefully "butterfly," splitting the root mass in half vertically, from the bottom halfway to the top.

Larger roots that encircle the rootball, sometimes working themselves up to the top of the pot, need to be untangled before transplanting or they'll continue to choke the plant. Cut apart if you can't loosen them with your fingers. Splay the unbound roots outward when you plant.

If a plant is severely rootbound, also make several ¼- to ½-inch-deep cuts in the rootball from top to bottom (as shown below) to encourage the development of new feeder roots.

Cut back some of the top growth to compensate for the reduction in root mass, even if it means sacrificing a few flowers. —*S. C.*

CURTIS ANDERSON

JOHN TRAGER

Sourwood: A sweet autumn beauty

■ Sourwood (*Oxydendrum arboreum*) is a deciduous tree native to the hardwood forests of the eastern United States. But don't let its origin put you off: this tree is perfectly suited for small gardens in the Pacific Northwest. It grows slowly (rarely more than 6 inches a year) to a height of 15 to 25 feet (given perfect conditions, it might reach 50 feet in a century).

In winter, when the tree is leafless, it displays its slender, statuesque form. In spring, its foliage unfolds with a bronzy tint that turns to a rich green as the 5- to 8-inch leaves reach maturity. In July, when most flowering trees have finished blooming, it bears clusters of creamy, bell-shaped blossoms along 10-inch stems.

These traits are reason enough to grow this tree. Still another bonus comes in October, when the flower tassels burst into green seed pods and the leaves turn brilliant scarlet (see the photo on page 278). The fiery autumn leaves cling to the tree for a good long time, dropping over an extended period much as the leaves of a liquidambar do.

Hardy in *Sunset* climate zones 3 through 7, sourwood needs ample water and rich, acid soil with good drainage. Allow open ground around the base of the tree so its delicate roots won't have to compete with grass, ground covers, or other plants for nutrients.

Nurseries sell sourwood trees in 5-gallon and larger containers. Plant now and water them well until fall rains begin. — *S. R. L.*

Pumpkin-orange gladiolus for autumn

■ *Gladiolus dalenii* is a catch-22 plant. This late-blooming gladiolus would be a welcome addition to fall gardens. Picture it, for instance, against the lavender-blue of asters. Native to South Africa and adapted to our climate, this species gladiolus would naturalize as readily in our gardens as freesias do. But growers don't propagate *G. dalenii*. There's no demand for it. And there's no demand because no one sees it.

You can remedy that situation this month. *G. dalenii* will be in glorious bloom in the perennial borders at the University of California, Irvine, Arboretum and on the subtropical hill at the Huntington Gardens. And both gardens sell *G. dalenii* as potted plants at their fall sales. For information on the arboretum's sale, call (714) 824-5833. To learn more about the Huntington's sale, call (818) 405-2141. One wholesale grower, Suncrest Nursery, is propagating *G. dalenii* and expects to offer plants in small quantities to nurseries this fall. — *S. C.*

CURTIS ANDERSON

Helping trees stand tall

■ Inventors are constantly dreaming up new and better products, including ways to stake a tree. The latest invention by a group of horticultural professionals is the Bio-Tie, a single-stake tree support designed to eliminate less attractive dual stakes. This new device allows the trunk to sway in the wind (making it stronger and stimulating root growth), so a young tree can stand on its own soon, usually after only one season of growth.

Unlike the black rubber straps normally used to support a tree, Bio-Tie's strap breaks as the trunk grows larger, so there's no chance of it strangling the trunk. The plastic housing is reusable; only the flexible strap needs replacement.

To order Bio-Tie, call (800) 958-4832. Each one costs $5.99, including shipping. — *L. B. S.*

CHARLES MANN

Wildflower secrets

■ The Desert Botanical Garden in Phoenix has nearly perfected the art of wildflower displays (one is shown above). But even if you don't have the space to plant a whole meadow, you can still enjoy wildflowers by planting them in small patches.

In *Sunset* climate zones 11 through 13 (Las Vegas, Tucson, Phoenix), early October through mid-November is the best time to sow wildflower seed or set out plants.

Resident horticulturist Michelle Rauscher offers some planting tips.

•**Choose a sunny spot,** then loosen the soil to a depth of 3 to 4 inches. Soil amendments are generally not necessary for native wildflowers.

•**Water the area** to encourage weed seeds to germinate. Pull or hoe the weeds as soon as they appear.

•**Scatter a mix of annual and perennial seeds** over the area. Use about ¼ ounce of seed for a 25-square-foot garden. Lightly rake the soil to cover the seeds. As a quicker (but costlier) alternative, set out 1-gallon-size plants of perennial wildflowers.

•**Water right away** and as often as needed to keep the soil moist until wildflower seedlings appear. Then reduce watering to two or three times a week. Pull weeds by hand as soon as you can tell them from the wildflowers.

•**Protect the garden** with a ring of chicken wire if rabbits or other rodents are a problem in your area.

One good source for seeds of many regional wildflower species is Wild Seed, Box 27751, Tempe, AZ 85285; (602) 276-3536 (catalog is free).

— *Judy Mielke*

Pacific Northwest Garden Notebook

by **STEVEN R. LORTON**

*A*utumn is my favorite season. I love everything about it. The cool weather, the smell of dry foliage, and, of course, the fall colors. Flip a calendar to October and you'll likely see a hillside in Vermont covered in a blaze of sugar maples. It's a glorious sight, but it's not my autumn scene. I prefer to gaze at dark green Northwest landscapes dotted with spots of color and, in my garden, at the glowing oranges and yellows of trees, shrubs—and perennials.

In fact, a surprising number of perennials put on a fall foliage show. Consider the leafy, low-growing *Geranium macrorrhizum* this month. British horticultural writer Graham Stuart Thomas calls it "a splendid dense weed-proof ground-cover which can be relied upon absolutely." Its lobed leaves flourish in sun or shade, and the plant bears delicate pink flowers. But in autumn, when the frost is on the pumpkin, the blush is on *Geranium macrorrhizum*; its leaves acquire a strong reddish and orange flush. The colorful foliage sometimes lasts through the winter. When crushed, its leaves have a strong cedarlike fragrance. One source for *G. macrorrhizum* is Heronswood Nursery, 7530 N.E. 288th St., Kingston, WA 98346; (360) 297-4172.

Another fine perennial with a fall-color bonus is the oak-leaf hydrangea (*H. quercifolia*). I first saw this plant blooming in the Deep South one summer: a big, rounded 6-foot shrub, with rugged, rusty bark and thick green leaves that closely resembled oak leaves, it was filled with big cones of sparkling white flowers. When I returned to the Northwest, I bought three plants locally and planted them in my country garden in Washington's Skagit Valley. When fall arrived, the leaves turned dark burgundy, and after the first frost hit, some leaves took on a deep burnt-orange color. Many nurseries sell this beautiful plant.

So now whenever I go plant shopping in October, I head to the spot where the nursery has shoved the bloomed-out perennials. As I browse among the stock, I often find another specimen of unexpected autumn color.

that's a good question ...

Q: My fruit trees have a lot of moss on them. Some people tell me the moss will kill the trees and to spray with chemical moss killer. Others say the moss feeds off nutrients in the air and to leave it alone. What do you think? — *Ron Samuelson, Portland*

A: Gary Moulton, pomologist at Washington State University, advises against spraying. The moss and lichen will not hurt the trees, but they are likely a sign that the trees are not getting enough light and air circulation. So you may want to prune your trees to open them up. Personally, I think trees with a bit of moss on them are beautiful, especially in the winter garden.

MARINA THOMPSON

Northern California Garden Notebook

by LAUREN BONAR SWEZEY

One of the great perks of working at *Sunset* is my picturesque view of our 4-acre garden designed by the famous landscape architect Thomas Church. Magnificent oaks dot the landscape, redwoods and pines frame the long-distance view, and flowers bloom year-round. Head gardener Rick LaFrentz works magic with the seasonal beds of color, bringing in a wonderful array of annuals, perennials, and bulbs.

This past spring in the bed right outside my window appeared the most glorious combination of deep maroon 'Queen of Night' tulips (from Van Dyck's, 800/248-2852) overplanted with bright yellow calendulas.

I had watched LaFrentz plant the calendulas last fall; they bloomed first. Since I'm not particularly fond of golden yellow flowers, I barely took notice of them outside my window. But when the tulips poked up through the calendulas and burst into bloom, I couldn't take my eyes off the display. It was an interesting lesson in the use of color.

GARDENING THE LEAST TOXIC WAY

I'm a strong proponent of gardening without the use of highly toxic pesticides, which is why the new "Grow It!" guide from Marin County Stormwater Pollution Prevention Program (MCSTOPPP) appeals to me.

The 17-page, pocket-size fan guide (riveted together like a paint-chip selector) was produced in an effort to prevent toxic pollutants from entering storm drains and polluting streams and the San Francisco Bay. It features 17 plant pests, explain-

ing how to detect them, low-toxicity controls, and prevention techniques. On the flip side of the cards are plant lists, including deer-resistant plants, fire-resistant plants, invasive plants, and native plants that attract butterflies.

Six other Bay Area counties (all but Sonoma and Napa) have similar guides, though some are less comprehensive than Marin's. They're free and can be ordered by calling (888) 229-9473.

SOURCE FOR GINGER PLANTS

The phone number listed for Brudy's Exotics in the August issue is no longer in service. Try the Banana Tree, which sells 25 kinds of gingers (including kahili) and other tropical plants. To order, call (610) 253-9589, or check out the catalog on the firm's Web site: http://www.banana-tree.com.

that's a good question ...

Q: Do you know of a book or Web site that lists the names of nurseries and the specific plants they sell? I understand they have such a publication in Britain. — *Marge Tobias, Santa Rosa*

A: The closest publication we have is *Gardening by Mail,* by Barbara J. Barton (Houghton Mifflin Co., Boston, 1994; $21.95), updated monthly on the Virtual Garden Web site (http://vg.com/gbm). It's a wonderful sourcebook for almost anything related to gardening.

MARINA THOMPSON

Southern California Garden Notebook

by SHARON COHOON

i've wanted to add ribbon bush (*Hypoestes aristata*) to my garden ever since I saw it in Darwin Black's yard in Laguna Beach three years ago. Under a steel gray November sky, this shrubby perennial's magenta flowers glowed like neon. Now I won't have to go another winter without it. UC Riverside Botanic Gardens has ribbon bush on the plant list for its fall sale—along with 101 other temptations. All I have to figure out is what to plant with it. Will it work with *Cuphea* 'Buena Creek Red', a tall evergreen shrub that would be covered in orangy-red flowers about the same time? Or maybe woolly butterfly bush (*Buddleia marrubifolia*), with its small, fuzzy white leaves and big yellow flower clusters? And dare I add a mound of *Galvezia speciosa* 'Firecracker'—"gray-green foliage, handsome, compact habit, intense red flowers"—to the mix?

Oh, why not? Darwin's garden gives me courage. In spring, magenta, scarlet, and orange together would look like a circus costume. But in winter it's almost impossible to be gaudy. Leaden skies and oblique light temper everything. Maybe, just to be on the safe side, I'd better toss in the lemon yellow of *Reinwardtia indica,* too.

To get to the UC Riverside Botanic Gardens, take the Martin Luther King Boulevard exit off State Highway 60 in Riverside. Turn right, then right again on Canyon Crest Avenue,

and follow the signs directing you to the gardens. For more information, call (909) 787-4650.

TONIC TIME FOR PLANTS

I got a good gardening tip from Steve Brigham of Buena Creek Gardens in San Marcos. The soil pH in our gardens creeps up steadily all summer, he says, because of the alkalinity of our primary water supply, the Colorado River. This high pH makes it hard for plants to pull the minerals they need out of the soil. Applying an acid-based fertilizer throughout the garden this month reduces the pH, "unlocking" these minerals, says Brigham. He happens to use Super Iron by Best, but any camellia or azalea food will work.

that's a good question ...

Q: I love the aroma of chaparral plants, but I live in an apartment and my "yard" is a concrete patio. Are there natives I can plant in containers?

A: Surprisingly, yes. Though some natives are ultrasensitive to summer water, there are others that survive easily in containers. The following plants—all aromatic—are good ones to try: *Artemisia californica* 'Montara', *A. pycnocephala* 'David's Choice', Cleveland sage (*Salvia clevelandii*), hummingbird sage (*S. spathacea*), and coyote mint (*Monardella villosa*). Most native plant societies hold plant sales this month. Check your local newspaper's garden calendar for dates.

Westerner's Garden Notebook

by JIM McCAUSLAND

the Southwest harvest always includes one of my favorite foods: hot chilies. There are so many kinds, each with its own intensity of heat, that it's hard to know what to grow unless you've tasted several. That may be one of the best reasons to attend La Fiesta de los Chiles in Tucson, usually in mid-October at Tucson Botanical Gardens (2150 N. Alvernon Way; 520/326-9686). This event is sponsored by the gardens, Native Seeds/Search, and the *Tucson Weekly*. Admission costs $5, $3 in advance (look for listings in the *Tucson Weekly*). To order seed, pick up a Native Seeds/Search catalog ($1) at the event.

CONIFERS THAT WEAR AUTUMN COLOR

You don't expect to see conifers wearing autumn color, nor do you expect them to drop all their needles. But larches do both. These deciduous conifers have needles that turn gold in fall before dropping as the trees go into winter dormancy.

Most larches grow to great heights in forests, but a few species also make good trees for big gardens. Among these are European larch (*Larix decidua,* 30 to 60 feet in gardens), Japanese larch (*L. kaempferi,* 60 feet), and Western larch (*L. occidentalis,* 30 to 50 feet). Nurseries commonly offer larch trees in containers and sometimes as bare-root stock.

GUIDANCE FOR DESERT GARDENERS

Nothing accelerates learning like doing, and few things are as well worth doing as gardening. With that in mind, three Phoenix garden education specialists (Linda A. Guy, Cathy Cromell, and Lucy K. Bradley) wrote *Success with School Gardens: How to Create a Learning Oasis in the Desert* (Arizona Master Gardener Press, Phoenix, 1997; $14.95). Designed to show how to set up gardening programs in schools, the book is also a great primer for anyone who wants to grow vegetables, herbs, and flowers in Southwest deserts.

The first section of the book is aimed at teachers who want to start a gardening program in school. Of broader interest to all gardeners, the second section covers the nuts and bolts of starting a garden in the desert—from container gardening to organic techniques. An appendix lists planting times for almost every vegetable, flower, or herb you can grow in the desert. To obtain a copy, send $16.95 (includes shipping) to Arizona Master Gardeners, Box 200, Phoenix, AZ 85040.

IF YOU LOVE DIANTHUS, JOIN THE CLUB

With spicy-scented, old-fashioned flowers that look as if they were cut out with pinking shears, dianthus has a timeless appeal. So I suppose it was only a matter of time before a society formed to advance the dianthus cause. For 78 cents in postage, the American Dianthus Society will send you a brochure, sample newsletter, and membership information. Write to Rand B. Lee, Box 22232, Santa Fe, NM 87502.

that's a good question ...

Q: My husband and I have relocated to the Reno-Sparks area. We have been here just over a year, long enough to hear everyone complain about how difficult gardening is in Reno, and the growing season is a very short one. Where do we begin?
— *Tanya and Tim Richardson, Sparks, Nevada*

A. Before you start gardening in unfamiliar territory, first learn about your climate in the *Sunset Western Garden Book*. The book's Western Plant Encyclopedia lists the climate zones each plant thrives in. Reno is in *Sunset's* zone 3, so if you select plants whose range includes zone 3, they should do well in your garden. Native plants are also sure bets. Then do what I do: walk through your neighborhood and look for plants that catch your eye. Finally, stop by a local nursery and check out the offerings.

MARINA THOMPSON

Pacific Northwest Checklist

PLANTING

☑ **BULBS.** Nurseries and garden shops will be filled with bins of bulbs this month. Shop early to get the best selection, and get the bulbs into the ground—or containers—pronto so they won't wither or freeze.

☑ **PERENNIALS.** Throughout the Northwest, now (and into mid-November in zones 4–7) is prime time to plant perennials. Fall-planted stock has the winter to establish good root systems, then take off vigorously when warm weather arrives in spring. Also, spring- and summer-blooming plants are often sold at reduced prices in nurseries at this time. Since October can be dry and hot, be sure to water newly set-out plants well.

☑ **TREES AND SHRUBS.** It shouldn't surprise you that the best time to buy trees and shrubs for autumn color is now. Also, plants that bear fruits and berries are starting to color up.

MAINTENANCE

☑ **CARE FOR LAWNS.** After mowing the lawn, rough up bare spots, then scatter a generous amount of grass seed, cover with a fine layer of soil, water well, and keep the seedbed moist until fall rains begin. You'll have healthy new grass next spring.

☑ **GROOM ROSES.** Remove faded blooms. As you shape plants, cut flowers to take indoors. Allow a few flowers to form hips. This tells the plant that it's time to head into dormancy.

☑ **FUSS WITH FUCHSIAS.** Continue to snap off faded blooms and keep up with your feeding program until two weeks before the first frost is expected in your area.

☑ **MAKE COMPOST.** All the stuff you take out of the garden now—grass clippings, spent annuals, vegetable waste, prunings—will turn into rich compost this winter. Keep the pile moist and turn it regularly.

☑ **WATER.** Drought-stressed plants are more vulnerable to damage from freezing weather. Water permanent plants deeply until rains start.

PEST CONTROL

☑ **BATTLE SLUGS.** Whatever method you use to control slugs, consistency pays off. Eventually, you'll see a reduction in numbers and the remaining slugs will be smaller.

☑ **SET OUT MOUSETRAPS.** As the weather gets colder, mice and rats try to sneak indoors, especially into places where you store produce. They love to nibble on potatoes and squash. Set out traps and check them daily from now through the winter. ◆

Northern California Checklist

PLANTING

☑ **ORDER GRAPES, FRUIT TREES, BERRIES.** If you plan to purchase special varieties of fruit by mail, order soon. This way you will be sure to get the types of fruit you want and they'll arrive in time for dormant-season planting.

☑ **OVERPLANT BULB BEDS.** Zones 7–9, 14–17: Cool-season annuals planted over bulbs will give a colorful show during the winter before the bulbs pop up. Choose colors that complement the bulbs, such as blue violas with yellow or white daffodils, salmon *Primula obconica* with purple tulips, or purple and white *P. malacoides* with pink tulips.

☑ **PLANT BULBS FOR SPRING BLOOM.** Purchase bulbs as soon as possible, while there's still a good selection and bulbs are healthy. Some of your choices might be allium, anemone, crocus, daffodil, Dutch iris, freesia, hyacinth, muscari, ranunculus, scilla, and tulip. Lesser-known bulbs from Mediterranean climates are babiana, ixia, sparaxis, tritonia, and watsonia. These come back in greater profusion each year in mildwinter climates.

☑ **PLANT FOR PERMANENCE.** This is

Eureka
Redding
CALIFORNIA
Mendocino
Santa Rosa
Sacramento
Sunset
CLIMATE ZONES
San Francisco
San Jose
☐ Mountain (1-2)
☐ Valley (7-9)
☐ Inland (14)
☐ Coastal (15-17)
Monterey
Fresno
NEVADA
DEBRA LAMBERT

one of the best months for setting out any kind of plant that's not frost-tender. Ground covers, shrubs, trees, and flowers all benefit from fall planting; they get off to a fast start in still-warm soil and then have the long, cool months ahead to develop a healthy root system. Before buying plants, learn their ultimate height and spread. Allow plenty of room to grow, so you won't have to prune to keep them in bounds.

☑ **PLANT A SALAD POT.** Zones 7–9, 14–17: Start with a large pot (at least 18 inches in diameter and about a foot or so deep) filled with potting mix. Look for seedlings of green- or red-leaf, butter, or romaine lettuce. Plant two or three heads of lettuce along with arugula, curly endive, mâche, and mustard. Intersperse with chives and Johnny-jump-ups or other small-flowered violas (which are edible). Or start with seeds of a mesclun salad mix (available from Shepherd's Garden Seeds, 860/482-3638) and sow very thinly over the top of the soil. When seedlings need thinning, harvest and use in salad. Harvest additional greens when they're 3 to 5 inches long. Replant when the pot's been completely harvested.

MAINTENANCE

☑ **CLEAN UP THOROUGHLY.** To reduce the number of sites that harbor insects and diseases during winter, pull weeds, spent annuals, and vegetables. Clean up all fruit and leaves. Compost only pest-free plant debris, adding other material to your city's compost collection, if it has one (commercially made compost normally gets hot enough to kill insects and diseases), or toss.

☑ **WATER.** Fall weather is often very dry and warm, so continue to water if winter rains don't come this month, or appear infrequently. Check soil moisture before watering by digging down with a trowel. ◆

Southern California Checklist

PLANTING

☑ **PLANT COOL-SEASON ANNUALS.** Coastal and low-desert gardeners (zones 22–24 and 13, respectively) can set out winter- and spring-blooming bedding plants now. Choices include calendula, English daisy, Iceland poppy, lobelia, ornamental kale, pansy, snapdragon, stock, and viola. For shady areas, try cyclamen, cineraria, and primrose.

☑ **PLANT PERENNIALS.** Fall is the best time to plant perennials. Visible growth will be slow, but the roots will take hold and the plants will zoom into action come spring.

☑ **SOW ANNUALS.** Some cool-season annuals grow faster and perform better when directly seeded rather than transplanted. Starting from seed also gives you more choices. Try corn cockle, flax, forget-me-not, godetia, larkspur, lavatera, linaria, linum, nemesia, Shirley poppy, and sweet pea. Sow in raked-smooth, weed-free soil.

☑ **PLANT NATIVES AND MEDITER-RANEANS.** California natives like ceanothus and Mediterranean plants like rosemary are adapted to a climate of wet winters and dry summers, which means that fall is the best time to get them established in the garden. Let them take advantage of the winter

rains and these plants will develop deep roots before next summer.

☑ **PLANT COOL-SEASON CROPS.** Coastal and low-desert gardeners can sow seeds of beets, carrots, chard, onions, parsley, peas, radishes, and turnips and set out transplants of broccoli, cabbage, and other cole crops this month. Coastal gardeners can also start lettuces and other leaf crops from seed or transplants. This is also the month to start perennial crops like asparagus and artichokes.

☑ **OVERSEED BERMUDA.** For an emerald-green lawn by December, overseed Bermuda grass with annual winter ryegrass now.

MAINTENANCE

☑ **DIVIDE PERENNIALS.** To restrain fast-growing perennials, such as Shasta daisies, or to rejuvenate stagnating ones, like daylilies, circle plants with a shovel or spade and pop them out of the ground. Wash or shake off excess soil and divide plants with a knife or spade. Partially cut back foliage on divisions; replant immediately.

☑ **CARE FOR LAWNS.** Rake up thatch that has built up in your lawn. Fertilize cool-season lawns, such as tall fescue, with a high-nitrogren fertilizer.

☑ **PREPARE FOR SANTA ANA WINDS.** Prevent branch breakage by thinning top-heavy trees like jacaranda. When winds are predicted, give trees, shrubs, and ground covers a deep soaking. Once the winds come, mist plants frequently. Container plants are especially vulnerable.

PEST CONTROL

☑ **MANAGE PESTS.** Aphids and whiteflies, and snails and slugs multiply when the temperature drops. Combat the first pair with blasts from a hose or sprays of insecticidal soap. For the second deadly duo, set out traps at night, or handpick mornings or evenings. ◆

Mountain Garden Checklist

PLANTING & HARVEST

☑ **HARVEST AND STORE CROPS.** Pick broccoli, brussels sprouts, and tomatoes before a killing frost hits. Beets, carrots, potatoes, and turnips store best at 35° to 45° in barely damp sand. Onions need cool but dry storage in slotted crates or mesh bags. Leave a 2-inch stem on winter squash and pumpkins; store at 50° to 60°. Store apples and pears indoors in separate containers at around 40°. Carrots, horseradish, kale, parsnips, and turnips can tolerate heavy frost; mulched, they can stay in the ground all winter.

☑ **PLANT BULBS.** Before the ground freezes, set out bulbs of crocus, daffodil, hyacinth, scilla, and tulip. Plant daffodils and tulips 10 to 12 inches deep, smaller bulbs 5 inches deep.

☑ **PLANT FOR PERMANENCE.** Set out ground covers, trees, shrubs, and perennials. Water them well.

☑ **SOW WILDFLOWERS.** For bloom in spring, broadcast seed early in the month over rock gardens, hillsides, and fields. If possible, lightly rake and cover the seedbeds with a ¼-inch layer of organic matter. (In areas where winters are cold but snow cover is minimal, sow seeds in spring.)

Sunset
CLIMATE ZONES
☐ 1-3   ☐ 10-11

DEBRA LAMBERT

MAINTENANCE

☑ **CLEAN UP.** Collect diseased plant refuse, tie it up in plastic bags, and discard it. Compost most other plant material except leaves from ash, cottonwood, maple, oak, poplar, and willow trees, which do not break down readily; use them for mulch.

☑ **CUT BACK PERENNIALS.** After the first hard freeze, cut back flowering perennials such as aster, campanula, daylily, phlox, and veronica to about 2 inches above the ground.

☑ **MULCH FOR WINTER.** After a hard freeze, spread 2 to 3 inches of compost, straw, or other organic matter to protect bulbs, perennial flowers and vegetables, permanent plants, and strawberry beds. Mulch conserves soil moisture and helps minimize freezing and thawing of soil.

☑ **PREPARE PLANTING BEDS.** For earlier planting next spring, hand-dig beds now, working in generous amounts of organic matter such as compost. Leave soil rough so it will absorb winter moisture; the freezing-thawing cycle will break clods apart.

☑ **PROTECT YOUNG TREES.** Winter sunlight can make young tree trunks split and crack down their south sides. Protect them with a coat of white latex paint, tree wrap, or burlap. After trees are three or four years old, their thickening bark resists sunburn.

☑ **WATER.** After their leaves have fallen, water deciduous trees deeply—but only when the temperature is above freezing.

PEST CONTROL

☑ **PINE-BARK BEETLES.** Before spring, burn firewood cut from pines killed by these beetles. Otherwise, newly hatched beetles may infest pine trees when the weather warms. ◆

Southwest Checklist

PLANTING

✔ OVERSEED LAWNS. Zones 11–13: Mow Bermuda grass closely (at about ½ inch), overseed with perennial ryegrass, and water deeply.

✔ PLANT COOL-SEASON ANNUALS. Zones 10–11: Plant seedlings of common aubrieta, candytuft, English daisy, forget-me-not, primrose, snapdragon, and stock. Zones 12–13: Try seedlings of calendula, dianthus, English daisy, Iceland poppy, lobelia, nemesia, ornamental cabbage and kale, pansy, primrose, schizanthus, snapdragon, stock, and viola.

✔ PLANT COOL-SEASON VEGETABLES. Zones 12–13: Now is the time to plant beets, cabbage and its close relations (bok choy, broccoli, brussels sprouts, cauliflower, kale, kohlrabi), carrots, chard, endive, garlic, lettuce, onions, parsley, peas, radishes, and turnips. Many of these are sold as nursery seedlings; sow the root crops yourself.

✔ PLANT NATIVES. This is the best month of the year to start all kinds of native plants. Before planting container-grown trees and shrubs, loosen the soil to at least the depth of the rootball and five times as wide.

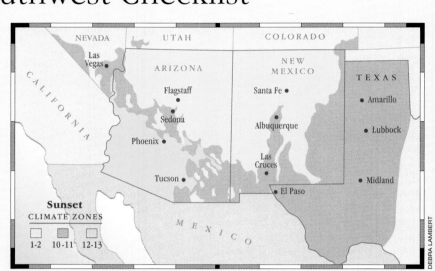

✔ PLANT SHRUBS, TREES. Plant all except frost-tender kinds.

✔ PLANT GROUND COVERS. Zones 10–11: There's still time to plant low-growing junipers. Zones 12–13: Plant *Acacia redolens,* Baja and Mexican evening primroses (plant Mexican evening primrose in a confined area or it will invade the garden), *Dalea greggii,* dwarf rosemary, gazania, lippia, low-growing junipers, snow-in-summer, and verbena.

✔ PLANT PERENNIALS. Plant perennials right away for spring bloom. Water them well until they become established.

✔ PLANT STRAWBERRIES. Plant any time after midmonth for a crop next spring. 'Sequoia' and 'Tioga' are two varieties that do well in zones 12–13. In zones 10–11, try 'Fort Laramie' and 'Ogallala'.

MAINTENANCE

✔ DIVIDE PERENNIALS. Zones 10–13: Dig and divide perennials such as daylily and Shasta daisy to reinvigorate plants and increase the size and number of blooms.

✔ FEED ESTABLISHED LAWNS. Zones 12–13: Apply 1 pound actual nitrogen per 1,000 square feet of lawn. ◆

NORMAN A. PLATE

Smart trees for fall planting

The right trees in the right place will give you
summer shade, winter sunlight, and energy savings

There's a shade tree revolution going on in the West. The battle cry is "Plant trees to conserve energy." And even though public utility companies—striving to reduce energy consumption—started the revolution, Westerners are joining in on a family-by-family, house-by-house basis.

Why? Because tree-shaded houses stay cooler, naturally, than unshaded houses. And because energy is a resource that is bound to become even more precious and more expensive in the future.

But trees do more than provide shade. They beautify houses and neighborhoods, increase property values, create refuge for wildlife, and reduce air pollution. And throughout much of the West, October is the ideal time of year to plant them.

To help homeowners choose and plant trees, Western cities from Tucson to Fresno have started their own shade tree programs (see page 299 for resources in your area). In Sacramento, for example, the Sacramento Municipal Utility District (SMUD) joined forces with the Sacramento Tree Foundation to start Sacramento Shade, a program

*Big trees for a big house: Grand old
sycamorpkeep this Sacramento
house cool.*

to encourage residents to plant and care for trees. Since 1990, it has been responsible for the planting of nearly 300,000 shade trees.

What Sacramento and other hot-summer cities have learned in their quest to chill out provides a valuable lesson for us all: Cooling your house with trees—the right trees, in the right spots—does save energy.

by **JIM McCAUSLAND** *and* **LANCE WALHEIM**

An Eastern redbud makes a brilliant spring show before flowers ever open.

LOCATION IS EVERYTHING

The path along which the sun travels across the sky from morning to afternoon—and also from winter to summer—determines the best locations for energy-saving trees.

In midsummer, the sun shines on the east side of your house in the morning, passes over the roof near midday, then beats down on the west side in the afternoon. It's in the afternoon, when temperatures are highest, that solar radiation heats the house most and air conditioners work the hardest. Consequently, the west side of your house is the most important side to shade. The east side, where sun can warm the house early in the day, is the second most important to shade.

As fall and winter approach, the sun is lower in the sky and shines more directly on the south side of your house. With cooler weather, however, the sun becomes a benefit rather than a liability. The warmth it provides reduces heating costs, so in most cases you don't want to shade the south side of the house. Even leafless deciduous trees can reduce sunlight falling on the south side of your house by as much as 40 percent. Leaving the southern exposure open also allows you to use solar collectors for heating water or your home.

There are a few exceptions to these rules. In hot, sunny climates (such as in Phoenix or Palm Springs), the weather can be quite warm in spring and fall. Shading the south side of a house in these areas can have some benefits as long as the trees don't block solar collectors. On the other hand, if you live in a cool- or foggy-summer climate (such as in San Francisco or Seattle), any sunshine is a blessing, and planting trees for shade may be a mistake.

In cold climates, a row of conifers that doesn't shade a house can break cold prevailing winds and help save money on heating. But to make the most of solar gain through south-facing windows, avoid planting any trees that would block sunlight falling on the south side of your house.

(Continued on page 298)

Where to plant shade trees

Shade windows first. Sun shining directly through a window heats a home quickly. Plant trees on the east or west side near any windows. If possible, position them just to the side of the window so you don't block the view but still provide shade.

Don't plant too close to the house. The closer you plant to your house, the more you'll shade it. But planting trees too close could cause the roots to damage the foundation. Small trees should be at least 5 feet from the foundation, larger trees at least 10 feet away.

Shade paved areas. The right shade tree can turn a patio into a special garden retreat. Shade trees also reduce the heat that's stored or reflected by paved surfaces, including patios and driveways. Reflected heat can increase the temperature of your home during the day, and stored heat can slow the cooling of your house after the sun has gone down.

Shade air conditioners. Keeping your air conditioner cool can reduce its workload and cut energy consumption.

Don't plant near utilities. Avoid planting trees where limbs will grow into power lines or where roots may damage underground utilities. If you have questions, contact your local utility company.

THE WEST'S BEST SHADE TREES

We asked tree experts to recommend the shade trees that best suit the size and climate conditions of most *Sunset* climate zones. All the trees illustrated here do the job, but the best choice depends on your situation: fruiting trees, for instance, may be too messy for a patio.

Color bars below indicate leaf color in each season. See the *Sunset Western Garden Book* for detailed descriptions.

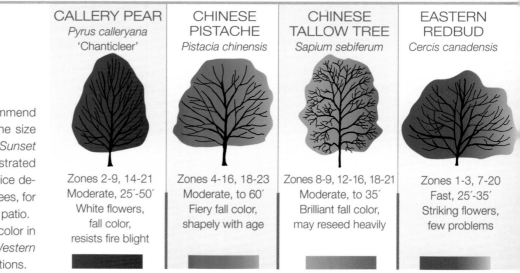

CALLERY PEAR
Pyrus calleryana
'Chanticleer'

Zones 2-9, 14-21
Moderate, 25´-50´
White flowers,
fall color,
resists fire blight

CHINESE PISTACHE
Pistacia chinensis

Zones 4-16, 18-23
Moderate, to 60´
Fiery fall color,
shapely with age

CHINESE TALLOW TREE
Sapium sebiferum

Zones 8-9, 12-16, 18-21
Moderate, to 35´
Brilliant fall color,
may reseed heavily

EASTERN REDBUD
Cercis canadensis

Zones 1-3, 7-20
Fast, 25´-35´
Striking flowers,
few problems

ANTHONY DAVIS

East

In the morning, three trees planted on the eastern side of the home help keep the interior cool.

In the late afternoon, two trees planted on the western side help keep the interior cool. A third tree partially shades the patio.

North

How much can you save?

How much energy and money can you save by planting trees around your house? Thanks to a computer program at the University of California at Davis, researchers for the U.S. Forest Service's Western Center for Urban Forest Research and Education can now predict both. Using a model of a 2,500-square-foot unshaded house in Sacramento, the computer predicted that shading the house's east and west sides (including windows) could reduce energy use for air-conditioning by as much as 40 percent, or $140 annually.

As a bonus, plant tall, narrow trees such as giant redwoods in a row to help block prevailing winds.

Prevailing Winds

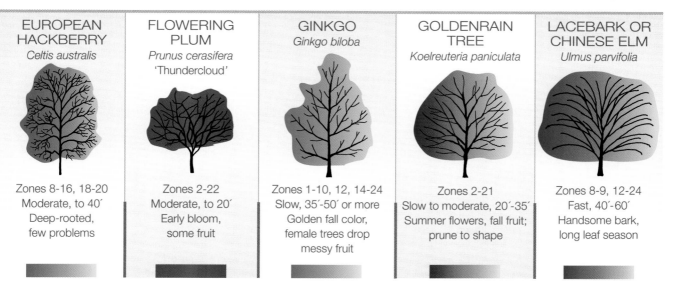

EUROPEAN HACKBERRY	FLOWERING PLUM	GINKGO	GOLDENRAIN TREE	LACEBARK OR CHINESE ELM
Celtis australis	*Prunus cerasifera* 'Thundercloud'	*Ginkgo biloba*	*Koelreuteria paniculata*	*Ulmus parvifolia*
Zones 8-16, 18-20 Moderate, to 40´ Deep-rooted, few problems	Zones 2-22 Moderate, to 20´ Early bloom, some fruit	Zones 1-10, 12, 14-24 Slow, 35´-50´ or more Golden fall color, female trees drop messy fruit	Zones 2-21 Slow to moderate, 20´-35´ Summer flowers, fall fruit; prune to shape	Zones 8-9, 12-24 Fast, 40´-60´ Handsome bark, long leaf season

SAXON HOLT

Same tree, different colors: Autumn turns the Chinese pistache on the left orange, the one on the right golden yellow. Expect some color variability in most species.

Seasonal shade patterns

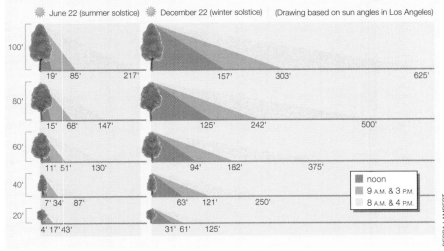

☀ June 22 (summer solstice)   ☀ December 22 (winter solstice)   (Drawing based on sun angles in Los Angeles)

■ noon
■ 9 A.M. & 3 P.M.
□ 8 A.M. & 4 P.M.

DEBRA LAMBERT

Evergreen trees cast shade farther in winter than in summer, when it's most needed.

WHAT TREE SHOULD YOU PLANT?

In most areas, the ideal shade tree is deciduous: the sun can shine through its leafless branches in winter. It should have a fairly dense round to spreading canopy, and reach 25 to 50 feet—anything much larger may be a liability on an average-size lot. Ideally, the tree will spread its limbs wide enough to partially shade the roof.

Small trees are appropriate where space is limited or when you want to shade only a single window. For narrow side yards, a row of columnar or upright trees works better than a single broad-canopied tree.

If you live in warm-winter climates, evergreen trees may be appropriate to provide year-round shade. But if you live in a cold climate, evergreen shade trees—especially on the south side of the house—can add as much as 20 percent to winter heating costs.

How many trees do you need? Often more than one. Because the sun rises and sets in different places at different times of year, you can get better shading if you plant a pair of trees outside each window that needs shade. (In San Francisco, for example, the sun sets 40° farther north in June than in October, so a tree that shades you well in summer may not help as much in fall.)

GETTING TREES OFF TO A FAST START

The sooner a tree starts reducing your energy bills and increasing your comfort, the better. Since trees grow fastest

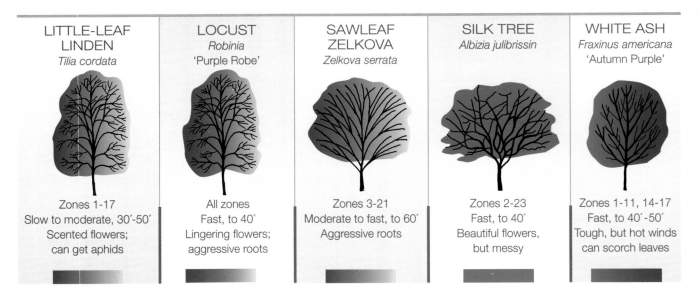

LITTLE-LEAF LINDEN
Tilia cordata

Zones 1-17
Slow to moderate, 30´-50´
Scented flowers;
can get aphids

LOCUST
Robinia
'Purple Robe'

All zones
Fast, to 40´
Lingering flowers;
aggressive roots

SAWLEAF ZELKOVA
Zelkova serrata

Zones 3-21
Moderate to fast, to 60´
Aggressive roots

SILK TREE
Albizia julibrissin

Zones 2-23
Fast, to 40´
Beautiful flowers,
but messy

WHITE ASH
Fraxinus americana
'Autumn Purple'

Zones 1-11, 14-17
Fast, to 40´-50´
Tough, but hot winds
can scorch leaves

Goldenrain trees (Koelreuteria paniculata) splash this house and lawn
with shade. Summer flowers are followed by buff-colored fruit.

when they're young, most of the trees
on our list will really start to pay off
within five years. (If you don't want to
wait, start with a tree that's already
roof-high when you buy it.) Here's how
to pick the best tree and get it off to a
good start.

Look before you buy. If the top of
the tree is healthy and well formed,
check the roots. They should penetrate
the rootball's edges, but not densely
circle the inside of the container or be

growing through the drain holes (a
common problem with a tree that's
been in the same pot or box for too
long). Check roots by sliding the plastic
container off the rootball, or if the tree
is in an extra-large container, dig down
a side of it and feel for a matted sheet
of roots against the container wall.
Avoid trees that have thick surface roots
encircling the trunk.

Dig the planting hole. Make it the
same depth as the rootball and two to
(Continued on page 300)

About prices and sizes

You can buy most kinds of trees three
ways from nurseries:
•Bare root (available in winter only)
for $15–$25 per tree.
•In standard-size containers (usually
5-gallon size) for $20–$35.
•As roof-high "specimen" trees in
2-foot-diameter containers for $100–
$500 (most cost $200–$250). You'll
probably also have to pay a delivery
charge, and perhaps even a planting
charge if the tree is too heavy for you
to handle by yourself.

According to some landscape contractors, larger, more mature trees are
slower to become established than their younger counterparts, so in the long
run, a smaller tree may be a better deal and actually surpass a specimen tree in
a few years. Because specimen trees are costly, it pays to get a tree with a replacement guarantee if you can. Many nurseries warrant the tree's survival for
a year after planting. Good care, of course, is assumed.

TREE-PLANTING HELP THROUGHOUT
THE WEST
The following organizations provide
information on selecting and planting
energy-saving trees in your region.

Arizona. Trees for Tucson supplies
site-selection advice, inexpensive
shade trees, and planting information
for Tucson residents. (520) 791-3109.

California. California ReLeaf dis-
tributes "California ReLeaf Network," a
free pamphlet that lists phone numbers for more than 50 tree groups
throughout the state, many with active
shade tree programs. (714) 557-2575.

TreePeople offers individual and
community-level help in Los Angeles
County, as well as a tree guide and four
trees for $25 annual membership. For
details, call (818) 753-4600.

Sacramento Tree Foundation.
(916) 924-8733.

Colorado. The Colorado State
Forest Service has useful, local tree advice. (970) 491-6303 or http://www.
colostate.edu/Depts/CSFS/index.html.

Denver Digs Trees offers selection
and planting information. (303) 722-
6262.

Idaho. Contact Canopi for information about siting and tree selection, and
referrals to county agents statewide, arborists, and others. (208) 424-0037.

Nevada. For shade-tree selection
and planting information, contact your
University of Nevada county extension
office. The Nevada Department of
Forestry offers low-cost windbreak
trees. (702) 687-4353.

New Mexico. Tree New Mexico can
give advice about site and tree selection, and tell you how to plant. (505)
265-4554.

Oregon. Friends of Trees offers
brochures on siting trees, planting, and
varieties. (503) 284-8733.

Utah. Tree Utah can help with site
selection, a tree selection list, and advice. (801) 364-2122.

Washington. For brochures to
guide you through the tree-selection
and planting process, call the Department of Natural Resources Urban and
Community Forestry Program, (800)
523-8733; outside Washington, (360)
902-1703.

Palo verde's tracery of branches provides shade even when tiny leaves drop.

three times as wide. Unless you have extremely sandy soil, you don't need to add amendments to the backfill; it's enough just to break it up. Plant the tree so its crown—the place where the trunk goes into the ground—is just slightly above ground level.

Water thoroughly. Build a berm of soil around the tree just outside the rootball. The berm should be at least 6 inches high and 18 to 24 inches wide.

Soak the newly planted tree and rock it gently by the trunk to settle it in. Then spread a 4-inch layer of organic mulch over the root zone (but don't let it rest against the trunk) and soak the tree twice a week for the first month and weekly after that until winter rains take over. Next year water the tree weekly during the growing season. In sandy soils or hot desert climates, trees may need deep watering more often.

Crape myrtle's rose-colored flowers appear in the heat of summer, stopping traffic wherever the tree grows.

MORE GREAT TREES

For the Northwest:

MOUNTAIN AREAS (ZONES 1–3)
- Hawthorn (*Crataegus* species)
- Hedge maple (*Acer campestre*)
- Maples (*Acer freemanii* 'Autumn Blaze', *A. grandidentatum*)

MILD AREAS (ZONES 4–7)
- *Acer freemanii* 'Autumn Blaze'
- Crabapple (*Malus* species)
- Hawthorn (*Crataegus* species)
- Hedge maple (*Acer campestre*)
- *Magnolia* 'Galaxy'
- Tupelo (*Nyssa sylvatica*)

For California:

MOUNTAIN AREAS (ZONES 1–3)
- Hawthorn (*Crataegus* species)
- Hedge maple (*Acer campestre*)
- Maples (*Acer freemanii* 'Autumn Blaze', *A. grandidentatum*)

CENTRAL VALLEY (ZONES 7–9)
- Chitalpa (*C. tashkentensis*)
- Crape myrtle (*Lagerstroemia indica*)
- Oriental persimmon (*Diospyros kaki*)

CENTRAL AND NORTHERN CALIFORNIA COAST (ZONES 14–17)
- Oriental persimmon (*Diospyros kaki*; best in zones 14–16)

SOUTHERN CALIFORNIA (ZONES 18–24)
- African sumac (*Rhus lancea*)*
- Australian willow (*Geijera parviflora*)*
- Chitalpa (*C. tashkentensis*)
- Crape myrtle (*Lagerstroemia indica*; best in zones 18–21)
- Jacaranda (*J. mimosifolia*)
- Strawberry tree (*Arbutus unedo*)*
- Victorian box (*Pittosporum undulatum*; best in zones 21–24)*

For mountain gardens:

- Hawthorn (*Crataegus* species)
- Hedge maple (*Acer campestre*)
- Maples (*Acer freemanii* 'Autumn Blaze', *A. grandidentatum*)

For desert gardens:

- *Acacia salicina* (best in zones 12–13)*
- *A. saligna* (best in zone 13)*
- *A. smallii* (best in zones 12–13)
- Arizona ash (*Fraxinus velutina*)
- Blue palo verde (*Cercidium floridum*)
- Chinese photinia (*P. serrulata*)*
- Crape myrtle (*Lagerstroemia indica*; best in zones 10, 12–13)
- Desert willow (*Chilopsis linearis*)
- Hawthorn (*Crataegus* species; best in zones 10–12)
- *Magnolia grandiflora* (best in zones 10–12)*
- Mesquite (*Prosopis*)
- Pines (*Pinus eldarica*, *P. halepensis*)*

*Evergreen

DON NORMARK

The Garden Cook

GROWING THE FRESHEST PRODUCE FOR USE IN THE KITCHEN

by RENEE SHEPHERD

Renee Shepherd harvests lavender for cooking and for bouquets.

Delicious lavenders

■ I've always felt a special affinity for lavender. Its heady sweet scent is my favorite floral perfume, and the soft color of the blossoms and the gray-green of the foliage are highlights in my garden.

Three years ago, I indulged my lavender fantasies by planting a 50-foot-long solid row along one side of my driveway. Throughout late June and July, this classic mounding hedge is truly glorious—with rich color and a fragrance that brings pleasure to the entire neighborhood—and it yields dozens of sweet-scented bouquets.

With such abundance at hand, I've also discovered the joys of cooking with fresh and dried lavender. Like many edible flowers, lavender is a time-honored cooking herb; its culinary use dates back to the Middle Ages. I love connecting with these centuries-old traditions, while finding new ways to flavor foods with the spicy blooms.

Lavender is such a romantic scent. While grilling pork and lamb on the barbecue during a recent dinner party, I threw a handful of flowers and stems onto the fire. As the lavender burned, it sent up an aromatic plume of smoke that spiced the air with earthy perfume. I put the lid on the grill and let the smoke infuse the meat for about five minutes. My guests loved the beautifully subtle flavor.

The best lavenders for cooking are the sweetest-scented kinds—for example, classic English lavender, *Lavandula angustifolia* (sometimes sold as *L. officinalis* or *L. vera*). This 2- to 3-foot-tall mounding subshrub with gray-green foliage has beautiful long spikes of richly colored florets. Compact varieties of *L. angustifolia* that have good culinary qualities include 'Munstead' (1½ feet tall) and 'Lady', a fast-blooming variety that grows just a foot tall. 'Hidcote', another fine cooking lavender, is semidwarf (1½ to 2 feet) with captivating deep violet-blue flower spikes and a richly fruity fragrance.

L. intermedia, currently the plant of choice for French perfume makers, has an intense, complex fragrance that is great in the kitchen. Varieties to look for include 'Provence' and 'Grosso'. These vigorous plants reach 3 feet tall with exceptional canopies of bloom.

For grilling, I add fresh or dried lavender flowers, stems, and leaves to the white-ashed coals during the last five minutes of cooking to give a mild but smoky aroma to lamb, pork, or salmon steaks. I often substitute fresh lavender for rosemary in savory dishes, too—using twice as much lavender as the prescribed rosemary. ◆

Favorite recipes

Lavender custard for fruit tarts. Start with a favorite recipe for custard but infuse the warmed milk with ¼ cup of chopped lavender flowers for each 2 cups of the liquid. Steep the mixture for an hour or two, then strain out the lavender before proceeding with the custard recipe. Fill tart shells with the custard, and top the custard with fresh fruit.

Lavender cookies. Add 1 to 2 tablespoons of finely chopped lavender flowers to a favorite sugar cookie or shortbread recipe.

Floral honey. Steep 4 teaspoons of chopped lavender flowers for an hour in a cup of warm honey with a tablespoon of lemon or lime juice. Reheat the honey until it is liquefied, then strain out the lavender. Drizzle the flavored honey onto fresh toast that's been spread with sweet butter or cream cheese.

Lavender marinade. Combine chopped fresh or dried lavender with lemon juice and olive oil as a rub for pork or lamb. Marinate the meat in this mixture for several hours before grilling.

GROWING TIPS

Lavenders are perennials that grow well in *Sunset* climate zones 4 through 24. They're drought-tolerant and deer-resistant.

• **Plant** in loose, fast-draining soil in a spot that gets full sun and good air circulation.

• **Water** plants until they're established (about a year), then irrigate mature plants about once a month.

• **Fertilizer isn't necessary** for lavenders; they can thrive without it.

• **Avoid using pesticides** on lavenders intended for culinary use. The plants shouldn't need them anyway.

• **Harvest** just as flowers open, and throughout the blooming season. Air-dry by hanging bunches upside down for a few days in a dark, cool place with good air circulation.

What's wrong with my compost?

Answers from an expert

by LAUREN BONAR SWEZEY

"Why does my compost smell bad?" "What are those ugly maggots in my compost?" If your compost pile prompts questions like these, you're not alone. Many beginning composters wonder what's causing problems in their piles.

Meghan Starkey, a specialist with the Home Composting Program in Alameda County, California, fields dozens of questions like these every week on the program's hotline. "When troubleshooting over the phone, I always go back to the basic concepts of composting," she says. "That often solves the problem."

In analyzing your own situation, Starkey recommends that you review the basics of composting (see "Easy basics," below). If a composting question has been nagging you, read on. Starkey answers the commonly asked questions and offers advice for correcting problems.

COMPOST QUESTIONS AND ANSWERS

Q. Why does the pile smell bad?
A. "It's often because there's too much food, or green waste, which means the pile is too moist. When it's too moist, the pile becomes anaerobic (no air) and the bacteria that work under these conditions are slower and stinkier. It's better to have an aerobic pile; your neighbors will thank you.

"Mix some browns [dry leaves] into the pile. If you don't have browns on hand, get some sawdust. Also, always bury kitchen scraps inside the pile or cover with additional browns."

Q. What are those bugs in the pile?
A. "A zillion mostly good insects live in the compost pile, and they all play a part in the decomposition cycle. Soldier fly larvae (maggots) are scary-looking but benign. They concentrate where there's too much food waste. If you add more brown material and give the pile a turn, they often disappear. If you're really grossed out by the larvae, just scoop them out and discard them.

"You'll also find ants, beetles, mites, red worms, and sow bugs in the pile. Ants nest in dry piles. Wet the pile down and turn it to get rid of them."

Q. When is compost ready to use?
A. "Finished compost should be brown and crumbly. But depending on the method you use, usable compost may still contain twigs. If you build a pile all at once and turn it every two to three days, the pile should heat up to 140° and everything will be broken down evenly. Cool piles [that don't heat up to 140°] and piles you build up slowly won't break down evenly.

"Remove and use the fine compost [by sifting the coarse matter through a $1/2$-inch screen], then add the rest back to the pile, or use all of it as a mulch."

Q. What can you compost?
A. "Most organic materials are compostable, but for safety you have to keep some of them out of the pile [see the "No-no's" listed in the box]. Also, some materials are more difficult to compost because they take a long time to break down. It's okay to compost oleander, but not poison oak. And don't compost ivy (which sprouts easily) or pernicious weeds. Blackberry thorns take forever to break down."

Q. Should you use a commercial compost activator?
A. "I say no. It's better to add manure from an herbivore, which is high in nitrogen and beneficial bacteria." ◆

Easy basics of perfect compost

FOUR MAIN INGREDIENTS

Brown matter (high in carbon) includes dry leaves, hay, sawdust, straw, wood chips, and woody prunings.

Green matter (high in nitrogen) includes grass clippings, fresh prunings, fruit and vegetable trimmings, manure (from cows, horses, goats, poultry, and rabbits), coffee grounds, tea bags, and rinsed-out eggshells.

Air. Bacteria need air to break down materials into compost. When building a pile, add a thin layer of larger prunings or cornstalks to create air pockets. To hasten decomposition, turn the pile every two to seven days.

Water. Bacteria need moisture.

No-no's: Do *not* add bones, cat or dog waste, charcoal ash, cooked food, dairy products, diseased or insect-infested plants, fats, grains, meat, or pernicious weeds (such as morning glory, oxalis, purslane, and thistle).

THREE BASIC STEPS

Chop materials into pieces no larger than $3/4$ to 1 inch by 6 inches.

Mix equal volumes of brown matter and green matter. Alternate layers of brown and green matter so that each layer is 2 to 8 inches deep (2 inches deep for grass). As you're layering, toss the materials with a pitchfork to mix. The optimal size of a pile is 3 feet tall by 3 feet wide by 3 feet deep.

Maintain moisture by adding water as often as needed to keep the pile as moist as a wrung-out sponge.

STEVEN GUNTHER

themselves up the steep slope unless they want to, she says.

Edwards inherited this natural canvas. Figuring out how to turn it into a picture, however, took 20 years.

Clearing German ivy to create a blank slate was the first step. Adding a series of terraces, held in place by retaining walls of redwood planks anchored with 8-foot-long steel pipes, came next. "I just stood at the bottom and directed— 'A foot higher, a little more to the left,'" she says. "There was no plan."

Terracing gave Edwards flat places to walk so she could plant the sloped beds. Adding a zigzag path to the top turned the garden into a satisfying composition. "Before, it was just a series of horizontal bands, but all these strong angles meeting in the middle made it dynamic."

Finding foundation plants that mirrored the lines of the composition— ground-hugging Korean and mondo grasses and plants like junipers that could be pruned to emphasize the lines—followed. Seasonal color adds ornamentation. But the strong pattern that gives the garden its structure makes it satisfying even in quieter seasons.

Unthirsty Korean grass (Zoysia tenuifolia) spills over retaining walls and creeps between steppingstones.

Virtually vertical

An artist's approach to an impossibly steep slope

Walking out into Betty Edwards's garden in Santa Monica is like stepping up to a giant painting. A steep slope heads straight for the sky just a few feet from her patio, rising high enough to block off views of neighboring property. This vertical plane is what you see, and it alone. Drawn across it are the strong horizontal lines of planting terraces and the slashes of a switchback path. A wash of bright green is the background for the pattern, and dots of color provide ornamentation. The scene reads like a painting; you take in the entire pattern, look to interesting details, then return to the whole again.

It's not the way we're usually encouraged to design gardens. Compose a garden like a mystery novel, revealing one segment at a time, we're told. But there are other ways to view the world, says Betty Edwards, a professor emeritus of art at California State University Long Beach and the author of *Drawing on the Right Side of the Brain* (Tarcher/Putnam, New York, 1989; $15.95) and *Drawing on the Artist Within* (Simon & Schuster/Fireside, New York, 1987; $14.98). "Garden rooms and meandering paths may appeal to mathematicians and musicians, who see things as a progression in time," Edwards says. "But painters like seeing whole compositions in a glance." Her garden suits an artist's temperament, it takes as long to absorb as if it were divided into segments, and visitors don't have to hoist

Gardening, Edwards has learned, is much like drawing. The subject doesn't matter as much as the execution. Plants are only there to serve the design, she says. "Composition is everything." And Edwards is convinced that all of us recognize a good composition when we create it. ◆

by **SHARON COHOON**

Inside the canopy of this Japanese maple, graceful branches stand out against crimson leaves. November is one of the best planting months; see page 308.

JANET LOUGHREY

November

gardenguide

A pretty, private courtyard in Tucson

■ When landscape architect Jeff Van Maren began remodeling his front yard in Tucson, he never expected that it would take five years due to the complexity of wall construction. But once he was done, he thought the courtyard garden was well worth the wait.

Building the courtyard wall was a labor of love. "I played around with the shape and design until I came up with something I liked," says Van Maren, "then I stacked dry concrete masonry block one by one. It's not your stan-

dard 8-inch-thick wall. It's very three-dimensional." He covered the blocks with stucco.

The 6-foot-high wall provides much more than privacy. Inside the courtyard, the wall is interrupted by an arched window with a fountain. The trickling water masks street noises and has a cooling effect on hot desert evenings. The water also supports lush green water plants such as horsetail (*Equisetum hyemale*) and water iris.

A low, L-shaped wall extends from

the main wall to provide extra, bench-style seating for entertaining. Behind one arm of the low wall is a raised bed for flowers and foliage plants. Pavers cover the patio. Around the patio and the fountain are container plants filled with cactus, succulents, and colorful seasonal flowers, such as the pansies and petunias in the foreground pot. Two large mesquite trees growing inside and outside the courtyard shade it in summer.

— *Lauren Bonar Swezey*

Leafy vines that last forever

■ The vines that twine up the entry gate of Susan Lutter's garden in Palo Alto bear everlasting leaves with an evergreen patina. They were crafted by metalsmith David Burns of Rough and Ready, California. He stalks recycling yards in search of old copper pipe and sheeting, then shapes the metal into leafy motifs for gates and garden ornaments. Burns also handcrafts bronze hinges and latches for the gates. He often uses fruitless mulberry as a model leaf, but can custom-design foliage to match clients' favorite plants: oak, rose, saguaro cactus, even grasses. He treats the copper with a substance that imparts a patina, which turns from chartreuse and turquoise hues to a rich verdigris.

In addition to gates (from $750, plus shipping), Burns makes pot hangers and stands ($60–$175), and wall-mounted plant holders ($65). For a free brochure and price list, call Copper Gardens at (888) 431-1001.

— *Dick Bushnell*

JAMIE HADLEY

Forcing narcissus for winter bloom

■ Perfuming whole rooms, paper white narcissus are wonderful winter-flowering indoor plants, and they make great gifts. Sold with spring bulbs at nurseries and garden centers, these daffodils flower in about two months if you plant them in containers.

Start by asking your nursery which daffodils it has for forcing (promoting early bloom). Paper whites (shown at left) and other Tazetta narcissus, including golden yellow 'Grand Soleil d'Or', are the most popular because they have multiple, fragrant flowers and don't have to be chilled before planting.

Related and almost equally foolproof bulbs that are easy to force include 'Chinese Sacred Lily' (with cream petals and a yellow cup) and 'Cragford' (white petals and a scarlet cup).

To plant the bulbs, fill a shallow pot with potting mix. Space the bulbs about an inch apart, with the tops just below the soil surface. Move them to a cool (below 50°), frost-free, dark place and keep them there until shoots emerge.

Allow the plants to grow under cool, bright conditions to keep their stems compact and strong. You may need to put them outside on mild days and bring them in at night, or set them on a bright, cool indoor porch. Water whenever the soil dries out, and stake flower stems if they start to flop over.

When buds appear, bring the plants indoors for display. Most varieties bloom for about two weeks.

— *Jim McCausland*

NORMAN A. PLATE

NORMAN A. PLATE

Dianthus ... for the scent of cloves

■ Tantalizing aromas of cinnamon and cloves wafted through the hallways of our Menlo Park, California, headquarters last spring, and they didn't all come from the test kitchen. Two dianthus tested in our gardens—a tall variety called 'Cinnamon Red Hots' (pictured above) and a short one called 'Pinkie'—smelled too good to simply pass by. Both got snipped and brought back to office desks frequently.

'Cinnamon Red Hots' has the bright red color and spicy scent of the hard candies it was named after, plus foot-long stems just right for the classic bud vase. 'Pinkie', less than half that size, isn't designed to be a cut flower at all. It makes a neat little clump of blue-green foliage and frilly rose-pink flowers meant to edge a border or fill a patio container. But its spicy-sweet fragrance is intense.

All dianthus need light, fast-draining soil and regular watering. 'Pinkie' seems to tolerate heat more than most dianthus. — *Sharon Cohoon*

PRUNING TIPS

Step inside a Japanese maple

■ Most of us view autumn foliage from the outside of a tree's canopy. But, if you want to gain a beautifully different perspective on a deciduous tree, step inside the canopy. That's what photographer Janet Loughrey did last fall at Portland's Japanese Garden when she encountered the picturesque Japanese maple (*Acer palmatum*) shown on page 304.

You can also gain valuable insight into pruning the tree. Although many home gardeners hire professionals to prune Japanese maples, pruning them is not a mysterious process, says Nancy Fiers, and she ought to know. Fiers grows 200 cultivars of Japanese maples at her Mountain Maples nursery in Laytonville, California (call 707/984-6522 for the $2 catalog). "To get that delicate look that maples are loved for, always be certain that you prune so that finer wood is at the edges and top of the plant, heavier wood is at the inside and bottom. And try to follow the tree's natural form," says Fiers, who also recommends that Japanese maples be pruned between mid-July and early August—a period when the sap won't run from cuts. She always makes a clean cut close to the next-largest branch.

If you're in the market for a Japanese maple, you don't have to wait—November is one of the best planting months. If you already have one, this is the time to study the tree as it defoliates; observe its structure so that when you prune at the optimum time next summer, you'll make the right cuts. — *Steven R. Lorton*

HARMONIOUS LANDSCAPE
Simple and elegant

■ When landscape architect Jana Ruzicka was asked to design a garden for this '60s-era tract home in Laguna Beach (see below), she wasn't particularly aiming for a Japanese-style garden to echo the house's shoji entrance, designed by architect Fred Briggs. Simple drama was what she was after.

She achieved it by carefully placing a few boulders so they would emerge like natural outcroppings from a bumpy sea of creeping fescue. And she chose plants just as deliberately—*Chrysanthemum pacificum* to echo the rounded shapes of the boulders and provide seasonal color, bamboo for the shadow patterns it makes on the plain walls, and yucca and its softer, shorter

counterpoint, Berkeley sedge (foreground), for their bristly energy. Just a few simply perfect things add up to an elegant garden. — *S. C.*

AMENDMENT TIP
Mix your own

■ Good soil is the key to healthy plants. That's why masterful gardener Dan Heims developed the following recipe for soil amendment. Fill a wheelbarrow two-thirds full with sandy loam; add 1 small bag of composted steer manure, 4 cups of green sand or 6 cups of sea kelp (available at stores that sell organic gardening supplies), and about 2 cups of granular controlled-release fertilizer (see photo at right). Stir well with a shovel, or small portable tiller, then work the mixture into your planting beds.

NORMAN A. PLATE (3)

The ideal potted tree?

■ There's no such thing as a maintenance-free container plant, but the pine pictured at right comes close. It's bristle-cone pine (*Pinus aristata*), a native of the West's high mountains, from the Sierra to the Rockies. In the wild, it grows slowly, often to a great age—some are thousands of years old.

Precisely because it is so hardy and slow-growing, the bristlecone is a fine candidate for a container. Plant it in loose potting soil in a generous-size pot with good drainage. In the driest climates, a weekly watering will help ensure steady growth. Fertilize lightly and infrequently, if at all.

Bristlecone pines are sometimes sold in nurseries, particularly during the holiday season. They are also available by mail from Forestfarm (990 Tetherow Rd., Williams, OR 97544; 541/846-7269); an 18- to 24-inch-tall plant in a 5-gallon can costs $26, plus shipping. — *S. R. L.*

BEN WOOLSEY

A grass with violet flowers

■ Perhaps because they're American natives, the muhly grasses (*Muhlenbergia* species) were initially overlooked when the ornamental grass rage swept onto the horticultural scene. But savvy Southwest gardeners have been finding and planting muhly grasses with spectacular results. One of the most attractive is *M. filipes* 'Regal Mist'. This variety is at its best in autumn, when a soft haze of violet flowers floats over a clump of stiff green blades.

Look for 'Regal Mist' in nurseries with a good selection of ornamental grasses. This plant handles drought, heat, salty soil, and wind with aplomb. The blades turn almond-brown after a killing frost. Use 'Regal Mist' as an accent in dry creek beds or beside a fence, as shown in the garden at left. Plants make a 2-foot-diameter clump in two to three years; divide established plants in spring to increase your stock. — *J. M.*

STEVEN GUNTHER

A chair fit for a king

■ Many gardeners become deeply attached to their trees. So when one dies, they often save the stump to use as a pedestal for a birdbath or container plants. When Mark Sahlberg's Douglas fir had to be removed from his garden in Port Orchard, Washington, he was left with a 2-foot-tall, 38-inch-diameter stump. Then inspiration struck; he turned the stump into a chair that looks like the throne of a woodland king.

He first made a paper template to outline the shape of the seat and arms. Then he transferred the chair's outline to the top of the stump with an indelible marker. Using a chain saw, he removed the wood in the center of the chair in small chunks. After carving out the contour of the chair, he smoothed out the irregularities with a rasp. To keep water from collecting in the seat, he cut a drain channel from the back of the chair to the front along one of the arms. A friend made seat and back cushions from vinyl stitched over foam to pad the chair (materials cost about $40). — *J. M.*

PATRICK BENNETT

Pacific Northwest Garden Notebook

by **STEVEN R. LORTON**

i consider November the best planting month in the Pacific Northwest. The weather is reliably cool, and if nature cooperates, rains quickly provide plants with ample water. On Saturday, November 1, my family will hear a resounding "Yahoo!" as I bound into the garden, shovel in hand, like a wild-eyed prospector headed for the Yukon. I'll make a beeline for my temporary holding area on the north

side of the house, where all the plants I've bought for the past several months have accumulated. At last, it's time to get them into the ground.

I'll start by planting Scotch heather (*Calluna vulgaris*). I love these plants, not only for their late-summer flowers but also for their winter foliage—many varieties turn fiery orange or rusty red. Three of my favorites are *C. v.* 'Hoyerhagen', a compact plant that turns bright red as freezing weather advances; *C. v.* 'Wickwar Flame', which turns rich orange to red; and *C. v.* 'Robert Chapman', which turns deep brick red. They look great spreading out among large, rounded river rocks interplanted with sword ferns. The contrast of dark greens and flame colors is one of the great treats of my winter garden. An

excellent source is Heaths & Heathers, 502 E. Haskell Hill Rd., Shelton, WA 98584; (360) 427-5318 (catalog $1).

Next, I'll plant another of my personal favorites for seasonal color—*Fothergilla monticola*. I'm proud to own four of these noble shrubs. In October and November, when the broad, oval leaves blaze orange-scarlet, few plants shine brighter in a mixed border. The plant, which is hardy in *Sunset* climate zones 3 through 7, eventually grows 3 to 4 feet tall and about one-half to two-thirds as wide. Even though it's deciduous, *F. monticola* provides year-round interest: I admire its attractive form in winter and new growth and brushlike clusters of small white flowers in spring, and its leathery, dark green leaves make an excellent background for flowers in summer.

that's a good question ...

Q. I'm having a rough time with *Melianthus major*. I keep losing it. I know it is marginally hardy. Any suggestions?
— *Marty Wingate, Seattle*

A. I share your frustration, having also tried and failed to grow *M. major*, which, as you note, is not reliably hardy in the Pacific Northwest. With its prehistoric-looking leaves, the plant looks great all winter, then croaks in spring, killed by a combination of cold and wet conditions. However, two of my friends, Val Easton and John Roberts, have mastered *M. major* and share their secret of success: They recommend cutting the plant back to the ground at Thanksgiving and laying the big leaves loosely over the crown of the plant. This keeps the crown somewhat dry and provides a bit of frost protection. Next spring, small shoots will appear, and *M. major* will spread its leaves again.

MARINA THOMPSON

Northern California Garden Notebook

by LAUREN BONAR SWEZEY

*W*henever I see a magnificent mature street tree in a city setting, like the California sycamore in my neighborhood, I gaze at it in awe. I am amazed that the tree has flourished under such difficult conditions—minimum root space, little summer watering, and probably no added nutrients. At least this tree hasn't fallen victim to poor pruning, construction, or other hazards of urban life.

I'm fortunate to live in the city of Palo Alto, where people care about their street trees. They've even formed a volunteer organization called Canopy "dedicated to planting, preserving, maintaining, and studying the Palo Alto urban forest, educating the public about the aesthetic and practical value of trees, and engaging the community in the process." What does that mean for the trees? It ensures that Palo Alto's trees will remain healthy, be cared for properly, and be replaced when necessary with appropriate trees. For more information about Canopy, call (415) 964-6110.

Other communities in Northern California have recognized the need and legislated for the renewal and preservation of their urban forests. (Read about Sacramento's success story on page 295.) For example, Santa Clara County's Our City Forest program (408/277-3969) has been operating for five years. To find out whether your community has a street-tree program in which you can participate, call your city arborist (often in the public works department).

TIME FOR A GOOD BOOK

One of my favorite pastimes on chilly evenings is to curl up beside a roaring fire with a fragrant cup of spicy cinnamon tea and a good gardening book.

One favorite, *Garden Flowers from Seed,* by Christopher Lloyd and Graham Rice (Timber Press, Portland, 1994; 800/327-5680; $22.95), gives useful advice on flowers to grow, how to germinate them, and how to use them in the garden—all in colorful, honest language. For instance, Rice says *Calendula officinalis* used to be 2 feet tall, with flowers on long stems, but the most recently developed varieties—'Fiesta Gitana' mixture and 'Apricot Bon-Bon'—are "short, dumpy little plants."

that's a good question ...

Q: Can you recommend how long grow lights should be left on for orchids? I live among the redwoods and believe my orchids would benefit from supplemental light in winter.
— *Christopher Milligan, Occidental, California*

A: The American Orchid Society (AOS) publishes a 64-page paperback called *Your First Orchid: A Guide for Beginners,* by Stephen R. Batchelor (AOS, West Palm Beach, FL, 1996; 561/585-2510; $7.95, plus $3 shipping). The book includes a chart that gives the lighting needs for various types of orchids.

MARINA THOMPSON

Southern California Garden Notebook

by **SHARON COHOON**

You don't get the opportunity to start a day at the zoo with an ike-bana demonstration very often. And that's too bad. Because I began a visit to the San Diego Wild Animal Park with one last November, and I'm convinced that such a novel beginning was responsible for the perfect day that followed. Ikebana, a Japanese style of floral arranging, is a form of meditation, according to our *senséi* (teacher), Rumi Rice. And it must work on audiences, too, because watching Rice assemble four papyrus stalks, five bronze-colored mums, three rusty-red proteas, and a lone banana leaf in a dramatic arrangement was so absorbing that all my mental clutter simply dissolved. (Rice's ritualistic, nearly wordless demonstration is proof you don't have to make a lot of noise to command attention.) With my head cleared, I was able to give the animals and gardens that followed my full concentration. I don't think I've had a day half as serene since.

If you missed Rice last year, you have another chance. She'll be giving weekend ikebana demonstrations as part of the park's annual Mum Festival this year. Other festival attractions: masses of chrysanthemums—a solid blanket of blazing color—in the entrance beds; thousands of cascading mums spilling like waterfalls from trellised walkways throughout the park; and a new "herd" of topiary animals constructed for the event.

The Mum Festival runs from November 1 through 30. The park is at 15500 San Pasqual Valley Road in Escondido. Call (760) 747-8702, ext. 5140, for more details.

FOIL THOSE WEEDS

Fall is a great time to plant a tree, but it's also when winter weeds start emerging. And those weeds seem to love the bare soil at the base of trees. Cultivating the soil under trees risks injuring surface roots, and weed whips can damage bark. But the Typar Tree Circle, a skirt of landscape fabric that acts as a weed barrier, eliminates the problem. Made by Reemay (800/367-9556), the spun-bonded polypropylene material is sold at garden centers and nurseries.

that's a good question ...

Q: "Despite healthy foliage, my chrysanthemum has never re-bloomed," an audience member complained to gardener Paul Maschka at his mum care lecture last year. "What's wrong?"

A: An outdoor light is probably the culprit, says Maschka. Shorter days, not cooler temperatures, tell a chrysanthemum when it's time to bloom. If a mum is planted near a streetlight or another form of artificial light, it thinks it's still summer. Move the plant to an unlit area, says Maschka, and it should behave like a fall bloomer again.

MARINA THOMPSON

Westerner's Garden Notebook

by JIM McCAUSLAND

every November I walk through my garden—pruning saw in hand—casting a critical eye on my trees. I think large, mature trees should have branches that either run clear to the ground, like those on my Korean fir, or are pruned up high enough to walk under, as on my Austrian pine.

Low horizontal branches are hard to work under when I'm weeding and mulching, and they're a pain to mow under. So, except on weeping trees, I remove any branch between ground level and the top of my head, unless a particular tree is too short for such radical surgery.

ARIZONA NATURE BY THE BOOK

One day, as I was hiking up Madera Canyon near Tucson, I found myself surrounded by unfamiliar flowers, trees, birds, butterflies, and reptiles. If only I'd had a copy of *Southern Arizona Nature Almanac: A Seasonal Guide to Pima County and Beyond,* by Roseann Beggy Hanson and Jonathan Hanson (Pruett Publishing Company, Boulder, CO, 1996, $21.95; call 800/247-8224 to order). This is a good book to keep by your window, because many of the creatures it identifies make their homes in gardens—or at least visit them. The book's month-by-month format can help you keep track of the seasonal progression: native plants, for example, are listed by month and flower color. You'll also learn about the weather patterns that affect your garden.

AMERICAN ARBORVITAE VS. CANADA HEMLOCK

The classic conifer for creating a screen is *Thuja occidentalis* 'Fastigiata'—a green, columnar form of American arborvitae that's usually sold as 'Pyramidalis'. But if you've seen how a load of snow can deform its branches, you've probably wondered whether there's a better alternative. Dick Rifkind, who works with a wide range of conifers at Bumble Bee Nursery in Kingston, Idaho, tells me he's increasingly recommending Canada hemlock (*Tsuga canadensis*). It takes well to shearing, develops a fairly dense, neat cloak of needles, tolerates cold down to -20°, and shrugs off snow without deforming.

By comparison, even in late summer my own American arborvitae hedge was still slightly deformed from last winter's wet snows. My arborvitae measures 4 feet wide and 10 feet tall—dimensions a Canada hemlock hedge can hold indefinitely with light annual shearing. The hemlock also holds its color during winter, when arborvitaes tend to become dull.

that's a good question ...

Q: Many needles on my pine tree are turning yellow-brown and falling off, but many others are green and seem fine. I can't find any great insect infestations, and otherwise the tree seems fine. What's wrong?

A: Pines are coniferous evergreens, but evergreen doesn't mean that pine trees never lose their needles. It means that instead of losing all their leaves (needles are leaves) every year, as deciduous trees do, they lose about a fifth of their leaves every fall and replace them the following spring. The new needles last about five years. The needles you see dropping are probably five-year-olds that have served their time.

MARION MCCAUSLAND

Pacific Northwest Checklist

PLANTING

☑ **ANNUALS.** Sown in autumn, the seeds of hardy annuals will germinate as soon as nature wakes them up in the spring. Sow candytuft, clarkia, larkspur, linaria, and wildflower mixes in well-tilled, weed-free soil.

☑ **BULBS.** Throughout the Northwest, there's still time to get spring-flowering bulbs into the ground. Nursery bins are full of crocus, daffodil, and tulip bulbs as well as less-common bulbs like allium, anemone, and scilla.

☑ **CAMELLIAS.** Zones 4–7: Shop nurseries for Sasanqua camellias in full bloom. Buy one and keep it in a decorative pot on a deck or patio or in an entryway, or plant it immediately in the ground. Sasanquas are especially effective when espaliered against an outside wall under an overhang where the blossoms get protection from pelting winter rains.

☑ **CONIFERS.** As leaves drop from deciduous trees and shrubs, you'll see where conifers can make a contribution to your landscape. Shop now, and plant immediately. When selecting a conifer, consider the ultimate size of the tree in your garden: a young Douglas fir looks adorable in a 5-gallon can, but in 10 years it may look as out of place as an eagle in a canary cage.

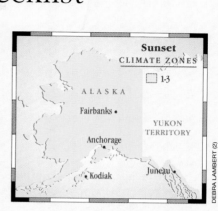

MAINTENANCE

☑ **DIVIDE PERENNIALS.** Zones 4–7: This is an excellent time to dig and divide perennials. Circle clumps with a shovel or spade, then pop the plants out of the ground. A plant the size of a dinner plate will divide neatly into three or four sections. Replant divisions immediately in soil amended with organic matter.

☑ **CUT BACK MUMS.** Once blooms fade, cut the plants back to within 6 inches of the ground. Next spring, they'll send up vigorous new shoots.

☑ **GROOM BORDERS.** Cut back plants as frost nips the flowers and foliage. You might want to leave plants with dried flowers or seed heads (sedums and Siberian irises, for example) to provide winter interest and food for birds. Rake up debris and pull any weeds.

☑ **GROOM LAWNS.** Mow and edge the lawn one last time. Rake leaves before they mat up and smother the grass underneath.

☑ **MAKE COMPOST.** As you rake, prune, mow, and pull out spent annuals and vegetables, throw the waste on the compost pile. Turn the pile one last time for the season.

☑ **PRUNE TREES AND SHRUBS.** Many plants respond well to pruning this month. First, remove dead, diseased, and injured wood and any branches that cross. Then, prune for shape. ◆

Northern California Checklist

PLANTING

☑ **GARLIC.** Artichoke (common white) types are easiest to grow. Rocambole has a wonderful, intense flavor. Choose a site in full sun with well-drained soil. If your soil is heavy and poorly drained, plant in raised beds. Mix in plenty of compost. Plant cloves so tips are about 1 to 2 inches deep. (Elephant garlic isn't a true garlic and is milder in flavor; plant cloves 4 to 6 inches deep.)

☑ **PERENNIALS.** Nurseries have a wide assortment in sixpacks and in 4-inch and 1-gallon containers. Some good choices include alstroemeria, artemisia, campanula, catmint, columbine, coral bells, dead nettle (*Lamium*), delphinium, dianthus, diascia, Oriental poppy, penstemon, perennial foxglove (*Digitalis mertonensis*), phlox, salvia, scaevola, and species geraniums.

☑ **SOW WILDFLOWERS.** For colorful spring bloom, choose a seed mix that's suited to your climate or buy individual kinds and create your own color combinations. You can also buy wildflower mixes for specific purposes, such as attracting butterflies or beneficial insects. Two regional seed sources are the Wildflower Seed Catalog in St. Helena (800/456-3359) and Clyde Robin Seed Company in Castro Valley (510/785-0425).

Sunset
CLIMATE ZONES
☐ Mountain (1-2)
☐ Valley (7-9)
☐ Inland (14)
☐ Coastal (15-17)

DEBRA LAMBERT

MAINTENANCE

☑ **CARE FOR POTTED BEGONIAS.** Zones 7–9, 14–24: Continue watering plants through the mild fall months. When new blooms stop developing and leaves begin to turn yellow with the onset of cool weather, reduce watering. Allow the soil to dry out when the stems fall off the tubers, then lift the tubers out of the ground, shake off the soil, and allow them to dry for a few days. Store the tubers in a cool, dry place.

☑ **CLEAN UP DEBRIS.** If you haven't rid your garden of fallen fruit, leaves, and faded summer annuals and vegetables, do so now. A clean garden, free of overwintering sites for insects and diseases, will be a healthy garden come spring.

☑ **FERTILIZE COOL-SEASON CROPS.** Zones 7–9, 14-17: If you didn't mix in a controlled-release fertilizer at planting time, your annuals and vegetables probably need feeding. You can use an organic fertilizer, such as fish emulsion, or another liquid or granular fertilizer.

PEST CONTROL

☑ **CONTROL SNAILS AND SLUGS.** Zones 7–9, 14–17: Protect newly planted annuals and emerging bulbs from snails and slugs this month. Handpick the pests at night, with a flashlight in hand. If you want to use a control with low toxicity to mammals, apply insecticidal diatomaceous earth (if the weather is dry). If you use a commercial snail bait, always apply it out of reach of children and pets.

☑ **SPRAY FRUIT TREES.** Zones 7–9, 14–17: After the leaves have fallen, spray peach and nectarine trees with lime sulfur to control peach leaf curl. For brown rot on apricots, use a fixed copper spray. Apply it on dry days when no rain is predicted for at least 36 hours. Cover the stems and trunk of each tree thoroughly. ◆

Southern California Checklist

PLANTING

☑ **PLANT COOL-SEASON ANNUALS.** Except in the mountains (zones 1–3), there's still time to set out early-blooming annuals such as African daisies, calendula, dianthus, Iceland poppies, ornamental cabbage and kale, pansies, snapdragons, stock, and viola. For shady areas, try cineraria, cyclamen, and English and fairy primroses. Some annuals perform best when seeded directly into the garden. Good annuals for direct sowing include flax, forget-me-nots, godetia, larkspur, linaria, linum, Shirley poppies, and sweet peas.

☑ **PLANT FOR FALL COLOR.** Yes, there are trees whose leaves will change color in mild-winter areas, even in frost-free coastal zones 22–24. Look for gold-leafed ginkgo, orange-red Chinese pistache, and various shades of liquidambar in nurseries now. Consider adding some late-blooming perennials—such as asters, rudbeckia, or salvias—to the garden as well. These underutilized perennials perform beautifully in our climate.

☑ **PLANT WINTER VEGETABLES.** Early November is a great time to start cool-season crops in most areas. In zones 13 and 18–24, sow seeds of beets, carrots, chard, onions, parsley, peas, radishes, and turnips and set out transplants of broccoli, cabbage, and other cole crops by midmonth.

Bishop

NEVADA

CALIFORNIA

San Luis
Obispo

Bakersfield

Tehachapi

Santa
Barbara

Lancaster

Los Angeles

Palm Springs

Sunset
CLIMATE ZONES

San Diego

1-3 7-9 11 13 14-24

MEXICO

DEBRA LAMBERT

Near the coast, continue to plant lettuce and other leaf crops from seed or transplants. Gardeners in zones 7–9 can sow peas and spinach and plant garlic and onions.

☑ **FIGHT EROSION.** Make sure you have enough plant material in place on slopes to prevent erosion during heavy winter rains. On bare or sparsely planted slopes, now is the time to sow a cool-season grass such as the mixture of fine fescues used in the garden shown on page 309. You can add native wildflower seed for color.

MAINTENANCE

☑ **OVERSEED BERMUDA.** Sow annual winter rye to cover up dormant Bermuda grass. Mow the Bermuda as low as possible first, then sow one pound ryegrass per 100 square feet of lawn. Cover with a light mulch and keep moist until seeds germinate.

☑ **TEND CHRYSANTHEMUMS.** Support still-blooming plants with stakes and ties. After bloom, cut back plants, leaving 6-inch stems. Lift and divide old clumps; cut roots apart and discard woody centers, then replant.

☑ **MULCH.** Put a 3- to 4-inch layer of organic mulch around half-hardy plants, trees, and shrubs, and on bulb beds that might heave during winter frosts at high elevations (zones 1–3) and in the high desert (zone 11).

PEST & WEED CONTROL

☑ **PROTECT CABBAGE CROPS.** Cover broccoli, cabbage, and other cole crops with row covers to keep cabbage white butterflies from laying eggs that hatch into leaf-chomping caterpillars. Or spray the uncovered plants with *Bacillus thuringiensis*. Focus the BT carefully to avoid spraying other plants, so you don't destroy the larvae of swallowtails and other butterflies you want in your garden.

☑ **SPRAY FRUIT TREES.** To avoid peach leaf curl, rake fallen leaves and remove old fruits from peach and nectarine trees. Then treat with lime sulfur or fixed copper spray. ◆

Mountain Checklist

PLANTING

☑ SPRING-FLOWERING BULBS. Nurseries and garden centers are well stocked with spring-flowering bulbs now. Buy before they're picked over, and plant immediately.

☑ WILDFLOWERS. Sow them in weed-free beds. Also sow a small amount of the same seed in a flat of sterile soil so you'll have a reference plot. Otherwise you won't know weeds from wildflower seedlings when they emerge next spring.

MAINTENANCE

☑ BRING IN HOUSE PLANTS. If you haven't done so yet, bring tender plants into the house for the winter. First check for insect pests, then rinse plants off with lukewarm water in the shower. Wait until spring to repot and fertilize. If your house has low humidity, mist plants twice a day or keep them near the kitchen sink or shower, where it's a bit more humid.

☑ LIFT AND STORE DAHLIA TUBERS. Stop watering dahlias a few days before digging tubers, then carefully unearth them with a spading fork. Discard tops, brush off soil, and let tubers cure for a few days in a dry, frost-free place. Store the tubers in boxes of peat, vermiculite, or sand.

☑ GROOM LAWNS. Mow and edge the lawn one last time. Rake leaves

MONTANA
Helena •
• Boise
IDAHO   WYOMING
Cheyenne •
NEVADA
Salt Lake
• Reno   City   Denver •
UTAH   COLORADO
Las
Vegas
Sunset
CLIMATE ZONES
☐ 1-3   ☐ 10-11

DEBRA LAMBERT

before they mat up and smother the grass underneath.

☑ GROOM PERENNIAL BORDERS. Be judicious as you cut back perennials, leaving ones with seed heads or dried flowers to provide winter interest—and food for birds.

☑ MAINTAIN TOOLS. Put an edge on all your tools, from hoes and shovels to pruning shears, then wipe them down with oil (use machine oil for metal parts, linseed oil for handles), and store them in a dry place for the winter.

☑ MAKE COMPOST. As the weather cools off, you can speed decomposition by grinding plants before you throw them into the compost pile.

☑ MULCH. Spread a 3-inch layer of organic mulch around half-hardy plants, under trees and shrubs, and over beds of bulbs that might otherwise be heaved out of the ground by hard freezes.

☑ PLAN NEXT YEAR'S GARDEN. While the memories of this year's successes and failures are still fresh, draw up plans for next year's plantings. When planning your vegetable patch, be sure to rotate crops so that you don't end up growing related plants in the same beds more than once every three years. For example, don't replant cabbage or its close relatives—including broccoli, cauliflower, and kale—in the same bed.

☑ PROTECT ROSES FROM FREEZING. Cut back 50 to 60 percent of the top growth, then mound fallen leaves over the plants (use screen to keep the leaves from blowing away).

☑ PRUNE. You can start pruning deciduous trees and shrubs after their leaves fall. Prune on a mild day when temperatures are above freezing. First, remove dead, diseased, and injured branches, watersprouts, and crossing or closely parallel branches, then prune for shape. ◆

Southwest Garden Checklist

PLANTING

☑ **ANNUAL COLOR.** Zones 12–13: In sunny places, set out ageratum, aster, bells-of-Ireland, calendula, candytuft, clarkia, cornflower, foxglove, larkspur, lobelia, painted daisy, petunia, phlox, snapdragon, stock, sweet alyssum, and sweet pea. In shade, set out dianthus, English daisy, pansy, primrose, and viola.

☑ **BULBS.** Zones 1–2, 10–11: Plant spring-blooming bulbs immediately. Zones 12–13: Chill crocus, hyacinth, and tulip bulbs in your refrigerator's crisper (away from apples) for six weeks before planting.

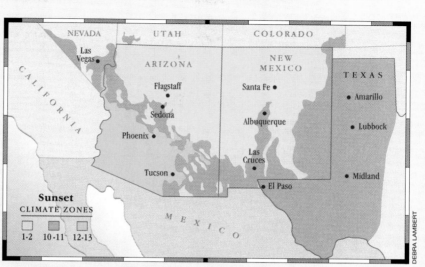

☑ **OVERSEED WARM-SEASON LAWNS.** Zones 12–13: Mow warm-season Bermuda grass at about ½ inch, then overseed it with 10 to 20 pounds of ryegrass per 1,000 square feet. You can use annual or perennial rye (coarser-leafed annual rye costs less but needs more frequent mowing than its perennial cousin). A month after sowing, fertilize the young ryegrass to encourage it to fill in quickly.

☑ **PERMANENT PLANTS.** Zones 10–13: Plant almost any kind of tree, shrub, or ground cover now.

☑ **VEGETABLES.** Zones 12–13: Sow or set out transplants of asparagus, beets, broccoli, brussels sprouts, cabbage, carrots, cauliflower, celery, endive, garlic, kale, kohlrabi, leeks, lettuce, mustard, parsley, peas, radishes, spinach, Swiss chard, and turnips.

☑ **WILDFLOWERS.** Zones 10–13: Sow blackfoot daisy (*Melampodium leucanthum*), California desert bluebells (*Phacelia campanularia*) desert globe mallow (*Sphaeralcea ambigua*), Indian blanket (*Gaillardia pulchella*), Mexican hat (*Ratibida columnaris*), Mexican tulip poppy (*Hunnemannia fumariifolia*), and owl's clover (*Orthocarpus purpurascens*). Keep moist until plants are at least 2 inches tall.

MAINTENANCE

☑ **PRUNE AND FEED ROSES.** Zones 12–13: Remove faded flowers, pruning lightly as you go. Take out dead, diseased, crossing, and injured canes, and prune for shape. Then apply a complete fertilizer and water it in well to encourage winter bloom.

PEST CONTROL

☑ **APHIDS.** Zones 12–13: Blast them off new growth with a jet of water from a hose, then spray with insecticidal soap.

☑ **SNAILS AND SLUGS.** Zones 12–13: Handpick them at night or in the morning after you've watered. Or set out poison bait where children and pets can't get at it. ◆

Outsmarting Bambi

You can have a beautiful garden in deer country by choosing plants that deer don't like

■ "How can a garden be so colorful in deer country?" ask visitors to Jack and Lisa Nelson's impressive flower and foliage display in North Fork, California, just 20 miles from Yosemite National Park's south entrance. The lush greenery and eye-catching blooms in this 2-acre English-style country garden are seldom, if ever, bothered by deer, even though small herds pass through the garden regularly.

There's no mystery to the Nelsons' success: they planned the garden for deer, with lots of help from Cindy and David Martin of Water Wise Landscape Architects, who live nearby.

"The deer were here first," says Lisa. "So we've tried to coexist with them by planting appropriate plants." "We don't feed the deer," adds Jack. "[They're] wild and should [stay] that way."

"People get discouraged and give up on gardening if they have to fight deer all of the time," explains Cindy, who has been designing gardens with her husband in deer country for years. "So we encourage them to grow plants that deer don't like. Or to fence in valuable plants that they *do* like. The Nelsons have a dog. That helps too."

The Nelsons' garden is designed for bloom and foliage color through the seasons. Beds and borders have a layered look: low plants such as moss pink (*Phlox subulata*) and creeping thyme grow in the foreground, medium-size plants like *Achillea taygetea* and 'Garnet' penstemon in the middle, and taller-growing plants such as foxglove and miscanthus in the rear.

Because gophers and ground squirrels are also a serious problem in the garden, the Nelsons line most of their planting holes with chicken wire cages. Deer can't yank these wire-protected plants out of the ground easily, since the chicken wire is secured to the soil with pins.

The Nelsons love to putter in the garden, and they spend plenty of time deadheading, pruning, and dividing perennials. But when it comes to deer, they're realistic. They have left parts of their property wild, with existing shrubs and grasses the deer can graze on. "We've been lucky," says Jack. "We've had good rains [in recent years], and there's been plenty for the deer to eat.

"But someday, if the deer get hungry enough, they may even eat our deer-tolerant plants."

THE NELSONS' TOP 10 DEER-RESISTANT PLANTS

California fuchsia (*Zauschneria californica*). Red flowers; *Sunset* climate zones 2–10, 12–24. "Blooms summer to fall."

Ceanothus gloriosus 'Fallen Skies'. Lavender-blue flowers; zones 4–7,

Tips from the garden

Use deer repellents. Young, lush plants—even some resistant plants—are attractive to deer. "We spray a bitter-tasting product called Ro-Pel on such plants, and respray when new growth appears," says Cindy. "Then deer seem to get the idea that things don't taste good in the garden, and they stay away."

Place tasty plants carefully. If you want roses in deer country, train the climbers on an arbor so the foliage and flowers grow above deer's reach. (Protect young climbers by spraying them with a repellent or temporarily surrounding them with fencing.)

by **LAUREN BONAR SWEZEY** *photographs by* **JACK NELSON**

Deer-resistant border (above) filled with colorful perennials and shrubs—including poppies, yellow yarrow, purple barberry, *Spiraea bumalda* 'Limemound', and pink foxglove—sweeps around the edge of the lawn and up to the house.

Purple *Verbena peruviana* and red sunrose tumble over the tops of rocks (left); pink common thrift and blue-eyed grass snuggle against their bases.

Spires of pink and white foxglove rise behind a colorful mix of California poppies, multicolored Iceland poppies, and white sweet alyssum. Deer apparently don't like the taste of these bright bloomers, since they leave them alone.

14–24. "Prostrate grower, good bloomer. Quite spectacular."

Cistus crispus. Pink flowers; zones 7–9, 12–24. "It blooms a long time and is neat and compact. It grows over our boulders, covering them like a blanket."

Coreopsis verticillata 'Moonbeam'. Yellow flowers; zones 1–24. "Continual bloomer."

Foxglove (*Digitalis purpurea*). Various colors; all zones. "Striking plant when in bloom."

Gaura lindheimeri. White or pink flowers resemble butterflies; all zones. "Another continual bloomer."

Pacific Coast iris hybrids. Various colors; zones 4–24.

Penstemon 'Beverly Johnson'. All zones.

Plumas monkey flower (*Mimulus bifidus*). Pale yellow to peach; zones 8–9, 14–24. "Handsome native plant."

Rudbeckia fulgida 'Goldstrum'. Yellow; all zones. "Rich color, dense bloom."

Brightly flowered perennials mingle with boulders. Purple Erysimum 'Bowles Mauve', yellow basket-of-gold, and pink sunrose grow in the foreground. Behind are purple verbena, light yellow sulfur flower, basket-of-gold, and moss pink.

How do other gardeners thwart deer?

Last fall we published a query in the magazine to find out how other gardeners prevent deer from devouring their plants. More than 200 readers responded, sharing their deer-foiling successes and failures. The thing all agreed on: deer are extremely unpredictable creatures with fickle taste buds. Nylon hosiery bags filled with blood meal and hung on plants deterred deer in Bremerton, Washington, but not in Belmont, California. Gardeners in Cheshire and Corvallis, Oregon, told us that deer never eat their rhododendrons, while a gardener in Sisters, Oregon, said they do eat rhododendron leaves and flower buds some years. Here's what worked:

Deer-resistant plants. The key to using deer-resistant plants is figuring out the likes and dislikes of your deer. "Often the bucks, does, and fawns eat (or at least taste) different things," says Ann Thompson of Sisters, Oregon. "Experience has taught me that you really have to plant a test garden and see what works in your area."

Some nurseries and cooperative extension services publish lists of deer-resistant plants. A particularly good one is Bob Tanem's 1993 *Deer Resistant Planting* (273 N. San Pedro Rd., San Rafael, CA 94903, 415/472-6121; $5.95, including shipping). You can also find a list in the latest (1995) edition of *Sunset Western Garden Book* (Sunset Publishing Corporation, Menlo Park, CA, 800/526-5111; $29.95). Consider these lists starting places for determining which plants will resist deer in your location.

Fences. According to respondents, fences provide the ultimate protection against deer, but effective materials and heights varied tremendously. A 7-foot metal fence proved adequate in one Washington garden, but it took a 10-foot electric fence to keep deer out of another garden in Bend, Oregon.

Double fencing, like that in the Nel-

Double barrier has an outside fence made of wire; surveyors' tape, raised well above the ground, serves as an inside fence.

sons' vegetable garden, worked for lots of respondents, probably because deer can't high-jump and broad-jump at the same time. The outside wire or wood fence should be 4 feet tall, with another fence 4 to 5 feet inside the first (surveyors' tape, placed 36 inches off the ground, could substitute for the inside fence as shown above). Penny Fryman of Shingle Springs, California, suggests building a double fence and using the space in between as a dog run.

Monofilament fishing line can make an unobtrusive deterrent. Dot Leistritz of Ridgefield, Washington, strings two lines, one 16 and one 32 inches high, between metal stakes set 6 feet apart around her rose garden. Sidni Battle of McKenna, Washington, adds 2-foot-tall chicken wire to the bottom of the stakes to keep out small creatures. Other readers reported that chicken wire helps keep the deer from crawling under.

Sprays. Homemade egg solutions seem to beat all others for effectiveness, although Deer-Away Big Game Repellent, made of egg solids, has worked for many gardeners.

Gerry Zalkovsky of Mill Valley, California, says she's tried everything

"short of a gun" (lion urine, lion manure, Zest and Irish Spring soaps, Ro-Pel, Hinder, Deer-Away, netting, deer-resistant plants). "Netting and green stakes made the place look like a suburban version of *Stalag 17*. Hinder worked until [the deer] acquired a taste for it." But Zalkovsky's home egg spray seems to work. Blend 2 cups water, 2 cups nonfat milk, 2 eggs (with shells), 2 tablespoons cayenne, 2 cloves garlic, and a couple of drops of spreader-sticker and sprinkle (or strain and spray) over plants. The effects last one to two months.

Simpler homemade egg solutions worked well for other gardeners. The most basic is 1 egg in 1 quart warm water, blended, strained, and sprayed on plants. Variations of the homemade spray include adding to the egg mixture some sort of hot pepper (1 teaspoon hot pepper oil or 1 tablespoon Tabasco per quart of water), milk ($\frac{1}{4}$ cup per quart of water), and cooking oil (1 teaspoon per quart of water). Strain egg white strings from such mixtures to help prevent the sprayer from clogging. And repeat spraying when new growth appears or when rain washes the solution off. ◆

Tropical plants including Chinese hibiscus (top), Spathiphyllum (left), and Caladium draw water from 8-inch containers with built-in reservoirs (about $15).

Smart pots that water themselves

They can go a week or longer between refills

by **JIM McCAUSLAND**

A potted plant's worst enemy is usually the hand that holds the watering can. When a plant gets too much to drink, it drowns; when it doesn't get enough, it dies of thirst. So how can you avoid the wet-dry cycles caused by hand-watering? Consider using a self-watering container. It supplies constant moisture to plants for an extended period. Self-watering containers also save time; all you do is fill their built-in reservoirs at weekly (or longer) intervals. This undemanding schedule may even relieve you of the need to find a plant sitter when you go on vacation.

HOW THEY WORK

Most self-watering containers draw water up into the soil from the reservoir through inlets at the bottom. Capillary action pulls the water into drier soil in much the same way that a kerosene lantern draws fuel up a wick.

Some containers, in fact, use wicks

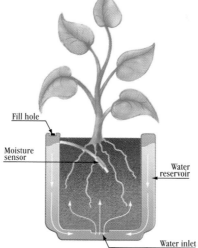

Fill hole

Moisture sensor

Water reservoir

Water inlet

to draw water from the reservoir. Others draw water directly from the reservoir. These versions keep the soil moist all the way to the surface.

More complex containers, like the ones shown on these pages, use a moisture sensor to regulate the water content in the soil (see drawing). The sensor is buried in the soil about a third of the way down the pot; when sufficient moisture reaches the sensor, it stops the flow of water up into the pot until the moisture level drops. The surface of the soil remains dry (that's a plus, since

it discourages the gnats that breed in moist potting soil).

To refill a reservoir, you pour water through a hole in the side or top rim of the pot.

Once, most self-watering containers were 8-inch units sold mainly for small indoor plants. But interior plant designers and landscape architects have spurred demand for larger planters— ones that can hold palms and other trees, indoors or out. To accommodate these big plants, manufacturers have come up with big, sturdy plastic containers that are strong yet light: a self-watering planter typically weighs only half what a terra-cotta planter weighs, and one-tenth that of concrete, so it's easy to move. And advances in plastic-molding technology have expanded the colors and textures available. Now choices include a variety of shades and textured finishes ranging from glossy black to faux stone and earthenware.

WHERE TO FIND THEM

Self-watering containers are sold in most major home improvement centers and some nurseries. The models shown on these pages are the Natural Springs brand by Planter Technology (999 Independence Ave., Suite E, Mountain View, CA 94043; call 800/542-2282 for a catalog and price list). Hanging baskets and pots are also sold under the Gardenware brand by Bemis Manufacturing Co.; call (800) 558-7651 for local dealers.

The containers come in a range of sizes and prices, from 8-inch models ($9 to $15) to 20-inch patio pots ($23 to $159) to 24-inch planters (about $280). You'll also find 9- to 12-inch hanging baskets in the $6 to $11 range.

WHAT PLANTS WORK

Many house plants (especially fuzzy-leafed kinds like African violets) and indoor trees do well in self-watering pots. Plants that need dry spells between waterings, such as cyclamen, cactus, succulents, and *Sansevieria,* do *not* do well in these containers. Plants with aggressive roots, including trees like *Ficus benjamina,* can be grown successfully in self-watering pots, but they may need more frequent repotting and root pruning to keep the water inlets open. ◆

Caring for self-watered plants

Soil mix. Self-watering containers work best when filled with professional potting mixes (never plain garden soil) that contain about one-third peat; one-third sand, perlite, or vermiculite; and one-third other organic matter such as leaf mold or redwood compost. Buy the best potting mix you can (ask your nursery staff what they use): it will have to support the plant between repottings.

Feeding. You must always use liquid fertilizer, putting it into the reservoir at one-fourth the recommended strength (never apply it directly to the soil).

Most fertilizer is salt, and excess salt is lethal to most plants. In open garden soil, fertilizer salts are flushed out of the root zone by rain and periodic deep watering. Since self-watering containers draw water from bottom to top, the salts end up in the top inch of soil. That makes it easy to get rid of them: once a year, scrape the top inch of soil off the plant and replace it with fresh mix.

Repotting. Every two to three years, repot the container plant. Gently rake away most of the soil from around the rootball and replace it with the same kind of fresh potting mix you started with. For potted trees, you may also need to prune the roots or replant them in a larger container.

PHOTO: NORMAN A. PLATE   ILLUSTRATION: DEBRA LAMBERT

The quieter, gentler poppies

California poppies may be show-stealers, but their less vibrant cousins mix better with other garden plants

NORMAN A. PLATE (2)

Tufted poppy (Eschscholzia caespitosa) bears small, pale yellow flowers.

As glorious as a field of California poppies can look from the freeway, that irrepressible orange can dominate a garden. It's shockingly visible, like the fluorescent safety vests worn by highway maintenance crews. Fortunately, other varieties with the same virtues as *Eschscholzia californica*—satiny petals, ferny foliage, simplicity of care—come in softer colors.

E. californica 'Maritima', a coastal version of the orange California poppy, has clear lemon yellow flowers with small orange blotches at the throats. It's compatible with a wide range of flower colors. A true perennial, it's an excellent choice for a border.

The plant's low mounding habit also makes it handsome in meadow lawns. Dave Fross of Native Sons Wholesale Nursery in Arroyo Grande, California, has grown 'Maritima' in his meadow for eight years. It reseeds freely, he says,

Red flowers of Eschscholzia californica 'Mahogany Red' have center tufts that echo the yellow poppies behind.

and it comes true from seed as long as its orange cousin isn't in the vicinity. When the two poppies cross, the orange throat blotches on 'Maritima' grow bigger with each generation until the flowers are pure orange.

'Moonglow', a cream-colored variety of *E. californica*, is mellow enough for an English garden. 'Mahogany Red', an English hybrid with deep rust-red flowers, is another attractive option.

A search through seed catalogs will turn up many other *E. californica* hybrids in a wide range of colors and as bicolors. Seed is usually sold mixed. Standouts are 'Mission Bells', semidoubles in a mix of cream, pink, and orange; 'Double Ballerina Mixed', doubles and semidoubles in shades of yellow, orange, rose, and scarlet; and 'Monarch Mixed', singles and semidoubles in a range from yellow to cerise. 'Thai Silk', a ruffled semidouble, is often available in single colors as well as in a mix of pinks.

The easiest *Eschscholzia* to blend into the garden is *E. caespitosa*, the tufted California poppy. This 6- to 12-inch-tall annual has pale yellow flowers with a faint lemon scent. Use it as an edging, mixed with other short wildflowers, or as a bulb cover.

WHEN AND HOW TO SOW POPPIES

In the West's mild-winter climates, sow seeds from mid-September through January (sow in fall for winter bloom or in late winter for spring bloom). In cold climates, wait until early spring to sow.

Hoe or pull weeds from areas you want to plant. Amend the soil lightly with compost, then water to force more weeds; hoe or pull this second crop.

Broadcast seeds over the amended soil. Cover them lightly with additional compost or potting soil.

Irrigate to begin germination, or wait for winter rains to do it for you.

WHERE TO BUY POPPY SEEDS

Catalogs are free unless noted.

Larner Seeds, Box 407, Bolinas, CA 94924; (415) 868-9407 (catalog $2).

Park Seed, Cokesbury Rd., Greenwood, SC 29647; (864) 223-7333.

Thompson & Morgan, Box 1308, Jackson, NJ 08527; (800) 274-7333. ◆

by **SHARON COHOON**

The Javanese stone Buddha seems to float above a jade green sea in the Lemon Grove, California, garden that Sinjen designed for Jim and Barbara Hartung. The bed of crunchy echeveria planted beneath it provides a deterrent to getting closer. You don't see the statue, you see the scene—and from exactly the vantage point you were intended to. "Create some distance [between the sculpture and the viewer]," Sinjen suggests, "and people will see things the way you want them to."

Sinjen: San Diego's garden magician

Sinjen, the landscape designer responsible for some of the most beautiful gardens created in San Diego during the post–World War II gardening boom, learned his trade in Europe, where he was a garden apprentice on the estate of a German count. In 1928, when he immigrated to the United States, he began working as a nurseryman and landscape designer in the Long Beach area. A stint in the Army during World War II landed him in San Diego. Here Sinjen quickly made a name for himself with the landscapes he installed during his off-duty hours. When the war ended, he became the area's premier designer, a role he maintained for decades. Though he's near 90, Sinjen isn't exactly retired. Homeowners lucky enough to have maintained or inherited his gardens still turn to him regularly for advice. And one of his most recent projects, the garden of Ann and John Hill in San Diego, was completed just two years ago.

Sinjen's magic carpets

A venerable landscape designer shares his secrets for using ground covers imaginatively

Aladdin and Sinjen have at least two things in common. First, both get by fine using a single name. Aladdin jettisoned his surname; Sinjen, his given name. To his friends and clients, he's just Sinjen. Actually he prefers "Sin." The other link between these two legends? Well, both happen to be wizards with carpets. Sinjen's, though, are composed of living plants, not silken threads. A distinctive way of using ground covers has long been one of this landscape designer's trademarks.

Take *Polygonum capitatum*, whose cloverlike blossoms provide a solid blanket of color from curbside to doorway at a home in San Diego, for instance. Sinjen used the wash of pale pink blooms as the background color in the garden, then superimposed bolder materials—such as *Tagetes lemmonii*, which bears clouds of sulfur yellow flowers, and bronzy red–leafed *Acalypha wilkesiana* 'Macrophylla'.

Appropriately, Sinjen got the idea for this landscaping style while sitting on a carpet. Years ago, a friend spread out an old Oriental rug on the grass for a picnic, he recalls, "and I immediately started figuring out how I could create the same effect with plants."

P. capitatum was his first success, and it's still his favorite background plant for Persian carpet–style gardens. The plant is frost-tender but otherwise tough, blooms nearly year-round, and stays flat and compact when kept on a lean diet. Yellow-flowered Cape weed (*Arctotheca calendula*) is another of Sinjen's staples. Silver- or golden-leafed liriope works too—"buy big plants and divide," he advises. Succulents such as the echeveria beneath the Buddha pictured at left make great carpets.

Sinjen's first experiments with "magic carpets" were in large gardens, but his idea may be even more useful in today's smaller gardens. "If you keep the upper plants laced out so you can see the underground color all the way from the street to the house," he says, "a solid-colored 'carpet' makes a small lot look a lot bigger." ◆

by **SHARON COHOON** *photographs by* **STEVEN GUNTHER**

TOM BEAN

Stately saguaro cactus shimmer like lighted sculptures against the night sky. For tips on adapting this idea to your own garden, see page 332.

December

gardenguide

In Mexico, many children enjoy Lotería, a bingo-style game played with brightly colored pasteboard cards depicting various folk characters, creatures, and objects, ranging from a palm tree and a rooster to El Diablito (the devil). Now, Lotería cards have found their way onto folk-art pots decorated by Chicano artists Kathy and Patrick Murillo of Phoenix. The Murillos paint ceramic pots in vivid colors, then affix different Lotería cards to the sides. The 7-inch-tall pots ($40 each) make suitable containers for plants such as small cactus, succulents, and lavender. The Murillos also use the cards on 12-inch-tall cactus planters ($85), but we couldn't resist filling one with festive ornamental peppers. The card for El Pajarito (the bird) goes on their hand-painted wood birdhouses ($55). The pots, planters, and birdhouses are sold by Southwest Gardener (Box 36894, Phoenix, AZ 85067). For a free catalog or to place an order, call (800) 769-4019.

— *Dick Bushnell*

gift

NORMAN A. PLATE (2)

A mahonia with holiday blooms

■ It's only natural that Northwest gardeners show great admiration for the genus *Mahonia* in general and for our native Oregon grape—*Mahonia aquifolium*—in particular. There's much to admire about this evergreen shrub, including its hollylike green leaves and handsome rough brown bark.

One variety that's well worth a search is 'Arthur Menzies' (shown at right). Discovered by Washington Park Arboretum in Seattle, it is a natural hybrid between *M. bealei* and *M. lomariifolia*. *M.* 'Arthur Menzies' is a multistemmed plant that reaches 12 feet or taller. It bears glistening yellow flower spikes around Christmastime.

Occasionally you'll spot *M.* 'Arthur Menzies' at a nursery. There's another source: Washington Park Arboretum will propagate a plant for you, but you'll have to wait two years (a 1- to 2-foot plant costs $25). To add your name to the waiting list, call (206) 726-1954. If you just can't wait, substitute *M. bealei*—it has similar form and foliage but bears less spectacular flowers later in the year. — *Steven R. Lorton*

DAVID McDONALD

Dappled dandies

Color-splashed poinsettias capture the spotlight.

■ Blotches and freckles are in. That's the word in the poinsettia world, where dozens of shades of true-red poinsettias and an equal range of novelty colors—from coral to gold to cream—have made up the poinsettia palette until now. The industry is moving from this well-explored territory of solids into the new frontier of bicolors. And customers are enthusiastically following. Growers can call the new varieties marbled, speckled, or splashed, it doesn't matter. If they're variegated, we're buying.

Two handsome varieties from the current crop are shown at left. Both are from the German breeder Fischer, a relative newcomer to the poinsettia market. The salmon-pink and white bicolor in the foreground is 'Marblestar'. The plant with red bracts and silver-green and white variegated leaves is 'Silverstar'. Trial plants of both have performed well in home and office settings: some lasted well into February. These and other Fischer plants should be readily available in nurseries this month.

For best performance, set plants in bright, indirect light. Keep soil moderately moist, but don't allow water to stand in the saucer or foil. Poinsettias do best when daytime temperatures stay below 70° and nighttime temperatures are from 60° to 65°—or no lower than the low 50s outdoors.

— *Sharon Coboon*

Cutting greens for decorations

■ Cuttings from evergreens such as fir, pine, holly, mahonia, and strawberry tree make fine wreaths and swags. But don't whack off snippets indiscriminately; take advantage of this annual opportunity to prune for shape. To reveal the plant's naturally handsome form, prune from the bottom up and from the inside out. Avoid ugly stubs by cutting back to the next-largest branch or the trunk. If the plant has grown too dense, selectively remove whole branches to allow more air and sunlight to reach into the plant.

After you've finished pruning, spray the greens with water to remove dust and insects. Trim cuttings to desired size. To keep them fresh, immerse the cut ends in a bucket of water and store outdoors in a shady spot until you're ready to decorate. Adding a commercial floral preservative to the water and spraying the cuttings with an anti-transpirant such as Wilt Pruf can also help preserve their freshness. If the greens are bound for bouquets, strip foliage from the portions of the stems that will be immersed in water. — S. R. L.

NORMAN A. PLATE

Light up a living sculpture

■ Little white lights don't need conifers or ivy to set them off handsomely. At the Festival of Lights in Phoenix's Ahwatukee-Foothills community, thousands of lights illuminate desert plants such as the stately saguaro cactus pictured on page 328. Gardeners throughout the West can adapt the idea; any plants with interesting curves or angles can shimmer like lighted sculptures against a night sky. Examples include:

• Harry Lauder's walking stick (*Corylus avellana* 'Contorta'), with fantastically gnarled and twisted branches and twigs.
• Mediterranean fan palm (*Chamaerops humilis*), a hardy, clumping palm with green to bluish green fan-shaped leaves.
• Prickly pear cactus (*Opuntia*), with branches like spiny beaver tails.

You can also light up colorful winter performers like *Camellia sasanqua* 'Yuletide', pyracantha, or 'Washington' navel orange. Use miniature lights approved for outdoor use, and wear sturdy leather gloves when stringing lights around cactus. — *Jim McCausland*

The secrets of Santa Fe's gardens

■ Santa Fe has long been a source of creative inspiration for artists and writers. The city provides an inspiring environment for gardeners, too. Charles Mann, a photographer who lives in Santa Fe and frequently contributes to *Sunset,* beautifully illustrates this point in a new book: *Secret Gardens of Santa Fe,* by Sydney LeBlanc (Rizzoli International Publications, New York, 1997; $45; 800/542-6657).

Mann and LeBlanc open the gates of 19 gardens—including Berry and Dianne Cash's garden, pictured at left—to reveal a rich assortment of landscapes filled with adaptable ideas. Chimney flue pipes serve as pedestals for terra-cotta pots; short lengths of aspen branches driven into the ground create a rustic edging around flower beds. What makes these gardens so enchanting are the colorful details: a cluster of blown-glass grapes tied to a stake, red chili ristras strung on a fence, painted wood bird cages arrayed on a patio wall.

These landscapes also succeed by making the most of a rather limited range of plants—those hardy enough to thrive in one of the West's harshest climates (Santa Fe records about 30 inches of snow in winter, but only 11 inches of rain in an average year). Indeed, after seeing pages of gardens dotted by recurrent blooms, you could easily conclude that Santa Fe is heaven for hollyhocks and sunflowers. — *D. B.*

CHARLES MANN

Northwest Garden Notebook

by STEVEN R. LORTON

i don't understand all the hand-wringing provoked by holiday shopping. It should be simple and fun. I use this season to share my favorite garden discoveries, buying gifts en masse. This year, all the gardeners on my list will receive one of two things. So, if you're expecting a present from me, close your eyes right now and turn the page.

My mother-in-law, Dorothy Turner, was one of the greatest gardeners I ever knew. Her favorite plant was the celandine poppy (*Stylophorum dipyllum*). A native of the eastern United States, this woodland plant grows well in partially shaded spots, reaching 15 inches tall. It bears deeply cut, bluish green leaves and profuse patches of bright yellow flowers over a long season. Dorothy gave me my first plant, and through the years, I've parsimoniously doled out tiny starts to friends who wanted to grow one. Now, at last, I've found a source: Wayside Gardens (800/845-1124) lists the plant in its fall catalog.

I'll bet there isn't a gardener out there who doesn't have moss growing someplace around. Yet we know so little about this soft, fuzzy subject. Now, a new book brings moss out of the cracks and into the light: *Moss Gardening,* by George Schenk (Timber Press, Portland, 1997). Schenk leads readers on a great adventure, from a moss garden on a backyard stone all the way to Saihoji, a moss temple garden in Kyoto, Japan. Page after page, Schenk plumbs the simplest ideas with Einsteinian flare and great sensitivity (he forgives the thrushes who pull moss from his rocks for nesting material because they eat snails in his garden). One chapter is an encyclopedic listing of moss, lichens, and liverworts by genus and species, from *Acarospora chlorophana* to *Xanthoria parietina*. To order *Moss Gardening,* send a check for $40.45 to Timber Press, 133 S.W. Second Ave., Suite 450, Portland, OR 97204; or call (800) 327-5680.

that's a good question ...

Q. I'm bored with the typical gift plant selection: poinsettias, cyclamen, even forced narcissus. Any ideas?
— *Howard Cohen, Seattle*

A. Any house plant can be spruced up for gift giving. Try decking the tall, snaky leaves of *Sansevieria* with some red balls. Or tie a big silver bow onto a potted Chinese evergreen (*Aglaonema modestum*) for an understated but festive touch. I once heard a story about Mae West from a neighbor of hers in the Hollywood apartment building where the actress kept a unit. West liked to tie lots of small gold bows and little gold balls all over a jade plant (*Crassula argentea*). I tried this once, and it certainly had a tinsel-town charm: "Merry Christmas! Why don't ya come up and see me sometime?"

MARINA THOMPSON

Northern California Garden Notebook

by LAUREN BONAR SWEZEY

Whenever I go shopping for a Christmas tree with my husband and son, fond memories of tree-hunting adventures with my parents and sisters come flooding back. We never went to a tree farm to chop down a tree; instead, every year we visited the same lot not too far from home in Palo Alto. The trees there—which came from Oregon—seemed superior to trees sold at the lots down the road.

As we looked over each tree, our liveliest discussions (some might say arguments) were always about the size of the tree, not the variety. Unsheared Douglas firs were the most common Christmas trees then; their branches were widely spaced so ornaments dangled handsomely between them. (Today's sheared trees don't leave much room for ornaments.) My mother, being the practical one in the family, always wanted a short tree that was easy to decorate. But my father and I preferred to think big, and always won out. We'd drive home with an 11- or 12-foot-tall tree tied on the roof of the station wagon.

After I left home, my parents bought smaller trees, and they started choosing different varieties.

So did I. Today, Nordmann fir (*Abies nordmanniana*) is one of my favorites. Its foliage is dense, but not so dense that there's no room for ornaments. The needles are dark green with white bands underneath. And its fragrance is wonderful.

My son is too young to argue with me about which tree to buy. But I'm waiting for the day. I bet he'll demand one of those bushy Douglas firs.

SAY GOOD-BYE TO ROUGH GARDENING HANDS

I'm always looking for useful but special gifts for my gardening friends. This year, Sweet Orange Hand and Body Lotion is at the top of my gift list. I think it's one of the best lotions around for dry, gardening-roughened hands.

I discovered it last season after digging in the soil too long. The creamy lotion so relieved the dryness in my skin that, if my hands could talk, they would have thanked me. (And my nose appreciated the unbelievably rich citrus fragrance.)

Made in San Rafael, the lotion is sold at Smith & Hawken stores and through the company's catalog (800/ 776-3336). An 8-ounce green glass bottle costs $24, a 9-ounce plastic bottle $21 (available only in stores).

that's a good question ...

Q. Can you suggest a peony that will do well in the Central Valley? — *Vinh Pham, Stockton*

A. Marde Ross & Company, a mail-order bulb nursery in Palo Alto, has been testing peony varieties for a number of years. It has found that Japanese single and early double peonies are most suited to the mild climates of California. The company offers nine varieties by mail. To obtain a listing, call (650) 328-5109.

MARINA THOMPSON

Southern California Garden Notebook

by **SHARON COHOON**

i'm thinking of a white Christmas. Maybe I'll fill the raised bed I reserve for seasonal plants with nothing but white cyclamen this year. That would definitely dress up the garden for the holidays. I like the way Janelle Wiley, color specialist for Sherman Gardens, uses this winter bulb. She treats cyclamen as a choreographer would treat the corps de ballet in *Swan Lake.* Dress them all in the same color, let them have the stage to themselves, and space them far enough apart so no one's tutu gets crushed, she suggests. The cheek-to-jowl color you get with pansies isn't the goal, she says. Cyclamen's ruffs of patterned foliage are half the show, so leave a bare circle of mulched earth around each plant to set them off. Despite their regal air, cyclamen are easy to care for as long as they have good drainage, says Wiley. Just make sure their crowns— the tops of their root systems—remain an inch or so above soil level.

But will an all-white bed leave me hungry for color? I sure liked the way my seasonal bed looked decked out in red last winter. Edible greens love this spot, and last year I tried out ruby chard. It turned out to be such a gorgeous plant—burgundy stems, red-veined, glossy leaves—it was hard to harvest. 'Charlotte', listed in the current catalog of the Cook's Garden (800/457-9703), sounds even more difficult to treat as a crop. "Breathtakingly bright scarlet chard … pretty enough for a place in the perennial border … color much superior to common ruby … chard," the copy reads.

I can't decide. But at least I know what I want for Christmas. Santa, a bigger garden, please.

LET'S HEAR FROM HARDIE

Wish you could incorporate poinsettia blossoms into mixed floral bouquets? Here's an idea from *Hardie Newton's Celebration of Flowers,* a new release from Storey Publishing (Pownal, Vermont, 1997; $27.95; 800/441-5700). Buy plants in 4-inch pots. Soak the potted plants in 6 inches of water in the kitchen sink for an hour, then drain overnight. Tap the plants out of the pots the next day, gently squeeze out the excess water from the rootballs, place the plants in plastic freezer bags, and securely twist and tie. Tuck the bagged plants into arrangements, hiding their plastic containers with greens or moss.

that's a good question …

Q. Is it too late to buy tulips this year? I missed the fall planting time.

A. No. You've still got time to chill bulbs in the refrigerator for six weeks (the minimum requirement) and get them planted in January. January is actually ideal, believes Gary Jones of Hortus nursery in Pasadena. December is still shirtsleeve weather in many areas. Colder, wetter January, he says, is more in line with a tulip's idea of spring.

MARINA THOMPSON

Westerner's Garden Notebook

by JIM McCAUSLAND

*t*he best gifts are the ones that give pleasure or service season after season. With that in mind, I did some early Christmas shopping this year. Here are two items I found that my family and I—and maybe you—will enjoy for many seasons to come.

A LIVELY GAME FOR GARDENERS

Even on those winter days when I can't be out in the garden, I can play at it with the Garden Game (Ampersand Press, Port Townsend, Washington; $26.95). This board game leads two to six players (ages 8 and up) through the virtual realities of growing flowers, vegetables, and herbs. Your game garden flourishes or languishes, depending on the effects of beneficial or pesky insects and fair- or foul-weather conditions (spin the dial and your garden could suffer from drought, flood, or storm). Players draw Gardener's Almanac cards that provide tips about good and bad gardening practices and assign consequences accordingly. ("Your compost pile is soggy and stinky … Lose one turn.") The information this game delivers is useful, the art (by Erica Thurston) is delightful, and—most important— my kids think the game is fun. It can be as short or as long as you choose; the player with the most points wins. To order a copy, call (800) 624-4263.

A LITTLE MUSIC TO SOOTHE THE SOUL

One of my favorite recordings is *In the Garden,* by guitarist Eric Tingstad and woodwind artist Nancy Rumbel (Narada Productions, 1991; $13.98). This is music to still the mind, but it isn't audio wallpaper: one number called "Big Weather" conjures up a spring storm. Recently the pair recorded another compact disc: *Pastorale* (Narada Media, 1997; $13.98). The peaceful sounds on this disc are almost pure guitar and woodwinds (oboe, English horn, double ocarina), with just a touch of synthesizer. Tingstad and Rumbel have both pursued music and gardening since childhood, and the resulting synergy comes through in works such as "Savannah" and "Roses and Lace." Look for both titles at record stores, or order by calling (800) 966-3699.

A GOOD LOOK AT COLD-HARDY PLANTS

My bookshelves already sag under the weight of volumes devoted to trees and shrubs, but I've managed to squeeze in yet another worthy title: *Dirr's Hardy Trees and Shrubs,* by Michael Dirr (Timber Press, Portland, 1997; $69.95; 800/327-5680). This pictorial encyclopedia contains 1,650 excellent color photos showing 500 species of trees, shrubs, and vines for cold country (*Sunset* climate zones 1–3). Dirr's plant list isn't comprehensive, but he offers expansive opinions of the plants he does include. Zelkova seedlings, he writes, "grow like a rabbit's hind legs." The best forms of common hackberry approach "the dignity of an American Elm; the worst, a worn-out broom." Though Dirr's orientation is clearly eastern (he lives in Georgia), the book is still a useful reference for gardeners in the cold-winter West.

that's a good question ...

Q: I've heard that you can water living Christmas trees with ice cubes. Is that a good idea?

A: Yes. As the ice cubes melt, they slowly release water, which is absorbed gradually by the root mass. (When you irrigate with water, it runs quickly through the container soil.) Each day, supply the tree with enough ice so that by the end of the day only a little water trickles out the drain holes (be sure to place a saucer under the container). During the tree's stay indoors, the melted water also keeps the roots cooler than the surrounding air.

CURTIS ANDERSON

Pacific Northwest Checklist

PLANTING

☑ AMARYLLIS. Nurseries and garden shops are bulging with amaryllis bulbs. Buy several and store them in a cool, dark place. Plant them at two-week intervals for a steady show of big, bold blossoms from Christmas through Valentine's Day.

☑ BUY CAMELLIAS. Zones 4–7: Shop for winter-flowering camellias. Slip plants in nursery cans into larger decorative pots for display. You can even trim them with small lights or ornaments. After the holidays, plant them in the garden.

☑ TREES AND SHRUBS. Zones 4–7: All but marginally hardy trees and shrubs can go into the ground this month. Water them thoroughly after planting.

MAINTENANCE

☑ CARE FOR HOUSE PLANTS. Snip off faded blooms and yellowing leaves. If leaves are dusty, give plants a shower in lukewarm water. Feed winter-flowering plants, but don't fertilize the others until early April.

☑ GROUND-LAYER EVERGREENS. You can propagate new evergreen shrubs by using a technique called ground-layering. First, scrape away a

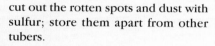

spot of bark (about the size of a fingernail) on the underside of a branch close to the ground. Dust the scraped portion, or wound, with rooting hormone. Scratch out a shallow hole in the soil under the area where the wound is. Push the branch down to the ground, fill in soil, and put a heavy stone atop the branch. Keep this area well watered. Roots will develop. Next fall, you can sever the branch from its parent and transplant it.

☑ INSPECT STORED BULBS. Frost-tender bulbs, corms, and tubers in storage for the winter should be examined for rot. Discard damaged ones. Dahlia tubers are the exception:

cut out the rotten spots and dust with sulfur; store them apart from other tubers.

☑ KEEP ON COMPOSTING. When holiday greens wither, put them on the compost pile along with fallen leaves and wind-downed debris.

☑ TEND GIFT PLANTS. To prolong bloom on Christmas cactus, cyclamen, kalanchoe, and poinsettias, water plants well but make sure they have adequate drainage (remove decorative foil from pots). Snip off faded leaves and flowers.

☑ WATER. Make sure plants in containers and under house eaves get enough water. When temperatures plunge, well-watered plants stand a better chance of surviving than dehydrated ones. ◆

Northern California Checklist

PLANTING

☑ **PLANT FRUITS AND VEGETA-BLES.** Zones 7–9, 14–17: Late this month, nurseries begin selling bare-root artichokes, asparagus, cane fruits (berries), grapes, rhubarb, and strawberries. Buy and plant early in the month while roots are still fresh. If the soil is too wet to plant, temporarily cover the roots with moistened mulch to keep them from drying out, or plant in containers.

☑ **PLANT BULBS.** Zones 7–9, 14–17: It's not too late to plant any bulbs you still have stored in the refrigerator or the garage. But if you shop for leftover bulbs at nurseries, choose them carefully. Avoid soft or molding bulbs. Plant healthy ones right away (tulips not chilled in the refrigerator will bloom on slightly shorter stems).

☑ **SET OUT CYCLAMEN.** Zones 8–9, 14–17: To protect the flowers from rain spots, set plants in containers, then put the pots under an overhang or on a covered porch. Give cyclamen partial shade or morning or late-afternoon sun. Set crowns (base of plants) slightly higher than the surrounding soil.

☑ **SHOP FOR BARE-ROOT ROSES.** Zones 7–9, 14–17: Bare-root roses start appearing in nurseries this month. Shop while selections are good. Look for the new All-America Rose Selection 'Sunset Celebration';

the warm apricot-umber flower with pleasing fragrance is a winner.

MAINTENANCE

☑ **CARE FOR LIVING CHRISTMAS TREES.** Most nurseries carry the following selection: aleppo pine, Colorado blue spruce, dwarf Alberta spruce, giant sequoia, and Monterey pine. Before bringing the tree indoors, water the pot thoroughly and hose down the foliage with water. Indoors, set the pot in a cool location in a waterproof plastic saucer. If the saucer is clay, set it on plastic or a waterproof cork mat. Check soil moisture daily.

☑ **FILL HUMMINGBIRD FEEDERS.** Zones 7–9, 14–17: These birds stay in Northern California through the winter. Since flowers are scarce in most gardens now, it's important to keep your feeder filled; clean and refill it every few days.

☑ **PRUNE FOR HOLIDAY GREENS.** Long-lasting choices include juniper, pine, and redwood. For tips on correct pruning techniques, see "Cutting greens for decorations" on page 332.

☑ **TEND GIFT PLANTS.** Place flowering gift plants in a cool spot with bright, indirect light. Don't let them sit in water; remove any decorative foil from the pot or perforate its bottom and set the pot in a saucer.

PEST CONTROL

☑ **SPRAY.** Zones 7–9, 14–17: After leaves have fallen, apply dormant oil to deciduous flowering and fruiting trees and roses. The oil will smother overwintering insects. Use fixed copper (in wettable powder form) or lime sulfur to control peach leaf curl. Spray on a dry day and follow label directions carefully. Spray again in January or early February. ◆

Southern California Checklist

PLANTING

☑ **BUY BARE-ROOT PLANTS.** Gardeners in coastal, inland, and low-desert regions (zones 22–24, 18–21, and 13, respectively) can begin planting bare-root this month. Roses show up at nurseries first. It's a good idea to shop early for the best selection. Later this month and early next month, deciduous fruit trees, cane berries and grapes, and perennial vegetables such as artichokes and asparagus will begin arriving. Plant all as soon as possible. Do not allow roots to dry out. If the ground is too wet for immediate planting, cover roots with soil or plant temporarily in containers.

☑ **PLANT WINTER VEGETABLES.** Plant replacements for the winter crops you harvest. Beets, carrots, chard, kale, head and leaf lettuces, mustard, peas, radishes, and spinach can go in from seed. Broccoli, brussels sprouts, cabbage, and cauliflower do best started as seedlings.

☑ **FINISH PLANTING BULBS.** Coastal, inland, and low-desert gardeners can continue to plant spring-blooming bulbs, including crocus, hyacinths, and tulips that have been prechilled at least six weeks.

Sunset
CLIMATE ZONES

1-3 7-9 11 13 14-24

DEBRA LAMBERT

MAINTENANCE

☑ **CARE FOR CHRISTMAS TREES.** To prolong the freshness of a cut tree, saw an inch off the bottom of the trunk, then store the tree in a bucket of water in a shady area outdoors. When ready to bring it indoors, saw off another inch of the trunk before setting the tree in a stand filled with water. Keep the reservoir full (check it daily during the first week). It's best to keep living trees outdoors until shortly before the holidays. Don't leave them indoors longer than two weeks.

☑ **PROTECT FROST-SENSITIVE PLANTS.** Move tender container plants under the eaves or indoors when cold weather is predicted. Cover plants in the ground with perforated plastic or burlap supported by some kind of frame that will keep the cover from touching the foliage (such as four tall stakes).

PEST CONTROL

☑ **APPLY DORMANT SPRAY.** As soon as their leaves fall, spray deciduous flowering and fruit trees with dormant oil to smother overwintering aphids, mites, and scale. If you haven't already treated trees for peach leaf curl, do so now. Add lime sulfur or fixed copper to the dormant oil. Spray branches, crotches, and trunk, as well as the ground beneath the tree's drip line. If it rains within 48 hours of spraying, repeat the treatment. Spray again at the height of dormancy and at the first bud swell. Gardeners at upper elevations (zones 1–3) or in the high desert (zone 11) can treat roses with dormant spray now, too.

☑ **PREVENT BEETLE DAMAGE.** Prune eucalyptus, pine, and other trees susceptible to bark beetles now, while beetles are inactive. Chip the prunings or cover the firewood tightly with a trap to prevent beetles from laying eggs. (Beetles lay eggs on dead as well as live wood.) ◆

Mountain Checklist

PLANTING & SHOPPING

☑ **BUY AND CARE FOR LIVING CHRISTMAS TREES.** Some good choices for mountain areas include alpine fir (*Abies lasiocarpa*), Douglas fir (*Pseudotsuga menziesii*), Colorado spruce (*Picea pungens* 'Fat Albert'), Colorado blue spruce (*P. pungens* 'Glauca'), and Engelmann spruce (*P. engelmannii*). Keep living trees away from fireplaces and heater vents. Water regularly.

☑ **PROPAGATE LEGGY HOUSE PLANTS.** As certain indoor plants, including Chinese evergreen, dracaena, and philodendron, get leggy in winter's low light, you can cut off elongated stems and root them in fresh potting soil to start new plants.

MAINTENANCE

☑ **CHECK STORED BULBS, PRODUCE.** Inspect stored summer bulbs such as gladiolus and tuberous begonias for signs of decay; throw out the rotten ones. You can save imperfect dahlia tubers by cutting out the bad spots, dusting with sulfur, and storing them away from the others. Also check stored squash, apples, and other produce, discarding those that show signs of rot.

☑ **MULCH.** It's not too late to put a 3- or 4-inch layer of mulch over perennial, bulb, and shrub beds to protect

Sunset
CLIMATE ZONES
☐ 1-3   ▨ 10-11

DEBRA LAMBERT

plants from damage due to alternate cycles of freezing and thawing.

☑ **PROTECT YOUNG TREES.** Young trees (any with less than a 4-inch-diameter trunk) need protection from sunscald. You can do the job with a corrugated tree-trunk protector, a PVC pipe that's split lengthwise. Get a size that's a little too large for the trunk so it won't hold water against the wood.

☑ **SAND ICY WALKWAYS.** Sand is a better choice than salt for use around plants, since it's nontoxic and can be swept into the garden when ice is gone. Don't, however, use sand on decks; it scars wood.

☑ **TEND GIFT PLANTS.** To prolong bloom on Christmas cactus, cyclamen, kalanchoe, and poinsettias, water plants well but make sure they have adequate drainage (remove decorative foil from pots). Snip off faded leaves and flowers.

☑ **WATER.** When the temperature is above freezing, water dry spots in the garden—especially plants in containers and under house eaves. When sustained subfreezing temperatures return, well-watered plants stand a better chance of surviving than dry ones.

PEST CONTROL

☑ **INSECTS ON HOUSE PLANTS.** If aphids, mites, or scale insects infest indoor plants, slip a plastic garment cover (the kind you get from the dry cleaners) over the plant, then spray the foliage with insecticidal soap; the plastic "tent" confines the spray.

☑ **OVERWINTERING INSECTS AND DISEASES.** On a clear day when the temperature is above freezing, spray deciduous fruit trees and roses with dormant oil mixed with lime sulfur or fixed copper. ◆

Southwest Checklist

PLANTING & SHOPPING

☑ **ANNUALS AND PERENNIALS.** Zones 12–13: Plant calendula, candytuft, cyclamen, dianthus, Iceland poppy, larkspur, pansy, petunia, primrose, snapdragon, stock, sweet alyssum, and viola. If you live in a frost-free place, set out bedding begonias and cineraria as well.

☑ **BARE-ROOT STOCK.** Roses and berries are usually the first bare-root plants to arrive in nurseries, followed by fruit trees and perennial vegetables like asparagus, horseradish, and rhubarb. Keep the roots from drying out between the nursery and your garden by wrapping them in wet burlap or packing the roots in damp sawdust. Plant as soon as you get home.

☑ **BULBS.** As early as possible this month, plant daffodils, gladiolus, ranunculus, and prechilled tulips.

☑ **PEPPERS, TOMATOES.** Zones 12–13: Start seeds of peppers and tomatoes in a warm indoor spot now and plants will be ready to set out in the garden by late February or early March.

☑ **SHOP AND CARE FOR LIVING CHRISTMAS TREES.** Some good choices for the Southwest include Afghan pine (*Pinus eldarica*) and

Aleppo pine (*P. halepensis*). Keep living trees away from fireplaces and heater vents. Water regularly.

MAINTENANCE

☑ **FERTILIZE DECIDUOUS FRUIT TREES.** Zones 10–13: For trees at least four years old, apply 9 pounds of 10-10-10 fertilizer now, then three more pounds right after harvest.

☑ **MULCH.** Zones 1–2, 10–11: It's not too late to spread mulch over bulb and perennial beds and over the root zones of permanent shrubs, especially those most vulnerable to cold.

☑ **WATER.** Irrigate dry spots in the garden, especially under house eaves.

PEST CONTROL

☑ **INSECTS ON HOUSE PLANTS.** If aphids, mites, or scale insects infest indoor plants, slip a plastic garment cover (the kind you get from the dry cleaners) over the plant, then spray the foliage with insecticidal soap; the plastic "tent" confines the spray.

☑ **OVERWINTERING INSECTS AND DISEASES.** On a clear day when the temperature is above freezing, spray deciduous fruit trees and roses with dormant oil mixed with lime sulfur or fixed copper. ◆

Gifts for the well-dressed gardener

A head-to-toe guide to garden apparel for all seasons

■ In business, dressing for success means wearing clothes that help you cut a big deal or plant your product in the right market. In the garden the concept is much the same. Whether it's time to cut big limbs or plant roses, wearing the proper apparel allows you to work more comfortably and efficiently, be it cold or hot, raining or sunny.

Which garb wears best for such chores? We surveyed professional and home gardeners around the West. Then we pored over catalogs to find their favorite items.

Their clothing choices are as diverse as gardeners are. Yet all who responded want apparel that allows maximum freedom of movement. Most of them keep two or more sets of garden clothes—one to wear while the other's in the wash. Here are some of their preferences, from head to toe. Any of these items could make a welcome gift. Sources are listed on page 345.

Head coverings. Headwear is important for protection from sun, rain, and scratchy branches. A well-designed hat should also have adequate ventilation to dissipate heat and perspiration. Favorites run the gamut from an heirloom straw hat to a pith helmet equipped with a built-in fan (shown on page 345).

Shirts, trousers, vests, jackets. More than anything else, gardeners say they want loose or baggy garments that can be tossed into the washer and dryer. "I buy everything two sizes too big," says one gardener. "I figure one size to give me plenty of room and one size to shrink in the dryer." Shirts of choice range from sturdy Ts to long-sleeved, button-up work shirts; pants, from baggy jeans to Japanese farmers' trousers. Sleeveless vests are popular for two reasons: they provide a layer of warmth without restricting arm movement, and they have plenty of pockets for toting seed packets, plant tags, and small tools. Among jackets and windbreakers, those made with fabrics that breathe, including Gore-Tex and Supplex nylon, are favored for their ability to shed rain without adding weight.

Gloves. Preferences depend on the task at hand. If you're only worried about keeping your hands clean, use a pair of inexpensive cotton knit gloves; they'll last through several washings. Flexible fabric and latex gloves are hits because they're made so thin that you can feel the texture of foliage and soil through them. For heavy work or handling prickly plants, thick leather gloves get the nod.

Footwear. Whatever the style—boots, clogs, or rain shoes—footwear should protect your toes, keep your feet dry, provide good traction on mud or wet grass, and wash off easily. In mild weather, clogs and rain shoes usually provide adequate protection. But when it's cold, rubber boots with liners supply the warmth you need.

Steve Lorton, chief of Sunset's Northwest bureau, gardens in Washington. He wears Dutch-style wood clogs over heavy socks. "They keep your feet dry and offer strong support for jobs that require standing for long periods. They take some getting used to, but once you learn to move around in them, you'll be hooked," he says. Cost is about $25 for a plain pair (for most sizes), $30 for a decorated pair. To order, trace the outline of each foot barefoot, then mail or fax the tracings to Wooden Shoe Factory (Box 2102, Holland, MI 49422; call 616/396-6513 or fax 396-0642).

LEFT: FRANCE RUFFENACH   RIGHT: NORMAN A. PLATE

by STEVEN R. LORTON

The heavy-duty gardener

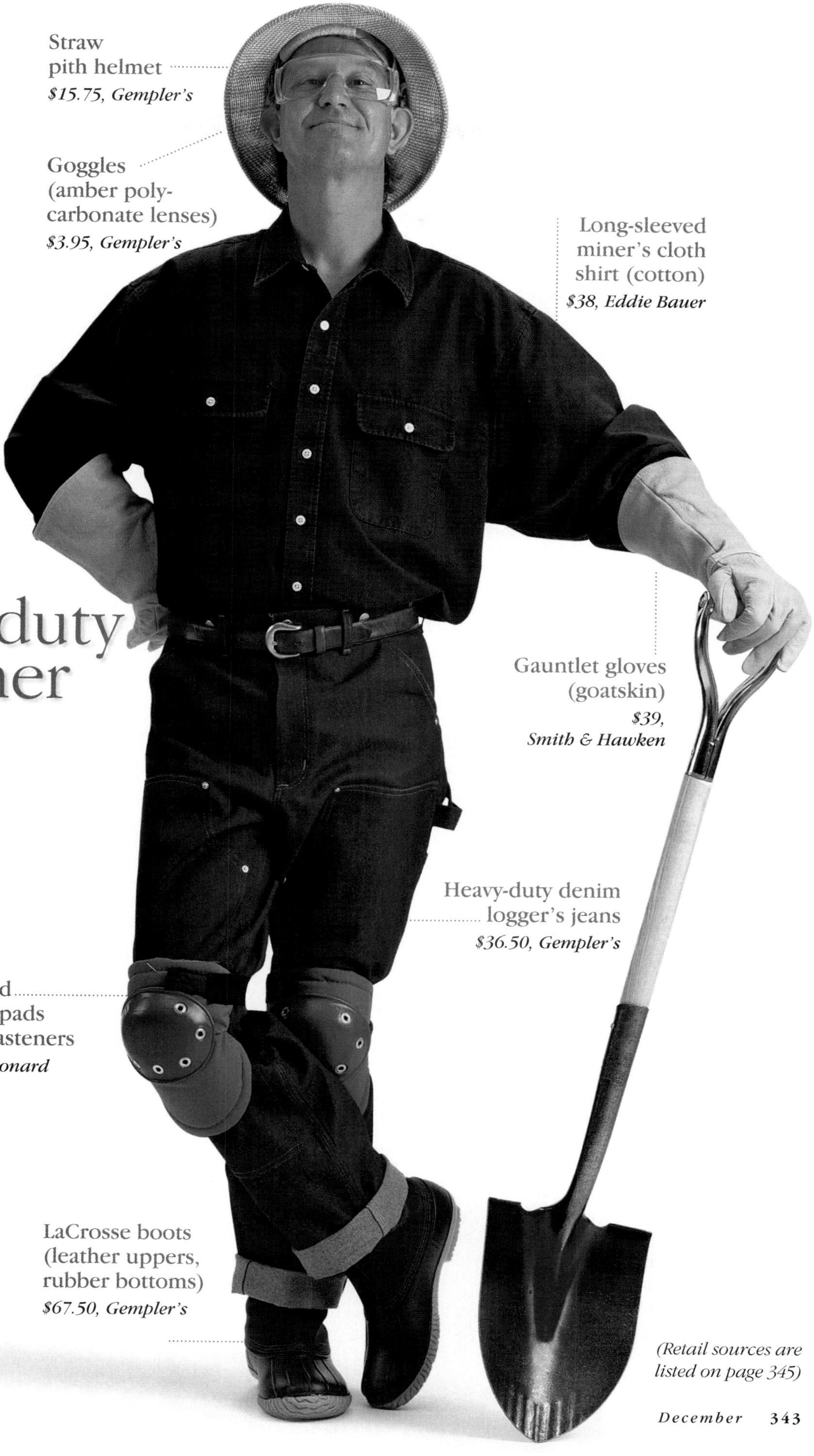

Straw
pith helmet
$15.75, Gempler's

Goggles
(amber poly-
carbonate lenses)
$3.95, Gempler's

Long-sleeved
miner's cloth
shirt (cotton)
$38, Eddie Bauer

Gauntlet gloves
(goatskin)
*$39,
Smith & Hawken*

Heavy-duty denim
logger's jeans
$36.50, Gempler's

Plastic-capped
rubber knee pads
with Velcro fasteners
$24.83, A. M. Leonard

LaCrosse boots
(leather uppers,
rubber bottoms)
$67.50, Gempler's

*(Retail sources are
listed on page 345)*

The foul-weather gardener

Sharon Cohoon, a Sunset writer who gardens in Southern California, explains why she prefers the Mud Glove: "Once wet, leather gloves dry out too stiff for comfort. Plain cotton gloves don't last. The Mud Glove, made of latex-coated cotton, is flexible, comfortable—and your fingernails don't pop through them." Cost is $8.95 a pair at many garden stores; you can order from Gardener's Supply Company (800/955-3370).

Packer hat of oil-finished cotton duck
$32.50,
C. C. Filson Co.

Thermal cotton T-shirt
$28,
Eddie Bauer

Plaid wool shirt
$61,
Pendleton Woolen Mills

Rose and cactus gloves (heavy cotton with synthetic coating)
$9.95,
Natural Gardening Company

"Tin" (oil-finished cotton) pants
$77.75,
C. C. Filson Co.

Supplex nylon windbreaker
$75,
Eddie Bauer

British rubber Wellies with flannel boot liners
$59 and $18, respectively,
Smith & Hawken

FAR LEFT AND FAR RIGHT: FRANCE RUFFENACH   CENTER : NORMAN A. PLATE (2)

The fair-weather gardener

Straw hat with chin strap ······
$45,
Smith & Hawken

Weathered cotton T-shirt
$18, Eddie Bauer

Cotton vest with six pockets ······
$49, Smith & Hawken

Armordillo gloves (Kevlar coated with rubber dots)
$19.50,
Natural Gardening Company

French rain shoes of molded PVC
$29, Smith & Hawken

Jack McKinnon, a gardener at Sunset's headquarters in Menlo Park, California, wears a whimsical but practical pith helmet with a built-in fan to cool his brow. "On a hot day, it keeps me going," he says. The fan is powered by a 3-volt solar panel or two AA batteries. Cost is $40, from Real Goods (800/762-7325).

SOURCES

Firms listed below accept mail orders. Eddie Bauer, Pendleton, and Smith & Hawken also have retail sites in the West. Call for free catalogs or store locations.

A. M. Leonard, Box 816, Piqua, OH 45356; (800) 543-8955. This firm offers dozens of kinds of gloves.

C. C. Filson Co., Box 34020, Seattle, WA 98124; (800) 299-1287. This company makes hardworking clothes, including "tin" (stiff, oil-impregnated fabric) hats and pants that wear well in the garden, particularly in wet weather.

Eddie Bauer, Box 182639, Columbus, OH 43218; (800) 426-8020. Check out the selection of sturdy, washable apparel, including shirts and trousers.

Gempler's, Box 270, Mount Horeb, WI 53572; (800) 382-8473. The catalog is well stocked with hats, gloves, boots, and heavy-duty garden wear.

Natural Gardening Company, 217 San Anselmo Ave., San Anselmo, CA 94960; (707) 766-9303. This firm sells hats, gloves, and footwear.

Pendleton Woolen Mills, Box 3030, Portland, OR 97208; (800) 760-4844. On a crisp winter day in the garden, no shirt feels—or looks—better than a classic plaid Pendleton.

Smith & Hawken, 2 Arbor Lane, Florence, KY 41022; (800) 776-3336. The catalog brims with stylish clothing made specifically for gardeners. ◆

OUR WESTERN WREATH

WHAT YOU NEED

- 18-inch grapevine wreath base (available at craft stores)
- Twigs (at least 15, each about 8 inches long)
- Evergreen boughs (at least three types), cut into 4- and 6-inch sprigs
- Florist's wire (green) • Wire cutter • 12 to 16 cinnamon sticks
- Raffia • 20 dried red chilies • 9 to 15 small apples
- Florist's picks (green) • 15 dried apple slices
- 20 dried orange slices • Eucalyptus twigs, in 4- to 6-inch lengths
- Fresh nandina and pepper tree berries (or other berries, such as holly)
- 15-inch-long curly willow twigs

(Directions on page 348)

Capture the season's abundance with fruits and greens

BY ANN BERTELSEN   PHOTOGRAPHS BY JAMES CARRIER

■ Last Christmas, we were captivated by the elegant wreaths designed by Jeff Thibodeaux for the Inn of the Anasazi in Santa Fe. They ranged from simple clusters of chilies to elaborate concoctions of exotic flowers and spiraling curly willows. He inspired us to make our own wreath that incorporates natural, easy-to-find materials and is a snap to make (in less than four hours).

"You don't have to be artistic [to make a wreath]," says Thibodeaux, who has taught classes on the subject. "What makes a wreath special is how you arrange the materials." Aim for a pleasing balance of foliage and fruit (or flowers), Thibodeaux suggests. If you space apples too symmetrically, a wreath will look stilted and formal. Opt for an uneven number of focal points, such as three or five clusters of fruit. Start at the 10 or 11 o'clock position and place large items casually around the circle, so the composition looks pleasantly balanced.

But just as important are the greens, fruits, and herbs you choose; different colors and textures are what give our wreath its richness.

For our wreath, we covered an 18-inch grapevine base with evergreens (Douglas fir, pine, and juniper, plus eucalyptus leaves to add paler shadings of green). Then we added twigs, small green lady apples, cinnamon sticks, red chilies, green (unripe) nandina berries and red pepper tree berries, and dried orange and apple slices, but you can use whatever seasonal foliage or fruits you like. Replace fresh ingredients (like apples) as needed.

DOOR FINISH BY MARGO FELICE

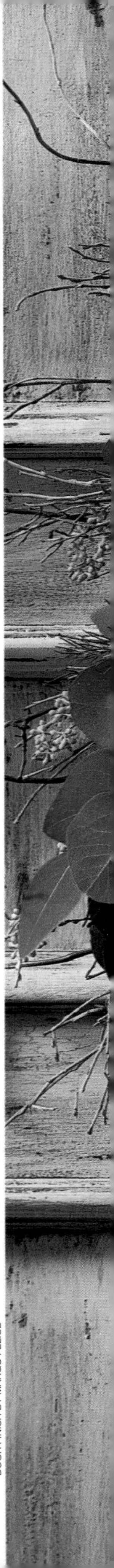

Light and dark evergreens add depth and texture to our wreath, forming a rich background for clusters of fruits and berries.

Assemble your wreath

Add twigs to the vine wreath base (a)
Space them evenly around the wreath's perimeter and set them at a slight angle (not straight out like the spokes of a wheel). Push them firmly between the vines.

Make a garland of greens (b)
1. Separate the evergreen sprigs into piles by type.
2. Make a bundle containing one sprig of each type of evergreen, with the lightest-colored greens on top. Secure the ends with a short piece of florist's wire. Repeat the process until you have enough evergreen bunches to encircle the wreath, allowing for the bundles to

overlap. (You should have about seven bunches.)
3. Cut a 6-foot-long piece of florist's wire and lay it straight on a flat surface.
4. Set a bunch of greens about 3 inches from one end of the 6-foot wire, with stems crossing the wire. Loop the long end of the wire several times around the stems to secure them.
5. Place a second bunch of evergreens about 4 inches from the first one, with its stems across the long wire. Wrap the long end of the wire several times around the stems. Repeat the process until the evergreen bunches are at 4-inch intervals all along the wire.

When finished, you should have a 3½- to 4-foot-long garland.
Attach the garland to the wreath base (c)
1. Place the garland on top of the grapevine base, bending it to fit the wreath's curves as you go.
2. Tie both ends of the garland to the vine base with florist's wire, concealing the wire beneath the overlapping greenery.
3. Tie the rest of the garland to the vine base, using a piece of florist's wire every 3 inches or so. Twist the wire at the back of the vine base, then snip off the ends.

Add a few finishing touches

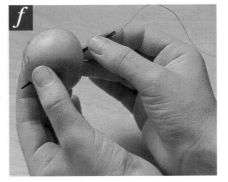

• Bundle three or four cinnamon sticks together and tie tightly with raffia; snip off raffia ends. If the tie seems loose on the bundle, insert another stick through the middle. Turn the bundle face down, slip a 12-inch piece of wire around the raffia, and twist it firmly. Make two more bunches of cinnamon sticks. Tie the bundles to the wreath *(d)* at the 2, 5, and 10 o'clock positions. Snip off wire ends.
• Add the chilies *(e)*. Wrap a piece of

wire around the stem of each chili (you can attach them to the wreath singly, or in groups of two or three) and tie the chilies to the wreath.
• Add whole apples. Push a florist's pick into an apple near the stem at a slight angle *(f)*, working it through the apple so only the wire ties show at the top. Gather three wired apples together; twist the wire ties together. Tie the apples to the wreath. Repeat with other apple bunches.

• Attach dried apple and orange slices to the greenery with wire.
• Poke 6-inch eucalyptus twigs in around the wreath's outside perimeter (using florist's picks to add strength to weaker stems) and 4-inch pieces around the inner perimeter.
• Attach nandina and pepper berries to the wreath with florist's picks.
• Weave curly willow twigs deep into the grapevine base at a slight angle, as shown in the photo on page 347. ◆

Article Titles Index

General Subject Index

If you are not already a subscriber to Sunset Magazine and would be interested in
subscribing, please call Sunset's subscriber service number, 1-800-777-0117.